Benjamin's -abilities

Benjamin's -abilities

SAMUEL WEBER

HARVARD UNIVERSITY PRESS

Cambridge, Massachusetts, and London, England   2008

Library of Congress Cataloging-in-Publication Data

Weber, Samuel, 1940–
  Benjamin's -abilities / Samuel Weber.
    p.   cm.
    "Appendix: Walter Benjamin's "Seagulls": a translation"—P.
    Includes bibliographical references (p.   ) and index.
    ISBN-13: 978-0-674-02837-1 (cloth : alk. paper)   1. Benjamin, Walter, 1892–1940.
I. Benjamin, Walter, 1892–1940. Möwen. English.   II. Title.
  B3209.B584W43 2008
  193—dc22   2007049785

Contents

List of Abbreviations   vii

I Benjamin's -abilities

1 Introduction   3

2 Prehistory: Kant, Hölderlin—et cetera   11

3 Criticizability—Calculability   20

4 Impart-ability: Language as Medium   31

5 Translatability I: Following *(Nachfolge)*   53

6 Translatability II: Afterlife   79

7 Citability—of Gesture   95

8 Ability and Style   115

9 An Afterlife of -abilities: Derrida   122

II Legibilities

10 Genealogy of Modernity: History, Myth, and Allegory
    in Benjamin's *Origin of the German Mourning Play*   131

11 Awakening   164

12 Taking Exception to Decision: Walter Benjamin and
    Carl Schmitt   176

13 Violence and Gesture: Agamben Reading Benjamin
    Reading Kafka Reading Cervantes . . .   195

14 Song and Glance: Walter Benjamin's Secret Names
    (*zugewandt—unverwandt*)   211

15 "Streets, Squares, Theaters": A City on the Move—
    Walter Benjamin's Paris   227

16 God and the Devil—in Detail   240

17 Closing the Net: "Capitalism as Religion" (Benjamin)   250

18 The *Ring* as *Trauerspiel*: Reading Wagner with Benjamin
    and Derrida   281

19 Reading Benjamin   297

20 "Seagulls"   310

    Appendix. Walter Benjamin's "Seagulls": A Translation   325
    Notes   327
    Acknowledgments   357
    Index   359

Abbreviations

AP	Walter Benjamin, *Arcades Project,* trans. Howard Eiland and Kevin McLaughlin (Cambridge: Harvard University Press, 2002)
CoJ	Immanuel Kant, *Critique of Judgment,* trans. W. Pluhar (Indianapolis: Hackett, 1987)
EE	Giorgio Agamben, *Etat d'Exception* (Paris: Editions du Seuil, 2003). English version in *State of Exception,* trans. Kevin Attell (Chicago: University of Chicago Press, 2005)
GS1, GS2, GS4	Walter Benjamin, *Gesammelte Schriften—Werkausgabe,* vols. 1–4 (Frankfurt am Main: Suhrkamp, 1980)
GS5	Walter Benjamin, *Gessammelte Schriften,* vol. 5 (Frankfurt am Main: Suhrkamp, 1982)
GS6	Walter Benjamin, *Gessammelte Schriften,* vol. 6 (Frankfurt am Main: Suhrkamp, 1988)
KdU	Immanuel Kant, *Kritik der Urteilskraft,* vol. 6 (Frankfurt am Main: Suhrkamp, 1981)
Origin	Walter Benjamin, *Origin of the German Tragic Drama,* trans. John Osborne (London: Verso, 1998)
Pdl	Jacques Derrida, *Politiques de l'Amitié* (Paris: Galilée, 1994)
PoF	Jacques Derrida, *Politics of Friendship,* trans. George Collins (London: Verso, 1997)
Politische Theologie	Carl Schmitt, *Politische Theologie, Vier Kapitel zur Lehre von der Souveränität* (Berlin: Duncker & Humblot, 1985)

PT	Carl Schmitt, *Political Theology: Four Chapters on the Concept of Sovereignty,* trans. George Schwab (Cambridge: MIT Press, 1985)
SW1	Walter Benjamin, *Selected Writings,* vol. 1: *1913–1926* (Cambridge: Harvard University Press, 1996)
SW2	Walter Benjamin, *Selected Writings,* vol. 2: *1927–1934* (Cambridge: Harvard University Press, 1999)
SW3	Walter Benjamin, *Selected Writings,* vol. 3: *1935–1938* (Cambridge: Harvard University Press, 2002)
SW4	Walter Benjamin, *Selected Writings,* vol. 4: *1938–1940* (Cambridge: Harvard University Press, 2003)

Benjamin's -abilities

PART ONE

Benjamin's -abilities

CHAPTER ONE

Introduction

Although Walter Benjamin was never timid when it came to writing, one practice he consistently avoided was that of creating neologisms.[1] It is therefore with all the more reluctance that I find myself compelled to resort to something similar, in order to sum up a motif that has imposed itself over the years in my reading of Benjamin. What is involved is, to be sure, not exactly a neologism, since it does not involve the creation of a new word, but rather the highlighting of a word-part, a suffix *(eine Nachsilbe)*. In English, to be sure, this suffix, when spoken, is indistinguishable from a word: what distinguishes it from a word is not audible, but only legible: a hyphen, marking a separation that is also a joining, a *Bindestrich* that does not bind it to anything in particular and yet requires it to be bound to something else. The suffix in question thus sounds deceptively familiar, since it coincides, audibly, with the word "abilities." Unlike that word, however, its first letter—which purely by accident happens to be the first letter of the alphabet—is preceded by a dash. When written in isolation, this gives it a somewhat bizarre appearance, to be sure, since suffixes are not usually encountered separately from the words they modify. But this bizarre appearance pales when compared to its German "original." If this book is ever translated into German—"back" into German I was tempted to write, since German here is of course the language in which Benjamin wrote and in which I generally read him—then its title, were it to be entirely faithful to the English, would indeed have to involve the creation of a neologism. For translated back into German, the German title would require its readers to "read, what was never written," namely: *"Benjamins -barkeiten."*

Let me, then, in what follows, begin to try to explain, if not justify, this bizarre title, whether as "Benjamins -barkeiten" or as "Benjamin's -abilities," by first of all tracing it back to what is a double—or split—origin. The first aspect is fairly obvious, at least to anyone who has read much of Benjamin's writings. Throughout his life, Benjamin tended to formulate many of his most significant concepts by nominalizing verbs, not in the usual manner but by adding the suffix *-barkeit* (which in English can be written either -ibility or -ability: for the sake of simplicity and clarity, I will in English use only the latter *Schreibweise*). To recall just the most prominent of these *-barkeiten* or *abilities*—and there are many more lurking in all corners of his texts, one of which I will discuss later in this chapter—I will mention only the following: *Mit-teil-barkeit* (from his 1916 "Language" essay), *Kritisier-barkeit* (from his dissertation "The Concept of Art Criticism in German Romanticism," published in 1920), *Übersetz-barkeit* (in "The Task of the Translator," 1923), *Reproduzier-barkeit* (in "The Work of Art in the Age of its Technical Reproducability," 1935), and finally, *Erkenn-barkeit,* but also *Les-barkeit* in Notebook "N" of the manuscripts concerning the Paris Passages. This widespread and persistent tendency to form concepts by recourse to this suffix, which even in German produces rather awkward nouns, provided a first indication that more had to be involved here than merely stylistic idiosyncrasy.

That was the first origin of my fascination with Benjamin's *-barkeiten.* A second inspiration came from quite a different source, although from one that for me has always been profoundly related to Benjamin's writing. I am speaking of the work of Jacques Derrida, and in particular of his celebrated—or notorious, depending on one's perspective—polemical exchange with the philosopher John Searle. Since I was involved in the English translation of what was to become known as *Limited Inc.,* I remember being especially impressed by one moment in Derrida's rejoinder to Searle's critique of an essay he had written on John Austin, the founder of speech-act philosophy. Let me briefly recall the context: in 1972 Derrida had published a reading of Austin under the title "Signature, Event, Context." The text was translated and published in English some years later. Soon after, word got around that Searle considered this essay extremely weak. He was therefore invited to respond to Derrida publicly, which he did, in a short text, to which Derrida in turn replied, but in an essay of over one hundred pages, entitled *Limited Inc.* One of the central issues discussed involved the relation of spoken to written language, and in particular, the role of the subject in relation to both. Searle's critique made it clear that he understood Derrida as claiming that a key difference between written and spoken language has to do with the absence or presence of the subject. As Searle put it, thinking he was thereby correcting Derrida: "Writing makes it *possible* to communicate with an absent receiver, *but* it is not *necessary* for the receiver to be absent. Written communication can exist *in the presence* of the receiver, as for example, when I compose a shopping list for myself."[2] In replying, Derrida brought to the fore a word that would remain one of only a few terminological constants throughout his subsequent writings—a sort of deconstructive "principle," if such were not a contradiction in terms; the term "iterability": "The response is easy and clear. *Sec* [the abbreviation used by Derrida for his essay on Husserl: "Signature, Event, Context"] *never said* that this absence is *necessary,* but only that it is *possible* [. . .] and that this possibility must therefore be taken into account: it pertains, *qua possibility,* to the structure of the mark as such, i.e. to the structure precisely of its iterability."[3]

It is in elaborating the nature of the "possibility" implied in the notion of "iterability" that Derrida explains why "itera*bility*" must not be confused with "iteration" but rather involves a very distinctive mode that is difficult to situate in terms of the traditional opposition—and hierarchy—that subordinates "possibility" to "reality" or "actuality":

> If one admits that writing (and the mark in general) *must be able* to function in the absence of the sender, the receiver, the context of production etc., this implies that this power, this *being able,* this *possibility* is *always* inscribed, hence *necessarily* inscribed as *possibility* in the functioning or the functional structure of the mark . . . It follows that this possibility is a *necessary* part of its structure . . . Inasmuch as it is essential and structural, this possibility is always at work marking *all the facts,* all the

events, even those that appear to disguise it. *Just as iterability, which is not iteration,* can be recognized even in a mark that *in fact* seems to have occurred only once. I say *seems,* because this one time is in itself divided or multiplied in advance by its structure of repeatability.[4]

Iterability, the power or potentiality to repeat or be repeated, is not the same as *repetition,* precisely because it is a *structural possibility* that is potentially "at work" even there where it seems factually not to have occurred. A "mark" can be identified, which is to say, apprehended as such, only by virtue of its being repeated, at least mentally, and compared to its earlier occurrence. Memory and repetition are thus constitutive elements of identity, which depends on iterability—that is to say, on the ability of any event to be iterated, repeated. The possibility of such repetition entails both alteration and sameness—sameness through alteration. This means that identification is only possible by averting one's regard, as it were, from what changes in order to apprehend what stays the same over time and space. As we shall see, something very similar also marks Benjamin's -abilities.

To be sure, Derrida's "ability" here is not simply that of Benjamin. Nevertheless, his distinction between "iterability" and "iteration," "repeatability" and "repetition," between empirically observable fact and structural possibility, can tell us much about Benjamin's penchant for forming key concepts in terms of their *-ability,* rather than their *actuality* as mere facts. Moreover, to argue, as Derrida does in the passage quoted, that this potentiality or ability involves a process by which what is ostensibly a single occurrence finds "itself divided or multiplied in advance by its [. . .] repeatability" is to undercut the usual definition of possibility itself, which, ever since Aristotle, has been understood to be a mode of actuality or of actualization, and thus has been defined by opposition to its negation, impossibility, which it is held to exclude. As we will see, this either-or binary logic does not hold for Benjamin any more than it does for Derrida.

Given the divided or double path by which the notion of "-ability," and in particular, its significance for Benjamin, imposed itself on me, it will not be surprising that the "-abilities" with which I am concerned cannot be considered as being the properties or attributes of a particular subject, Walter Benjamin, no matter how genial and fascinating that subject undoubtedly was. But what continues to provoke today, I am convinced, has less to do with the person of Walter Benjamin than with his writings, even if it is clear that one cannot fully separate the two. If those writings surprise us again and again by their seemingly inexhaustible ability to come up with striking, unexpected, and above all compelling formulations and insights, however enigmatic these may be, then I want to suggest that this is in part, at least, the result of a very distinctive way of *conceptualizing* that manifests itself in the tendency to resort to the suffix, -ability—"*-barkeit*"—in forming nouns from verbs. This mode of conceptualizing "virtualizes" the process of nominalization by referring it back to what in German is very appropriately designated as a *Zeitwort:* a "time-word," aka *verb*, that is inseparable from time insofar as it involves an ongoing, ever-unfinished, and unpredictable process: *Erkennbarkeit* thus names the virtual condition of *Erkennen*, *Benennbarkeit* that of *Benennen*, *Kritisierbarkeit* that of *Kritisieren*, and so on.[5]

In his "Epistemo-critical Preface" to the *Trauerspiel*-Book, Benjamin attempts to determine the specific mediating function *(Vermittlerrolle)* of the concept with respect to phenomena, on the one hand, and the idea on the other (*GS1*, 214; *Origin*, 34). The latter can only be presented or staged—*dargestellt*—by taking leave of the realm of pure ideas and descending to that of empirical, phenomenal experience, and this in turn can be accomplished only through a reordering or reorganization, a dismantling and dispersion effectuated by the concept on the "thing-like elements" *(dinglicher Elemente)* that constitute the phenomena. The concept accomplishes this rearrangement, which Benjamin designates as "virtual"—"*virtuelle Anordnung*"—by decomposing—today we might even say "deconstructing"—the preexisting empirical organization of the phenomena, thus allowing them to reorganize, albeit only "virtually." Moreover, Benjamin is quite precise in his account of how the concept accomplishes this decomposition and dissemination. It does this by departing from its traditional role of establishing sameness—which is to say, by identifying those traits of the phenomenon that make it similar to others, so that it can then be subsumed under an average common denominator; instead, the role of the concept as Benjamin understands and practices it is to discern not what makes phenomena like one another but rather what separates and distinguishes them from each other. The notion that Benjamin introduces here, in contradistinction to that of average—*Durchschnitt*—is that of the *extreme*. In the passages where he elaborates this *term*—which recurs frequently in the preface to the *Trauerspiel* book—Benjamin never defines or analyzes it. But what emerges from his use of the word is that he is using it quite literally as a *term:* which is to say, to stress that the delimitation of a phenomenon depends on a certain process of *termination,* through which it both occludes and exposes the outer edge of its scope, its *Tragweite,* thereby stabilizing itself, but only by *gesturing* toward what it excludes. The *extreme,* which it is the task of the concept to activate, thus marks the point where a phenomenon is constitutively implicated in what it is not, in what is other and external, in what resists comprehension and containment. The concept, one could say, dismantles the phenomenon by *exposing* it as a *term,* in the linguistic sense, but also in the semantic one. The concept, by determining the phenomenon, allows it to *part company with* itself. The phenomenon, determined as a "thing," is decomposed into its "thing-like elements," which have the potential, the ability, to recombine into something else.

And yet, it is also the function of the concept not just to transform phenomena, but also, in so doing, to "save" them. This notion of "saving" is extremely complex, and this is not the place to go into it in detail. Let me just note that it does not imply simply staying the same over time. This would be the aim of the subsumptive concept, which aims to save the individual by both subordinating and elevating it to a more general average, one that is less vulnerable to alterations of time and space. Benjamin clearly rejects this notion of the concept: "To want to describe the universal as something average is misdirected [*Das Allgemeine als ein Durchschnittliches darlegen zu wollen ist verkehrt*]," he writes (*GS1,* 215; *Origin,* 35). The "idea," which is his term in the "Epistemo-critical Preface" for the alternative use to which the concept is to be put, affirms the uniqueness of a certain singularity: "As the shaping of a complex in which the singular-extreme stands with its like, the idea is circumscribed [*Als Gestaltung des Zusammenhanges, in dem das Einmalig-Extreme mit seinesgleichen steht, ist die Idee umschrieben*]" (ibid.). The "virtual rearrangement" of phenomena by concepts into terms thus links their de-termination to their singularity, as "the singular-extreme [*das Einmalig-Extreme*]." The "uniquely extreme" in no way excludes repetition: as a "virtual rearrangement" it presupposes it. But it also determines it as a movement of differentiation, of variation, of alteration. By driving complex phenomena to their extremes, the concept reveals not what makes them like other phenomena, their common denominator, but rather what separates them, distinguishes them and makes them "einmalig-extrem": incommensurably once-and-for-all.[6]

The power of conceptualization, in this perspective, then, is one of *singularization*. In taking phenomena to their ever singular extreme, the concept causes them to part company with themselves, with their Self, not in order to dissolve them into some greater generality, but rather to reveal their distinctive, incommensurable spatial-temporal singularity as a measure of change and alteration.

But this conceptual "rearrangement" or "reordering" *(Anordnung)* remains both "virtual" and an "order" in the sense of a command, or better: a challenge, since what results is a configuration that can never be fully self-present, for such a presence would reduce the uniqueness—*das Einmalige*—by treating it as though it were identically or essentially repeatable *as the same*. It is only in the divergent convergence of appearance and disappearance, of coming-to-be and passing-away, like the *éclair* of Baudelaire's *"passante"*—but also like those three dots or periods that separate the flash from its reflection ("un éclair . . . puis la nuit")—that such phenomena can be "saved." Such "salvation" can therefore be named most precisely, in English at least, as: *coming to pass*. What is "saved" is not preserved unchanged, but only in the *traces* of what *comes to pass*. This is why the "idea" can only be "circumscribed"—*umschrieben*—but never simply *beschrieben,* described. For the idea is not simply visible or describable, except perhaps in the literal sense of writing and language: "The Idea belongs to language, namely to the essence of the word in which it is symbolic [*Die Idee ist ein Sprachliches, und zwar im Wesen des Wortes jeweils dasjenige Moment, in welchem es Symbol ist*]" (GS1, 216; *Origin,* 36). This "symbolic side" is always "more or less hidden." Since language must have a phenomenal existence, however, its hidden "symbolic" and "ideational" dimension is never present in pure form, but always associated with a "manifestly profane significance." "The task of philosophy"—since it cannot claim to reveal directly *(offenbarend zu reden)*—consists in a certain kind of originary listening *(Urvernehmen)* that in turn entails *remembrance*. Through such remembering words are "once again" given the ability "to reassert their rights to name."

This is why neologisms—which also entail a certain naming—are to be avoided: for by introducing new words, they ignore the historical memory of language. Rather than investing words, Benjamin's discussion, and his writing practice, advocates the reinscribing of established terms so that they part company with themselves—which is to say, with their previous identities. It is by virtue of such a movement of *parting-with* that words recover the ability to name, which is never reducible to any identifiable semantic content, least of all to that of a proper noun.

If the "presentation of an idea" can therefore never be fully accomplished, if it must remain *virtual*, one way of naming that does not invent but rather virtualizes is precisely that of making familiar *terms* depend on a sequel or a sequence, on a *Nachfolge* that de-termines those words by involving them in their *Nachgeschichte*: awakening them to an after-life in the *Nach-* or *Fortleben* of a *Nachsilbe*.

This, *perhaps,* begins to explain Benjamin's persistent recourse to *-barkeiten.*

CHAPTER TWO

Prehistory

Kant, Hölderlin—et cetera

To be sure, such -abilities were never Benjamin's alone. For the use of this suffix to form key concepts is by no means a practice invented by or limited to Walter Benjamin. Formation of philosophical concepts through the use of the suffix -*barkeit* marks the work of the thinker who had doubtless the greatest philosophical influence on Benjamin's thought, at least in its early, formative years: Kant. Benjamin's admiration for Kant was "extreme" in the sense already alluded to: not simply as the thinker of a philosophical system, but as one who struggled to push philosophy to its extreme, as the following passage from a 1917 letter to Gershom Scholem attests: "Whoever doesn't feel the *thinking of instruction* [*Lehre*] itself struggling in Kant, and therefore does not treat him with the utmost respect, literally, as a *tradendum*—to be transmitted and passed down (no matter how much he must subsequently be reshaped), understands absolutely nothing of philosophy. Therefore all carping against his philosophical style is pure philistinism and profane chatter."[1] Nowhere perhaps is the tradition that Benjamin alludes to here, including its potential for *Umbildung*, more in evidence than in the last of Kant's "critical" works, usually translated in English as the *Critique of Judgment*. The word used by Kant in his title, of course, is *Urteilskraft*, a term that Werner Pluhar has rightly reminded his readers signifies not judgment but the "power" or "ability" to judge.[2] The contrast between the German title of the Third Critique, which names a "Kraft," and that of the first two Critiques, which name a species of reason ("pure" or "practical"), underscores the ambiguous mode of being of the main object of Kant's last Critique: a *use* of "judgment" that is not really a "judgment" in the traditional sense, but something far more difficult to qualify, since "aesthetic judgment" claims the universal validity otherwise reserved for cognitive "judgments," but without conveying any knowledge at all. It is in this Third Critique, where Kant addresses the problem of whether there are a priori and universally valid rules governing the representation of radical singularities—which is to say, of events that do not fit in or under the available stock of general concepts (as in so-called determining judgments)—that he resorts at certain key points to the kind of conceptual formation with which we are here concerned. In this chapter I will limit myself to recalling briefly two of them, since both will resonate in Benjamin's early writings and beyond.

Toward the end of the *Introduction* to the *Critique of Judgment,* Kant sums up the relation of the three "faculties"—and therefore of his three Critiques—as follows:

> The understanding, inasmuch as it can give laws to nature a priori, proves that we cognize nature only as appearance, and hence at the same time points to a supersensible substrate of nature; but it leaves this substrate wholly *undetermined.* Judgment, through its a priori principle of judging nature in terms of possible particular laws of nature, provides nature's supersensible substrate (within as well as outside us) with *determinability* [*Bestimmbarkeit*] *by the intellectual power.* But reason, through its a priori practical law, gives this same substrate *determination.* Thus judgment makes possible the transition from the domain of the concept of nature to that of the concept of freedom.[3]

Kant's effort to find an a priori principle that would allow "nature" to be "judged" even in its most heterogeneous particularity—which here is also its singularity—involves nothing more nor less than establishing the *determinability—Bestimmbarkeit—*of nature as it is in and of itself, which is to say, in its "supersensible substrate." And yet, as is clear from the passage just quoted, such *determinability* is to be distinguished from actual *determination,* since nothing in nature is effectively determined by the *ability to judge.* No objective concept is produced or invoked, nothing is cognized. Only an abstract principle is produced—purposiveness without purpose—which however demon-

strates its universal validity as principle through its link to two other
-abilities. The first is perhaps the strangest of all -barkeiten, for it is the
one most clearly separated from any subjective faculty. It is the term
Unmittelbarkeit, in English: immediacy (the -ability disappears in this
translation). In an aesthetic judgment of taste, of beauty, or of the sublime, the pleasure or displeasure called up is immediately attached to
the judgment, without mediation of a concept. Normally, this immediate link of pleasure or displeasure to a representation would mark it as
strictly subjective, in the sense of being individual, empirical, and of
limited validity. But the pleasure or displeasure attached to an aesthetic
judgment of taste claims universal validity despite, or rather because of,
this immediacy. Its ability to stake this claim depends on the third major ability of Kant's Third Critique, and it is one that we will find ech-
oed, albeit transformed, in the early writings of Benjamin. This term is
Mitteilbarkeit, usually translated in English as "communicability," but
which might be more accurately rendered as "impart-ability." An even
more literal translation would be the ability to part-with; but given the
difficulty of actually using this phrase, I will limit myself to the first two
translations.

In the Third Critique, such "communicability" or "impart-ability" is
what takes the place of the objective, conceptual universality that
defines judgment in the familiar sense, involving the determination of
the particular by the general. In the case of what Kant designates as "reflecting judgments," including the "aesthetic judgments of taste," the
particular is not determined but only experienced as determinable insofar as feelings of pleasure (or displeasure) associated with its apprehension are felt to be immediately and universally communicable.
Determinability thus depends on communicability. But just as he distinguished determinability from determination, Kant distinguishes communicability from actual communication: "Nothing, however, can be
communicated universally [allgemein mitgeteilt werden] except cognition, as well as presentation insofar as it pertains to cognition" (KdU,
131; CoJ, 61). No knowledge, however, is actually communicated in
the aesthetic judgment of beauty or of the sublime: rather, a certain
state of mind (Gemütszustand) that is felt to be indissolubly linked to a
singular representation is experienced as being potentially communicable, which is to say, capable of being communicated universally. This
experience is in turn associated with pleasure or displeasure.[4]

In these two instances, then, Kant invokes his -abilities not merely to designate a possibility in the sense of a mode of or means of actualization, but rather to define an experience that is related to cognition but is nevertheless non-cognitive; indeed, it could be called *affective*, although Kant does not use this term, since it involves a "feeling" or a "state of mind" that is produced from without: from the encounter with a singularity that is apprehended, perceived, or represented in a way that renders it universalizable.

Both of these two Kantian -abilities—*Bestimmbarkeit* and *Mitteilbarkeit*—reemerge in Benjamin's early writings, but with a decisive shift: for now they are situated not primarily within a horizon of knowledge, but within one of language.[5] In this chapter I will only be able to deal with the first of these, although as we will see, the two are ultimately inseparable.

Determinability appears in Benjamin's essay on "Two Poems of Friedrich Hölderlin," written in the winter of 1916–1917. I will limit my analysis to the specific way in which this Kantian -ability is re-inscribed by the young Benjamin, mindful of the fact that this question would by rights require a much more elaborate account than I can give here.

Let me begin by anticipating the result of the analysis. Whereas in Kant the effort is to describe *-abilities* as constituting the conditions of a possibility in view of its full realization, while acknowledging that such realization can never be fully accessible to (theoretical) knowledge—for Benjamin the primary question no longer concerns *Erkenntnisvermögen* but rather *Sprachvermögen,* the potentialities of language, which, qua signifying process, entail *impossibility* no less than *possibility.* This difference can be interpreted negatively, as the impossibility of ever realizing, in a full and self-present act of cognition, the "abilities" involved; or it can be interpreted positively, as a *virtuality* that, precisely because it can never hope to be fully instantiated or exhausted in any one realization, remains open to the future, which is to say, to what Benjamin in the title of another essay of this period calls *das Kommende (Über das Programm der kommenden Philosophie).*[6] In other words, already in these early writings, the *"Jetzt der Erkennbarkeit"* is implicitly distinguished from anything like a meaningful present, which is also why it cannot be identified with an object of knowledge. Benjamin is thus faithful—perhaps more faithful than Kant himself—to the Kantian distinction between "thinking" and "knowing."[7] It entails a virtuality that is never fully actualizable and therefore involves an "experience" of movement and alteration rather than a reproduction of the same—or of the self.

Turning now to the essay on Hölderlin, Benjamin introduces the term *Bestimmbarkeit* in the opening pages, when he attempts to define his procedure, which he designates as an "aesthetic commentary [*ästhetischer Kommentar*]" (*GS2*, 105; *SW1*, 18), aimed at elaborating the "inner form" of the two poems involved. This "inner form" he then goes on to identify with the "poetic task" *(dichterische Aufgabe),* in which the "evaluation" of the poem by the critic is grounded. What is decisive here, Benjamin insists, is not the degree to which the poet has *accomplished* this poetic task, but rather "the seriousness and greatness of the task" itself. This task has to be derived from a reading of the poem, although at the same time—and here a certain circularity emerges—it serves as the "premise" *(Voraussetzung)* of the poem, "as the intellectual-regardable *(geistig-anschaulich)* structure of the world to which the poem bears witness" (ibid.).

Benjamin does not explicitly discuss the circularity that here begins to link task, poem, and commentary, but he clearly rejects any attempt to resolve such circularity by recurring to ostensibly non-circular empirical instances, such as the "person or world-view of the creator." In place of this traditional appeal to an authorial intention or person, he introduces the term that will guide him in his introductory methodological discussion—the "sphere" that is both "product and object of the investigation" can neither be equated with the poet, nor with the poem: "This sphere, which for every poem [*Dichtung*] has its own shape [*Gestalt*] shall be designated as the poetized [*das Gedichtete*]" (ibid.). This sphere of the "poetized," in which Benjamin situates the "truth" of the poem (and of poetry: *Dichtung*), is thus peculiar to each singular poem, and receives its particular "shape" as its "inner form."

But if the poetized is thus manifested as the inner form of the poem, it is not entirely inherent in it either. Rather, Benjamin describes it as a "borderline concept" *(Grenzbegriff),* and this in a "dual respect" *(doppelter Hinsicht).* The first and most obvious aspect concerns the poem itself. The "poetized" is a borderline concept with respect to the "poem," from which it distinguishes itself as a "category of aesthetic investigation" *(ästhetischer Untersuchung).* On the other side of the "border" is "life," which Benjamin also identifies as the origin of the "poetic task." As borderline concept, "the poetized reveals itself to be the transition from the functional unity of life to that of the poem" (*GS2*, 107; *SW1*, 19–20). Yet if Benjamin writes that "life is the poetized of the poem," it is not the personal life of the poet that is meant but rather a "context of life [*Lebenszusammenhang*] determined through art" (*GS2*, 107; *SW1*, 20).

The question then becomes just how "art"—here the poem—"determines" the "context of life." And so it is no wonder that the category of "determination"—*Bestimmung*—is at the core of Benjamin's discussion of the poems, and also the basis of his contrasting evaluation of them. It is not necessary to go into the details of that evaluation here, and it is also not my main concern. Rather, it is the *ability to determine and be determined* that is of interest in this context, and it is precisely this term—*Bestimmbarkeit*—that Benjamin invokes to distinguish the poetized—*das Gedichtete*, sphere of the poem's truth—from the poem itself, as well as from "life," that sets the poem its "task." After having asserted that the *Gedichtete* shares with the poem itself the unity of form and content, Benjamin goes on to attempt to describe the decisive distinction between the two as a difference not in "principle," but in degree. This degree, however, turns out to be of a rather unusual, non-quantitative kind:

> [The poetized] differs from the poem as a limit concept [*Grenzbegriff*], as the concept of its task, not simply through some fundamental characteristic but solely through its greater determinability [*Bestimmbarkeit*]; not through a quantitative lack of determinations but rather through the potential existence of those that are effectively [*aktuell*] present in the poem—and others [*und anderer*]. The poetized is a loosening up of the firm functional coherence that reigns in the poem itself, and it cannot arise otherwise than by disregarding certain determinations, so that the meshing, the functional unity of the other elements is made evident [*sichtbar*]. (*GS2*, 106; *SW1*, 19)[8]

The stylistic movement of this passage is extremely characteristic of what I would call the discontinuous mode of argumentation that marks so many of Benjamin's texts.[9] It also explains why he should have been so appreciative of Kant's torturous, if not tortured, philosophical style of writing, which as we have seen he defended against all criticism. If such barely grammatical phrases could be seen as emblematic of the "*Ringen*"—the struggle—that Benjamin so valued in Kant, the same can be discerned in his own writing, and perhaps particularly in those texts that were never published in his lifetime, such as the essay on Hölderlin. For in those texts Benjamin allows himself to think and write things out to an extreme that he cannot necessarily resolve or synthesize into grammatically or stylistically "correct" formulations and phrases. That process is particularly in evidence here, at the end of the second sentence quoted, where Benjamin strives to describe positively that wherein the distinctive quality of the poetized consists. He has already stated what it does *not* consist in: it does not consist in a *"prinzipielles Merkmal"* but rather in a "greater determinability"; that "determinability," however, is not "greater" in a simply quantitative sense. On the contrary, if one can take Benjamin's formulation here literally, it seems as if the poetized has *fewer* determinations than does the poem. But those fewer determinations nevertheless contribute to a "greater determinability." How is this possible? Precisely through the predominance of *possibility* in the poetized, which is constituted by the "potential existence" *(potentielles Dasein)* of determinations that in the poem are "actually present" *(aktuell vorhanden).* This is also why the poetized does not distinguish itself from the poem by any "principled mark or trait" *(prinzipielles Merkmal).* For there is nothing "principled" about the poetized: it merely takes its cue from the poem—or looking ahead, to the essays on the "Task of the Translator" and on "The Work of Art in the Age of its Technical Reproducibility"—we could also say that it takes its cue from its "original." But it does so, already here, in a way that anticipates and perhaps even transcends many of the theorems unfolded in the later essays. For the "potential" determinability of the poetized virtualizes not merely the determinations that are actually present in the poem, but "others" as well. It is here that we stumble on the most awkward formulation of the entire essay, one that Benjamin would perhaps have expunged had he revised it for publication. But he did not do so, and what remains is as "intellectually provocative," as *denkwürdig,* as it is stylistically and philosophically monstrous. Since the passage was previously cited in English, I will now cite the full German sentence, in which Benjamin tries to provide a positive determination of how the poetized distinguishes itself from the poem: not in principle, but "Vielmehr lediglich durch seine größere Bestimmbarkeit: nicht durch eine quantitative Mangel an Bestimmungen, sondern durch das potentielle Dasein derjenigen, die im

Gedicht aktuell vorhanden sind *und anderer*" (*GS2*, 106; *SW1*, 19; my emphasis). Note the last two words: *und anderer.* They are appended, *angehängt*, at the end of the sentence as a kind of afterthought, a kind of suffix not to a word this time but to the sentence.[10] What it does, however, is very similar to what Benjamin has described as the effect of the poetized on the poem: it brings about *"eine Auflockerung der festen funktionellen Verbundenheit, die im Gedichte* (here: in Benjamin's sentence—SW) *selbst waltet."* Let me try to paraphrase and in the process sum up the result of this all too brief reading: The "greater determinability" of the poetized—which is the object of the aesthetic commentary—consists first in the fact that it reinscribes the determinations that are "actually present" in the poem in a text that renders those determinations "possible," "potential," virtual perhaps. But in so doing—in potentializing and virtualizing determination as determinability—the poetized cannot limit itself simply to the determinations *actually present* in the poem: it must also take into account *"anderer."* What those "other" determinations are Benjamin does not say—not here at least. But by suggesting that the poem is an attempt to resolve a task set by "life," he makes clear that the "inner form" of the poem cannot simply be internal to the poem itself, since the poem is a *response* to a challenge and task that antedates and transcends its singularity, while at the same time calling it into being.

The paradox here, as Benjamin puts it toward the conclusion of this very long and complex paragraph, is that if the poem (and "life") are characterized by "functional unity," "insight into the function presupposes the multiplicity of combinatorial *possibilities* [*Verbindungsmöglichkeiten*]." Such an insight, however, is not construed by Benjamin as a synoptic view, but rather as the problematic result of an *Absehen—a looking away from, rather than a looking toward: "Sie kann nicht anders entstehen als durch ein Absehen von gewissen Bestimmungen."* The result is that in order to approach the poem with ever greater determinacy *(Bestimmtheit),* "das Gedichtete [muß] von gewissen Bestimmungen absehen" (*GS2*, 106; *SW1*, 19).[11]

We see here how the ability to be determined—the "greater determinability" of the poetized—depends directly on the ability to indetermine: to avert one's view from what cannot be taken in. Looking at and looking away are not mutually exclusive, but rather inseparable. This suggests how and why determinability, and Benjamin's -abilities more generally, go hand and hand with the negotiation of inability, and why looking up—*der Augenaufschlag,* as he writes in the *Trauerspiel* book[12]—always also means looking away.

Perhaps it is this convergence of looking at, looking-away, and looking-up that explains why the primary of Benjamin's -abilities is readability. And also why the now of knowability—*das Jetzt der Erkennbarkeit*—is also the moment in which readability parts company with determinate meaning and knowledge, not by dissolving its relation to it, but by acknowledging the irreducible immediacy—the *Un-mittel-barkeit*—of its medium of language to be the greatest -ability of all.

CHAPTER THREE

Criticizability—Calculability

Walter Benjamin's Ph.D. thesis, "The Concept of Criticism in German Romanticism," written at the University of Bern during the First World War, was to be his first, and last, academic success. The book's apparently straightforward title calls for a few preliminary terminological clarifications. Such clarifications will have to be preliminary not least of all because the very notion of "terminology" itself will turn out to constitute one of the most significant aspects of the Romanticism with which Benjamin is concerned. In a letter written in November 1918 to his friend Gerhard Scholem, Benjamin remarks that although it is "out of the Romantic concept of criticism that the modern notion has emerged," the term was nevertheless used by the Romantics in a way very different from that which is familiar today, namely as "an entirely esoteric concept (one of the most hidden), based upon mystical presuppositions insofar as knowledge is concerned."[1] We will return to this "esoteric" and "mystical" aspect shortly. Before we do, however, it should be noted that "Romanticism" in this book is largely identified with the writings of only two of its German proponents: first of all, Friedrich Schlegel, and second, Novalis. Moreover, the work of Schlegel held to be exemplary by Benjamin is largely that published during the relatively short period from 1799 to 1801, that is, the work centered on the brief life of the periodical he founded and edited, the *Athenaeum* (1798–1800).[2]

If, then, one of the most insistent motifs that will emerge from his study of German Romanticism can be described as the *problem of self-delimitation* [*Selbstbeschränkung*], then Benjamin's book itself provides an exemplary performance of such self-limiting. Not merely insofar as it limits its source materials, both primary and secondary, to a minuscule fraction of German Romantic writing on the notion of criticism—not to mention its literary production as such (poetry, narrative fiction, theater)—but also in that it defines its own scope and style. The result is what Peter Demetz has called "a professionally done dissertation,"[3] although precisely as such it stopped just short of what Benjamin himself considered to be the essential issues at stake—issues that are inscribed both in his letters of the period and also in the margins and interstices of the thesis itself.

Thus Benjamin describes his study as an attempt not "to present the historical essence of Romanticism" as such, but rather to collect "materials" that might contribute to such a definition. That essence itself, he adds in a footnote, "should presumably be sought after in the . . . messianism" of the Romantics, which he characterizes by citing the following short passage from a contemporary critic: "The thought of an ideal humanity perfecting itself ad infinitum is rejected; instead, what is demanded is the 'kingdom of God' now, in time and on earth . . . an ideal realized at every level of life—out of this categorical demand emerges Schlegel's new religion" (*GS1*, 12–13, fn. 3; *SW1*, 185, fn. 5).[4] Benjamin's "professionally done dissertation" was thus intended to lead its readers to the limits of its explicitly treated subject-matter and point them beyond, in the direction of an "esoteric" dimension that transcends the purview of traditional scholarly discourse. All the more interesting, therefore, is that the "subject-matter" which was to perform this function was held by Benjamin to be the antecedent of what in the English-speaking world has come to be the primary meaning of the word "criticism" as well as its "theory."[5] But precisely this esoteric-mystical genealogy that Benjamin begins to elaborate in his dissertation is also what may well render the ostensible familiarity of "critical theory" strange, if not downright uncanny, to many of its writers and readers. For what turns out to distinguish this particular "subject-matter" is that it ultimately derives neither from the "subject" nor from "matter": or rather, it only "matters" insofar as it ceases to be purely subjective. And this in turn will have considerable significance for Benjamin's subsequent writings.

The starting-point, and perhaps also the end-point, of this uncanny genealogy is one that has since become quite familiar under the guise of "reception theory." It is the notion that criticism constitutes an integral and essential element of the artistic process, of no less importance or dignity than the work of art itself. Benjamin sums up the distinctive specificity of Romantic Critical Theory in two tenets: first, that the individual work of art has an intrinsically coherent structure. And second, that an essential characteristic of this structure, and hence of the work itself, is that it is "criticizable" *(kritisierbar)*. Which is to say, that it requires critical reflection in order to fulfill its artistic function. Criticism, so conceived, does not involve primarily the "evaluation" of individual works—this might be called the classical or neoclassical conception—but rather their "fulfillment," or, as Novalis writes, their *"Vollendung."* This German word, Benjamin emphasizes, must be read in the double sense, entailing on the one hand the *completion* or *consummation* of the work, and on the other, its *consumption or dissolution:* its *Voll-endung.* If the work is finite, criticism infinitizes it; were the work a living being, and hence, mortal, criticism would thus be its salvation and transfiguration.

This double aspect of Romantic Critical Theory—its elevation of the work to the status of a highly organized, autonomous structure, determined by its own, intrinsic laws, and the concomitant elevation of the critical process, as the culmination, continuation, and confirmation of those laws above and beyond the limitations of the original work—allows Schlegel and Novalis to be considered the founders of modern criticism. But it also indicates that the "secular" nature of such criticism is not as far removed from its origins in Biblical criticism (and in particular, Christian interpretation of the Old Testament as preparation for the New), as is commonly supposed. Nor would it be farfetched or difficult to extend Benjamin's analysis of Romantic criticism to contemporary criticism, whether in its formalist heritage, focusing on the immanent analysis of individual works, or in its more recent, more pragmatic, historicist versions, which construe the literary text to be an artifact that both consumes and fulfills itself in the reception or readings it receives. In this sense, not as much has changed in the eighty-five years or so since Benjamin wrote his dissertation. Except— and this is hardly trivial—that the subjectivism of such criticism was probably more self-conscious in a Germany dominated by neo-

Kantianism than it is today, when many critics believe they have left the subject behind in appealing to ostensibly more "material" or "historical" notions—as though such "objective" perspectives were conceivable independently of the subjective vantage-point that remains the epistemological (and historical) condition of their possibility.

Nevertheless, whether conscious or unconscious, it is precisely such subjectivism that renders the contemporary heirs of Romanticism so unable to grasp the thrust of its criticism. "These Romantics," Benjamin writes, citing Erwin Kircher, "sought precisely to distance themselves from what was then called Romanticism, and what still is today."[6] What modern critics fail to see, argues Benjamin, is the importance of the notion of *work*, which, for Schlegel and Novalis, is not the mere by-product of subjectivity, as it is often misconstrued by modern authors, but rather its corrective. The "determinate, immanent structure" attributed by the early Romantics to the individual work is no longer conceived in neoclassical categories such as "harmony or organization." Instead, the relative autonomy of the individual work and its structure now depends on "a general notion of art as a reflective medium and of the work as a center of reflection" (*GS1,* 71–72; *SW1,* 155). It is this notion of art as a *medium of reflection* that leads Benjamin to assert that Romantic Critical Theory is not in essence subjective, that it "has to do exclusively with the objective structure of art—as idea, [and] with its manifestations [*Gebilde*]—as works" (*GS1,* 13; *SW1,* 118). And again: "Criticism, which today is grasped as the most subjective of activities, was for the Romantics a regulative of subjectivity, contingency and arbitrariness in the emergence of works" (*GS1,* 80; *SW1,* 160).

What is at stake, then, in Benjamin's account of German Romantic Critical Theory is nothing less usual, idiosyncratic—or, if you will, original—than the effort to elaborate a notion or practice of "reflexivity" that would not be rooted ultimately in a constitutive subject. His first move is to define the way in which the Romantic use of reflection both depends on and diverges from its most immediate philosophical antecedent, Johann Fichte. Schlegel's conception of reflection, as Benjamin describes it, consists in three moments or "levels." First there is thought in its immediate form, thought of an object—what Schlegel calls "sense" *(Sinn).* Second, there is what he calls "reason": thinking that takes as its object the sense, or *Sinn,* of the first, immediate thought. This level could also be called reflection proper. In the relationship of the Romantics to Fichte, the decisive difference emerges in the varying ways in which this second level of reflection is interpreted. For Fichte, such reflection only makes sense, only "exists correlative to an act of positing [*Setzen*]," which in turn implies an I *(Ich)* as its origin and agent: "Fichtean reflection resides in absolute positing . . . outside of which it means nothing, because it leads into the void" (*GS1*, 29; *SW1*, 128). "With Fichte reflection relates to the I, with the Romantics it relates to pure thinking," Benjamin adds, emphasizing that such reflection is unbounded by any being or entity such as an Ego: "Romantic thinking absorbs *(hebt . . . auf)* being and positing into reflection" (ibid.). This is why for the Romantics the essence of thought as reflection is not limited by the positional act of an I to its second form of reflection "proper" but instead entails necessarily and structurally a third and far more ambivalent level: "The thinking of thinking of thinking (and so on)" (*GS1*, 30; *SW1*, 129). In short, without the self-positing I to limit and contain reflection, the latter initiates a movement that entails the "decomposition" *(Zersetzung)* of what Benjamin calls the "archetypal, canonical form of reflection" (ibid.) into a "peculiar ambiguity [*eigentümliche Doppeldeutigkeit*]": reflection proper finds itself split, as it were, into either an object or a subject, or rather into both: the "thinking of thinking" functions both as an object (of third-level thoughts) and/or as a subject—the thinking of thinking—which has "thinking," in its initial form, as its object (ibid.). This equivocation or ambiguity is what led philosophers, from Fichte to Hegel, to search for a way of transcending mere reflection in order to avoid the vicious circle, the *regressus ad infinitum* that reflection in its "pure" and unadulterated form would entail.

The Romantics as Benjamin describes them do not draw back from this danger: on the contrary, even before Hegel, Schlegel sees Fichte's attempt to enclose reflection within the opposition of a self-positing I and a counter-posited not-I as precisely falling prey to the infinite regress: "Whenever the thought of the I is not at one with the concept of the world, such pure thinking of the thought of the I leads only to eternal self-mirroring, to an infinite series of mirror-images that contains only the same and never anything new" (*GS1*, 35; *SW1*, 131–132). The response of the Romantics is to construe reflection not as the act of an I, but as the process of a Self that can no longer be contained or comprehended in terms of the opposition of being and positing, I and not-I, subject and object, but only in terms of the Absolute: "Reflection expands itself without limit and the thinking thus formed in reflection becomes a formless thought that is directed at the Absolute" (*GS1, 31; SW1, 129*). This "Absolute," unlike that of Fichte, however, is determined "not as the consciousness of an I but as reflection in the medium of art" (*GS1, 39; SW1, 134*). Such reflection has two manifestations: the first is the individual work of art itself; the second, criticism. Criticism is "second" logically and chronologically, since it addresses already existing works. But its very secondariness makes it the exemplary manifestation of art as a "medium of absolute reflection" since the individuation of reflection in the work arrests the process at the same time that it determines it. If criticism arises out of the work, and in that sense depends on it, the work in turn depends on an "idea" of absolute reflection that it restricts and dissimulates by giving it finite shape. This restriction is raised and reflection reinstated through the process of criticism.

The problems that emerge from such an account are of course obvious and not neglected by Benjamin. In a word they focus on the question of "self-limitation." A remark of Novalis cited by Benjamin demonstrates that the Romantics themselves were well aware of the difficulty: "The possibility of self-limitation is the possibility of all synthesis, of all miracle. And the world began with a miracle" (*GS1, 35; SW1, 132*). Everything depends on the way in which art, as the medium of absolute reflection, limits itself in this account. The key term here is the notion of "context," "coherence," or "structure," all of which are partial translations of the Romantic notion of *Zusammenhang* (literally: hanging-together). By calling attention to the "systematic" character of Romantic thought in general, Benjamin emphasizes that the notion of the Absolute as artistic reflection is essentially synchronic, not diachronic, despite Schlegel's famous definition of "romantic poetry" as "progressive universal poetry" (*GS1, 93; SW1, 168*). This definition, Benjamin argues, has nothing to do with the notion of a temporal progress or "becoming"—a notion sharply criticized by Schlegel (ibid.). Instead, it seeks to articulate the essentially unfinished process by which the reflective medium differentiates itself: "What is essential is rather that the task of progressive universal poetry is given in the most determinate way in a medium of forms, as the latter's increasingly exact and pervasive ordering [*dessen fortschreitend genauere Durchwaltung und Ordnung*]" (*GS1*, 92; *SW1*, 168). What the absolute infinitude of art involves, then, is not the progressive realization of a self-identical ideal or entity, but the articulation of a medium understood to consist in a "continuum of forms." This medium can be said to "unfold" in the individual work qua "system" or "Zusammenhang" (complex), and criticism, as an "experiment" performed on the work, continues this process of "unfolding." The question now to be confronted is how such an "unfolding" is to be construed.

Benjamin's response is not, to be sure, given explicitly in this text, since it would inevitably have led him to address directly the issue that exceeds the bounds he set himself for his thesis. Not surprisingly, however, it is implicit in his reflections on the Romantic approach to the question of form. "Practical, i.e. determinate reflection, self-limitation, comprise the individuality and form of the work" (*GS1*, 73; *SW1*, 156). Form is thus conceived not as a means of exhibiting or of representing *(darstellen)* content, but as "a peculiar modification of reflection, limiting itself" (*GS1*, 76; *SW1*, 158). Criticism reflects and thereby de-limits—that is, dissolves—the "positive" form of the individual work by exposing its appurtenance to the more general medium of reflection, which for the Romantics comprises the determining Idea of art itself. The problem remains, however, that of explaining just how such a general idea of reflection can *limit itself* in individual works and still remain pure reflection. The problem is clear to the Romantics, as the following remark, once again of Novalis, cited by Benjamin, indicates: "A work is formed when it is sharply limited everywhere, but within its limits [it is] limitless . . . everywhere the same and yet sublimely beyond itself" (ibid.). As individuation of the general medium of reflection, the individual work can fulfill its function only insofar as it is driven out of and beyond itself, and thus is ultimately dissolved in— and into—the critical process. The "value" of the work can thus be measured by the degree to which it allows this process—that is, criticism—to take place: by the degree, that is, to which it is "criticizable" (*GS1*, 79; *SW1*, 160). Such criticism, Benjamin insists, "is not bent primarily on judging [*beurteilend*] the individual work, but rather on exposing its relations to all other works and finally to the idea of art" (*GS1*, 78; *SW1*, 159–160).

Precisely how the exposure *(Darstellung)* of such "relations" is to lead to "the idea of art" as a general medium of absolute reflection remains an open question in Benjamin's account of Romantic Critical Theory. And yet the possibility of a response can be glimpsed in Benjamin's discussion of Romantic irony. Benjamin distinguishes between two kinds of irony. The first, the more familiar, is felt to demonstrate the sovereignty of the author, who thereby shows himself to be free of all material constraint. This irony, which is generally identified with Romantic subjectivism, if not subjectivity, Benjamin designates as "material irony" in order to distinguish it from a second variety, which he finds both more "positive" in character and less subjective: the irony of form. Unlike material irony, that of form cannot be identified with the sheer freedom of the subject, since all art is "subordinated" to the "objective lawfulness" of a certain formality (GS1, 83; SW1, 162). Such irony thus "attacks" the "illusoriness" of the form of a work, without however utterly abandoning it. In thus undermining the integrity of the individual work, formal irony resembles criticism, which also tends ultimately to annihilate the work. All the more revealing, then, is the difference that Benjamin elaborates when he compares the two, formal irony and criticism:

> How does irony's destruction of illusion in artistic form relate to the destruction of the work through criticism? Criticism sacrifices the work utterly to the will of the One Cohesive Context [um des Einen Zusammenhanges willen]. [Formal irony] on the contrary does not merely not destroy the work that it attacks: it tends to render it indestructible . . . Formal irony is not, like fortitude or rectitude, an intentional behavior of an author. It cannot, as is usually done, be considered the index of a subjective lack of limits; rather it must be valued as an objective moment in the work itself. It represents the paradoxical attempt to continue building a structure even as one tears it down [Sie stellt den paradoxen Versuch dar, am Gebilde noch durch Abbruch zu bauen]: the effort to demonstrate the work's relation to the idea in the work itself. (GS1, 86–87; SW1, 164)

Although in an age familiar with "deconstruction" such "paradoxical attempts" may seem less daring than at the time they were written, Benjamin's description here of the Romantic "ironizing of form" marks a decisive point in his interpretation of Romantic Critical Theory—and beyond. With respect to Benjamin's later work, this discussion of *formal irony* foreshadows the theory of "allegory" that he will articulate some six years later in his second, and this time definitively unsuccessful, attempt at academic writing—his "Habilitationsschrift, the Origins of the German Mourning Play." In terms of the dissertation itself, the account of formal irony contains the germs of an alternative to the impasse of Romantic Critical Theory, which, as Benjamin makes clear in no uncertain terms, lies precisely in its tendency to conflate "the profane with the symbolic form . . . Only at the cost of such imprecise demarcations can all the concepts of critical theory be integrated into the realm of the Absolute, as the Romantics intended" (GS1, 98; SW1, 172). Although Benjamin himself does not spell it out, what he calls here the "profane" form can be identified with the "positive" form of the individualized work, a form that can never be adequately understood as the manifestation of the self-delimitation of the absolute, which is to say, of reflection itself.[7] To distinguish between a "profane" and a "symbolic form" is to take into account that any "positive" or profane aesthetic form of reflection can never "contain" the Absolute within its borders or lead to it by any continuous path. In contrast to the immanence of the symbol (which, as Benjamin will later state in his discussion of allegory, is only at home in theology, not in aesthetics), the "profane" form of the individual work of art involves a process of delimitation that can never, as such, be assimilated to the Absolute: whether as reflection or in any other guise. The Romantic attempt to define criticism in precisely such terms is thus forced to rely ultimately on an "axiomatic presupposition" that sidesteps rather than addresses the decisive relation of reflection and form by advancing, as an article of belief, "that reflection is in itself substantial and fulfilled, and does not run off into an empty infinity" (GS1, 31; SW1, 129). This is why the "formal irony" to which Benjamin refers is not really a part of Romantic Critical Theory proper, but rather of Romantic literary practice, here identified with the theatrical writing of Ludwig Tieck rather than with Schlegel or Novalis. The unmistakable implication is that the only way out of the impasse of Romantic criticism—which is also that of modern criticism tout court—lies not in the effort to dissolve the work in an absolute and ultimately self-identical critical reflection, but in a practice of writing that, precisely by undermining the integrity of the individual "form," at the same time allows the singular work to "survive." But it "survives" as a different kind of writing—as a writing of difference and of alteration. Such writing would be "critical" in that it would "reflect"—and hence, alter—an already "given" "positive" form or set of delimitations. But such alteration would not be the transfiguration of a "profane" form into a symbolic one envisaged by the Romantics when they wrote of "the pure expression of reflective self-limitation," since the "ironization of form" would remain as profane as the form it "survives" (the verb here to be understood both transitively and intransitively). To insist, as does Benjamin, discreetly but firmly, on the necessary distinction between "profane" and "symbolic form" is to emphasize that the reflective delimitations that constitute "form" can never be grasped entirely or essentially in terms of a "self." The Romantics sought to disengage reflection from the subject in replacing the Fichtean opposition of I and Not-I with an Absolute Self. Benjamin seeks to demonstrate how this movement cannot and does not stop at this "axiomatic presupposition" either. Thus, although the Romantics insist that the general medium of reflection that constitutes the determining "idea" of art must be conceived as a "continuum of forms," when they set about interpreting the kind of language and writing that most powerfully exemplifies "the highest of all symbolic forms" and "the Romantic idea of poetry itself" (*GS1*, 99; *SW1*, 173), they privilege a mode of writing that they themselves describe as discontinuous, the prosaic writing of the novel: "The writing style of the novel must not form a continuum, it must be a structure articulated in each of its periods. Each small piece must be detached, limited, its own whole" (quoted by Benjamin in *GS1*, 99; *SW1*, 172). Such a discontinuous style of writing culminates in the Romantics' notion of "prose" as the highest "idea of poetry": in prose, "poetry expands itself . . . by contracting, abandoning its combustion [*Feuerstoff*], congealing" and thus "assuming a prosaic appearance" in which its components "no longer form the same intimate community" as in poetry but are therefore all the more capable of "presenting the limited." The movement of phrase becomes "simpler, more monotonous, quieter," the context "more flexible," the expression "more transparent and colorless" (Novalis, quoted by Benjamin in *GS1*, 101; *SW1*, 174). Thus the entire Romantic "philosophy of art" is determined by an "idea of poetry as prose" that in turns leads to an idea that marks both the culmination and the limits of Romanticism: the idea of the *Nüchternheit* or "sobriety of art" (*GS1*, 103; *SW1*, 175). This proposition, which is "the essentially new and fundamental thought of the Romantic philosophy of art," is most fully articulated outside of Romanticism proper, in the work of Hölderlin. The notion of "sobriety," which Benjamin affirms is "even today powerfully at work with unforeseeable consequences," exceeds the scope of his study; he therefore merely indicates Hölderlin's emphasis on the "calculability" and hence the element of *repetition* at work in the procedures of poetry. It is such calculable repetition that explains the effect of formal irony in assuring a certain survival of the work: "What disintegrates in the ironic ray is strictly the illusion, what remains indestructible however is the nucleus of the work, consisting not in ecstasy, which can be decomposed, but in the unassailably [*unantastbar*] prosaic figure" (*GS1*, 106; *SW1*, 176). Everything depends, we discover, on the way in which the "calculable laws" and rhythms of a certain repetitive language—both prosaic and poetic—are to be conceived, and even more, practiced. Here this question will bring Benjamin to a term that defines the limits of his thesis but also the horizon of his future work on the *Origin of the Mourning Play* and on allegory. That term is *Darstellung*: usually translated as "presentation" or "exposition." Here however, toward the conclusion of the book, it is used in a different way to describe the function of criticism in light of the "sobriety of art." Since Benjamin will define the word himself, I will cite it in German: "Criticism is the *Darstellung* of the prosaic nucleus in each work. The concept *Darstellung* is thereby to be understood in the chemical sense, as the production of one substance [*Erzeugung des Stoffes*] through a determinate process to which others are *subjected*. This is what Schlegel meant when he said of Wilhelm Meister that the work does not merely judge itself, it also sets itself forth [*stellt sich dar*]" (*GS1*, 109; *SW1*, 178, my emphasis).

The Romantic idea of criticism thus turns out to consist in a process of recombination, through which "others" are subjected so that something can matter. Criticism, in this sense perhaps indistinguishable from poetry, reveals its essence to reside in a process that leads from the criticizability of works to the calculability of subjection that stages *(stellt dar)* its self-transformation in a movement that breaks with the vicious circle of self-reflection by generating something else. Out of the *mise en abyme* of self-reflection emerges the uncanny recurrence of what is like but never the same.

CHAPTER FOUR

Impart-ability

Language as Medium

Possibility, Virtuality, and the Politics of Actualization (Gilles Deleuze)

"The more closely one looks at a word, the more distantly it looks back"—this aphorism of Karl Kraus, cited by Walter Benjamin,[1] seems nowhere more applicable today than with respect to the words "media" and "virtuality." We live increasingly in a world of virtualities: not just images are "virtual," but "reality" itself, including libraries, universities, and indeed, "virtually" anything at all. That words should become increasingly imprecise the more widely they are used is not particularly surprising. But when they assume a scope and significance affecting "virtually" all walks of life, such a situation can be cause for concern. In the following remarks I will attempt to address this predicament by reviewing certain aspects of the recent and not so recent history of these two words.

I begin with one of the most astute and prolific French theoreticians of the media, Pierre Lévy, who argues that "virtualization" distinguishes itself above all through "a movement of becoming-other or heterogenesis,"[2] which he in turn opposes, following Gilles Deleuze, to the "here and now," or what in French is called *actualité*. This approach to the virtual derives from what is perhaps the first extended philosophical examination of this term, in Deleuze's book, *Difference and Repetition*, first published in 1968.[3] In the fourth chapter of this book, "Synthesis of Difference," Deleuze reflects on his previous use of the word "virtual" and comes to the following conclusions:

1. The *virtual* must above all be clearly distinguished from the *possible*. Whereas the possible is generally used to designate the "subsequently produced" image of a reality, with which it is associated through the category of "similarity," the virtual possesses its distinctive and proper reality.

2. This reality of the virtual Deleuze designates as its "structure."[4] Qua *structure* the virtual is not vague, but "fully defined." It consists of a manifold of elements that are both *singular* and *differential*.

3. Since the virtual, in contrast to the possible, already possesses a certain reality in itself, it cannot be simply defined in opposition to the real. It is already "real," although not in terms of its representational content or reference. The virtual is not oriented on or directed toward a reality existing outside of itself: rather, it is defined, negatively, with respect to the "actual," the here-and-now. This relation to the "actual" must be clearly distinguished from the relation of the possible to the real. The latter rests on similitude and identity, the former on alteration and differentiation. Whereas the possible therefore is expected to realize itself in the continuity of an entelechy, the virtual becomes actual, but only in *altering itself*. It realizes itself not in staying what it was, but in becoming something different: "Actualization, differentiation is in this sense continually a veritable creation."[5]

Deleuze's assimilation of "actualization" here not just to "differentiation" but also to "creation" is no empty rhetorical phrase. In regard to the transition from virtual to actual, Deleuze writes, four terms must be considered as synonymous: "Actualizing, differentiating, integrating, resolving. The nature of the virtual is so constructed that actualization signifies differentiation for it. Each differentiation is a local integration that converges with others in the entirety of the resolution in the global integration."[6] In the context of this definition of the actualization of the virtual as the global resolution of a problem, Deleuze invokes the notion of the *living* organism as being exemplary: "In this way the actualization process shows itself in the realm of the living to be the local differentiation of parts, *global formation of an inner mi-*

lieu, resolution of a problem . . ."[7] Deleuze shows himself here not only as the thinker who anticipates the significance of the virtual, but also as one who thinks of the notion of actualization, in however differential, singular, and heterogeneous a way, as the *global and integrative resolution* of problems. And since he considers the exemplary model of this global process of integration to be found in the *living being*, there is a certain consistency in the fact that he designates the overall process as *creative*. For what is involved here is nothing neither more nor less than the process by which living beings emerge as unified and whole. Despite his emphasis on difference and alteration, the horizon that informs Deleuze's elaboration of the notion of virtuality can thus be assimilated to what Heidegger has designated as "onto-theology," an approach that construes being in terms of identity and self-presence, however transcendent. "Life" is conceived from the perspective of unity, wholeness, and "global integration."

In the passages I have quoted, Deleuze defines actualization as local differentiation, and yet *at the same time* as the "global formation of an internal milieu," which in turn is equated with "global integration." As long as the virtual is construed primarily in the horizon of actualization qua "global integration," however, the notion will depend on an analogical conception of representation and of identity, all appeals to "digitalization" notwithstanding. This explains the ease with which Pierre Lévy transforms the Deleuzian notion of the virtual qua actualization into a theory of virtualization qua "humanization,"[8] a concept that Deleuze presumably would have categorically rejected. For as long as "local differentiation" can be said to operate in the service of "global integration," the concept of the virtual remains dependent on a notion of the whole that is traditionally associated with the privileged status of "man" whose image reflects and embodies the unity of the Creation deriving from a single Creator. If the "virtual" is thus understood as a moment in a process of "global integration," it reveals itself as the contemporary version of what in fact is a very ancient story. As we will see, however, that story of the virtual need not, as with Deleuze, confirm the tradition from which it emerges: it can also challenge and disrupt it. But it will do so only in conjunction with the second term I want to discuss, and that has become no less of a buzz-word these days, the notion of "media." I will begin with a brief recapitulation of what might be called "the classical concept of the medium," in order to then proceed to a thinker who transforms this notion in ways that both resemble and diverge from the approach of Deleuze.

The Classical Concept of "Medium"

In his discussion of the "virtual," Deleuze does not use the word "medium" but instead associates it with a related if distinct term, "milieu." The appeal to the notion of "milieu" has a dubious and indeed dangerous political progeny, going back to Hippolyte Taine, to whom of course Deleuze does not refer explicitly. Rather, he uses the word to situate the process of "integration," which provides the horizon of the "virtual." The "milieu" thus emerges in *Difference and Repetition* as the medium of the virtual. This approach to the notion of medium continues a venerable tradition that goes back at least as far as Aristotle's discussion of sense perception in his treatise *On the Soul (peri psyche).* The following passage indicates the conception of medium that informs his discussion:

> Democritus misrepresents the facts when he expresses the opinion that if the interspace [*to metaxou:* the medium as interval, that which is in between—SW] were empty, one could distinctly see an ant on the vault of the sky; that is an impossibility. Seeing is due to an affection or change of what has the perceptive faculty and it cannot be affected by the seen color itself; it remains that it must be affected by what comes between. Hence it is indispensable that there be *something* in between—if there were nothing, so far from seeing with greater distinctness, we should see nothing at all.[9]

The notion of "medium" here is already distinguished from a simple vacuum or a passive interval. But it is also demarcated from the opacity of matter. Only so can it fulfill its function, which entails both separation and connection, or rather, connection across a certain separation. The medium here is conceived as a separation that nonetheless binds, joins, not directly, but by means of a movement, a transmission, a transformation. In order to be perceived, visible phenomena—and it is no accident that the favored example of sense perception, and of the medium, always seems to be visual, or audiovisual—require a "medium" *through which they can move.* This is why the defining property of the medium, in this discussion of Aristotle, but perhaps also far more generally, is that of *transparency.* The medium must, as he puts it, be diaphanous *(to diaphanes).* It provides the element "in" and "through" which the data of sense pass on their way to their addressees. As we will see shortly, it is precisely this notion of medium that Walter Benjamin will criticize in elaborating a radically alternative approach to the notion of medium. In the case of Deleuze, on the contrary, the medium, qua milieu, constitutes a space that modifies itself, to be sure, but primarily in order to provide the internal coherence necessary for the "global integration" that defines the *telos* of virtuality as actualization.

There is every reason to believe that this Aristotelian approach to the medium as interval and as transmission still governs much of the discourse on it even today. For instance, the French theoretician Pierre Sorlin introduces his study of *Mass Media* by describing the generalized notion of "media" in order to warn against its simplifications:

> Originally, a medium is something lying in a middle or intermediate position—an agent, an object through which a purpose is accomplished. In other words there are two poles (for instance, two people) and between them a medium (for instance, a telephone or a fax). Nowadays, the media are the means by which information or entertainment is diffused. Who are they linking and to whom? Again, we are trapped by words. Whenever there is a medium, there is necessarily someone who acts and someone who receives and we cannot refrain from referring to the image conveyed by the term "medium" which means "something between." It was partially to counteract this stereotype that Marshall McLuhan launched his famous paradox, "the medium is the message." What he wanted to clarify was that any medium, because it is an instrument, modifies our hold over the world and consequently our interpretation of experience . . . It is helpful to emphasize the fact that what is known as "the media" includes a large variety of components and that study of the media must not follow the oversimplified scheme: sender/medium/destination.[10]

In these words of caution, Sorlin still seems to accept the notion of "medium" as an "instrument" that "modifies our hold over the world"—and hence, the notion that assisting "us" to get a "hold" on the world constitutes the primary object of this instrumentality. This notion, however, was problematized long before McLuhan, at the culmination of Western philosophy, in the dialectics of Hegel. For the dialectical process by which conceptual thinking determines itself, according to Hegel, proceeds through a dynamics that he designates, in German, as *Vermittlung* (in English: "mediation"). And although it is no secret that Hegel in general and this notion in particular builds on the Aristotelian tradition, it also modifies it in certain significant respects. Perhaps the most important of these is that for Hegel, the process of mediation no longer takes place "between" two entities or "poles," as Sorlin puts it, which could be construed as existing independently of it. Aristotle's (or Democritus's) ant, for instance, presumably does not depend on its being-seen, and hence on the medium of visibility, to exist. This is no longer true of the notion of dialectical "mediation." For what it brings to light is that individual entities indeed can only be constituted as what they are, as self-identical, by relating, negatively, to what they are not. It is through a specific set of such "not-nesses" that each entity acquires its positive properties. This in turn means that the "medium" of negativity and its "mediation" go on not simply "outside" or "between" objects, but *within* them. And it also means that the medium is not merely an "instrument," much less an interval, for "getting a hold on the world," but rather the movement through which that world constitutes itself. For Hegel, then, the theological notion of "creation" is replaced by the dialectical one of "mediation," functioning through "determinate negation." The medium, qua mediation, is already for Hegel the "message" and indeed much more: it quite literally in-forms the object by turning it *virtually* inside-out. Or rather, and this nuance is decisive: by *having turned it inside-out*. For the temporality and the tense are critical. The Hegelian mediation defines virtuality as the "past perfect" realizing itself as the determinate negation of the present. As Hegel describes it in his *Encyclopedia of Philosophical Sciences,* mediation is constituted through the contradiction of any one item *both* as a "beginning and having-advanced to a second, so that this second only is [what it is] insofar as it [in turn] has been reached from something other than itself."[11] The decisive parts of this difficult passage situate the movement of mediation ultimately in the presence of the past perfect. The individual entity is what it is only in its "having gone over" into a second entity or state: in German, *Fortgegangensein zu einem Zweiten.* And this second, other state in turn can only be understood for what it is to the extent that it condenses the process that has always already arrived at it coming from that other, first item: in German, *so daß dies Zweite nur ist, insofern zu demselben von einem gegen dasselbe Anderen gekommen worden ist.* In English this phrase is impossible to render exactly because there is not, as in German, a single verb that combines a *movement toward* something (and *away from* something else) with the *state* of having arrived or reached the goal: in short which combines *movement* with its *completion*. In German that word is supplied by the verb *to be,* which is used as an "auxiliary verb" in conjugating the present with the past, in forming the past perfect tense. Thus, in German one says that something or someone "*is* arrived" or "*is* come" rather than "*has* come or arrived." And it is precisely this grammatical rule that Hegel exploits in defining the dialectical movement of mediation as something that *will always already have taken place,* in the future perfect of the concept. Or, as Hegel describes this movement, as "a circle returning to itself."

The image of the circle indicates the two properties of the Hegelian conception of medium as mediation: it is infinite and it is self-enclosed. In the context of such mediation, "virtuality," a word that Hegel does not employ, is everywhere, and above all, "here and now" insofar as the unmediated present is always only a "moment" on the way to becoming what it "virtually" will always have been: a future perfecting itself as the presence of the past (perfect).

This Hegelian notion of medium qua mediation thus can be seen as anticipating, and perhaps encompassing, the "global integration" that Deleuze defines as the "actualization" of the "virtual." Universal mediation reduces every present to a moment of "differentiation" or of "alteration" in a process of totalization that will never simply be present, except as the reflected-anticipated medium of the future perfect. And this Hegelian universalization of the medium, qua mediation, also suggests how and why certain discourses on, and practices of, the "media" could today have come to supplant or to supplement religious discourse in its more traditional forms. For the Hegelian notion of mediation as an infinite process of becoming other in order to become the same, presents a strategy of safeguarding finitude from an alterity, and from a future that would not come full circle as a return of the same. To the extent to which the theory and practice of "the media" must conform to a logic and economy of appropriation in which the realization of "value" remains the dominant goal, the Hegelian dialectic remains, even today perhaps, the most powerful model of what might be described as "media theology," in which "mediation" takes over the function of "creatio ex nihilo." The "singularization" and simplification of the complex and plural notion of "the media" would be a symptom of this theology, whose aim can be interpreted as the legitimization of a world whose horizon is *informed* by "appropriation." It is a world in which one can "reasonably" hope to "get a hold on" on the future, indeed, in which reason is defined precisely in terms of such a project, which in turn depends on the control *of* "the media" (subjective *and* objective genitive).

The Immediacy of Impart-ability: Language as Medium (Walter Benjamin)

And yet, what distinguishes our epoch, at the beginning of the twenty-first century, is the paradox that precisely to the extent that this hold strives to extend its scope over the entire globe, it appears to *lose its grip*. And since "the media" seem to be part and parcel of this process, involving ever greater power and ever greater vulnerability, it is reasonable to search for alternative approaches to "the media" better able to take into account developments that seem to conform neither to the Hegelian nor to the Aristotelian models of virtuality and mediality. One such approach is that elaborated by Walter Benjamin, and perhaps nowhere more powerfully and more directly than in his early essay "On Language as Such and on the Language of Man" (1916). It is surely not fortuitous that Benjamin's initial confrontation with the problem of the "medium" concerns the question of "language 'overall' [*überhaupt*] and human language" in particular. For it is only with respect to language that the "medium" cannot be approached simply as though it were a self-contained or detached "object" of study. Like Ferdinand de Saussure, Benjamin begins his essay by stressing that the notion of language cannot be restricted to verbal discourse but is as much a trait of "things" and of institutions—law, politics, technology—as of persons. But the problem of objectifying language goes further for Benjamin: it is not simply extensive, but also intensive. A theory of language, he writes, must avoid the two tendencies hitherto prevalent in the conception of language: the "bourgeois" approach, which construes language as an instrument or a *means* [*Mittel*] to an end; and the "theological-mystical" approach, which hypothesizes and hypostasizes language as an *end in itself*. It is this latter temptation that is clearly the stronger one for Benjamin, who calls it "the great abyss to which all theory of language threatens to succumb" if it does not succeed in "holding itself suspended [*schwebend*] above it" (*GS2*, 141). This effort leads Benjamin to one of the intellectual and stylistic peculiarities that will distinguish his writing from beginning to end and that institutes a certain *virtualization* in the formulation of many of the key concepts he elaborates. If Deleuze, as we have seen, describes "structure as the reality of the virtual," one could say that Benjamin construes the virtual as the reality of structure—here, that of the concept. The mark of this virtualization of the concept is Benjamin's distinctive use of the German suffix *-bar,* which in English would have to be translated either as *-able* (or *-ible*). This tendency first emerges in this essay, and as we have noted, it will persist throughout Benjamin's entire, although abbreviated, career. To recapitulate, what results is a series of concepts that are all constructed around this suffix: "Criticizability," "Translatability," "Citability," "Reproducibility," and "Recognizability" in the *Arcades Project*; and "impart-ability" in the essay on language.[12] These are Benjamin's *-barkeiten,* his *"-abilities,"* which define his major concepts in terms of what Derrida has called *structural possibility* rather than in view of their actual realization. The philosophical predecessor of this unusual move is probably to be found in Kant's use of the suffix *-mäßigkeit* in the *Critique of the Power to Judge.* It is no accident that this formulation is invented by Kant in order to articulate a type of judgment that provides no actual knowledge, determines nothing, and is therefore not cognitive, precisely to the extent that it remains tied to a certain *singularity.* Kant designates this non-conceptual, non-cognitive judgment as "reflective," since it merely reflects the movement of the mind judging, rather than executing an act of judgment itself. The chief example of such judgment is, of course, the aesthetic "judgment" of beauty, which treats its object as a manifestation of "purposiveness without purpose," *Zweckmäßigkeit ohne Zweck.* Such a state is "objectively" fictional, in the sense of being non-actualizable, since it pertains not to the object ostensibly so judged, but to the operation of judgment itself: it feigns judgment without actually judging. Or rather, it does in fact judge, but not in a way that is logically demonstrable, since it has no cognitive or objective content.

This reference to Kant also serves to highlight the difference that Benjamin brings to the concept as a *"-barkeit"* or *"-ability."* For, to put it succinctly, a *-maß* is not a *-bar.* In German, a *Maß* is a measure, something that organizes and contains. The importance, for Kant, of a judgment of "purposiveness without purpose" is that its actualization may be impossible, but it still provides the horizon for its absence. The aesthetic judgment of beauty defines itself by resemblance to what it is not: it *resembles* a cognitive judgment in its claim to objective universality, despite its indemonstrable quality and despite its indissoluble link to a singular situation. Benjamin's *-barkeiten,* however, do something different: they do not simply define their own virtuality in terms of the *absence* of what they name, but rather in terms of its radical alteration: the terms struck by the suffix *-barkeit* become something radically different from what they were, from their conventional use. And in this becoming-different, the question of the medium, and of mediality, begins to emerge.

The rejection of the notion of "measure" with respect to language is explicit in Benjamin's essay, and explains why the temptation of the "mystical" hypostasis of language should constitute for him the great "abyss"—one that should not simply be avoided, but over which thinking must "suspend itself." This hovering self-suspension involves first the insight that language exceeds all possibility of subordinating it to an external criterion or measure: "That which imparts itself *in* language [and never simply *through* it—SW] can not be measured or limited from without, and thus each language is invested with its incommensurable, singular infinity [*ihre inkommensurable, einziggeartete Unendlichkeit*]" (*GS2,* 143, *SW1,* 64). In its "incommensurable singularity," language cannot even be measured in terms of itself, as a simple and self-identical noun or name. However important the notion of "naming" is in this essay, and also later for Benjamin, he insists that any "identification of naming language with language overall deprives the theory of language of the most profound insights" (ibid.).

The word that Benjamin employs to describe the linguisticity of language is ostensibly familiar, especially in its English translation, which however turns out to be extremely misleading precisely in this apparent familiarity. The word, in German, is *Mitteilung,* which in English would and generally is translated as *communication.* Today, one would doubtless think of Habermas's "communicative competence." And yet nothing could be further from Benjamin's use of the term. The word *Mitteilung* is composed of two parts: the root, formed from the verb *teilen* (to separate or partition), and the adverbial prefix *mit-* ("with"). Literally, then, the word suggests "partitioning with," or also, "sharing." But to share, I must first divide, and it is precisely this double movement that is reflected in the English word, to *impart*. As the following passage indicates, it is such "imparting" that Benjamin seems to be describing with the verb *mitteilen*:

> What does language 'communicate' or impart? It imparts the spiritual being that speaks to it . . . Spiritual being imparts itself *in* a language and not *through* a language . . . Spiritual being is identical with linguistic being, only *insofar* as it is impart*able*. Whatever of a spiritual being is impartable, *is* its linguistic being . . . That which is impartable about a spiritual being, *is* its language. On this "is" (equals "is immediately") hangs everything . . . This impart*able* [Mitteil*bare*] is immediately [*unmittelbar*] language itself . . . This means: each language imparts itself [*teilt sich mit*]. Or more precisely: each language imparts itself *in* itself, it is in the purest sense the "medium" of imparting. The medial, which is to say, the *immed*iacy [*Unmittel*barkeit: unmedia-bility] of all spiritual imparting, is the basic problem of all theory of language, and if one calls this immediacy magic, then the fundamental problem of language is its magic. At the same time the phrase, magic of language, points toward something else: toward its infinitude. The latter is conditioned by immediacy. For precisely because nothing imparts itself *through* language, that which imparts itself *in* language cannot be limited or measured from without, and this is why each language is imbued with its incommensurable, unique infinitude. Its linguistic being, not its verbal contents, designates its limit. (*GS2*, 142–143; *SW1*, 63–64)

The first thing to notice about this decisive passage is that Benjamin does not simply use the familiar noun *Mitteilung*, but rather its virtual possibility: *Mitteilbarkeit*. Indeed, the suffix *-bare* (-able), is set in italics in the first occurrence of the word "Mitteil*bare*," impart-able or communicable, in the phrase "the impart*able* is immediately language itself." This was done in order to stress, in a complementary gesture, the lack of mediation in the medium of language by italicizing the first two syllables of the word *immed-iate* (*unmittel*bar) in the phrase: "The medial is the *immed*iacy (*Unmittel*barkeit) of all spiritual imparting." In other words, Benjamin himself is explicitly attentive to the play of prefixes and suffixes in the two words, impart-able and immediacy, *mitteilbar* and *unmittelbar*, two words that resemble each other phonetically in German, and that in combination determine Benjamin's theory of media, not just in this early essay but in general.

But this double use of the suffix *-bar*, which Benjamin will go on to employ precisely to define the mediality of language—language *as medium*—enacts the very virtualization it also describes and designates. For there is a striking discrepancy, or incommensurability, between the two words *mitteilbar* and *unmittelbar*. The first is derived from the verb *mitteilen,* which I translate here as *impart.* The second, however, on which Benjamin insists equally, is derived from the noun *Mittel,* in its negated form, designated by the prefix *-un.* The impart-ability that constitutes language as medium is un-mediated, im-mediate: not a means to an end, nor a middle between poles or periphery, but also not simply the opposite of a means, which is to say, an end in itself. Rather, language still retains one decisive aspect of the means, which is that it is not self-contained, complete, perfect, or perfectible. It is simply *there,* but as something that splits off from itself, takes leave of itself, *parts with* what it was to become something else, to be transposed, transmitted, or translated into something else. Morphologically, it can be noted that the root of the word *unmittelbar*—the noun *Mittel*—takes leave of its nominal character to become not a verb, as with *mitteilen,* but an *adverb, unmittelbar,* and what is more, an adverb whose mode of existence is virtual in three senses. It is virtual first of all in never existing in and of itself, as is true of any adverb or adjective; second, it is virtual in being designated as a kind of negation and yet as one that does not simply efface or transcend that which it negates, the *means.* And finally, perhaps most significantly, it is virtual in never being present to itself, insofar as it modifies *mitteilbar,* the *impartable.* What is "immediate" is that which is defined by the potentiality of taking leave of itself, of its place and position, of altering itself. In thus being named, the language of names takes leave of itself, of its nominal character, not by actually becoming something else but by naming the structural potentiality of such leave-taking. In short, as medium, language *parts with itself* and can thus be said to constitute a medium of virtuality, a virtual medium that cannot be *measured* by the possibility of self-fulfillment but by its constitutive alterability.

The fact that such alterability never consummates or realizes itself fully is reflected toward the end of the essay in Benjamin's insistence that the impart-ability of language always leaves a certain residue of in-communability, *Unmitteilbarkeit,* behind. The immediacy, *Unmittelbarkeit,* of the impart-ability, *Mitteilbarkeit,* of language as medium is thus inseparable from the Incommunicable, the

Unmitteilbare. As Benjamin writes: "Language is namely [!] in each case not simply imparting of the impartable [*Mitteilung des Mitteilbaren*] but at the same time Symbol of the non-impartable [*Symbol des Nicht-Mitteilbaren*]," and he associates this with the "nameless, unacoustic languages . . . of material" and of "things" (*GS2*, 156). This "mute language" traverses "nature" as the "residue of the creative word of God" he suggests at the end of the essay, concluding with the notion that this silent "language of nature" calls for translation. This ending anticipates the essay he will write several years later, "The Task of the Translator," whose own final remark perhaps provides a response to the enigmatic conclusion of the earlier essay. The great resource and potentiality—*Vermögen*—of translation, Benjamin writes there, is to take the "symbolizing"—which always symbolizes the incommunicable—and turn it into the "symbolized," thereby recovering "pure language" for the "movement of language" *(Sprachbewegung).*[13]

This *Vermögen* (potentiality) of translation is designated as "*gewaltig,*" violent, to the extent that it entails a paradox and an impossibility: that of rendering the "symbolizing" of the incommunicable itself as the "symbolized." To be brief, I would argue that, like the "un" of "immediacy," *Unmittelbarkeit,* it does not involve the transformation of the "symbolizing" into its polar opposite, the "symbolized," but rather their paradoxical and violent convergence in translation, as that which sets the mediality of the language-medium into motion, going nowhere and yet never standing still. Impartibility becomes immediate not as a self-contained work or original, but as the tangent that touches the original at a single, incommensurable point, glancing off it to follow "its own course." But this course is set by that single point of contact where what Benjamin calls the "way of meaning" takes leave from meaning as such but without simply forsaking or negating it. "Translatability"—another of Benjamin's "-abilities"—involves the move of meaning from self-contained concept to on-going way, which is configured in what Benjamin, with great precision, calls "word-for-word transmission of syntax" *(Wörtlichkeit in der Übertragung der Syntax)* that he finds epitomized in Hölderlin's translations of Sophocles. Such transmission, *Übertragung,* gives a new direction to the word "*über,*" which no longer means simply "above" or "higher"—as in "language *überhaupt*"—and thus no longer conforms to the ontotheological verticality that is still present in the early language essay. Fidelity to the syntactical arrangement of words, rather than to the grammatical ordering of meaning, respects the "incommensurable singularity" that is common both to the text and to the medium, as Benjamin construes them. The "over-" of "over-naming" and "over-determination" mentioned in the Language essay, as well as the "over" of language *"überhaupt"* (language "overhead"), designates in the translation essay a movement of language taking leave of itself, glancing off its "original," on its way elsewhere. This leave-taking, in which language parts with itself, not to become something entirely different but also not to stay simply the same—this, perhaps, is what Benjamin thinks of as the mediality of the medium.

Let us now try to resume the sense of the argument we have been reviewing. Language, Benjamin states, "is in the purest sense the 'medium' of imparting." "In the purest sense" refers here to the fact that according to Benjamin—and in contradistinction to most major theories of language—language communicates or "imparts" nothing outside of itself. It therefore can be said to impart itself "immediately," without any further mediation. It only "is" in and as the immediacy of that which is impartable, *mitteilbar.* Immediate means here: without additional intervention from without. Language *is (immediately)* the ability or the capacity to impart without recourse to anything else. Impart here entails what the word in English, as in German, implies: a process of *partitioning,* of *parceling out* "oneself," thereby becoming something else.[14] This relation to something or someone else is underscored in German by the prefix *mit-* (*mit-teilen:* to separate and share *with*).

Therefore the impartable cannot simply be equated with that which is actually communicated or the act of communication itself. The latter are acts or processes that actually take place, or that could take place, once and for all. The impart*able,* by contrast, has another mode of being, another dynamic, which consists in its transformation, its becoming-other. It is out of this tendency to be altered that the "virtual" arises. The impartable entails virtuality but not necessarily one that is equivalent to a potential act of communication. The latter could be construed as an act that may not have happened, but that could happen once and for all. Its reality would thus be identical with its potential implementation, with its actualization. This is not, however, how Benjamin construes the impartable. Rather, it is *immediately* effective qua possibility itself, and not merely as an anticipation of a possible realization.

The question remains: how can anything be conceived as being "immediately impartable"? If "impart-able" signifies the capacity to be imparted, to impart oneself by dividing and displacing oneself so as to enter into contact "with" others, in what sense can such a process be understood as being "immediate," devoid of all mediacy, and precisely therein as being "medial"? Benjamin's response to this paradox is to be found in his rereading of the Biblical story of Genesis—a rereading that problematizes the process of *naming* by suggesting that all naming must amount to an *overnaming*, to an *Überbenennung*, a term that recalls Freud's term "overdetermination" in *The Interpretation of Dreams*. Like Freud, Benjamin is convinced that the problem of language requires one to go back beyond the usual discourse of self-consciousness to a more archaic situation. But unlike Freud, he finds that situation articulated, however allegorically, in the Biblical story of the creation: "In it language is presupposed as an ultimate, inexplicable and mystical reality that can only be observed in its development" (*GS2*, 147; *SW1*, 67). In this "development," human beings occupy a special place. The Bible states that man was "made out of earth." As Benjamin comments: "In the entire story of creation, this is the only place where a material is mentioned in which the Creator expresses his will, which otherwise is construed as being immediately creative. [And] this human being, who is not created directly by the Word, is now endowed with the *gift* of language and thereby elevated above the rest of nature" (*GS2*, 148; *SW1*, 67). This privileged position of man is thus by implication ambivalent. On the one hand man is elevated above the rest of creation: he is not created directly through the word of God, but indirectly, through the mediation of earth, out of material. He must therefore *receive* language as a *gift,* because he does not stem directly from it. Language remains alien to man, and paradoxically this brings him closest to it, since it "is" only the capacity of im-parting itself. Man im-parts himself qua language in naming the others. Human beings are thus the only living beings that are not entirely homogeneous and whose distance from language remains the sign of this irremediable heterogeneity. Only through such distance can humans name themselves as well as other beings. But on the other hand, in naming others man imposes a certain sameness on them. Such domination can avoid turning into tyranny only insofar as both ruler and ruled, namer and named, are situated within the continuous confines of a unified and divine creation: "God made things recognizable in their names. But Man names them by means of knowledge (*GS2*, 148; *SW1*, 68).

Why this qualifying "but" in the phrase just quoted: "But man names them by means of knowledge"? It is this "but" that distinguishes Benjamin's approach to language, media, and virtuality from all of those we have hitherto discussed: Deleuze, Aristotle, and Hegel. For there can be no "global integration" for Benjamin, and he retells the story of a divinely created universe to demonstrate this. For the Creation, precisely in its divine origins, remains heterogeneous and this is what renders the name both so fascinating and so problematic: "The absolute relation of the name to knowledge exists only in God, only there is the name the pure medium of knowledge, because only there is it intimately identical with the creative word" (*GS2*, 148; *SW1*, 68). Only *there*, in a place to which human beings as such cannot accede, is language "the pure medium of knowledge." Here, on earth, by contrast, naming is inevitably "overnaming," too much and too little at once. The "theory of the proper name" marks "the border that sets off finite from infinite language" (*GS2*, 149; *SW1*, 69), as well as "the community of human beings with the *creative* word of God" (*GS2*, 150; *SW1*, 69). But this community is defined by its heterogeneity: man's naming is not infinite and creative, but finite and cognitive: "Things in themselves have no words, they are created out of God's word and recognized in their names by human language. This cognition of things is not however spontaneous creation, it happens not from an absolutely unlimited and infinite language like the divine; rather, the name that humans give to things reposes on the way they impart themselves to humans. In the name the word of God has not remained creative, but has become in part receptive, even if receptive of language" (ibid.). The "imparting" that constitutes the immediacy of the medium of language is one that places man in a position of receiving a gift and responding to that gift by naming. But it is a very particular kind of naming that is radically distinct from the creative Word of God. The medium of languages in which man is inscribed is thus defined not so much by naming as by something more like renaming, through "the translatability of languages into one another" (*GS2*, 151; *SW1*, 70). And where the relation of humans to the non-human is involved, such translatability, in turn, entails a relation of incommensurability: "It is the translation of the nameless into names" (*GS2*, 151; *SW1*, 70).

What defines the world in its heterogeneity—divine, human, non-human—is precisely the diversity of translatability, which in turn entails the ability to impart: to partition, take leave of oneself in order to transpose a part of that self elsewhere, thereby altering it. The world, thus described, consists not of a single, continuous medium, nor even of different media that resemble one another, but rather of a network of media whose sole shared trait is the ability to "part with" in im-parting. "Differentiation," perhaps, but not one that produces anything like "global integration." Rather, global disintegration. For the effort to actualize such im-partability leads inexorably to its polarization in "judgment," the stable opposition of Good and Evil, the "fall" of language from a medium of immediate imparting into an intermediate position as mediation and as means (*"Mittelbarmachung der Sprache,"* GS2, 154; SW1, 71).

Benjamin's discussion can thus be summed up as follows: The "pure" medium as the imparting of an identical being never actualizes itself as a process of creation. For between the creation, the creative word of God, and actualization lies the fall "into the abyss of the mediacy of all imparting *(der Mittelbarkeit aller Mitteilung)*, of the word as means." After the Fall, language actualizes itself creatively only as a means of judging and of cognition, but no longer as a medium of imparting or as a medium that parts-with. Judgment and knowledge are inseparable from the instrumentalizing of language and from the mediatizing of its mediality.

From this emerges the paradox that all actualization of the medial, whether linguistic or other, tends to mediate the linguistic aspect of the medial, its impart-ability, by institutionalizing and codifying it. Such codification is exemplified in the work, and in particular, in the artwork.

Against the claims of the integrative artwork Benjamin insists on the medial imparting as the historical heritage of the work. Works are not self-enclosed or complete, but live on, survive themselves as something else, for instance, as criticism or as translations. Or as theatrical performances. In such performances, they are no longer the same as they were: they take leave to become something else.

Creativity and integration do not describe such a movement, which is rather an interruption of the given, whether of the "work" or of the "word," through the transformational force of the imparting medium. Like languages after Babel, the media proliferate. Names that "overname" are no longer entirely proper; words that are overdetermined, are no longer simply words. Elsewhere Benjamin will write of "constellations," "configurations," networks of images that do not resemble as much as they dissemble. Such images demand not just to be seen, but also to be read, in their relation to other elements and media that are not simply visible. Only insofar as they are legible, *lesbar,* do such images become recognizable. But recognition is, as we shall see, not simply the same as cognition, any more than legibility is the same as reading. For both involve virtual possibilities, *-abilities,* that tend to depart in being put to the test. One such phenomenon Benjamin calls "the dialectical image," which "ignites in the now of cognizability." Such an apparition, which disappears in appearing, which takes leave in arriving, becomes the epitome of a certain mediality in the later texts of Benjamin. We will therefore, in conclusion, take a quick look at one such text: the "Notebook 'N' of the Arcades Project."[15]

Recognizability and Legibility: Notebook "N" of the Arcades Project

The notes that have become known as "Notebook 'N'" [On Epistemology, Theory of Progress] are directly concerned neither with the concept of media nor with that of the virtual. And still they throw considerable light on both. For they are grouped around two concepts that bear the mark of the medial in Benjamin's own writing: "recognizability" *(Erkennbarkeit)* and "legibility" *(Lesbarkeit):*

> What distinguishes images from the "essences" of Phenomenology is their historical index . . . These images must be thoroughly demarcated from "humanistic" [*geisteswissenschaftlichen*] categories such as the so-called 'habitus,' 'style' etc. The historical index of images tells us not only that they belong to a particular time: it says above all, that they only become legible at a particular time. And such "becoming legible" in turn entails a particular critical point of movement within them. Every present (period)

is defined through those images that are synchronic with it: each now is the now of a particular recognizability. In it truth is charged to the breaking point with time. This breaking, nothing else, is the death of intention, which therefore coincides with the birth of genuine historical time, the time of truth. It is not that the past casts its light upon the present, or the present throws its light on the past, but rather the image is that wherein what has been converges in a flash to form a constellation with the now. In other words: image is dialectics at a standstill. For while the relation of the present to the past is purely temporal, the relation of what has been to the now is dialectical: not temporal in nature but imagistic [*bildhaft*]. Only dialectical images are genuinely historical, i.e. not archaic images. The legible image, which is to say, the image in the now of recognizability, bears to the greatest degree the stamp of the critical, dangerous moment, which underlies all reading. (*GS5, 577–578; N 3,1*)

In one of his earliest writings, "On the Program of the Coming Philosophy," Benjamin had predicted that "in addition to the concept of synthesis, also that of a certain non-synthesis of two concepts in an another is bound to gain increasing systematic importance, since outside of synthesis another relation between thesis and antithesis is possible" (*GS2, 166; SW1, 106*). A notion of non-synthesis recurs in his later writings in the concept of the dialectical image, as it is described in the passage just cited. "Image" for Benjamin is something very different from the familiar conception; indeed, it is something unheard-of. Image, as here used, signifies not the illustrative depiction of an external object. Rather, as something to be read rather than merely seen, the image is construed by Benjamin as both disjunctive and medial in its structure—which is to say, as both actual and virtual at the same time. Such images become a point of convergence, which Benjamin here designates as "now." This *now* coexists with the "time" from which it simultaneously sets itself apart. Time, one could say, imparts itself as now, and in a historical sense. For history signifies not a temporal continuum, nor even the continuity of an expected or sought-after meaning. Rather it contributes to the explosion of all meaning, as that "death of intention" that never ceased to fascinate Benjamin and that he here ascribes to the mode of being of the image, marking the "birth of a genuinely historical time as the time of truth."[16] Such historical truth should not be conceived as a preserving of truth, understood as the correspondence or adequation theory, but rather as a dissolving, non-integrative dialectics of explosive convergence or coincidence.

This moment of explosiveness has two aspects. First it designates the way in which integration and integrity are interrupted. Second, it describes how the exploded elements recombine as an image. They are never simply "there," nor do they establish a new continuum. They remain virtual. Their virtuality expresses itself in virtual concepts, Benjamin's -*abilities*. Here those abilities are designated as "legibility" and as "recognizability."

The way Benjamin introduces the concept of the "legibility" of "images" is highly significant. First of all, he clearly demarcates his use of these terms from the usual practice, by stressing that the discourse involved is not one of the "humanities," the *Geisteswissenschaften*. Another kind of discourse is at work here, and it cannot be adequately described simply through the addition of some other predicate. What is at stake is rather the manner in which such predicates are used. Images, as Benjamin conceives them, are not simply to be thought of as being "legible": rather they come to be readable—not as one might expect, through the fact that they take place at a particular historical time or because they "express" that period, but rather through a "movement within them," at a "particular, critical point." Such a point is "critical" in the most literal sense, since it designates not only the arresting of a movement, the interruption of its progression, but at the same time and above all the separation or division of its "interior." For the constellation of "what has been and the now" completes itself not only within the image: it constitutes this interior through the "lightening" intervention of a certain "outside." The tendency of the "movement within" is precisely designed to explode every inwardness and immanence, every type of interior space. The interior turned inside-out marks the movement of medialization in Benjamin and stamps it at once as one of virtualization.[17] Therefore what is involved in this passage is not so much the act of reading as the virtuality of images becoming-readable.

The fact that this movement of becoming-readable remains virtual does not prevent it from having its specific *actuality*, which Benjamin designates as the "dialectical exposition" *(dialektische Darstellung)* of history and which he *describes* as follows:

> The pre- and post-history of an historical situation [*Tatbestand*] are revealed by its dialectical exposition to be part of the situation itself. Even more: each dialectically exposed conjuncture [*Sachverhalt*] polarizes and becomes a force-field in which the confrontation between its prehistory and post-history plays itself out. The conjuncture becomes a force-field

when penetrated by the actuality of the present [*Aktualität*]. And so the historical situation polarizes into pre- and post-history *ever anew, never in the same way.* And it does this outside of itself, in the present; as a line [*Strecke*] divided according to the golden mean [*apollinischen Schnitt*] encounters its division outside of itself. (*GS5*, 587–588; N 7a,1, my emphasis)

As Deleuze will later, Benjamin here emphasizes the divisive effects of "actuality," which can "penetrate" a historical situation once the latter has been "exposed dialectically," setting it apart into pre- and post-history. The Deleuzian concept of "disparity" probably marks the point where his thinking comes closest to that of Benjamin. But with his notion of the "historical" Benjamin moves away from Deleuze. For Benjamin's concept of history knows neither goal nor "global integration" but at best, an "end."[18] This end does not come "at the end"; rather it is always *actual,* always *now.* The actuality of this "now," however, is never self-contained, integrated, simply present: rather it is a divider, a dividing-line or point, producing a "cut" that is never in-between but always *outside* of that which it divides. History emerges, for Benjamin, only insofar as the "here and now" imparts itself as a "there and then," encountering its innermost division outside itself: "before" itself, in a past that opens—imparts itself—to the future. The future "is" nothing but this explosive imparting of the past. It is this explosive imparting that endows the "present" with its virtuality, with its -abilities to become other than it is and has been. It is this becoming-other through explosive imparting that defines "the media" in their singular plurality for Benjamin. And in this his thought perhaps anticipates a demand recently articulated by Derrida:

If I had time, I would insist on another trait of "actuality," of what is happening today and of what is happening today *to actuality.* I would insist not only on the *artificial* synthesis (synthetic images, synthetic voices, all the prosthetic supplements that can take the place of real actuality) but first of all on a concept of *virtuality* (virtual image, virtual space and thus virtual event) that can no longer simply be opposed, in total philosophical serenity, to actual reality, as one formerly distinguished between potentiality and act, between *dynamis* and *energeia,* between the potentiality of matter and the defining form of a *telos,* and hence also of a *progress,* etc. This virtuality impresses itself even upon the structure of the produced event, it affects the time as well as the space of the image, of discourse, of "information." In short, everything that relates us to the said actuality, to the implacable reality of its supposed presence. A philosopher who "thinks his time" should today, among other things, be attentive to the implications and the consequences of such virtual time. To the novelties of its technical implementation [*mise en oeuvre technique*] but also to what its radical innovations [*l'inédit*] recalls of possibilities that are far more ancient.[19]

CHAPTER FIVE

Translatability I

Following *(Nachfolge)*

It may seem surprising to juxtapose two texts as different in tone and spirit as *The Life and Opinions of Tristram Shandy, Gentleman* and "The Task of the Translator." The serious, indeed often prophetic tone of Benjamin's discussion of translation contrasts with the studied self-mockery of Sterne's novel. And yet, more binds Walter Benjamin to Walter Shandy than their common first name. Indeed, their shared concern with the power of names in general is indicative of a concern with language that permeates the two texts, although certainly in very different ways.

It is, at any rate, just this concern with naming that leads us to the scene from which the epigraph to this discussion is chosen. Walter Shandy's newly born son has just been christened, but the name that he has received—"Tristram"—is from Walter's point of view the worst one possible. Walter is deeply convinced that names determine the destiny of those who bear them, and he has gone to great trouble to choose a name for his son that would most help him on his way: "Trismegistus," meaning "thrice great." But through an unfortunate concatenation of circumstances all too characteristic of the world of the Shandys, the name "Trismegistus" is misunderstood and transformed in the process of its transfer, or "translation," from the mouth of Walter to that of the pastor charged with christening the child.

Walter Shandy is thunderstruck to learn that his second son has been named "Tristram" rather than "Trismegistus." In desperation he visits the learned scholar Didius to see if the misnaming might not yet be undone. During the course of the evening, the conversation drifts slightly from the question of naming to that of kinship, and it is in relation to this latter question that the following exchange—which will serve as my epigraph—takes place:

> 'Tis a ground and principle in the law, said Triptolemus, that things do not ascend, but descend in it; and I make no doubt 'tis for this cause, that however true it is, that the child may be of the blood or seed of its parents—that the parents, nevertheless, are not of the blood and seed of it; inasmuch as the parents are not begot by the child, but the child by the parents—For so they write, *Liberi sunt de sanguine patris & matris, sed pater et mater non sunt de sanguine liberorum.*
>
>   —But this, Triptolemus, cried Didius, proves too much—for from this authority cited it would follow, not only what indeed is granted on all sides, that the mother is not of kin to her child—but the father likewise— It is held, said Triptolemus, the better opinion.[1]

This parody of the belief in the irreversible linearity of a certain conception of time and of history raises questions that are not at all absent from "The Task of the Translator," even if the temper in which they are approached by Walter Benjamin differs radically from that of Tristram Shandy (if not always from that of his namesake, Walter Shandy). One of those questions is precisely that of kinship, which haunts both Walters. To be sure, Walter Benjamin is not concerned with his physical progeny so much as with that of language in general, or more precisely, with the kinship between languages. For translation, as he construes it in this essay, is a function of just that relationship, although in a different way from what one might expect: "In truth however the kinship of languages manifests itself in a translation in a far more profound and defined a manner than as the superficial and indefinable similarity of two poetical works."[2] Kinship, according to Benjamin, should not be confused with resemblance or similarity: it can consist in a project, a function, or a tendency. One such that marks both Tristram Shandy and "The Task of the Translator" could be described as a tendency toward paradox, in particular in respect to the operation of language. Where language is concerned, paradox often prevails over logical consistency. And this prevalence contributes to the affinity or kinship

(Verwandtschaft) of languages among themselves to which Benjamin alludes.

But we are getting ahead of ourselves. The invocation of Sterne's ironic, reflective, language-game-playing novel right at the outset of these remarks is designed to throw a light, however oblique, on Benjamin's text, which in terms of intellectual history at least, would seem to have more in common with German Romanticism than with British satire of the eighteenth century. If Benjamin's text were exclusively a theoretical essay, this sort of classification would be pertinent and it would indeed be out of place to juxtapose it with Tristram Shandy. But as is well known, Benjamin's discussion of translation, despite its very high level of abstraction, followed his experience of translating Baudelaire's *Tableaux parisiens,* to which it was to serve as an introduction. The practical dimension of Benjamin's text has been largely underestimated, probably because of the extremely speculative and at times theological character of certain arguments. Nevertheless, "The Task of the Translator" remains a very practical text, not in spite of its abstractions but because of them. As we will see, the essay has some very concrete things to say about just how translations should be construed, although it is striking that most of the translations of Benjamin's essay—not to mention most theories and practices of translation in general—ignore this aspect of Benjamin's text. It is symptomatic of the "reception"—one is tempted even to speak of "canonization"—of Benjamin that his essay on translation has been translated as though the specific conception of translation it articulates had never been written. In view of this situation, one can legitimately wonder whether it is justified to say that this essay has been "translated" at all.

The practical thrust of "The Task of the Translator" is not restricted simply to its initial relation to the Baudelaire translation Benjamin had undertaken. Rather, it is manifest in the emphasis placed by Benjamin on the category that determines his overall approach to translation: "the way of meaning" (*Art des Meinens*). This is what establishes the specific differences of languages and at the same time their relationship to one another. Later I will discuss this key concept at some length. For the moment I want only to raise the question of whether this notion should not have practical consequences for the reading of Benjamin's writing—whether his texts in general and this one in particular should be considered not simply in terms of what they say explicitly, but also and perhaps above all from the perspective of how they say what they say: their distinctive way of meaning. In other words, does this category not establish a bridge between a theory of translation and a practice of writing and reading, whether translative or interpretive? The reference to Tristram Shandy is also meant to remind us that the way a text means may well be a decisive determinant of whatever it has to say, above and beyond the explicit content of its assertions taken individually and in isolation from one another.

And yet, at first sight "The Task of the Translator" seems to do everything possible to remove the reader from this insight. It would be difficult to find another essay of Benjamin's that begins with such an overwhelming series of apodictic assertions (couched in the form of negations): "No poem is meant for the reader, no picture for the viewer, no symphony for the listeners" (GS4, 9; SW1, 253). With this fanfare the essay begins (somewhat reminiscent of the style of Carl Schmitt) and rapidly moves to the conclusion that, similarly, no translation can be explained strictly in terms of the needs of readers unable to read the work in its original language. The reason for this, Benjamin asserts, is that neither poetry (Dichtung) nor translation is primarily concerned with communication or understanding. "What does a work of poetry say? What does it communicate? Very little to one who understands it. Its essence is not communicating, not assertion" (ibid.). Thus asserting the irrelevance of assertion to poetry and to translation, Benjamin multiplies and intensifies his own assertiveness: "What distinguishes poor translation," he argues, is that it is "an inexact transmission of an inessential content" (ibid.). But what then can be said positively about translation? Benjamin's initial response: "Translation is a form" (GS4, 9; SW1, 254). At the very latest, this is the point in the essay where the reader, having been overwhelmed and borne along by the string of powerful if unargued propositions, is suddenly called on to react. For what, after all, can Benjamin mean by describing translation as a "form"? That is, what can he intend by using a term generally reserved for the various poetical genres themselves to designate their secondary reproduction through and as translation?

Characteristically, Benjamin never defines just what he means by the term "form." In so doing, he continues a long and illustrious tradition, one that goes back to the philosopher to whom Benjamin's thought is most deeply indebted: Kant. Kant's *Critique of Judgment*, a text that can be seen as the origin of modern aesthetics and critical theory, revolves in great part around precisely the very same term that Benjamin employs here to distinguish translation. The object of aesthetic judgment, in the Third Critique, is defined as nothing other than "beautiful form." And yet Kant too throughout the *Critique of Judgment* never stops to discuss the concept of form, much less give any sort of definition of it—with the partial but significant exception of a remark made almost in passing, in which form is described as "the agreement of the manifold with a unity, leaving undetermined what this is supposed to be."[3] This is not much, but it is sufficient to indicate what Benjamin is driving at in using the term and also why his American translator feels impelled to avoid the word. In the first American translation, by Harry Zohn, Benjamin's lapidary assertion was translated as follows: "Translation is a mode."[4] Although this has since been corrected in the Harvard edition, Zohn's initial rendering was symptomatically suggestive. The translator was obviously unsatisfied or highly uncomfortable with the word "form" in this context. Why? The very next phrase suggests a possible response: "To comprehend it as a mode one must go back to the original. For in it resides the law of that form as the original's translatability" (ibid.). The reason why "mode" is substituted for "form" is because the translator senses a tension between the autonomy and integrity associated with form, on the one hand—remember Kant's definition of it as "the agreement of a manifold with a unity"—and the subordination or dependence generally associated with translation and endorsed here by Benjamin: a translation is precisely not autonomous, self-contained, integral—it consists in a relationship to something outside of it, to something it is not and yet to which it owes its existence, the "original" work. "Mode" suggests a way of being, a modification, rather than any sort of independent structure. And yet it is just such independence that Benjamin endorses, provocatively, in extending the term "form" to cover not only the original work but that of "translation" as well. It is this extension that is unusual, that shocks, and this is reflected in the initial translation of "form" as "mode." What disappears in this translation, however, is precisely the provocative tension between the relative independence of translation and its dependency on something other than itself—an "original," a work—that is, the tension that informs Benjamin's effort to articulate "The Task of the Translator." That task is an ambiguous one, traversed by tensions and conflicts, and as such is remote from the notions of harmony and wholeness traditionally dominant in the realm of aesthetic theory. The translation of "form" as "mode" tends to efface or at least reduce that tension and to reinstate the very ideal of harmony that Benjamin's thought and writing are constantly calling into question.

Translation, then, for Benjamin, is indeed a form. But its formal quality is not something inherent in itself. Rather, it consists in a relationship with at least two dimensions. First of all, it entails the relationship of the translation to the original. Second, and far more significantly, it entails a relationship of the original itself: a relationship of the original to itself. The original is not simply self-contained, not a whole. The formal quality of the original work in which the form of translation is rooted is designated by Benjamin, in the passage already quoted, with a rather awkward, but once again highly characteristic term: translatability. What is "translatability"?

In his response it is helpful to recall the distinction made by Derrida between "iteration" and "iterability" in his polemical critique of John Searle, in *Limited Inc.* Derrida emphasizes that the suffix -ability marks not a fact but what he calls a "necessary possibility":[5] writing is constituted by the irreducible possibility of being-repeated, not by the manifest fact of repetition. The fact that this distinction should have escaped Searle is indicative not so much of personal obtuseness as of the unfamiliarity of a certain American philosophical tradition with the Kantian notion of the "transcendental," used to designate universal, structurally necessary traits that are of a different order from empirical acts or facts. Thus, in the perspective of Western phonologocentrism, writing is constituted by the necessary structural possibility of its being repeated: as writing, being is subordinated and determined by its ability to be repeated. The suffix -ability marks this structurally necessary possibility. It is a necessary possibility because it is inseparable from the practice of writing, even if one never actually repeats something by writing it down.

The reason that I have spent so much time discussing the transcendental dimension implied in this suffix -ability is not simply because Benjamin resorts to this rather awkward, rather unaccustomed word-form to articulate his thinking about "The Task of the Translator," but also because his use of this form is by no means limited to this particular essay. As mentioned earlier, there are many other instances in which he similarly resorts to the same suffix in order to explain key concepts, and these instances generally turn out, as here, to be of decisive importance for his thinking overall. Indeed, one could even trace the trajectory of Benjamin's thinking by using these markers. One of the first is criticizability (*Kritisierbarkeit*), a second is translatability, and a third, and doubtless best known, is reproducibility.

The first, criticizability, plays a decisive role in Benjamin's first major critical work, his dissertation on "The Concept of Criticism in German Romanticism" *(Der Begriff der Kunstkritik in der deutschen Romantik)*. The last, reproducibility, will be familiar to many since it is included in the title of one of Benjamin's best-known essays: "The Work of Art in the Age of its Technical Reproducibility" *(Das Kunstwerk im Zeitalter ihrer technischen Reproduzierbarkeit)*. Although I will come back to these terms later in this chapter, let me make two points here. First, what they all have in common is their tendency to form substantives out of verbs: criticize, translate, reproduce. Second, the processes that these nominalized verbs designate are all traditionally considered to be ancillary, secondary, supplementary. To therefore define these processes as quasi-transcendental, structuring possibilities is to shift the emphasis from the ostensibly self-contained work to a relational dynamic that is precisely not self-identical but perpetually in the process of alteration, transformation, becoming-other.

This tendency is palpable in Benjamin's discussion of translatability. "If translation is a form, then translatability must be an essential feature of certain works" (*GS4*, 10; *SW1*, 254). Translatability does not depend on a relationship of the original to a particular audience, according to Benjamin: rather, it is an intrinsic trait of certain works themselves. This is the direction, then, in which Benjamin will seek an alternative approach to translation from that which has hitherto been prevalent and which, in the context of his discussion, could be designated as the "humanistic" or anthropological approach. This approach results in what Benjamin calls "superficial thinking." What defines the "superficiality" of such thinking is, surprisingly enough, its tendency to reduce or interpret all relations to human relations. It is precisely with this notion that Benjamin takes issue:

> The question of whether a work is translatable has a dual meaning. Either: Will an adequate translator ever be found among the totality of its readers? Or, more pertinently: Does its nature lend itself to translation and, therefore, in view of the significance of the form, call for it? . . . Only superficial thinking will deny the independent meaning of the latter and declare both questions to be of equal significance . . . It should be pointed

out that certain correlative concepts retain their meaning, and possibly their foremost significance, if they are not referred exclusively to man. One might, for example, speak of an unforgettable life or moment even if all men had forgotten it . . . Analogously, the translatability of linguistic creations ought to be considered even if men should prove unable to translate them. (*GS4*, 9–10; *SW1*, 254, translation modified here as throughout)

What seems to be at stake here is the concept of relation: it changes depending on whether or not relations are construed on the model of human relations. In short, the question is whether or not the "human" must be used to define "relation," or whether the latter transcends all attempts to define it in purely human terms. In regard to this question Benjamin never wavered: his response, from his earliest writings to his latest ones, was always to refuse any determination of the "human" that sought to elevate it to the measure of all things, or rather, to the norm of all relations. Significant in this context is his use of the word "God." The transcendental status of a "translatability" that Benjamin refuses to reduce to the dimension of "the human" is defined in terms of "a reference to a realm in which it is fulfilled" even if human beings do not fulfill it—namely, to "the commemoration of God" (*GS4*, 9–10; *SW1*, 254).

The "commemoration of God" presupposes a separation, indeed an irreducible distance, between the process of commemoration and its object. Benjamin's allusion to "a commemoration of God" is meant to remind his readers that the demand or appeal of translation—translatability—cannot be measured in exclusively human terms. "A commemoration of God" is, first and foremost, a reminder of the limits of the human. It is therefore almost a contradiction in terms to translate "ein Gedenken Gottes" as "God's remembrance." God does not remember, for He does not forget. Man does not "remember" God either, at least not so long as remembering implies forgetting, since man cannot forget what he could never have known. Rather than a "remembrance," the "thought of God" is a reminder and challenge to *commemorate* the enabling limitations of the human. And these limitations include that which the human produces itself, its works. The limits of man are also those of the work. With this insistence on delimitation, already powerfully at work in the philosophy of Kant, Benjamin begins to drive a wedge into traditional aesthetic theory and pry it free from its moorings, thereby opening the space for something radically different, which we will not be in a hurry to name. For one of the things that is going on in this opening-up is precisely the rethinking of the status of naming as such, and perhaps above all its relation to what we call the "verb." To concretize this in the passage we are considering: the naming of "God" is relativized by a context that renders it the object of a relationship involving not just a "thought" *(Gedanke)*, but a *Gedenken,* which is to say, a process of commemorating that entails referring. This move, in which the status of the name emerges as an effect of a dynamic relationship associated grammatically with verbs rather than with nouns, is paradigmatic for the entire argumentation that will determine "The Task of the Translator," and beyond that, Benjamin's thinking and writing in general.

It is precisely this shift in focus from name to verb that distinguishes Benjamin's essay on translation from a text he had written ten years earlier, but which was published only posthumously, "On Language as Such and on the Language of Man" (*Über die Sprache überhaupt und über die Sprache des Menschen,* 1915).[6] In that early essay, the question of naming is absolutely central, but in a way that also renders it deeply problematic. Naming is the prerogative of man but the creation that is named is also one that mourns *(trauert)*. The naming of the creation by man is, already, a prelude to the baroque *Trauerspiel* (mourning play) that will so absorb Benjamin some ten years later, shortly after he writes "The Task of the Translator."

Although we cannot go into this text extensively here, that which causes the named creation to mourn is not unrelated to the fate of the work, as Benjamin begins to describe it in respect to the quality of "translatability." For if the call for translation is in some sense rooted in the structure of the works themselves, then these can no longer be considered self-sufficient, independent, autonomous, or self-contained. The paradox resides in the fact that the work can only *be itself* insofar as it is *transported elsewhere,* altered, transformed—in short, *translated.* Put another way, the work can only make a name for itself—keep its name—by having that name travel, *take leave,* go elsewhere and become another name, in another language. The original can only be itself by becoming something different. Or, to sharpen the paradox: the original work can only survive insofar as it is able to take leave of itself and become something else. This is its quality of "being-translatable," its "translatability." Its being converges with its being-translated. And yet here again we see the paradoxical tension that marks Benjamin's writing and keeps it in motion—the "convergence" never comes full circle, never fully arrives. Benjamin insists that the relation between original and translation—however indispensable and intrinsic the latter may be for the former—is never simply reciprocal or mutual: "That a translation can never—however good it may be—signify anything for the original is evident [*leuchtet ein*]. Nevertheless it stands in the most intimate connection to the original work. Indeed, this connection is all the more intimate for the fact that it [the translation] no longer signifies anything for the original" (*GS4*, 10; *SW1*, 254). If translation "no longer signifies anything for the original"—and "signifies" is not equivalent with "important," as the translation suggests: signifying is not simply "being important for"—then this implies that the original is no longer present; it has taken leave. But it is still part of a relation. Benjamin insists that the translation still "stands in the most intimate connection" to "the original work." The paradoxical nature of this relationship is intensified as Benjamin, toward the end of the same paragraph, asserts that in translation "the life of the original" attains "its ever-renewed, latest and most comprehensive unfolding"—comprehensive unfolding and not "abundant flowering," as the published translation would have it. There is no trace here of anything organic, which in regard to translation will emerge later in a very different context. The question that arises here, both from Benjamin's text and from the slippages of the translation, concerns the role of "signifying" and its relation to "life," as Benjamin is using the term here.

By now we may begin to see how Benjamin's notion of "translatability" is related to the two other adverbial nouns that frame his own writing career, as it were, and that are formed through use of the same suffix: that of "criticizability," at the heart of his discussion of the Romantic concept of criticism (1919), and that of "reproducibility," which informs his discussion of film (1936). What is common to all three of these concepts is already clearly delineated by Benjamin in his discussion of the German Romantics and of Friedrich Schlegel in particular: the individual work is considered neither self-contained nor self-sufficient; it acquires significance only through what comes after it in order to become what alone it can never be.[7] What is this "being" that requires the subsequent intervention of something else, something other—whether criticism, translation, or technical reproduction—in order to become "itself"? Perhaps as good an answer as any would be: significance. A work can only "work," do its work, have effects, be *significant,* insofar as it goes outside of itself and is transformed, by and into something else, something other. This is why "to signify" is not simply the same as to "be important." To signify is to be transformed.

In any case, the problematizing of the status of the individual work that begins, in Benjamin's writing career at least, with the German Romantics, raises a question that will guide and influence his thinking increasingly as he progresses: the question of the relation of the individual work to the spatial-temporal *medium* in which it exists, of which it forms a part. In the case of the German Romantics, there is a tendency, or a disposition, to subordinate the work qua an individual phenomenon to the more general, generative power of the medium of critical reflection. Against this tendency, however, Benjamin defends the irreducible element of the "contingent" or "accidental" in the work of art: "The Romantics wanted to render the lawfulness [*Gesetzmäßigkeit*] of the work of art absolute. But the moment of the accidental, of the contingent, can only be dissolved—or rather, rendered lawful, necessary— insofar as the work of art itself is dissolved" (*GS1,* 115; *SW1,* 182). As much as he is fascinated by the idea of the dislocation of the meaningful, self-contained, self-sufficient work, Benjamin remains suspicious of any effort to subordinate it to a higher law or necessity. Indeed, the tendency of the Romantics to dissolve the work by emphasizing its "criticizability" can be clearly distinguished from that of the "reproducibility" that reigns in the medium of film, for instance. In film, the "reproducibility" of the individual work does not produce any sort of "absolute," not at least in the sense of a totality or a continuity. This, however, is precisely what the Romantics envisaged and this is also why Benjamin, in his discussion of the Romantic concept of criticism, felt it necessary to contrast the Romantics with two other approaches to the work of art: that of Goethe, diametrically opposed to the Romantics, which emphasized the irreducible singularity of the individual work, which for Goethe had no need of critical reflection or transformation in order to fulfill itself. And the notion of the "sobriety or prosaic" quality—the *Nüchternheit*—of poetry articulated by Hölderlin, a poet who for Benjamin (as later for de Man) stands emphatically outside both German Romanticism and its classical antipode, Goethe. We will return later to Benjamin's interpretation of Hölderlin and to this notion of "sobriety."

For the moment, however, we should note that what drew Benjamin toward the German Romantic concept of criticism in the first place was its tendency to introduce a dynamic and indeed, a historical dimension into the aesthetic domain: "What I am learning through it," he wrote of his study of German Romanticism, is "insight into the relation of a truth to history" an aspect of his interest that would remain largely implicit in his thesis, "although hopefully apparent to attentive readers."[8] It is precisely the notion of "history," although transformed, that returns increasingly in his effort to define "The Task of the Translator." Thus while this notion underscores Benjamin's indebtedness to the early German Romantics, it also marks the beginning of his decisive distancing from them, one that a few years later will reach a polemical high point in his introduction to the question of allegory in *The Origin of the German Mourning Play*:

> For more than a hundred years the domination of a usurper weighs upon the philosophy of art, a usurpation that rose to power during the confusion of Romanticism. The frantic efforts of the Romantic aestheticians to achieve a radiant and ultimately noncommittal cognition of the Absolute has allowed a conception of the symbol to dominate aesthetic debates, a conception which outside of its name has nothing in common with the authentic notion of symbolism . . . As a symbolic structure, the Beautiful is supposed to grow without interruption [*bruchlos*] into the Divine. The limitless immanence of the moral world in that of the beautiful was developed by the theosophical aesthetics of the Romantics. But its foundation had long been laid. The tendency of classicism towards an apotheosis of existence [*Daseins*] in the perfected individual—and not just morally perfected—is clear enough. Typically romantic however is the insertion of this perfected individual into an infinite, but at the same time eschatological, indeed sacred progression. (*GS1*, 336–337; *Origin*, 159–160)

Romanticism and Classicism are here placed back to back, as it were, with regard to a tendency that Benjamin finds particularly nefarious: the progressive subordination of theology under aesthetics, with as a concomitant effect the progressive confusion of transcendence and immanence. What most disturbs Benjamin in this confusion or confounding is that it obscures a dimension of history that he takes to be decisive: what might be called the finitude of history.[9] The classical, Goethean emphasis on the work as something that requires no intervention through criticism because it is already a perfect embodiment of immanence is here characterized by Benjamin as an "apotheosis of existence in the not just morally consummate individual" (*GS1*, 337; *Origin*, 160). Goethean classicism is thus understood as an anticipation of the Romantic identification of art and criticism, aesthetics and eschatology. In both cases, a theological notion of perfection and totality—embodied in the theological notion of the symbol—is transferred to a profane, worldly domain, that of art, thereby denying the difference between the two domains: the difference between finitude and infinity, between mortality and eternity. The return of the repressed that Benjamin discovers already at work in spiritual and political crisis that haunts and drives the German baroque—that is, long before the Romantics burst upon the scene—is the discovery that history is finite, traversed by mortality, and that no transcendent, eschatological scheme can effect that singular fact or alter its reality. This return of the repressed—mortality, finitude—articulates itself precisely as allegory, which Benjamin much later, in his Arcades manuscript, will describe as "the sign that is sharply set off from its significance" (J 83 a,3).

Between the Romantic notion of "criticizability," then, and Benjamin's subsequent concept of "technical reproducibility," the idea of "translatability" occupies a middle ground, and not just chronologically. Unlike "criticizability," it does not simply imply a notion of history that represses or seeks to transcend the mortality of profane, worldly individuals by inserting them into an infinite progression. But unlike "reproducibility," it does not yet entirely abandon the idea of fulfillment and totality, although it does relegate them to a dimension that seems to be unattainable for postlapserian mortals in a word of post-Babelian linguistic diversity. All of this is not just thematized but rather played out in the sequence or syntax of Benjamin's argumentation, which first organizes itself around the notion of "life" in order then to subordinate "life" to "history." Let us summarize a few of the steps of this shift.

First, "translatability" is defined as a function of the "nexus of life" *(Zusammenhang des Lebens)*. Second, this nexus is described in terms not of "life" as such, but rather as what Benjamin calls the living *(das Lebendige)*. This, of course, tends to get effaced in the translation (although it could easily enough have been preserved): "Just as the utterances [*Äußerungen*] of life are most intimately tied to the living [not "the phenomenon of life"—SW], without signifying anything for it, so translation issues from the original. Not so much from its life as from its 'after-life'" (*GS4*, 10; *SW1*, 254). What characterizes Benjamin's language, in German, and what once again tends to get lost in the English translation, is the critical movement of departure, of taking-leave, a movement that moves outward and away. The word that is translated in the published version simply as "phenomena" is in fact literally constructed around the prefix "out-" *(aus)* and the adjective or adverb *außer,* meaning "outside of," "except." This movement outward is then taken up in the shift from the familiar noun "life" (*Leben*) and the gerundive, built on the present participle, which I translate as "the living"; in German, "das Lebendige." In the published translation, the substantive "life" displays its "manifestations," and these "manifestations of life" are then repeated and rendered redundant as "the phenomenon of life." In Benjamin's text, life is taking leave already from the start: instead of displaying itself in its manifestations, it begins to lose itself in its "utterances," a movement that is then intensified in the shift from "life" to "the living." For "the living" names a movement in which life, paradoxically enough, is only rendered "present" by expending itself, that is, by opening itself to a movement of iteration in which it is constantly being altered. This is the enigmatic mystery and resource of the present participle: it is present only in departing, present only partially, never fully, never completely present. It is present to the quick, right now, but in an ongoing recurrence that is always also on the verge of taking leave, of departing. This strange movement is then named in a noun that Benjamin puts into quotes as "afterlife." Not simply as that which comes "after" life has gone, but a life that is "after" itself—that is, constantly in pursuit of what it will never be.

The reason, in short, why works are translatable, is that they have an afterlife. And they have an afterlife because in the process of living, they are also dying, or at least, departing, taking-leave from themselves and this from their birth. Translation does not alter this leave-taking; it does not overcome it or "signify" anything that would nullify the departure of the original. Rather, it confirms that departure through its own non-translatability. It is finally finite. And as such, it remains "intimately" connected or related to the original insofar as its own finitude singularizes this leave-taking by localizing it and giving it a determinate structure and inflection. The original "survives"—the literal meaning of *"überleben"*—in and as the translation. But this survival confirms finitude rather than transcending it, since the translation, unlike the original, will have a limited "after-life"; it itself cannot be retranslated, at least according to Benjamin. Translation transports the original into a sphere of limited reproducibility, in which it cannot live very long. Afterlife is not eternal life.

This, perhaps, is why Benjamin introduces another German word to describe it: not just *Nachleben* but *Fortleben:* living on, but also living away. *Fortleben* is a life that already is moving elsewhere: a life lost in translation. But this important shift is itself lost in the published English translation, which translates *Fortleben* simply as "afterlife," as in the following passage, which I modify for the reasons indicated:

> In its living-on, which would not be called thus did it not involve transformation and renewal of the living, the original undergoes a change. There is an after-ripening even of fixed words . . . To locate the essence of such transformations as well as the no less constant (change) of meaning in the subjectivity of posterity instead of in the ownmost life of language and of its works would be, even allowing for the crudest psychologism, to deny one of the most powerful and most fruitful historical processes through weakness of thinking." (*GS4,* 12–13; *SW1,* 256, my translation)

The original "undergoes a change" because it belongs to a medium that itself is always in the process of changing: the medium of language. Because it is linguistic, the original work is historical. Ultimately the notion of "life" itself must be understood historically: "For it is from the vantage-point of history, not from that of nature, much less that of sensation and soul, that the circle of life is determined. For the philosopher the task thus becomes that of understanding all natural life from the more comprehensive one of history" (*GS4,* 11; *SW1,* 255). But if all Benjamin means by "life" thus turns out to be "history," in the familiar sense of this word, then why does he bother to speak of life and its various derivatives and versions in the first place? Why not just of history? The answer should now be clear: to speak of history independently of life, as Benjamin understands it, would run the (quintessential modern, Christian) risk of confounding the theological with the profane, the infinite with the finite, the immortal with the mortal. The history that emerges out of this discussion of "life," "afterlife," "living-on" is a history that is mindful of mortality, a history that does not try to overcome or transfigure the finitude of what today we call, perhaps too easily, its "agents." Benjamin's "way of meaning" has taken us from the notion of life through that of death toward a strange kind of hybrid: the after-life or living-on that constitutes the curious form of survival identified with translation. What survives, survives in a modified form. Can it thereby be said to "outlive" itself? What might it mean to outlive oneself? In no case does it mean to be simply immortal. Rather, it is a form in which the uniquely modern relation of life and death defines its own ambiguous, ambivalent character. The classical "apotheosis" of the perfect individual existence, qua work; the Romantic apotheosis of the Absolute, the symbol that sought to preserve the two, individual and absolute, in perfect harmony—all this is supplanted by a vision of history that is far closer to the German baroque than to its classical and Romantic successors. For what marks this vision of history is precisely its subjugation to death, what Benjamin calls its *Todverfallenheit*: "That is the nucleus of allegorical observation, of the baroque, worldly exposition of history as the history of the suffering of the world; it is significant only in the stations of its decline. However much significance, that much subjugation to death [*Todverfallenheit*], because death draws the jagged line of demarcation between physis [*Natur*] and significance [*Bedeutung*]" (*GS1,* 343; *Origin,* 166). Although it is clear that the situation of translation and that of baroque allegory are not simply identical, both bear the mark of an irreducible finitude. Translation proceeds "not from the life of the original," Benjamin reminds us, but from its "afterlife." At the same time, translation, as we have seen, "no longer signifies anything for the original itself." It proceeds or issues out of the original, but unlike Orpheus, it never looks back.

This paradox also links the kinship of translation and original in Benjamin's essay to the discussion of kinship in *Tristram Shandy.* In both cases, what is being called into question is a certain linear continuity based on equivalence and reciprocity—that held to bind child and parents, or translation and original. The child is thus presented as related to its parents, while the parents are said to be unrelated to the child (since all things descend in law). Similarly, the translation is intimately related to the original, out of whose "translatability" it emerges, but in a way that bears absolutely no significance for the original, its "parent" as it were. In both cases, what is lacking is reciprocity, symmetry, equivalence. The original can be said to outlive itself in its own language, while being condemned to live on and away in the foreign language only as a component of its "history." As a singular event, the translation is destined to "go under" and be absorbed into the history of the "foreign" language. Translation—the event and the process—calls attention to the limitations of singularity in language: "While the word of the poet endures and survives in its language, even the greatest translation is destined to be absorbed in the growth of its language, and to disappear fully in the renewed language. Translation is so far removed from being the deaf equation of two dead languages that precisely its most specific task becomes that of calling attention to the after-ripening [*Nachreife*] of the alien word, as well as to the pangs of its own" (*GS4*, 13; *SW1*, 256). On the one hand translation embodies that which is most alive in language: its historical dynamic, which drives each given state beyond itself and makes it something else. On the other hand, and at the same time, translation confirms its own limitations, its mortality, for "even the greatest translation is destined to disappear into the growth of its language." Similarly, the survival of the original in its language is that of a "Nachreife," a ripening that announces decline. What emerges out of this strange hybrid of the living and the dead can no longer be understood either in terms of individual works, be they the original or the translation. Nor can it be understood in terms of a relationship between these two types of works. Rather there is something in the idea, or even the word "translation," that suggests that what is at stake here is a relationship not between *individual works* so much as between *singularly dividual languages*. In short, translatability defines language as the medium of singularly dividual events, rather than of universally meaningful *works*.

In this sense the relationship of translation to the original is not the manifest relation of two works but rather the "hidden relationship" "of languages to one another" (*GS4*, 12; *SW1*, 255). This contrasts sharply with the relationship that constitutes the original work of poetry, which is directed "not at language as such" but rather "at the particular contents of language."[10] Once again we see how significant it is that Benjamin begins by writing of translation as a *form:* compared to the original work of poetry, translation focuses on the form of language, as distinct from its relation to, subordination under, or unification with a specific content or meaning. And once again we see the Romantic indebtedness of Benjamin's approach to language. The "original" is clearly construed on the basis of the Goethean conception of the work as the fusion of form and content, whereas "translation" as the prevalence of form over content is more closely related to the Romantic notion of the work as a pretext and occasion for infinite (that is, immortal) reflection. Except that as we have seen, for Benjamin, the movement of translation cannot be understood as being infinite. Since translations cannot themselves be further translated, the buck stops here. Translation is not the goal but the end of translation and this end is inscribed in it as its translatability. Its translatability both elevates it and condemns it:

> In translation the original rises into a higher and purer linguistic air, as it were. It cannot live there permanently, to be sure, and it certainly does not reach it in its entirety. Yet, in a singularly impressive manner, at least it points the way to this region: the predestined, hitherto inaccessible realm of reconciliation and fulfillment of languages. The transfer can never be total, but what reaches this region is that element in a translation that goes beyond transmission of subject matter. This nucleus is best defined as the element that does not lend itself to translation. Unlike the words of the original, it is not translatable, because the relationship between content and language is quite different in the original and the translation. While content and language form a certain unity in the original, like a fruit and its skin, the language of the translation envelops its content like a royal robe with ample folds. For it signifies a more exalted language than its own and thus remains unsuited to its content, overpowering and alien. (*GS4*, 14–15; *SW1*, 257–258)

The "nucleus" of the translation is its *untranslatability*. And yet this "nucleus" *(Kern)* toward which it gestures, but can never contain or attain, is what Benjamin calls "pure language."

The notion of "pure language" is at first a negative notion: "pure" means purged of elements that are external. What are such elements and where do we find them? Paradoxically, we find them in the original works of poetry, insofar as these are determined by their relation to extra-linguistic "contents" and "contexts." The original can only singularize itself as a work inasmuch as it is determined by its relation to nonlinguistic entities. This, once again, is what Benjamin—in the appendix to his thesis in which he opposes the Goethean conception of the work to that of the Romantics—associates with the Goethean "Ideal" as opposed to the Romantic "Idea" of poetry. The Goethean ideal resides in the individualized work of art, as the organic unity of form and content, whereas the Romantic "idea" of poetry, involving a process of infinite critical reflection, is associated with translation. The intention of the poet is described as "naive, primary, visual and intuitive," whereas "that of the translator" is characterized as a "derived, ultimate, idea-bound Intention" (*GS4*, 16; *SW1*, 259). It should be noted that the very use of the word "intention"—which had been popularized by Husserl at the time Benjamin wrote—stresses the discontinuous separation between movement of mind or language, between a pointing-at, and that at which one is pointing. In this sense, the notion of "intention" is already, in and of itself, opposed to or distinct from the kind of unity of form and content that Benjamin associates with the poet and with the poetic work. It is true that Benjamin also uses the term in regard to the poet. But it is here that the basis of the distinction between intention as separation and intention as fulfillment and fusion becomes clear. The basis of poetic fulfillment is described in this text as "anschaulich"; visual and intuitive, it looks at an object *(an-schaut)*. The intention of the translator, by contrast, does not aim at an object, much less a visual one. Rather, it addresses something that cannot be seen as such, but only read: a difference. The intention of the translator aims at the difference between languages, not in general, but in their specifically different ways of meaning the same things. And this difference between languages is in turn related to an intra-linguistic differentiation, through which the work tends, as a temporal-historical event, to separate from the referents that initially made it meaning-ful.

And it is here, at the interface of intra- and inter-linguistic alteration, both based on language as signifying process, that Benjamin introduces what is perhaps the key conceptual distinction in his essay: that between "the meant" and "the way of meaning." Languages, he argues, are identical in what they mean: they all mean the same things, they all have the same "Gemeinte." What distinguishes them is the way they mean these things, their *Art des Meinens*. It is the relation of different *ways of meaning*, tied to the differences between and within languages, that constitutes the true object of the translator. The task of the translator consists, first, in relating the distinctive ways of meaning in different languages to one another, and secondly and correlatively, in bringing out what is ultimately "meant"—signified—by these different but related ways of meaning: namely, "pure language" itself.

Everything, we see, hinges on this notion of the "way of meaning." The term is an almost literal translation of the scholastic concept known, in Latin, as the *modus significandi*. Whereas the scholastics, for instance Thomas of Erfurt in his famous treatise on the modes of signification, interpreted the modus significandi as the expression of a conscious intention, Benjamin gives the notion a different spin. He considers it not as a framework for producing meaning—this was the interest of the scholastics—but rather, in a more Saussurean manner, as a movement of language that is prior to the communication or constitution of meaning. In thus separating the "way of meaning" from "the meant" (that is, from meaning as concept, object, or referent), Benjamin develops an argumentation that had already been explored in a book that Benjamin had read, although with very mixed feelings.

For before discovering this book in 1920, Benjamin had himself planned to write his *Habilitationsschrift*—which would have qualified him for an academic position—on precisely the same subject. Although Benjamin disliked the book intensely, he ultimately had to admit that there was enough in it to eliminate the subject as a possible thesis topic for him. The author of the book in question was of course none other than Martin Heidegger. Benjamin's initial reaction to the book is not without interest in the context of our discussion: in a letter to his friend, Gershom Scholem, he rejects it as nothing more than "a piece of good translation" masquerading as a work of scholarship.[11] Shortly after writing this letter, however, he admits, once again to Scholem, that "the text of Heidegger nevertheless perhaps covers what is most essential in Scholastic thought for my problem—although in an entirely unanalyzed manner—and yet still manages to point out what the real problem is."[12]

The argument that seems to have been decisive for "The Task of the Translator" is formulated by Heidegger in a style that could hardly be more remote from that of Benjamin:

> The modi significandi constitute a particular order within the realm of meaning. This a priori organized connection of meanings into semantic complexions does not suffice to constitute what we call valid meaning. In the semantic complexions as such, as they are organized through the modi significandi, the truth-value, which is tied to judgment, is not yet realized. Insofar however as the valid sense of judgment, which is expressible in sentences, is determined through the structure of such modes of signifying, something is realized already within the mere realm of meaning, which we, following Lotze, can call "syntactical value."[13]

It is precisely this relationship between modi significandi and syntax that becomes the nucleus of Benjamin's theory of translation—and also the point where this theory itself becomes eminently practical. This insight is announced in the provocative slogan that maps the task of the translator: "Fidelity to the word, freedom toward the meaning!" But precisely this distancing of word from meaning seems to confront Benjamin with irresolvable problems: "Indeed, this problem of bringing the seed of pure language to fruition in translation seems to be insoluble, determinable in no solution. For is not the ground cut from under such a solution if the reproduction of sense ceases to be decisive? And yet, nothing else is, negatively understood, the meaning of all the foregoing" (GS4, 17; SW1, 259). One should not simplify what Benjamin is suggesting here, with respect to the significance of meaning in translation. When he writes that the meaning of all the foregoing is that "the reproduction of sense" cannot be held to be "decisive" for translation, this is not tantamount to asserting that meaning is utterly unimportant and that it should be ignored. Rather, what he is suggesting is that such meaning cannot simply be equated with the sum of the meanings of individual words and phrases. And this holds not just for the translation but also for the original work: "For with respect to its poetical significance in regard to the original, this (meaning) does not exhaust itself in the meant, but rather accedes to the latter through the way in which the meant is bound to the way of meaning in the individual word. One customarily expresses this by saying that words carry with them an affective tone" (GS4, 17; SW1, 260). For Benjamin, this "emotional connotation," as the English translation reads, is a reality that derives not from the psyches of individual subjects, but from the heterogeneity of language—not however as the unity of form and content, but as their disunity, their divergence. Language here names the irreducibility of the way of meaning to what is meant, the non-equivalence of the What (meaning) and the How (signifying). Disjunction, non-equivalence, divergence of the meant from the way of meaning— all that does not efface the semantic dimension of language. On the contrary, it makes absolutely no sense to speak of a "way of meaning" without a meant, a meaning or sense. But such a "sense" indicates a direction rather than a point of arrival. For the semantic dimension of fixed meaning does not exhaust language. When Benjamin writes that the specifically poetical signification cannot be identified simply with what is meant, with the meaning of a phrase, but rather has to do with "how the meant is bound to the way of meaning in the determinate word," he indicates both that the semantic dimension of meaning plays a role in *binding* the way of meaning to particular words, and that the configuration of such binding is not itself determined semantically. Rather, it is syntactical. For what is decisive is *how* an object or concept is bound to an individual word, and through it, to a particular way of being-meant. And this idea of being bound to or up with individual words depends on a spatial arrangement that can be designated both as syntactical and as singular.

The result is what Benjamin calls "word-by-word syntax." "Wordliness (translated in English as 'literalness') with respect to syntax gets rid fully of every sort of reproduction of meaning and threatens to lead straight into the unintelligible. For the nineteenth century, Hölderlin's translations of Sophocles stood as the monstrous example of such wordliness (literalness)" (*GS4*, 17; *SW1*, 260). None other than Hölderlin, however, exemplifies the ideal of Benjamin's "Task of the Translator," just as he already stood as the unattainable, unanalyzed ideal of Benjamin's thesis on German Romanticism. What appears to fascinate Benjamin above all is the risk of madness: subordinating the sense to the signifying can easily lead to the loss of sense, to senselessness. The linguistic correlative of such a subjective risk of madness is the undermining of that relatively stable system of rules we call "grammar." What goes on when a text is translated as Benjamin suggests—namely verbatim, or with word-by-word literalness—is that it begins to lose its support in stable, self-identical meaning and instead, as syntax begins to take precedence over grammar, the way of meaning begins to gain independence with respect to that which is meant.

This sheds light on what is meant by "pure language": "True translation is translucent, it does not cover the original, or stand between it and the light, but allows pure language, intensified through its own medium, to shine all the more fully on the original. This can be done best through word-by-word transmission of syntax and precisely this reveals the word, rather than the sentence, to be the basic element of the translator. For the sentence is the wall before the language of the original, wordliness the arcade" (*GS4*, 18; *SW1*, 260). Word-by-word transmission of syntax forms the arcade, the passageways (already here, in 1923, Benjamin is already fascinated with passages and arcades) that lead not so much back to the original as "forward" to its medium, language. Or rather, linguistic difference. And it is here that we begin to approach what "pure language" might mean: language that is pure of

everything that is outside it is a language that would consist of pure signifying, something that is aporetical, to be sure, since signifying always
entails a signified and hence cannot be entirely pure. But a relation
to language in which syntax—the sequential arrangement of words—
takes precedence over the time-and-space transcending rules of grammar and semantics; in which the ways of meaning, their distribution
and relations, have priority over what is meant—this would be a language that seems to approach what Benjamin "means" by "pure language." This would be a language that performs by signifying without
being absorbed or determined by entities that appear to exist independently of all signifying.

How this is to be conceived, concretely, remains elusive. For this
reason, I propose to look more closely at the curious centerpiece of this
essay, where Benjamin cites a passage from Stéphane Mallarmé's *Crise
de vers*; he cites the phrase in French, without translating it, perhaps
because it is already, in a certain sense, a translation and hence untranslatable. In any case, the text seems to exemplify what can happen when
a way of meaning takes precedence over what is being meant. Let
me illustrate by citing it first in French, and then, in a word-by-word
translation: "Les langues imparfaites en cela que plusieurs, manque la
suprême: penser étant écrire sans accessoires, ni chuchotement mais
tacite encore l'immortelle parole, la diversité, sur terre, des idiomes
empêche personne de proférer les mots qui, sinon se trouveraient, par
une frappe unique, matériellement elle-même la vérité" (*GS4*, 17; *SW1*,
259). Now, my translation: "Languages, imperfect insofar as many,
lacking the highest: thinking being writing without accessories, neither
whispering but silent still the immortal word, the diversity, on earth, of
idioms prevents no one from offering the words which, if not, would
find themselves, in a single stroke, itself materially the truth."

Benjamin obviously knew why he did not want to translate this passage of Mallarmé. The text is clearly untranslatable. Not because what
it has to say—its meant—is incomprehensible or impossible to render.
On the contrary: to "translate" what Mallarmé has to say here would
be the least difficult problem to resolve with regard to the passage. The
published translation gives you an idea, and I will try my hand at a
paraphrase: "Since languages are many, the highest (that is, the supreme language, which would have to be a single language) is missing.
Since thinking is writing without accessories, whereby the immortal

word does not even whisper but rather is silent, the plurality of individual languages prevents those words from being uttered, which otherwise, in one stroke, would materially be truth itself." What is missing in this kind of paraphrase, one that seeks to render meaning faithfully, is nothing less than what is essential: namely, the way in which this meaning is meant, by virtue of being bound up with individual words and their relations to one another. To be brief: the way this passage means is marked repeatedly by a threefold interruption through which the expectation of a grammatically correct statement is derailed again and again. We expect to find the sequence: subject, verb, object (or complement). Instead, this expectation is disappointed. The apparently plural subject of this sentence, "les langues imparfaites en cela que plusieurs," does not accord with the form of the verb, since this verb stands in the singular: "manque le suprême." Through this disharmony the continuity of the progression of the phrase is jolted: the ostensible subject, "les langues imparfaites," reveals itself to be the object, while the expected object, "la suprême," shows itself to be the subject. This movement repeats itself three times in the sentence, revealing that the time of reading is not simply linear, progressive, and irreversible, but is rather effective only belatedly: what comes afterward— Kant's *Nachfolge*—determines what comes before. In distinction to that "ground and principle of the law" that was cited in the scene from *Tristram Shandy,* the law of reading prescribes a movement that goes in divergent directions at once: progressive and regressive, or, as Sterne calls it, progressive-digressive. The notion of "digression" here is particularly pertinent, for it suggests that what is involved is not simply a linear movement along a single axis, either forward or backward. Rather, what reveals itself at the end of the sentence to be the subject takes on a different value than it would have had, had it come at the beginning, where we were expecting it. It remains out of place, odd, alien, defying grammatical expectation. What is thereby revealed is the capacity of language to defy the general rules that allow it to function as medium of communication. In particular, the position of the subject will always depend on the singularity of the particular situation and will thus retain a certain eccentricity with respect to the generally prescribed positions of accepted systems of rules.

Naturally the semantic content of individual words and sentences is not thereby rendered indifferent. But their significance is not determined through their intrinsic, conceptual content, but rather through the way in which the individual elements are syntactically related or positioned with respect to the other elements of the phrase. Two consequences emerge from this, both of which are clearly marked in Mallarmé's text. The first concerns the "frappe unique," that singular stroke or blow that may also mark a turning-point. The "frappe unique" designates the moment at which words suddenly and materially become truth. Or rather, would become truth, if only . . . if only what? This question brings us to the second point. The words that would materially, with a single blow, become truth itself, cannot be proffered by anyone, so long as the highest language is lacking. This seems to be what the text of Mallarmé wants to say. But the way it says it leaves room for doubt. "La diversité, sur terre, des idiomes empêche personne, de proférer les mots qui etc." The turn of phrase "empêche personne" means literally, "hinders no one from proffering those words, etc." With one blow or stroke what is said is that nothing hinders us, or rather that no one is prevented from saying the words that would materially become truth. But does this not suggest that we are saying them all the time? That we are speaking "pure language"? And would that in turn not contradict everything that Benjamin seems to be saying, above all, about the transcendence of "pure language"? The answer to this question depends on how one construes the relation between transcendence and immanence, pure and impure language: Do we think of them as mutually exclusive opposites, or could they possibly overlap with one another? How does Benjamin describe "pure language"?

To begin with, negatively. Pure language, he writes, "which no longer means anything and no longer expresses anything" (GS4, 19; SW1, 261), is at the same time the "inexpressive and creative word that is meant in all languages." Although in this essay Benjamin remains largely caught in such purely negative determinations, he still asserts that pure language is not situated in another world, in a Beyond, but rather in the "distance," remote from us, although strangely enough it is one that is also contained "intensively, in a nutshell [Keimhaft intensiv]" in translation, which "realizes it," although in a concealed manner. Pure language is thus a kind of internal distance contained in translation. The question is: how?[14] Benjamin gives us at least a hint, not in this essay but in one written shortly thereafter, a study of Goethe's novel Elective Affinities (Die Wahlverwandtschaften). Once again it is a question of kinship, relatedness, relations. In the middle of this essay Benjamin reintroduces the notion of the "inexpressive," which he had used to characterize "pure language," and once again he uses Hölderlin both as example and as source. From Hölderlin's writings on tragedy, which grew out of his translations of Sophocles, Benjamin cites the following: "Tragical transport is namely actually empty, and the most untrammeled.—Thereby what develops in the rhythmic sequence of ideas wherein the transport presents itself is that which is called in prosody a caesura, the pure word, the counter-rhythmic interruption, necessary, in order to meet the rush of ideas, at its height, so that not merely the change in ideas appears but the idea itself" (quoted by Benjamin in *GS1*, 181–182; *SW1*, 340–341). Pure language as the word that is without expression, pure word, is here designated as the caesura that, all of a sudden, stems the rush of ideas, arrests its flow, impedes its progression, cuts against the grain of the grammatical expectation of meaning. In the Mallarmé text, this inexpressive, meaningless caesura can be seen in the punctuation, in those commas that do not so much articulate a meaningful phrase as mark the interruption of the expectation of meaning: "Les langues imparfaites en cela que plusieurs, manque la suprême." "Les mots qui, sinon se trouveraient, par une frappe unique, elle-même matériellement la vérité." If pure language consists in such inexpressiveness, in in-significance, then the reference to Hölderlin and Mallarmé suggests that the material embodiment of such pure language goes on all the time, more or less, as the countless interruptions that scan our utterances even if we generally choose to ignore them for the sake of both our self-preservation and a sense of sociability.

We are all constantly interrupting ourselves even though, as Freud argues, we have good reasons not to want to notice it. By transporting the ways words mean from one language to another, the translator, like the writer in general, challenges our desire not to notice just how profoundly, if silently, the caesura of "pure language" is intensively at work in everything we say and do.

CHAPTER SIX

Translatability II

Afterlife

If one were to search today for a way of reflecting on the destiny of language and literature in an age increasingly dominated by electronic media, there is probably no better place to start—and perhaps even to end—than with the question of translation. This might seem a somewhat surprising assertion to make, given the widespread tendency to associate the rise of electronic media with what is usually called the "audiovisual," as distinct from the linguistic, discursive, or textual. Such an association is, of course, by no means simply arbitrary. In 1999, the dollar value produced by the sales of products related to video games, considered on a global scale, for the first time surpassed that of non-game related personal computer software and hardware—and to be sure, sales of printed matter were not even close to either.[1] Given such developments in this age of electronic media, how is it possible to claim that the question of translation can serve as a valuable index of the changing signification of language and literature?

The answer to this apparent paradox cannot be simple, of course. Translation as such covers a great variety of activities, most of which are aimed at making texts accessible to people who do not know the language in which the text is written. Thus, for most translation activities in this sense, what is decisive is the goal of rendering a text written in one language understandable in another language. Meaning is thus the informing goal, a meaning generally held to transcend individual languages the way universality transcends particularity. There are, however, other kinds of translation—poetic, literary, philosophical—in which the transmission of meaning cannot be separated from the way in which meaning is articulated or signified. And although this sort of translation may be statistically and economically far less important than the first kind, it may also in many ways be more revealing of the relationship between the linguistic medium and other media.

At any rate, my initial assertion is concerned with this latter type of translation, in which the "what" cannot be separated from the "how." The *what*—that is, meaning—may be conceived as existing *apart* from its specific linguistic localization; the *how* is not. Its transmission, transport, or translation thus inevitably raises the question of how one moves from one relatively restricted linguistic system to another. Usually, the linguistic systems between which translations move are designated as "natural" or "national" languages. These terms, however, are anything but precise or satisfactory. "Portuguese," for instance, although named for a specific nation, is no more a "national" language than is "English," "French," "German," or "Spanish." Yet to call these languages "natural" is perhaps even more unsatisfactory than to designate them as "national." The imprecision of such terms is in direct proportion to the linguistic diversity they seek to subsume. To be sure, such diversity does not exclude the fact that individual language-systems exist and are distinct from one another. But such distinctions, and the language-systems they differentiate, are by no means as homogeneous as their names might suggest. The difficulty of finding a generic term that would accurately designate the class to which individual languages belong is indicative of the larger problem of determining the principles that give those languages their relative unity or coherence—assuming, that is, that such principles really exist.

The fact that the names of individual language-systems are not generally considered problematic is indicative not of the absence of such problems but rather of an established but largely unconscious decision not to acknowledge them in everyday practice. This decision is destabilized, potentially at least, whenever anything like "translation" is attempted. Such destabilization has to do with the fact, already mentioned, that translation always involves not merely the movement from one *language* to another, but from one *instance*—a text already existing in one language—to another instance, that does not previously exist, but that is brought into being in the other language. The tension between the generality of the language-systems and the singularity of the individual texts is reflected, but also *concealed,* by the ambiguity of the very word "translation" itself, which designates both a *general process,* involving a change of place, and a *singular result* of that process: *translating* in general, and (a) translation in particular. The tension between the general process and the individual product tends to be obscured by an attitude that regards translation as an instrument in the service of the "communication" of meaning or of a message. This attitude privileges the generality of the process at the expense of its singularity.

Such a tendency is reinforced today by the spread of what is called "globalization." The figure of the *globe* suggests an all-encompassing immanence in which singular differences are absorbed into a generalized whole. Nevertheless, precisely because of its homogenizing tendencies, "globalization" also exacerbates the need for differentiation. In facilitating circulation, transmission, and contact, globalization brings the most remote and diverse areas and languages into contact with one another. Such contact, while clearly increasing the need for translation, does it in a way that is no less ambivalent than globalization itself. The following remarks seek to explore certain aspects of the ambivalent contact of languages that are never very far from the surface when they are touched by translation.

The history of translation is marked by a tension between two inseparable and yet incompatible motifs: fidelity and betrayal. Both result from the split relationship of translation to its own history, which is to say, to its "origin." Translation, *translatio,* does not merely signify carrying-across, transporting, transferring *in general:* it also entails a specific, singular relation of texts to one another, and more particularly, of a text to that which it transports, its origin or *original.* The status of this *terminus ab quo,* the *original,* has been radically transformed by the spread of electronic media, and in particular, by the development of digital modes of presentation and transmission. The very notion of "medium" is changed by this extension of digitalization. Aristotle, for instance, defined a medium *(metaxos)* as a *diaphanous* interval that allows a certain transmission to take place.[2] The *medium* was thus construed as an intermediary *between* two places. Movement through the medium was—and in most people's minds still is—defined through implicit reference to and contrast with the *fixity* of the *places between* which it moves.

This, then, becomes the model of what is known as the "senses" and their "perception." The classical example cited by Aristotle in his definition of a medium is that of an ant in the sky being visible only by virtue of the action of the intervening medium, which allows light to pass through.

The discussion of the medium is thus associated, from the very beginnings of Western philosophy, with sense-impressions in general, and with the sense of sight in particular. The continuing power of this association is reflected even today in the widespread use of a term such as "television" to designate a process that involves audition as much as vision. This privileging of the visual can also be observed in the current tendency to equate "multimedia" with "audiovisual."

With the development of media technology over the past half century, the traditional conception of the medium as an interval both separating and linking a subject to an object via the physical senses has become increasingly problematic.[3] Correlatively, the notion of "origin" and of "original" has also been affected. The ramifications of this change, however, can only be correctly evaluated by contrast with that which it is altering: the traditional notion of origin. Doubtless the most influential articulation of this notion for the cultural tradition of the "West" is to be found in the book of Genesis, where origin is understood as creation. I propose therefore to reread briefly a few passages from this text, in order to discern certain traits that will continue, until today, to leave their imprint on what we call "translation."

I begin, therefore, with "the beginning," as it is rendered in the King James Version of the Bible: "In the beginning, God created the heaven and the earth, and the earth was without form, and void; and darkness was upon the face of the deep. And the Spirit of God moved upon the face of the waters" (Gen. 1:1). Creation, in the biblical account, operates above all through a series of dichotomies, beginning with the distinction between unbounded space ("heaven") and limited place ("earth"). At first, the limitation of place, "earth," is purely abstract, establishing the minimal dichotomy necessary for a distinction, but one that is otherwise wholly indeterminate, "without form and void" and hence totally obscure. Only in a second phase, as it were, is the abstract dichotomy of heaven and earth defined through a series of oppositions that progressively differentiate the *place* called "earth." In addition to this general tendency to describe the creation of the world through a series of dichotomies, there is another aspect that does not exactly fit in, but that will turn out to be quite significant. The second sentence of Genesis 1:1 recounts how, after the initial creation of heaven and earth, "the spirit (*ruach:* breath) of God moved upon the face of the waters." This kind of movement is very different from that implied by the oppositions that otherwise predominate: it suggests a quasi-tactile moment, in which Creator and Creation no longer are clearly distinguished or separated from one another. Rather, there is a certain convergence and contact between the two, without any sort of merging or fusion taking place. This unusual event is quickly submerged, as it were, by the introduction of temporal succession as the medium through which the creation moves toward completion. This temporal progression culminates, on the Sixth Day, with the creation of man: "God said, Let us make man in our image, after our likeness . . . So God created man in his own image, in the image of God created he him; male and female created he them" (Gen. 1:26–27). The Biblical account of the creation of "man" introduces two conditions that will be of particular significance for the problem of translation. Taken separately, each is familiar enough by itself, but their interaction has perhaps not been sufficiently considered. First, in contrast to all other living beings, "man" is made in the "image" of God, a relationship that is interpreted, in the King James Version at least, as "likeness." In more contemporary terms, one could say that the ruling role of Man in the Creation is a consequence of his "analogical" relation to his divine origin.

This, however, is only half of the story. For there is a second trait that distinguishes human beings from other animate beings in the Biblical account: gender ("Male and female created he them"). To be sure, the distinction of gender can be judged as already implied in the creation of other living beings, insofar as they are admonished by the Creator to be "fruitful and multiply." The fact remains, however, that it is only with respect to Man that gender is mentioned explicitly.

That the gendered creation of human beings is anything but self-evident is suggested in the Biblical text by the somewhat awkward addition of a second, more elaborate version of the creation of man in Chapter 2. In this expanded account, Man is created not directly by the word of God, but indirectly, formed out of "the dust of the ground."

The association of man with earth and "dust" anticipates the Fall, the expulsion from Eden and the advent of human mortality. At the same time, however, this second version of the creation links man's destiny to his origin, now understood to be not purely divine, but also earthly and hence bound up with a *place*. To be earthbound is above all to be determined by one's *location*.

This topographical aspect of the second story of the creation of man is reinforced by the geographical details and place-names that proliferate there. Man is "put" into a "garden" that is "planted . . . eastward in Eden." Through this garden a river flows that subsequently divides "into four heads." Each of these four rivers receives a proper name linked to the name of a country or region. In this second account of man's creation, woman is created from a rib "taken from man," in short, as the result of a bodily mutilation.

All of this complicates the initially "analogical" relationship of man as the image and likeness of the Creator. It introduces an unbridgeable distance and difference that clashes with the relationship of man to God implied by the notion of "image" as "likeness." Man and woman are not created *ex nihilo,* as in the first chapter of Genesis, but rather out of already existing matter: dust and rib, earth and body. Creation, in this second version, is a process of transformation. It no longer implies an absolute beginning or a pure performance, but rather almost a translation—almost, but not quite. It is not *yet* a translation for two interrelated reasons. First, because there is still no place available that would make a traversal—the "trans-" of *translation*—either necessary or even thinkable. Despite the growing sense of separation of the created from the Creator, the only place inhabited by Man is still the Garden of Eden. Second and correlatively, just as there is still only one place, so there is still only one language: the language of the Creator is the language of man.

This situation changes radically, of course, with the expulsion from the Garden of Eden. Of this momentous event, I want here to point out only one or two traits that are pertinent for our discussion. First, when Eve, having been accosted by the serpent, responds, she repeats the words of the Creator prohibiting her and Adam from eating of the Tree of Knowledge. But when she recites the divine prohibition, which modern Biblical translations usually render as a direct citation, she adds something not found in the "original" version of God's words: "And the woman said unto the serpent, We may eat of the fruit of the trees of the garden: But of the fruit of the tree which is in the midst of the garden, God hath said, Ye shall not eat of it, *neither shall ye touch it,* lest ye die" (Gen. 3:3, my emphasis). Here is the original account: "But of the tree of the knowledge of good and evil, thou shalt not eat of it: for in the day that thou eatest thereof thou shalt surely die" (Gen. 2:17). What Eve, herself the product of a bodily transformation, adds in her ostensible citation of the words of God, is the apparently anodyne detail of *touch:* "Ye shall not eat of it, neither shall ye touch it, lest ye die." Could this be the first case, in the Western tradition at least, of the famous formula, *traduttore—tradditore?* Yes and no. No, insofar as Eve's quotation is not "properly" a translation, insofar as the repetition takes place *within* a single language rather than *between* different ones. Yes, insofar as her rendering of the words of God involves a change of place, even if that place is still the Garden of Eden.[4]

In short, the divine prohibition, as re-cited by Eve at least, involves not just *eating* from the tree of knowledge, but *touching* it as well. A second instance of touching, which like the first we will leave suspended, but not for long.

Shortly thereafter, when God has discovered that Adam and Eve have eaten from the tree of knowledge, he responds: "And the Lord God said, Behold, the man is become as one of us, to know good and evil: and now, *lest he put forth his hand, and take* also of the tree of life, and eat, and live for ever: / Therefore the Lord God sent him forth from the garden of Eden" (Gen. 3:22–23, my emphasis). Adam and Eve are banished from the Garden of Eden not just as a punishment for what they have done, but as a way of preventing them from doing what Eve precisely had already acknowledged in her response to the serpent: *touching* and not simply *eating.*

Yet this is a very different kind of "touching" from that encountered at the beginning of the creation, when the "spirit of God moved upon the face of the waters." For the "touching" of the Tree of Life is a means of *taking possession,* and thereby of becoming "as one of us." Touching here, then, becomes a form of taking, turning *likeness* into *sameness.*[5] It is also associated with a certain form of knowledge: the dichotomous-hierarchical knowledge that distinguishes Good from Evil. This sort of knowledge turns touching into taking, thus collapsing analogy into equality, likeness into sameness, difference into identity, and it is this that causes God to intervene once again, in the process redefining what is involved in *touching:* "And the Lord God said unto the serpent, Because thou hast done this, thou art cursed above all cattle, and above every beast of the field; upon thy belly shalt thou go, and dust shalt thou eat all the days of thy life" (Gen. 3:14). The serpent will thus "crawl on its belly and eat dust" (New Jerusalem Bible), *touching* the earth but *not taking* it. Similarly, man will no longer touch the earth in order to possess it, but rather be touched and taken by it, back to the formless form of *dust:*[6] "In the sweat of thy face shalt thou eat bread, till thou return unto the ground; for out of it wast thou taken: for dust thou art, and unto dust shalt thou return" (Gen. 3:19). Conflict and struggle thus seem to be programmed by the Biblical story of the creation. On the one hand, man is said to be created in the image of God, or at least as his likeness. On the other, however *like* the Creator he may be, man is still part of the creation and hence irrevocably different from its Author. The first chapters of Genesis tell the story of man's efforts to reduce the difference that separate the human from the divine, and the ensuing reinforcement of that separation. In the process, the first of two necessary conditions for translation emerges: a certain distance. Yet another condition is still required, and this brings us to the second Biblical event commonly associated with translation: the Tower of Babel, which in a certain sense is a replay of the Fall:

And the whole earth was of one language, and of one speech.

And it came to pass, as they journeyed from the east, that they found a plain in the land of Shinar; and they dwelt there. . .

And they said, Go to, let us build us a city and a tower, whose top may reach unto heaven; and let us make us a name, lest we be scattered abroad upon the face of the whole earth.

And the Lord came down to see the city and the tower, which the children of men builded.

And the Lord said, Behold, the people is one, and they have all one language; and this they begin to do: and now nothing will be restrained from them, which they have imagined to do.

Go to, let us go down, and there confound their language, that they may not understand one another's speech.

So the Lord scattered them abroad from thence upon the face of all the earth: and they left off to build the city.

Therefore is the name of it called Babel; because the Lord did there confound the language of all the earth; and from thence did the Lord scatter them abroad upon the face of all the earth. (Gen. 11:1–9)

If the original Fall befell "man" and "woman" *as such*, its repetition now affects fallen *men* and *women* as members of a clan, community, or group. Their project now is not to avoid touching and eating from the Tree of Knowledge, but rather to build both a "city" and a "tower, whose top may reach unto heaven." The effort here is to re-create a place that will be as perfectly self-sufficient as that from which they have been banned. Once again, then, they seek to be like God, who is One, only this time as a "people." To be united, however, a "people" must possess a proper place, a city, but also a "name, lest we be scattered abroad." One people, one city, one name, and one tower reaching to the Heavens. But above all, one language. It is this ambition that provokes the second intervention of God, after the expulsion from the Garden of Eden, but with a similar result. The result is another expulsion, "scattering" the people "abroad," all over the "face of the earth." Such scattering, however, is the result not of brute force, as it were, but of the "confounding" of what until then was the single language of man. The institution of *languages,* in the plural, is thus tied to the dispersion of the community. No longer do they dwell in one place but in many. No longer do they bear one name, but many; no longer do they speak one language, but different languages. It is this splintering of human unity, which at once entails a dispersal of political unity, that marks the origin not of "language" in the singular, but of languages in the plural.

It is only from this point on that *translation* will become an inevitable, but also an *impossible*—that is, never fully achievable—condition of human existence. This, however, in turn means that "human" existence is no longer simply "human" because it has no single proper name. "Man" is now one name among many, ambiguously designating diversity, particularity, singularity—of peoples and communities and groups as much as of individuals.

This significance of "Babel" and of its consequences can be gauged in terms of the transformations it imposes on the "name." The initial project aims at constructing a city and a tower that would reach to—which is to say, *touch*—the skies. In this respect, it recalls the transgression committed in the Garden of Eden, that of touching of the Tree of Knowledge. To touch is to reduce the distance and difference between human and divine, created and Creator, to the barest minimum. Such touching is thus the effacing of the most decisive and constitutive of all limits: that between mortals and immortal, as the latter recognizes: "They have all one language; and this they begin to do: and now nothing will be restrained from them, which they have imagined to do." To touch the skies means to surmount diversity and acquire the attribute reserved to the One God: unity. It also means to have the power to make a name that is proper. The divine response, therefore, is to "confound" all names and languages, thereby instituting a medium in which *touching* will never simply be a means of *taking (possession)*. This transformation begins with the name of Babel itself, which means both confusion, imposed by God on language, and "gate of the god."[7] In this name, meanings touch one another but do not fuse into unity. Rather, they stand in tension to one another. The gate of the god is thus marked by the confusion of names and languages. It is a gate that does not lead back to the single language of Eden, but rather opens onto the impossible and henceforth ineluctable task of translation. In view of this history, the task of translation can be described as that of *touching* without *taking*.

The phrase "task of translation" touches on the last text to be discussed in this chapter, one that in a certain sense has already informed much of the previous discussion, without being named or quoted directly: "The Task of the Translator," written by Benjamin in 1921 to accompany his translation of Baudelaire's *Tableaux parisiens*. Were there space enough, I would have liked to introduce this discussion via a somewhat later text of Benjamin's in which he elaborates a notion of "origin" that is very helpful in understanding the way he construes the relation of translation to the "original." Instead, however, I will simply quote a short passage in order to suggest the rather unusual way in which Benjamin construes the notion of origin. This passage is found in the "Epistemo-critical Preface" to his ill-fated study of German baroque theater, written in 1924. In this passage, Benjamin insists that the notion of origin must be understood *historically*. What he means by "history," however, turns out to be quite different from the way that word is commonly understood:

> Origin, although an historical category through and through, has nevertheless nothing in common with emergence [*Entstehen*]. In origin what is meant is not the becoming of something that has sprung forth [*das Werden des Entsprungenen*], but rather the springing-forth that emerges out of coming-to-be and passing away [*dem Werden und Vergehen Entspringendes*]. Origin stands in the flow of becoming as a maelstrom [*Strudel*] that irresistibly tears [*reißt*] the stuff of emergence into its rhythm. In the bare manifestation of the factual, the original is never dis-

cernible, and its rhythm is accessible only to a dual insight. It is recognizable on the one hand as restoration, as reinstatement, and on the other, precisely therein as incomplete, unfinished.[8]

The concept of *origin* that Benjamin articulates in this passage contrasts sharply with the *creatio ex nihilo*—or more precisely, creation out of formlessness—that informs the biblical text of Genesis. Instead, the notion of *origin*—and hence, the notion of the *original*—is construed not as an absolute beginning, nor as the passage from formlessness to form, nor as the result of anything like the intervention of a divine logos. It is also not conceived as a function of *becoming (Werden)* or of its dialectical counterpart, passing away *(Vergehen)*.

As something that neither "comes to be" nor "passes away," which Benjamin designates with a participial noun as *"Entspringendes,"*[9] the origin is an *event* involving both singularity and repetition. This paradoxical combination is never to be found in the merely "factual," Benjamin asserts, since what it entails is less a self-contained phenomenon than a complex *relationship* that is described as a "rhythm," thus emphasizing both its repetitive and temporal aspect. This "rhythm" of the "origin," he states, in what can only be a deliberate mixing of metaphors (and senses), is accessible "only to a dual insight. It is recognizable on the one hand as restoration, as reinstatement, and precisely in this, as on the other hand, incomplete, unfinished" (*GS1*, 226; *Origin*, 45). An "origin" is historical in that it seeks to repeat, restore, reinstate something anterior to it. In so doing, however, it never succeeds and therefore remains "incomplete, unfinished." Yet it is precisely such *incompleteness* that renders origin *historical*. Its historicality resides not in its ability to give rise to a progressive, teleological movement, but rather in its power to return incessantly to the past and through the rhythm of its ever-changing repetitions set the pace for the future.

By thus determining "origin" as the insistent but unachievable attempt to restore an anterior state, Benjamin's 1924 text suggests that something like "translation" is already at work in the "rhythm" of the original, insofar as it is historical. This account of origin thus illuminates, retroactively, the discussion of translation he had undertaken three years earlier, in the "Task of the Translator." The necessarily incomplete attempt to restore and reinstate what has been, which defines the *original*, indicates how and why translation can never attain an existence that would be independent of its origin. Since the original defines itself historically through the ever-incomplete attempt to restore and reinstate itself, it is from the start, as it were, caught up in a process of repetition that involves alteration and transformation, dislocation and displacement. This conception of the "original" explains why Benjamin should approach "The Task of the Translator" not in terms of "translation," understood as a self-contained process or structure, but in terms of what he calls the "translatability" of "the original." *Translatability* is not simply a property of the original work, but rather a *potentiality* that can be realized or achieved, and that therefore has less to do with the enduring life usually attributed to the *work* than with what Benjamin calls its "after-life" or its "survival" *(Nachleben, Fortleben, Überleben)*. With respect to this afterlife, the original is already irrevocably departed and is thus not directly affected by the factual history of its translations. Its historical significance, however, is inseparable from its *translatability*. This is because translatability is never the property of an *entity*, such as a *work*, but rather of a *relation*. And relations, Benjamin warns, should not necessarily be judged in exclusively human terms, for instance the needs of actual human beings to understand works written in a foreign language: "Only superficial thinking could declare both for essentially the same . . . Against such a conception it must be pointed out that certain relational concepts [*Relationsbegriffe*] receive their good, indeed best meaning when they are not a priori and exclusively applied to human beings . . . Correspondingly, the translatability of linguistic structures [*Gebilde*] would still deserve consideration even if these were untranslatable for human beings" (*GS4*, 10; *SW1*, 254). If, then, "translatability" is to be understood as a "relational concept," but not as one that cannot be "a priori and exclusively applied to human beings," how is it to be thought? To what does translatability *relate?*

Benjamin's response is double. First, he argues, languages relate to one another. Second, they relate not to human needs, which is to say, to meanings or messages, but to what Benjamin calls "pure language." Contrary to what one might suppose, "pure language" is not prelapsarian language, not the unified and performative language of the Creative Logos. Pure language emerges out of the interplay of what Benjamin calls their "way (or mode) of signifying," *Art des Meinens*. As discussed in the previous chapter, languages, he argues, are distinguished not by their referents but by the way they refer to them, by their mode of signifying. It is the differential interplay of these diverse ways of signifying that constitutes the medium of translation, and the "task of the translator" is to render this interplay legible by revealing how *each self-contained unit of meaning* is always exceeded by the *way* it is *meant*:

> There remains in all language and its manifest structures [*Gebilden*] apart from that which is communicable something incommunicable, which, always according to the (specific) context in which it occurs can be either Symbolizing or Symbolized. Symbolizing merely in the finite structures of languages; symbolized, however, in the becoming of the languages themselves. And that which strives to expose itself, indeed to produce itself [*sich darzustellen, ja herzustellen sucht*] in the becoming of languages is the nucleus of pure language itself . . . If that ultimate essence, that is, pure language itself, is in language bound only to language and its transformations, in works it is charged with heavy and alien meaning. To free it from this charge, to make the Symbolizing into the Symbolized itself, to reconquer pure language in structured form [*gestaltet*] for the movement of language—this is the powerful and singular ability [*Vermögen*] of translation. (*GS4*, 19; *SW1*, 261)

Although it cannot be demonstrated here, the distinction Benjamin draws between the "movement of language" as signification on the one hand, and the resulting work as a repository of meaning on the other, continues a line of thinking that he developed first in his thesis on German Romanticism and continued in his study of German baroque theater. In both cases, Benjamin sought to uncover the dynamics hidden within the ostensibly stable status of the self-contained, meaningful work—whether as the work of art or as the "good works" of redemption. At the same time, he never mistook the necessity of some sort of instantiation or *taking place*. This is why "translation," or rather "translatability," functions in his writings as a kind of paradigm indicating the necessity of defining a work or construct that would *not* be self-contained or lasting, but rather "only" the stopping-place of an ongoing movement. Since the passage under discussion is obviously extremely enigmatic and dense, and would require much more time and space to unpack than is available here, I will simply present my interpretation of its main gist, by focusing on the formula "make the Symbolizing into the Symbolized." What translation does is not to communicate meaning but to point to—signify—the movement of symbolization itself, as it is at work already in the original, and then more obviously *between* the original and its displacement, between repetition and dislocation by and as translation. Translatability is the never realizable potential of a meaning and as such constitutes a *way*—a way of signifying—rather than a *what*.

But if it is a way, if it makes its way, where is it headed? Not simply back to the original or to the origin, but rather *away* from it. In moving away from the original, translation unfolds *the ways* of meaning by moving words *away* from the meanings habitually attached to them, and which are generally construed as points of arrival rather than of departure. Meaning is generally conceived as a self-contained, self-standing universally valid entity, one that precedes the words that express it. Translation's way to go, by contrast, leads in the direction of other words and other meanings, exposing a complex and multidimensional network of signification in which word-occurrences are inevitably inscribed. The ways of meaning that emerge in and as translation assign a determining function to *syntax* over *semantics*. Benjamin's formula for this decisive aspect of translation—one that despite its speculative character has eminently practical implications—is, as we have seen, the "literalness (wordliness) of syntax."[10]

Benjamin's syntactical notion of the word, although it echoes the celebrated beginning of the Gospel of St. John, "In the Beginning was the Word," is therefore anything but traditionally theological. For the word to which Benjamin here refers is not the Creative Word of God but a word that *gestures toward other words* and that is therefore defined not by its semantic content but by its relational position.

The syntactical literalness of the interlinear translation is his model. The interlinear translation comes close to its original, almost touching it, yet remains irreducibly distant from it. For the repetition of syntax excludes semantic resemblance. It results not in an analogical relation of translation to original, based on shared meanings, but rather in a positioning that inevitably strains the grammatical coherence of the translation. This relation of words to one another, no longer governed by sentence grammar, results in a relation of translation to original that Benjamin describes with a remarkable figure, one that sums up much of our previous discussion:

The pure language that is banned in the foreign tongue—to redeem it in one's own . . . that is the task of the translator. For its sake he breaks the brittle limits of his own language: Luther, Voss, Hölderlin, George have extended the limits of German.—What remains of this for the relation of translation and original can be formulated in a figure. *As the tangent fleetingly touches* [flüchtig berührt] *the circle only in one point and as it is this contact* [Berührung], *not the point, that governs its trajectory into the infinite, so the translation touches the original fleetingly and only in the infinitely minute point of its meaning, in order to pursue its own course* [Bahn] *following the law of fidelity, in the freedom of the movement of language.* (GS4, 19–20; SW1, 261, my emphasis)

Practically speaking, this does not mean that translation simply ignores the meaning of the original, something that would be hard to imagine. It means precisely what Benjamin states that it means: namely, that the translation which follows "syntactical literalness" pursues a course that leads it to touch fleetingly—glancing off—the meaning of the original and then to follow the trajectory that results. The angle of that trajectory is determined by the tangential encounter of two different languages *at a singular historical time and place.* The vector that results from this tangential encounter involves the interplay of the different *possible* meanings of the original text and of the translation. That interplay results not in a single meaning but rather in a *difference of meanings,* which, like a difference of opinion, signifies precisely through its disunity. Since this point remains rather abstract, it may be helpful to close with an example. In the previous discussion, I have translated Benjamin's German word "Berührung" variously as "contact" and "glancing." But in German, it can also signify, paradoxically, the "state of being moved," as by an *emotion.* In his essay, Benjamin links his remarks on "way of meaning" to what is called an "affective" or "emotional" tone [*Gefühlston*] (GS4, 17; SW1, 260). The glancing movement of translation moves—and is moved by—whatever it touches; but above all, it moves the language in which it takes place and those who depend on it.

And yet translation "moves" only by arresting movement. By reproducing the syntactic arrangement of words from one language to another according to the precept of "syntactic literalness," the movement of translation disrupts the grammatical rules that create meaning and institutes in their stead a sequence that does not add up to a whole.

Translation thus grazes the original, touches it without taking hold, like the interlinear translation that runs parallel to the original text without ever merging or resembling it. What it resembles, by reassembling it, is the spacing of the words, a certain positioning. By reassembling and dispersing the original, the translation touches a chord in it that causes it to resonate, "like an Aeolian harp is touched by the wind of language" (GS4, 21; SW1, 262). Or like that wind, *ruach*, rippling or "sweeping over the waters" (New Jerusalem Bible) before the creation of the world.

Translation thus suggests a conception of medium that would be very different from that of the transparent interval between two fixed points. Instead of diaphanous transmission and transparency, translation brushes up against a past and in so doing opens itself to the future. Any attempt to interpret the media today would do well to reckon with the drafts that such an encounter can produce.

CHAPTER SEVEN

Citability—of Gesture

Walter Benjamin is acknowledged as one of the most innovative think-ers and critics of the twentieth century and is known in particular as a remarkable theoretician of modern media. His elaboration of the rad-ical transformations brought about in perception and politics by the advent of new technologies entails a fundamental questioning of the status of art and aesthetics in a world increasingly dominated by media. The fact that Benjamin's conception of those media was restricted to a technology that during his lifetime was still largely characterized by its *mechanical* dimension (radio being the most notable exception) makes the continued fascination with his texts all the more remarkable. Benjamin was not born a media specialist, nor did he receive any spe-cialized training in that area. There were no departments of media studies at the universities he attended: the subjects that occupied him as a student were above all philosophy, aesthetics, literature, and art. And although his relation to all of these "fields" remained problematic, he would never have been able to interpret the new media in their radi-cal singularity had he not been immersed in those fields, if not necessar-ily in their corresponding academic disciplines. A *break*, to be radi-cal, must involve a very distinctive kind of *relation* to that from which it is set off. Benjamin's ability to describe and interpret the *new* media presupposed a distinctive understanding of the *old* media. More specifically, Benjamin recognized that historical change was itself embedded in a process of repetition and reproduction: the novelty of the "new" was not absolute but rather profoundly related to the conflictual dynamics of the "old." The decisive *break* did not intervene simply *between* tradition and its transformation; rather, it was already at work *within* that tradition itself. Contrary to the general conceptions of esthetical theory, traditional art forms were already traversed by conflicts and divisions and it was against the dynamics evolving from this constitutive instability that Benjamin sought to grasp the transformations brought about by the new media. Benjamin's interest and training in philosophy, aesthetics, and language gave him the wherewithal to articulate this complex and conflictual relation of old and new, tradition and transformation. And nowhere, perhaps, is this relation more instructively conceptualized and *performed* than in his essays on Brecht's Epic Theater.

The history of Benjamin's attempt to pose the question, "What is Epic Theater?" is marked by the very traits that constitute his response to it: *gesture, interruption,* and *citability.* The philological situation of "What is Epic Theater?" is organized around an interruption and a suspension. For Benjamin provided not one answer to the question of epic theater, but several: two essays, a suspended publication, two lectures, and several unpublished shorter texts. The first essay, "What is Epic Theater?" dates from 1931, the period of Benjamin's most intense direct contact with Brecht. The text was written, according to Benjamin, at the request of the *Frankfurter Zeitung,* which never printed it. Eight years later, in 1939,[1] Benjamin returned to the article, revised it. and finally published it, anonymously, in the exile review *Mass und Wert* (Measure and Value). In the intervening period, parts of the original text were cited and reworked for other occasions and texts, the best known of these being the lecture "The Author as Producer."

The trajectory of the work "proper" was thus interrupted, suspended for almost a decade, albeit a most productive one, before finally reaching a kind of completion in the 1939 version. But a completion of what kind? Benjamin himself spoke of his revision of the earlier text in terms of "minor alterations" *(geringfügige Änderungen).* Rolf Tiedemann, his editor, finds this qualification "not entirely accurate" *(nicht ganz zutreffend):* "In reality what we have here are two distinct works, of which the latter merely borrows individual formulations [from the former] and places them in a new context."[2] I find the relation between the two texts, or versions, considerably less clear-cut than Tiedemann asserts. To construe the relationship of these two texts in terms of the simple alternative, identity or difference, is to overlook that the problem with which both of these texts were ultimately concerned— that of the *citability of gesture*—requires a different type of logic, in which identity and difference, repetition and transformation are not construed as mutually exclusive. Not forgetting this is all the more urgent since the *citability of gesture* for Benjamin is not merely a theoretical issue. Rather it is one that organizes all of his writing, including the texts that articulate its principle. The second text on epic theater cites the first, even without placing quotation marks. The citability of gesture also recurs in the essay "The Work of Art in the Age of Its Technical Reproducibility," as the notion of *montage*. Through this history of citation and recitation, reinscription and transformation, the earlier versions take on a significance that they otherwise might not have had. What I am about to argue, however, is that if Benjamin's own writing can be read as an instantiation of that about which he is writing, it is perhaps because the *citability of gesture* already entails a mode of writing. But lest I get ahead of myself with these speculations, let me try to begin at the beginning.

In the 1931 version of the essay, the phrase "making gestures citable" is invoked by Benjamin as designating "the most important achievement of the actor" (*GS2,529*). He glosses this function through an arresting comparison to typography: the actor "must be able to block out *(sperren)* his gestures the way a typesetter spaces words."[3] This comparison, like so many of Benjamin's, surprises by virtue of its ostensible *dissimilitude* with that with which it is being compared. It suggests that an essential dimension of Brecht's theater can be compared to what would generally be considered to be an extrinsic and instrumental typographical procedure. What does the spacing of type have to do with the gestural quality of Brecht's Epic Theater? One might be tempted to elude the question by pointing out that Benjamin associates gestural citability only with the performance of the actor, and not necessarily with Epic Theater as such. But what is implicit already in the first version of the essay becomes explicit in the text of 1939. In this later version, "making gestures citable" is described by Benjamin as being "one of the essential achievements" not just of the Brechtian *actor*, but "of Epic Theater" itself (*GS2, 536; SW4, 305*).

But this re-citation only spells out what was already clearly implied in the earlier text: the distinguishing trait of Brecht's Epic Theater is its ability not just to produce gestures, but to produce them in a way that makes them *citable*. And indeed, closer attention to the two terms reveals that they describe two sides of the same process: the essence of gesture, in Brecht's theater, is fulfilled only insofar as it is rendered citable; and the process of citation, in turn, is inseparable from that of gesticulation. Already the etymology of both words suggests a certain affinity. Both stem from words designating a kind of movement: *citare, cire,* deriving from the Greek *kinein,* designate not just movement, but in their composites—in-cite, ex-cite—a *bringing into* movement. And *gesture,* stemming from *gerere, gestum,* designates the action of *bearing, carrying.*

What such references underscore is that the dynamic aspect of the two terms has over the past centuries come to be understood as the property of a self-identical subject, as the following definition of *gesture* in a contemporary American dictionary makes clear:

1. An expressive movement of any part of the body.
2. Something done to convey one's intentions or attitude, *a gesture of friendship.*[4]

This definition is undoubtedly an accurate summary of the most widely held understanding of the word "gesture." It is precisely such an understanding, however, that Benjamin's use of the term challenges. For "gesture" as he employs it with respect to Epic Theater, and in general, involves not the fulfillment or realization of an intention or of an expectation but rather its disruption and suspension. It entails not so much expression as interruption. And it is this that makes it eminently theatrical.

Gesture, as Benjamin uses the term, defines itself at first through two traits. First, it *interrupts*. What does it interrupt? It interrupts that which ever since Aristotle has been considered to form the primary object of theater as a dramatic *genre:* namely, *action.* Or more precisely: *plot.* Ironic, perhaps, that precisely a theater designated as "epic" should be the occasion for a "Western" theory of theater to challenge its traditional subordination to plot and action. Ever since Aristotle's *Poetics,* theater in the West has been largely understood as the representation of an action, not directly, to be sure, but through its representational arrangement into a *plot*, a *mythos*. Correlative to what can therefore be called a *mythological* conception of theater is the tendency to determine it as a *genre:* which is to say, a mode of representation defined first by what it represents (a unified action), and second, by its manner of narration, its *mythos*.

It is precisely such an action and its narrative representation that Brecht's Epic Theater, as a theater of *gesture, interrupts*. "Conclusion: the more an acting subject [*einen Handelnden*] is interrupted, the more gestures we have" (*GS2*, 521, 536; *SW4*, 305).[5] And since it is the actor who serves as the vehicle of such gestures, we can even say—Benjamin does not, to be sure—that for Brecht's Epic Theater, *acting* consists in the *interruption of action* by gesture. Epic Theater is thus situated in the singular zone that stretches from the noun, *action*, to the gerund, *acting*. (In this context therefore it may not be entirely superfluous to recall that *gerund* and *gesture* have the same antecedent: *gerere*.

Let us look a bit more closely at this unusual zone. On the one hand, or side, it is bounded and defined by a gesticulation that, far from expressing or fulfilling an intention, suspends or interrupts it. We usually think of such "interruptions" as a hindrance, an obstacle, as something negative or deficient. Benjamin is well aware of this attitude and addresses it explicitly in his 1939 text: "One should go further here and meditate on the fact that interruption is one of the fundamental procedures constitutive of form [*eines der fundamentalen Verfahren aller Formgebung*]. It extends far beyond the orbit of art. It lies at the root— to take only one example—of citation. To cite a text means to interrupt its context. It is thus comprehensible that epic theater, which is based on interruption, should be citable theater in a specific sense" (*GS2, 536; SW4*, 305). In the lines that follow, Benjamin goes on to indicate precisely wherein the specific citability of epic theater is to be sought: "The citability of its texts would not be peculiar to it. The situation is entirely different when gestures are involved" (ibid.). Thus a careful reading of Benjamin's texts leads to the conclusion that neither gestures as such, nor citability as such, are sufficient to define the specificity of epic theater. And indeed, elsewhere, Benjamin speaks of gestures as the "material" (*GS2*, 521)[6]—or even, in another fragment, as the "raw material"[7]—of epic theater. Conversely, "citability" alone is also not sufficient to determine the specificity of this theater. We must therefore examine more closely just what it is that distinguishes the citability of "gesture" from the more familiar forms of textual citation, involving words and sentences.

Gestures, Benjamin argues, emerge *in* and *through* the process of interrupting action. They are therefore constituted by and as interruptions. Benjamin will later designate interruption, rather than contradiction, as "the mother of dialectics." He assigns to the notion of interruption a structuring force that in the more Hegelian perspective of Brecht would be ascribed to negation. This in turn affects the structure of gesture itself. Benjamin describes this structure as a peculiar kind of *fixation:* "In contrast to the actions and undertakings of people [gesture] has a fixable beginning and a fixable end. This strict, framelike closure of every element in an attitude [*Haltung*], which at the same time is entirely inserted in a living flux, constitutes one of the fundamental dialectical components [*Grundphänomene*] of gesture . . . The retarding character of interruption, the episodic character of framing [*Umrahmung*], are what endow gestural theater with its epic quality" (*GS2*, 521).[8] Gesture is "form-giving," shaping, insofar as it not only "interrupts" an ongoing sequence, but at the same time *fixes* it by enclosing it in a relatively determined space, one with a discernible "beginning" and "end." But *at the same time,* the closure brought about by gesture remains caught up in that from which it has partially extricated itself: in the "living flux" of a certain temporality. The "strict, framelike closure" embodied in gesture is thus held together by a tension that Benjamin does not hesitate at times to designate as "dialectical." As we will see, however, Benjamin's "dialectic," here as elsewhere, is very different from the more familiar Hegelian category, which always has the synthesis of conceptual comprehension as its informing and ultimate goal.

Indeed, as we will see, the "epic" quality of such gestural delimitation endows it both with an extension and with an instantaneousness that distinguishes it not only from a "moment" in the sense of the Hegelian dialectic, but also from the Aristotelian conception of theater with which both Brecht and Benjamin are constantly in dialogue. "In dialogue," however, in a most complex way. Indeed, one can argue that precisely the relation of "gesture" to its environment is repeated, anticipated, or reflected in the relationship of Benjamin's conception of theater to the Aristotelian tradition. It interrupts it, arrests its progress, suspends its claim to totality, but at the same time remains all the more profoundly bound up with that from which it demarcates itself.

It will be useful to recall certain aspects of Aristotle's discussion of theater, or rather, of tragedy and comedy, in his *Poetics,* in order to see just how intimate its "interruption" through Benjamin (and perhaps through Brecht) really is. In the passage just quoted, Benjamin calls attention to the fact that it is the "retarding character" of the gestural interruption, and above all, the "episodic character of the framing" it produces, that gives Brecht's theater its specifically *epic* quality. This affirmation is part of a larger argument elaborated by Benjamin in these texts, in which he invokes the distinction between "epic" and "dramatic" to describe what is peculiar to Epic Theater. This is apparent in one of the most striking passages in Benjamin's essays: one that begins the 1931 essay and that, in condensed form, concludes the 1939 text. In the latter text, Benjamin asserts that "what epic theater is about is easier to define with reference to the concept of the *stage* than to that of a new *drama*" (*GS2,* 539; *SW4,* 307). But in the earlier, more speculative text, he is even more categorical: "What theater today is about can be more exactly determined in terms of the stage than in those of drama" (*GS2,* 519).[9]

Later we will return to analyze the entire passage from which this assertion is taken. First, however, it is necessary to reconstruct a certain context within which the general approach to theater here being announced takes place. Benjamin is quite clear that Brecht's insistence on the epic quality of his theater is directed first and foremost against the dominant Aristotelian tradition that identifies theater with *drama,* which is to say, with the representation of a conflicted, but ultimately unified and meaningful *action.* Along lines not unrelated to those expounded by Antonin Artaud, Benjamin—following not just Brecht, but a tradition going back at least to Nietzsche and to Kierkegaard—challenges the Aristotelian valorization of theater as a *dramatic genre,* epitomized in tragedy and comedy, insofar as such an approach devalorizes theater as *medium,* and above all as *scene* and as *stage.* It is with this Aristotelian "mythological" and "dramatic" conception of theater that Benjamin breaks in his elaboration of the "epic" quality of Brechtian theater. But he accomplishes this break not by simply rejecting the terms of the debate but rather through a strategy that itself mirrors and performs one of the central themes of the essays themselves. This strategy can be designated as one of *transformational citation*. Through such citation Benjamin retains many of Aristotle's terms while at the same time altering the value traditionally attributed to them.

Thus, when Benjamin singles out "the episodic quality of the framing" through gesture as peculiar to epic theater, he is implicitly taking issue with the Aristotelian notion of *mythos,* plot, for instance as it is expressed in the following passage from the *Poetics:* "Among simple plots and actions the episodic are the worst. By 'episodic' plot I mean one in which there is no probability or necessity for the order in which the episodes follow one another."[10] Aristotle does not merely condemn the notion of episode out of hand, as a decontextualized reading of this passage might suggest. Episodes are acceptable and even necessary to drama, but only insofar as they do not compromise the coherence and *unity* of action, which, Aristotle insists, must remain the defining object of theater. And that unity, as we have just seen, entails the recognition of a "probability" or a "necessity for the order in which the episodes follow one another." The sequence of events must thus be presented as *konsequent,* comprising an organic whole. The same holds also for the epic, Aristotle asserts, but its unity must still be distinguished from that of tragedy—and it should be noted how the discussion of *theater* in Aristotle tends to become above all a discussion of *tragedy.* In tragedy, "it must be possible for the beginning and the end to be seen together in one view." The epic, by contrast, "has a very strongly marked special tendency towards extra extension of its bulk."[11] This extension of the epic is excluded, Aristotle argues, by the limited scope of the stage, by the scene that delimits the field of representation in the theater. This limitation, however, is immediately placed by Aristotle within a horizon of unification: the limited spatial and temporal representation of tragedy is *unified* by the possibility of "beginning and end" being "seen together in one view." For Aristotle, then, the scenic medium of theater is legitimated as a condition of *synopsis;* the essence of the *theatron* is located in the synthesis of perception that it permits.

It is worth remarking that Benjamin couches his discussion of the relation of epic and dramatic in much the same terms, albeit with a very different interpretation and evaluation. He writes of "epic extension" (*epische Streckung:* literally, "stretching") as a distinguishing characteristic of Brecht's theater. But such "stretching" is not understood in the Aristotelian (or Cartesian) terms of *extension:* it also includes an *intensive* component, as is made clear in the following passage in which Benjamin ostensibly elucidates the concept of "epic stretching": "Brecht has raised the question of whether the incidents staged by epic theater must already be familiar. His theater relates to plot the way a ballet teacher relates to a pupil; his primary task is to loosen up her articulations to the limit of the possible" (*GS2*, 533; *SW4*, 303). The "stretching exercises" of the ballet pupil thus become a model for the stretching of dramatic action in epic theater; such stretching, Benjamin adds, is intended to reveal the articulations that structure what is apparently a unified plot. It thereby reveals a *tension (Spannung)* very different from the conflict of tragedy. Unlike the latter, which derives from uncertainty about origins and "outcomes," that of epic theater concerns "events in the singular [*die Begebenheiten im einzelnen*]" (ibid.). It is directed less at "ends" than at the "middle," at the "members," but in their singularity and not simply as parts of an organic whole.

This insight permits us to discern a bit more clearly wherein the "dialectical" dimension of gesture resides: the "fixation" it establishes through its interruption of an intentional, goal-directed movement toward meaning and totality remains *singularly ex-tended,* defined by and as the tension of separation and suspension. Epic Theater, it could be said, turns the traditional claims of drama *inside out.* This is why gesture *as such* is only the "raw material" of theater, and why Benjamin, citing Brecht, singles out the citability of gesture as the defining principle and resource of his theater. For "gesture" does not merely interrupt something external to it: the expressive intentionality of an action, the teleology of a narrative, or the causal necessity or probability of a sequence of events. It does all of this, but it also does something more: insofar as it is citable, it interrupts *itself,* and indeed, only "is" in its possibility of becoming other, of being transported elsewhere.

But this possibility is in turn not determined by the horizon of its realization. Rather, it in turn is arrested, "fixed" in what Benjamin, once again citing Brecht, calls, in German, a *Zustand.* By interrupting "actions" *(Handlungen),* epic theater forces *Zustände* to emerge. Yet the familiar English translations of this word, *condition, state,* miss precisely what is decisive in Benjamin's use of the term: the prefix *zu-:* to or toward. This prefix marks the "stand" of the *Zustand* as a *stance,* or perhaps also as a *di-stance:* which is to say, as a configuration that is not simply stable or self-contained but above all *relational,* determined

by the *tension* of its *ex-tension,* by its relation to that which it has interrupted and from which it has separated itself. The result is a highly unstable state of affairs marked by what Benjamin, in a felicitous formulation, describes as the "trembling of its contours" *(das Zittern ihrer
Umrisse).* Such trembling of these *Zustände* "betrays how much more
intimate the proximity is from which they have torn themselves free in
order to become visible" *(GS2, 525).*[12]

The *Zustand,* then, exposes the ambivalent unity of the theatrical
phenomenon as gesture. It *arrests* the forward movement of expectation, intention, action, and narrative; suspends the rush to judgment;
and deranges the desire for identification, for empathy, for *Einfühlung.*
But in so interrupting this movement and impeding its progress, it initiates a different sort of movement: that of the *after-thought,* the disjunctive and belated movement of *Nachdenken.*

What distinguishes this movement of *Nachdenken* from the usual effect and affect of Aristotelian and Western drama? The latter, according to both Benjamin and Brecht, is marked by a *catharsis* or discharge
made possible through empathetic identification. The German word
for such identification is enviably precise; indeed, its prefix says it all:
Ein-fühlung, literally: feeling *in* or *into.* In English, we would probably
express this as "identifying *with,*" but it is precisely the *with* that is
in question here. To be able to "purify" oneself through the discharge
of conflictual feelings presupposes that one can, for a time, put oneself
in the place of the other. This in turn presupposes two things about
that place. First, that it is roughly commensurable to one's own. Whatever is radically other, whatever resists or challenges assimilation, will
be ignored or assimilated. And second, it presupposes that the place
of the other is sufficiently stable and self-contained to allow possession to *take place.* Its borders must be fixed in a univocal and enduring fashion. It is, however, precisely these two presuppositions that
Benjamin's account of epic theater questions. The place established by
the suspensive and interruptive gesture is not simply "fixed" once and
for all. Its edges "tremble," it remains determined by the tension and
ex-tension that tie it to that from which it has partially detached itself.
Recalling the German of Brecht and Benjamin, one could say that the
Zustand determines itself as a *stance-toward* something else. Its stability is the precarious and problematic result of a momentary blockage.
And it is precisely this that leads Benjamin to insist that it is not the ges-

ture *per se,* nor its immediate fixating effect, that defines epic theater, but rather its capacity to be *cited:* its *citability.* The citability of gesture interrupts its immediate manifestation and constitutes it as interruption, which is to say, as something that cannot simply be seen, but that can give rise to *Nachdenken,* to after-thoughts. Such thoughts consider the "after," the aftermath, the *citability* of the gesture as disjunctive and discontinuous. Through this disjunction, the essence of the gesture resides in its tendency to always come too late, and yet at the same time never to arrive fully; it belongs to the future, never simply to the present or to the past.

The mode of being that characterizes this disjunctive theater of the future, therefore, is not that of "necessity" or of "probability," as Aristotle insisted, but rather that of "possibility" both as potentiality and as alterity: the possibility of becoming other than what is currently present or presented. But this future is not that which one expects, which one hopes to foresee, to calculate or even to bring about. It is unforeseeable, unpredictable, unfathomable. Writing of the indispensable freedom of such theater to alter "historical processes" in their staging, Benjamin observes that the "accents must be placed not upon those momentous decisions that are located at the vanishing points of expectation [*Fluchtlinien der Erwartung*], but on the incommensurable, the singular. 'It can happen this way, but it can also come about in an entirely different manner'—this is the basic attitude of anyone writing epic theater" (*GS2,* 525).[13] Paradoxically, perhaps, what epic theater does in bringing a certain history to a standstill, to a *Zustand,* is to keep open the possibility of what is yet *to come,* which in German, as in French, is the name assigned the future: *Zu-kunft, a-venir.* And yet the place of this future, which cannot be reduced to a present that has yet to arrive, is, paradoxically, nowhere if not *now.* In his 1934 lecture "The Author as Producer," held before the Paris-based Institute for the Study of Fascism, Benjamin found a formulation that designates the singularity of this strange now. In that talk, he noted that Brecht's staging of the *Zustand* recurs to "the great and venerable chance of theater—that of *exposing the present* [*die Exponierung des Anwesenden*]."[14] The future of theater consists in this ability to expose the goings-on of being-present: *des Anwesenden.*

What form does this exposure assume? None other than that of the *breach* that structures the present itself, as participle and as gerund: a present that is irreducible to the indicative, to the "is," since it must constantly repeat and renew itself and in so doing split its unity, turning itself inside out, suspending its movement and ex-posing its situation in and as the "di-stance" of the *Zustand*. For the *stance* consists not in a self-contained moment but in an *instant* determined as an *interval*. As with that blocked and spaced-out type *(Sperrdruck)* to which Benjamin compares the gestures of the actor in epic theater, the *interval* defines the space in which events *take place*. And events that take place in and as intervals are felt as *shocks:* "Epic theater advances, comparable to the pictures of a filmstrip, in jerks and jolts [*rückt . . . in Stößen vor*]. Its basic form is that of the shock with which the individual, clearly de-marcated situations of the play collide with one another. The songs, legends, gestural conventions demarcate one situation from the others. In this way, intervals arise which tend rather to limit the illusions of the audience. They paralyze its readiness to identify [*zur Einfühlung*]. Such intervals are reserved for its critical disposition" (*GS2*, 537–538; *SW4*, 306). It is difficult to "identify" with an *interval*, especially if "identi-fication" is understood as *Einfühlung*, Benjamin's word for *empathy*. Through shocks and surprises, epic theater deprives empathy of its es-sential prerequisite: a well-defined, self-contained place *into* which it can *feel* and project itself, or unload its feelings. The representative, mi-metic activity of epic theater thus splits and turns back on itself, retrac-ing in this *double-take* an interval and a gap between the function of representing and that which is being represented.[15] The latter can never be fully absorbed into, or obscured by, the former, never allowed to be-come fully identical with it. And this must be seen not as a defect of the-ater, but as its resource and its reserve. This is why the notion that brings us closest to epic theater, Benjamin suggests, is that of "play-act-ing," *Theaterspielen* (*GS2*, 538; *SW4*, 306): the style of acting should expose this dimension, which always involves a divergence. This is why the foregrounding of the actors in epic theater should not be under-stood as an appeal to subjective authenticity or interiority: it is not the *individuality* of the actor that is involved, as distinct from that of the character or situation that is being staged. Rather, it is the *dividuality* of both actor and action that is at stake in the citability of gesture. What interests Benjamin in *play-acting* is the rupture of interiority as such, the foregrounding not of the actor as opposed to the role, but of the constitutive *split* between actor and part, a split that, in epic theater at least, constitutes the movement of *acting* itself. Benjamin describes this movement as the ability "to fall out of the role, artfully [*mit Kunst aus der Rolle zu fallen*]" (ibid.).

Benjamin's notion of "shock"—which pervades his writings of the thirties—is absent from the earlier text. In its stead there is a description of the effect of the interruptive *Zustand* on the audience—an effect designated by a term that once again recalls the citational inscription of Benjamin's writing in the tradition from which it is simultaneously taking its distance. The key word used to describe the effect of what later will be called "shock" is *wonder, amazement, Staunen:* "Epic theater continually retains a lively and productive awareness of the fact that it is theater. This consciousness enables it to treat elements of the real as part of an experimental arrangement [*Versuchsanordnung*] and the situations [*Zustände*] stand at the end, not at the beginning. They are thus not brought closer to the audience but rather removed from it. They are recognized not with complacency, as in naturalist theater, but with amazement [*Staunen*]" (*GS2*, 522).[16] Benjamin here refers this use of "amazement" to Socrates—"With this amazement epic theater pays Socratic practice a hard and chaste tribute" (ibid.). But the term is no less decisive for Aristotle, whose famous observation (from the beginning of the *Metaphysics)* that philosophy is born in "wonder" *(thaumazein)* Benjamin alludes to in his "Theses on the Concept of History."[17] The notion also plays an important role in Aristotle's discussion of tragedy in the *Poetics* and it provides an illuminating contrast to its reworking, or reciting, by Benjamin.

What Aristotle's discussion of theater shares with Benjamin's is a certain emphasis on its pedagogical function. Against the Platonic condemnation, which forms the background of the *Poetics,* Aristotle defends mimesis in general, and theatrical mimesis in particular, as a process not merely of deception, but also of learning. We learn, Aristotle argues, by imitating and theater is one such form of learning. Hence the emphasis placed on the unity of action: for only a unified action can be meaningful. To be sure, the process of learning from theater—and of course, tragedy is Aristotle's primary focus—is not simply intellectual. It involves the discharge of feelings, the famous *catharsis,* as a process of purgation. But obviously not every discharge of feelings is necessarily purgative, and this is why the bulk of Aristotle's discussion has to do with the dramaturgical process of presenting conflicts in a meaningful manner. This Aristotle exemplifies in his analysis of what he calls "complex" plots, as opposed to the previously discussed "simple" ones. The complex plot of a tragedy relies above all on two distinct, but for Aristotle interrelated, devices. The first he designates as *peripeteia;* the second, *anagnoresis.* Peripeteia names the sudden and unexpected turn: either of events, or of the perceptions of them. This unexpected turn or surprise is characteristic of tragedy, but it should also be noted that something like it is indispensable to every mimetic experience understood as a process of learning. For how can one *learn* anything without brushing up against the unknown? Within the structure of the tragic plot, this irruption of the unknown, this sudden transformation of what one thought one knew, constitutes the decisive turn, the *peripeteia.*

We can see that what Benjamin refers to as the interruptive effect of epic theater is part of a long tradition extending back to the Aristotelian peripeteia: in both cases, an intentional expectation, a narrative sequence, is interrupted, arrested, suspended. But what results is very different. For Aristotle, what results is the purity of the tragic act, the *pathos,* and that purity is assured not simply by the peripeteia, but by what for Aristotle is its indispensable accompaniment: *anagnoresis* or recognition, which, "as indeed the name indicates," is constituted by "a shift from ignorance to knowledge."[18] Benjamin too, as we have seen, writes of a recognition provoked by the *Zustände* of epic theater, but it is one, he insists, that is characterized not by "complacency" *(Süffisance)* but by *amazement, Staunen.* In short, recognition for Benjamin does not mark the shift from ignorance to positive knowledge as much as it does that from self-evidence to wonder. The result is that the learning experience of epic theater is constantly compared to a certain type of *experimentation,* to a "laboratory."[19]

But this laboratory has very little in common with that of modern science. For the goal that informs each is almost diametrically opposed. In the case of the scientific experiment, the goal is to produce sequences that can be replicated universally with identical results. The notion of experiment to which Benjamin, citing Brecht, here recurs also entails a certain iterability, but not one that involves the reproduction of the identical. Rather, the goal of the theatrical experiment is the instantaneous emergence of the singular, the incommensurable, the irreducibly different. This notion of experiment has a long progeny, stretching back past Nietzsche at least to Kierkegaard, whose staging of *Repetition* bears the subtitle *A Venture in Experimenting Psychology*. Nor is it entirely accidental that this experimental venture places a discussion of theater at the center of its first section (although this discussion has long been overlooked or neglected in favor of the more doctrinal discussion of the Book of Job in the second half of the text). Nevertheless, at the center of Kierkegaard's text stands, however tenuously, the intimate connection between repetition, theater, and experiment, a connection that returns in Nietzsche's staging of the Eternal Return, and then, once again, in Benjamin's essays on epic theater. In all of these instances, theater emerges as the singular and structurally problematic localization of a possibility that cannot be measured either in terms of reality, identity, or self-presence, be it that of a subject, an object, or their dialectic as self-consciousness.

The "knowledge" to which the theatrical experiment leads, according to Benjamin, is not primarily theoretical or conceptual, but rather practical. With respect to the actor in epic theater, he explains: "In epic theater the actor must be educated to play in a manner that is directed at knowledge; his knowledge, in turn, determines his entire acting [*sein ganzes Spiel*] not alone in terms of content, but through tempi, pauses and intonations" (*GS2*, 528–529).[20] "Tempi, pauses and intonations" are, as it were, syntactic rather than semantic categories. They describe relations of arrangement and of placement rather than meaningful content. The supreme category implied in all the other syntactical terms, however, is repetition. Not repetition as the confirmation of an original identity, but rather as its transformation. It is this that endows the gesture with its singular *citability*. Gestures are always citable, in principle because they are themselves the result of a repetition and a separation. It is the structural convergence of gesture and citability that allows Benjamin to remark that "in epic theater" it is "not the contradictory course of utterances or of actions" that is "the mother of dialectics but rather gesture itself" (*GS2*, 530).[21] And "gesture itself" can play this part only because its "self" is constituted in and through the irremediable split of its iterability: "One and the same (gesture) summons Galy Gay to the wall, first to have his clothes changed, and then again to be shot. One and the same (gesture) gets him to renounce the fish and to accept the elephant" (ibid.). "One and the same": this is precisely what the citable gesture both situates and unhinges in an instant that does not come full circle, no more than the title of Brecht's play, "Man Is Man," actually completes its predication in the tautological circle it seems to announce. Between tautology and fulfillment, however, something else emerges, something to which Benjamin gives two names.

The first is "podium." According to Benjamin, this word best designates the distinctive space or scene of epic theater. Its announcement and description begin the essay of 1931, and close that of 1939. One can therefore describe it as in a certain sense the beginning and end, the frame, of the two texts. Here is the initial version:

> What is at stake in theater today can be determined more precisely with reference to the stage than to the drama. What is at stake is the filling in of the orchestra pit [*die Verschüttung der Orchestra*]. The bottomless pit [*Abgrund*] that separates the actors from the audience like the dead from the living . . . this abyss, which among all the elements of the stage bears most indelibly traces of its sacred origin, has lost its function. The stage is still elevated, but it no longer rises out of unfathomable depths; it has become a podium. On this podium one must learn to take one's place [*Auf diesem Podium gilt es, sich einzurichten*]. (GS2, 519)[22]

Benjamin's concluding sentence here is difficult if not impossible to translate. "*Sich einrichten*" is used to designate the process of "moving into," as into a new apartment or house. It suggests arranging a place of residence and yet also arranging *oneself* to fit into a new place. One must adapt to the new site of theater, as well as adapting that site to one's needs. As a "podium" that site is no longer sacred, no longer based on an inseparable gap separating humans from gods, the dead from the living. A podium is a place from which one can address a gathering, as in a political meeting, no doubt Benjamin's primary association here. But as is so characteristic of his style of writing, figures that seem merely to illustrate and to elucidate in fact interrupt themselves, resist explanation, erupt as enigmas often producing a belated shock effect. For although what Benjamin seems to be saying here is that theater, like so much else in the modern period, has lost its religious and sacred character in becoming fully secularized, what he in fact describes is somewhat different. The "level playing field" that emerges in the "filling up" of the orchestra pit—and the German word, *Verschüttung*, suggests nothing as much as the filling in of a grave—doesn't so much eliminate the difference between the human and the divine as confound the living with the dead. The actors now relate to the audience as the dead do to the living. On this level playing field, the living affront the dead.

And indeed, the surprising analogy echoes the functions attributed to epic theater, above all, that of *interruption* and *separation*. The actors in epic theater interrupt the temporal flow in its progress, arresting and suspending it, "fixating" it in a gesture. But such a gesture defines itself not merely in terms of what it is, but in terms of its potential extension, its virtual separation from itself: its *citability*. Such "ex-posing of the present" in which Benjamin glimpsed the "venerable chance of theater" as such, thus ex-poses the present not just to the future, but to its finitude. The possibility that epic theater seeks to demonstrate: that everything can happen differently, that what is, is not necessarily what *must* be or what *will* be *eternally*—this possibility means that the living cannot simply *separate* themselves from the dead, any more than the "public" or "audience" can separate itself entirely from the actors. Not because there is no separation, but because separability is everywhere, and because, being everywhere, it joins as much as it isolates: joins *in* isolating. This is why, in another of his dizzyingly suggestive figures, Benjamin can compare Brecht's "non-Aristotelian dramaturgy" with the "non-Euclidean geometry" of a Riemann and then conclude: "This analogy should make clear that the two forms of theater in question do not stand in a competitive relation to one another. With Riemann the parallel postulate dropped out. What dropped away in Brecht's dramas was the Aristotelian catharsis, the discharge of feelings through identification [*Einfühlung*] with the moving destiny of the hero" (*GS2, 535; SW4, 304*).

The pre-Riemannian, "Euclidean" condition of Aristotelian catharsis is a conception of space (as Benjamin writes of time in his text on history) as "homogeneous" and "empty." This "Euclidean" space is one in which one position is in principle equivalent to and exchangeable with another, a space in which separation is defined in terms of the opposition of identity and alterity. The space of Brecht's Epic Theater, by contrast, is neither empty nor homogeneous, neither infinite nor unbounded. It constitutes a singularly heterogeneous medium, a curved Riemannian space defined and punctuated by those interruptions of continuity that Benjamin calls *Zustände*, di-stances that gesticulate and whose being *here and now* is determined by their virtual capacity to be *there and then*,[23] to be moved elsewhere and transformed by their citability.

The "podium" is one such problematic locale: it is a site from which discourse is directed at *others*, but at others who are bound up with it in and through their separation and distance, through the incommensurability of their singular locations. From the standpoint of the podium, the opposition between "actors" and "audience" tends to break down, since "acting" is defined in terms of being heard and seen, whereas listening and seeing become themselves a form of action qua transformation.

The theater in which the opposition of stage and audience is replaced by a podium that no longer admits a clear-cut separation of actor and audience—such theater involves a radical transformation not merely of space, but of time. And this brings me to my second and final point—or rather, *passage*. The passage is extremely complex, consisting both of Benjamin's "own" words and passages cited from Brecht. It concludes the essay of 1931, but was then dropped in the later versions. Permit me to quote it therefore in full:

> The blockage [*Stauung*] in the real flow of life, the instant [*Augenblick*] where its course comes to a standstill [*zum Stehen kommt*], can be felt [*macht sich . . . fühlbar*] as an ebb [*Rückflut*]: amazement is this ebb. Its actual object is dialectics at a standstill [*Dialektik im Stillstand*]. It is the cliff from whose heights one looks [*der Blick*] down into that stream of things, about which those in the city of Jehoo, "which is always full and where no one stays" can sing a song, "which begins with:
>
> Don't cling to the wave,
> Which breaks at your foot,
> As long as it stands in water
> New waves will break upon it."
>
> When, however, the stream of things breaks on this cliff of amazement, then there is no difference between a human life and a word. In epic theater both are only the crest of the wave. It lets being there and then [*Dasein*] spray up from the bed of time and stand glistening for an instant in the void, before bedding down once again. (GS2, 531)[24]

It is hardly possible within the bounds of this chapter to do justice to this amazing passage about amazement. I will therefore be brief and unjust. Theater, as here described, involves something other than simply a form or genre of art. It has to do with a rhythm of existence, with the ebb and flow of life, with a being *there and then,* but, paradoxically perhaps, even more with its blockage than with its progress. Theater interrupts the announcements of everyday life to bring us a special message. That message is little short of amazing. One of the things it tells us is that, from the point of view of a certain amazement, "there is no difference between a human life and a word." Their difference disappears in the spray of a cresting wave, suspending animation and striking life to the quick.

It is this suspended animation, the interruption of the flow of everyday events, this bringing to a standstill of what we commonly think of as the "flow" of "life." And it is this *coming-to-a-standstill* that constitutes what, for Benjamin, from his very earliest writings to his last, can be designated as the *virtuality of media,* media *as* virtuality. The medium is never simply actual, never simply real or present, much less "the message" that it seems to convey. Rather, it consists in the suspension of all messaging and in the virtuality that ensues. Such virtuality makes its force felt as *intervention:* the media is what *comes between,* stretching apart everything that would be present to itself. This is why the medium, in this sense, is never an *element in* which things would take place, would take *their* place. As intervention, it causes the borders of all interiority—and be they those of the interval itself—to tremble. This "trembling" also delineates the enabling limits of the theatrical stage as a scene that both separates and joins whatever comes together in and around it. Such trembling and tremors summon its audience to do more than merely hear, its spectators to do more than merely see, its actors to do more than merely act. It exposes them to the afterthought that, *after all,* they share the *same* trembling space of singularity. It is a space not of *Einfühlung* but of *Exponierung,* of exposure to the possibility of separation and detachment. Thus exposed, the situation of the spectator can no longer be considered simply as a stable state (of contemplation or of identification) but rather, as a *stance of reading,* another word for the activity of *Nachdenken,* which might also be rendered here as "retarded thinking."[25]

It is the ability to impose this shift from *state* to *stance* that constitutes the power of the media and their fascination for Benjamin. Even today, especially today, it has not lost its force. It is commonplace to speak of the delocalizing effects of the electronic media that "globalize" even as they deracinate. But as long as we attempt to grasp this process in terms of a traditional logic of identity and its correlative conceptions of space, time, place, and body, we risk overlooking what is truly distinctive about this movement. What is changing through the spread of the electronic media, and what Benjamin was one of the first to see and to analyze, is the nature of the *situation,* of the ways in which people, things, and events are localized and hence, determined, perceived, and understood. And all this is changing because the structure of place itself is being altered. Or perhaps, being revealed as that which it always has been. Long construed as a self-contained site, *on* and *in* which subjects and objects could take place, take *their* place, be *themselves,* the experience of place is changing. Whether as a podium, stage, or even as a *Zustand:* a *stance,* standing *in, out,* and *for* something other than itself, gesticulating toward an elsewhere.

If this is so, then Benjamin's concatenation of *Zustand,* gesture, citability, and above all, theater, can help us better approach the question of what it means to be *situated* in and by a world organized by "the media," a world that itself is increasingly being organized *as medium.* Perhaps what this entails is nothing more nor less than acknowledging what has probably always obtained: that we only take place from place to place, from time to time, between places rather than in them, in the instant of an intervening interval—and that this is what we are all *about.* To read Benjamin is to open oneself to the virtual power of such instants that overtake us by surprise and leave us wondering in their wake.

CHAPTER EIGHT

Ability and Style

If, as Walter Benjamin once remarked, "style is the jump-rope [*Sprungseil*] thought must take in order to push forward into the realm of writing,"[1] it is worth noting how little attention has been paid to Benjamin's own style of writing in the massive amount of secondary literature that his work has elicited. Perhaps the rest of his un-published fragment, "Thought and Style," suggests why this is so: "Thought must pull all its forces together. But style [must] meet it halfway and [yet] stay supple, like the rope in the hands of the children swinging it as one of them gets ready to jump" (*GS6*, 202). "Style" must both respond to the most extreme concentration of thinking and yet at the same time stay loose in its recurrence, never rigidifying into regularity, always leaving room for the *Sprung*: the leap, to be sure, but also the crack.

One such leap or crack that may offer a privileged access to Benjamin's thinking is, as we have seen, his propensity to formulate certain key concepts by adding the suffix -ability or -ibility (in German, -*barkeit*) to verbs. These concepts include: communicability (*Mitteilbarkeit*) in his early essay "On Language in General and on Human Language" (or "On Language as Such and on the Language of Man" [1915]); criticizability (*Kritisierbarkeit*) in his doctoral dissertation, "The Concept of Criticism in German Romanticism" (1920); translatability (*Übersetzbarkeit*) in "The Task of the Translator"

(1923); reproducibility, in "The Work of Art in the Age of Its Technical Reproducibility" (or "The Work of Art in the Age of Mechanical Reproduction" [1936]); and knowability *(Erkennbarkeit)* in the posthumously published notes "On the Concept of History" (or "Theses on the Philosophy of History" [1940]). In this chapter I will discuss communicability and reproducibility, thereby foregrounding certain aspects of Benjamin's thought as well as the "jump rope" by which it articulates itself.

Before turning to Benjamin's use of these terms, however, it might be helpful to reflect briefly on some of the more general implications of the suffix -ability/-ibility. Nouns formed in this way refer to a possibility or a potentiality, to a capacity rather than to an actually existing reality. Communicability, for instance, does not refer to an accomplished act as does communication; the same holds true for knowability, which is by no means equivalent to knowledge. Benjamin himself discusses this difference in introducing the notion of the "translatability" of works, which, he emphasizes, does not depend on the empirical fact of whether or not a work has or ever will be actually translated. Benjamin's -abilities, then, refer to what Jacques Derrida, writing in *Limited Inc.* (1988) of his quasi-concept, "iterability," called "structural possibilities," the necessity of which does not depend on actual fact or probable implementation.

This emphasis on a possibility that is structurally necessary without being necessarily real disposes Benjamin to make use of such terms, even where they are rather uncommon. In "On Language as Such and on the Language of Man," Benjamin distinguishes "linguistic" from "spiritual" being by defining it in terms of "communicability": "That in a spiritual being which is communicable is its linguistic being" (*GS2*, 142; *SW1*, 63). This is tantamount to saying that the "being" (or "essence": Benjamin uses the German word *Wesen*, which can mean both) of language does not have the character of a determinate, self-contained entity. It is precisely in order to highlight this difference between spiritual, intellectual, or semantic being on the one hand, and language on the other, that Benjamin makes emphatic use of the suffix -ability, which is stressed in the text: "It is not that whatever is communicable in a spiritual being appears most clearly in its language . . . but rather that this communicable [*dieses Mitteilbare*] is immediately [*unmittelbar*] language itself" (ibid.). The -ability that distinguishes language from spirit or intellect has less to do with a what than with a how. "Language," although a noun, names something that is more like an adjective or an adverb: a property or attribute that is not self-contained but that requires something else in order to be, just as every how requires a what. Language, in short, names a modality rather than a substance or a substantive. It describes the possibility of a particular way of being: that of being communicated, of "communicability."

But the English word communicability is not the only translation possible of the German word used by Benjamin, *Mitteilbarkeit*. Another, perhaps more literal, translation would be impart-ability. This rendering would be more literal for several reasons. First, its root, like the German word, stresses the partiality of the process of *Mit-teil-ung*, something that does not necessarily come across in the English communication. The being of language, which is to say the particular way of being that constitutes language, has more to do with parts, and indeed with partitioning, than with wholes. Second, this way of being involves not simply "communicating," in the sense of conveying a meaning by means of something else. If Benjamin insists not simply that "impart-ability" is what constitutes language, but that it constitutes it "immediately" *(unmittelbar)*, it is in order to highlight the decisive relationship between two German words that sound and look almost identical although they mean very different things: between *mitteilbar* (impartable) and *unmittelbar* (immediate[ly]). The difference is decisive because *unmittelbar* means not just "immediate[ly]" but also, more literally, without means or instrumentality. Language, in short, is to be understood not as a "means" to some other goal, but as the immediate possibility of being imparted: "This impartable is language itself."

But this -ability can never be found in a vacuum, all by itself. It is not a thing, not a substance, nor a property—nothing that could be aptly designated by a straightforward substantive. In other words, it requires something else in order to be: it requires beings. Language requires beings and yet is not essentially determined by them; for what language "communicates" is nothing but itself: it communicates, or better, im-parts itself. In this way, language operates as a "medium," and moreover, one that is given immediately, as we have already discussed.[2] The reason such "immediacy" defines a "problem," and indeed even a "paradox"—the "paradox of all theory of language"—is that Benjamin will not resort to the expedient of saying that "the medium is the message." The fact that the medium operates in an "immediate" manner signifies, for Benjamin, that an essential understanding of medium must above all else avoid confounding it with the notion of message. It is this irreducible difference that his notion of "impart-ability" seeks, in however preliminary a fashion, to articulate.

Benjamin's insistence, in this essay of 1916, on the irreducible mediality of language qua impart-ability, indicates that his concern with the "media" originates not in his later studies of radio, film, and photography, but rather in his effort to elaborate a noninstrumental conception of language. It is this that leads Benjamin to insist on the irreducible immediacy of the medial. The "medial" is "immediate" in the sense of not being instrumental. The media must above all be distinguished from the means. This does not, however, make it an *end in itself,* unless "end" is understood not as *goal,* but as *interruption.*

It is characteristic that Benjamin should seek to elucidate this distinction through the use of prepositions with strong spatial connotations. Considered as a "means" of communication, language would be something "through" which something else was conveyed; language would be a more or less neutral vehicle of something essentially external to it. But as a "medium," language is itself a dynamic space "in" which something happens. Yet what happens tends to disrupt the usual meaning of "in." For this ostensibly well-defined, containing, and self-contained space of the medium consists precisely in the *self parting company from itself by imparting itself.* In thus refusing the instrumentalist conception of language as a medium through which something is communicated by someone to someone else, Benjamin does not introduce an alternative version of immanence or identity—for instance, the medium itself as the message, or as end in itself. Rather, he opens a highly volatile space in which all "spiritual being"—which is to say, all identity, whether of subjects, objects, things, or meanings—appears only in and through the process of parting company with itself, and in so doing, imparting itself to others. It is only in parting company with itself, in im-parting itself, that communication can take place. The "com-" of communication thus presupposes the parting of imparting, which alone opens up the space "in" which relations, whether social, semantic, or semiotic, can "take place."

It is precisely the ambivalent ramifications of "the immediacy of the medial," as end without self—that is, of the originating crack or fracture first described as imparting, that drive Benjamin's thinking and writing. They are marked by a double (or "cracked") tone. On the one hand, that of melancholy, sadness, and mourning (*Trauer* is a leitmotif from first to last); on the other hand, and inseparable from the first because its consequence, that of energetic engagement, militancy, and hope, because the very same fracture that is felt as loss also opens up the (linguistic) possibility of this loss itself being lost, imparting and thus altering itself and thereby keeping the way open for the coming of something radically different.

This is how the ostensible transcendentalism of Benjamin's -abilities comes to acquire historical, political, and cultural significance. Everything that contributes to dislodging that which is—by forcing it into a mode of self-imparting, self-departing, by wrenching it free from its established sites—is both painful, creating a sense of loss (that of the "aura," for instance, provoked by the spread of techniques of "reproducibility") and at the same time the bearer of messianic hope.

This ambivalent movement of imparting is perhaps nowhere more striking than in one of Benjamin's last writings, where he focuses on the notion of "time" itself, or rather on the key concept that has traditionally determined how time has been construed: that of the "present" or the "now." As "now," Benjamin reveals the -ability of time to part company from itself, thereby opening up nothing less than a messianic space in which mourning and melancholy converge in vengeful hope. It is in the context of Benjamin's discussion of the "concept of history" that he elaborates what will be one of his last -abilities: "knowability."

The question of history was one that occupied Benjamin from his very earliest writings. In the 1918 essay "On the Program of the Coming Philosophy," for instance, he called for a critical transformation of the Kantian philosophical heritage through renewed reflection on the "singular temporality" of finite experience and its significance for cognition. The direction such reflection should take, he urged, was toward the "systematic" elaboration of "a certain non-synthesis of two concepts in one another" (*GS2, 166; SW1, 106*), which was to be one of the most urgent tasks of the "coming philosophy." The "coming philosophy," in short, would be the philosophy of a certain "coming"— and going.

In this sense, all of Benjamin's writing and thinking can be productively studied in light of the task of elaborating the "non-synthesis of

. . . concepts in one another." Probably the most extended attempt is to be found in the "Epistemo-critical Preface" to his major published work, *The Origin of the German Mourning Play*. By replacing the consecrated philosophical and Kantian term epistemological with "epistemo-critical" in the title of that preface, Benjamin indicates that his task is not simply to reflect on the conditions under which cognition is produced, but to explore the way his writing questions critically the notion of knowledge itself. His (Nietzschean) determination of all knowledge as a "having," and his effort to develop the mourning play not as a concept in which phenomena are subsumed under universals, but as an "idea" in which their distinctive singularity is saved through a "configuration" of "extremes," constitutes a practical effort to develop a "nonsynthetic," nonsubsumptive form of knowledge. It is significant that this effort culminates in a discussion of "philosophical style," a form of "presentation" characterized by discontinuity, interruption, and renewed effort. These considerations return in Benjamin's discussion of the "knowability" of history and the status of historical knowledge. The following passage from section five of "On the Concept of History" indicates the manner in which the question is framed: "The true image of the past rushes by. Only as an image that just barely flashes its nevermore in the instant of its knowability can the past be retained" (*GS1*, 695; *SW4*, 390). As is clear, or should be, from this turn of phrase, Benjamin's often noted penchant for figural language has little to do with illustration or elucidation. Rather, what he describes here as the "nevermore" *(Nimmerwiedersehen*: "never to be seen again") of the image that disappears so rapidly that it can only be glimpsed in—and with—an *Augenblick*, articulates practically, graphically, the "singular temporality" of the "coming philosophy." Benjamin, so far removed in so many ways from the United States, treats the notion "phenomenon" in a sense accorded the word by American slang, as a manifestation of the extra-ordinary ("it's phenomenal!") whose coming to light converges with its disappearance.

If Benjamin designates this image as "dialectical," the reference is less to Hegel than to his own earlier demand, in the "Program," that the "coming philosophy" introduce "a certain non-synthesis" into the Kantian triad, one that, however, would "hardly lead to a quartet [*Vierheit*] of relational categories" (*GS1*, 166; *SW1*, 106). Benjamin's "dialectical image" thus heightens precisely what Hegelian dialectics seek to over-come: the "disjunctive relation" of the "synthesis." The dialectical image does this by arresting the forward flow of time, but it can only do so by interrupting its "own" intentionality qua representation and signification. In short, the "dialectical" image disrupts the horizon of expectation to which it ostensibly responds and thereby makes way for something else.

Such an interruption does not therefore install the *nunc stans* of a mystical *kairos*. Rather, it dislocates the self-perception of "the present" as unified and self-identical. In a fragment not included in the published version of "Theses on the Philosophy of History" or "On the Concept of History," titled precisely "The Now of Knowability," Benjamin quotes Turgot: "Before we are able to inform ourselves about a given state of things, it has already changed many times. Therefore we are always too late when we learn what has transpired. And thus one can say that politics is obliged, as it were, to predict the present" (*GS5.1*, 598; N 12a,1). For Benjamin, it is "just such a concept of the present that must be the basis of the actuality of genuine historiography" (ibid.).

The "now of knowability" thus presupposes an awareness of time not as a medium of becoming but as one of alteration and passing; what Benjamin calls the "image," therefore, is not simply the stable representation of a self-identical content but an allegorical figure that explodes the semblance of teleological progression by bringing its movement to a standstill while simultaneously moving in a different, less linear manner: as signification and repetition. Its temporality is that of the "calendar," which Benjamin distinguishes from that of "clocks." The time of the calendar, unlike chronological time, is neither homogeneous nor irreversible. Rather it is commemorative, discontinuous, repetitive. But such repetition turns out to be as ambivalent as all of Benjamin's other -abilities. It opens the possibility of a deadening (but also hypnotic) routine no less than that of messianic redemption, at times even leaving the impression that the two possibilities may not be entirely separable.

Such ambivalent -abilities—splinters of a word—endow Walter Benjamin's writings with much of the enigmatic fascination that has made them increasingly difficult to ignore but even more difficult to respond to. Melancholic and yet revolutionary, sober and yet scholarly, his texts challenge readers to measure their certitudes and prowess in a strange game of jump rope that they solemnly and prosaically reenact.

CHAPTER NINE

An Afterlife of -abilities

Derrida

The thinker who more than any other has taken up the legacy of Benjamin's "-abilities" is doubtless Jacques Derrida. This was not the result of a conscious or deliberate decision on Derrida's part. His concern with "-abilities" developed most immediately out of his encounter with Husserl, and in particular with Husserl's notion of "idealization" as constituted through a process of repetition. But whereas Husserl construed such repetition as demarcating the "ideality" of thought from all contamination by empirical exteriority, Derrida, in *Speech and Phenomenon,* argued that precisely this very same repetition necessarily contaminated the ideality it was held, by Husserl, to protect. Without mentioning Kierkegaard at that point by name, Derrida's deconstruction of Husserlian ideality was informed by a notion of repetition that Kierkegaard had elaborated in his essay of the same name, and that Nietzsche had reformulated as the "eternal return of the same." Some years later, in *Limited Inc.,* Derrida went on to elaborate this notion of repetition as an irreducible trait not only of language, but of every identifiable "mark." He called it "iterability," which he distinguished sharply from "iteration"—just as Benjamin had distinguished "reproducibility" from "reproduction," "translatability" from "translation," and all the other "-abilities" as possibilities from their realization as acts or entities.

But what had been largely implicit in Benjamin now became explicit in Derrida's reworking of such "-abilities," namely, the convergence of what in *Limited Inc.* he still designated as "structural possibility" with a no less structural, or rather destructuring, "impossibility." Precisely this convergence—which to be sure never was understood as establishing a simple identity—determines the way in which Derridean deconstruction took up the legacy of Benjamin's -abilities. "A legacy," Derrida writes in an essay that first appeared in 1998, "would only be possible where it becomes impossible." He continues: "This is one of the possible definitions of deconstruction—precisely as Legacy . . . Deconstruction might perhaps be 'the experience of the impossible.'"[1]

"Perhaps." It is around this word that the legacy of Benjamin's -abilities receives a decisive turn in the writings of Derrida. The convergence of the possible with the impossible is one of the driving motifs of the book *Politics of Friendship,* and it crystallizes around a discussion of the word "perhaps," as it is emphatically used by Nietzsche at the beginning of *Beyond Good and Evil.* There, in a passage that marks a major event in the legacy we have been retracing, Nietzsche envisages "philosophers of the future" who would no longer be bound by the hierarchical logic of mutually exclusive opposites that has hitherto dominated Western metaphysics, but who instead would negotiate with the inseparability of oppositional values in a way that would unseat the hierarchy and unsettle its certitudes. These would be "philosophers of the dangerous perhaps," a phrase that Derrida takes up first in the context of his ongoing dialogue with Heidegger, and in particular with Heidegger's notion of "questioning as the piety of thought." In *Of Spirit: On Heidegger and the Question* he had already indicated that at one point in Heidegger's writing Heidegger himself admits—but without drawing the necessary consequences—that all questioning must be preceded by an appeal, a *Zusage,* to which the question responds—but which it also dissimulates. In *Of Spirit,* Derrida had interpreted such an "appeal" as entailing a "gage"—a wager and engagement—in affirming the other inevitably addressed by every act of language (and whose irreducible alterity prevents language from every fully actualizing itself in such an "act"). A few years later, however, in *Politics of Friendship,* he went on to associate the conditions under which such a "gage" had to operate explicitly with the "dangerous perhaps" that for Nietzsche defined the "philosophers of the future" and that for Derrida now defined the future tout court:

> The *perhaps* that is coming will have always forewarned [*prévenu*] the question . . . At the moment when it forms itself, a *perhaps* will have opened it. It will have always prevented it from closing, just as it is forming. No response, no responsibility could ever abolish the *perhaps*. That a *perhaps* forever opens and precedes the questioning that it suspends in advance, not in order to neutralize or inhibit but to render possible all the determined and determining orders that depend upon *questioning* (research, knowledge, science and philosophy, logic, law, politics and ethics, language itself and in general)—that is a necessity to which we are attempting to do justice in various ways.[2]

How does one "do justice" to a "perhaps" that as the untranscendable condition of all questioning both underlies and destabilizes "all the *determined and determining orders*" of knowledge, politics, ethics, and language? It is in responding to this question that Derrida reinscribes, and transforms, the legacy of "-abilities" we have retraced from Kant to Benjamin. He begins with an "example" of the "justice" that exceeds all simple exemplarity, and it recalls his earlier discussion of Heidegger's "Zusage" in *Of Spirit*:

> For example, in recalling the acquiescence [*Zusage*] that is more originary than the question, which, without saying *yes* to anything positive, can affirm the possibility of the future only by opening itself to *determinability*, thus by welcoming that which still remains *undetermined and indeterminable*. It is indeed a *perhaps* that perhaps cannot be determined yet [*ne peut-être encore déterminé*] as dubitative or skeptical, the perhaps that is *left* [*reste*] to think, to do, to live (to death). But this perhaps does not come simply "before" the question (investigation, research, knowledge, theory, philosophy); it would come, making it possible, "before" the originary acquiescence through which all questioning is in advance involved with the other.[3]

Before all questioning, as "the piety of thinking," there is the *Zusage:* the "originary acquiescence" that acquiesces to nothing in particular but rather "affirm[s] the possibility of the future . . . by opening itself to a certain "indeterminability"—which is to say, to "that which still remains undetermined and indeterminable." The "still" in the preceding formulation—in French, *encore*—marks the convergence of both continuity and discontinuity; that is, it marks the temporality of what is to come as a possibility that can no longer be considered a negative or deficient mode of actualization. This is the strange and singular -ability of the "perhaps": it is inseparable from an *inability,* an "indeterminacy" that is not simply a negative form of determination. *Indeterminability* thus emerges as the condition of possibility of all determination, but also its condition of impossibility. This is why Derrida prefers the English (or German) versions of the word to its French "equivalent": "Perhaps [*peut-être*], although the French *peut-être* is perhaps here too rich in its two *verbs* [the *pouvoir* and the *être*]. Would not the original possibility of which we are speaking efface itself better in the *adverbs* of other languages (*vielleicht* or *perhaps,* for example)?" (*PoF,* 39; *Pdl,* 59). Marking the irreducibility of a certain indeterminability, the perhaps announces an -ability that is not that of a subject, much less that of an object, but of an event that in its singularity can happen but can never be reliably predicted or foreseen. The perhaps marks the difference between the ability to think and the ability to know, which in turn entails the difference between the irreducible spatial-temporal singularity of "there is" and the space-time transcending generality of "it is or exists":

> It is the moment when the disjunction between thinking and knowing is de rigueur. It is the moment when one can think sense or non-sense only by ceasing to be certain that the thing ever occurs or that even if there is such, that it would ever be accessible to theoretical knowledge or to a determining judgment, to any assurance of discourse or of naming whatsoever. This does not amount to conceding a hypothetical or conditional dimension ("if, suppose that, etc.") but rather marks the difference between "there is" [*il y a*] and "is" or "exists," which is to say, words of presence. Whatever there is, if there is any, need not necessarily *be.* Perhaps it will never *exist* or *present* itself, and nevertheless there is such [*il y en a*], there could be. Perhaps . . . (*PoF,* 39; *Pdl,* 59)

The English translation of Derrida's French here is confronted with a serious obstacle: the difference that is being marked depends on linguistic turns that are available in French and most other Romance languages, as well as in German, but not in English. The French *il y a,* and the German *es gibt,* are both ways of pointing toward something that need not exist, either materially or in the larger sense of being-present to itself, of being-as-presence. Instead of a timeless, spaceless, locationless, and self-contained *self-presence,* the French and German expressions designate some *thing* that can be *thought* without being *known, cognized* in the sense of being identified in a way that would transcend the limitations of a singular situatedness.

This is precisely the situation that Kant confronts at the outset of his Third Critique, designed to establish the decisive bridge between the theoretical and the practical, the phenomenal and the noumenal, the concept and the idea. And it is in response to this situation that he introduces the distinction between "determining" and "reflecting" judgments. Derrida's elaboration of the "perhaps" announces an experience that can never "be accessible to theoretical knowledge or to a determining judgment" (ibid.) and yet is not simply the negation of such knowledge or such judgment. The "opening to *determinability*" that accepts the latter precisely as an -ability—as a suffix, rather than as a noun (as a form of naming)—is thus here linked to the move from the name or noun, and the verb, as a subject-oriented activity, to those "*adverbs* in other languages" that instead of the French "can-be"—*peut-être*—designate the indeterminable as that which may "easily" happen (German: *viel-leicht*), but if it does, will never eliminate the element of chance *(per-haps)*.

Chance—in French, but also in English—signifies here both human calculation and control, as well as the possibility of alteration and change. Chance is necessary, and this is why Derrida's -abilities, like Benjamin's, can never be construed as properties of a subject or a self-consciousness. Acknowledging the convergence and interdependence of determinability and indeterminability prepares the way for insight into the "law of an aporia, of an undecidability, of a double-bind" (ibid.) that imposes itself in the irreducible gap that separates the general *concept* from the singular event. Together with iterability and (in)determinability, "undecidability" emerges as the third—but surely not the last—of Derrida's -abilities. It is that which takes up the cause that Kant sought to address with his notion of the "aesthetic judgment of beauty" and of "the sublime" as "reflecting judgment." But it takes it up only to take it elsewhere, reinscribing it in a chain that is no longer anchored in a constitutive subject. The "law" of "undecidability" is thus like the Kantian moral law in that it is inaccessible to theoretical knowledge. But it does not result in anything that can still be called a "judgment"—whether epistemological or juridical. It does not pronounce a "verdict" but instead engages in a "decision," a term that

Derrida borrows from Kierkegaard and at the same time demarcates from its use in the subjectively oriented "decisionism" of Carl Schmitt—to whom several chapters and an intensively deconstructive reading are devoted in *Politics of Friendship*.[4] Taking exception to the decisionism of Schmitt, Derrida argues that the decision itself can only be understood as that which takes exception to the subject. Far from abolishing undecidability, it singularizes it:

> It would thus recall the type or silhouette of the classical concept of decision: the latter must interrupt, marking an absolute beginning. It signifies therefore the other in me who decides and rends asunder. The passive decision, condition of the event, is always in me, structurally, another decision, a decision that tears apart as the decision of the other. Of the absolute other in me, of the other as the absolute that decides in me of me. Absolutely singular in principle, according to its most traditional concept, the decision is not only always exceptional, it *takes exception to me*. (*PoF*, 68–69; *Pdl*, 87)

The decision, in its character of passive response, singularizes undecid*ability* by actualizing it in a way that renders it indistinguishable from an inability. "The decisive or decisional moment of responsibility supposes a leap through which an act gets carried away, ceasing instantly to follow the consequence of *what* is, which is to say, that which is determinable by science or consciousness and thereby frees itself (this is what is called freedom)" (ibid.). But this is a freedom very different from the liberty of the subject to which we are accustomed: in being both "unconscious" and yet "responsible," what it responds to is the "heartbeat of the other." And Derrida stresses the "beat": "not just the heart, but the heartbeat [*pas seulement le coeur, mais le battement de coeur*], the movement through which the heart separates itself from its static state and at the same time marks its finitude" (*PoF*, 69; *Pdl*, 88). Belonging always to the other, this heart takes a beating.

Although the decision should be "preceded by all the science and all the consciousness that is possible," such knowledge and consciousness will never be able to determine "the leap of decision without transforming it into the irresponsible application of a program and thus depriving it of what makes it a free and sovereign decision [. . .] if there ever is such a thing" (*PoF*, 219; *Pdl*, 247).

This is why the appeal that is involved in all responsibility, which involves not just reacting to an appeal, but also repeating and transforming it, entails the ability to endure what Derrida calls the "test and trial [*l'épreuve*] of the perhaps" (*PoF,* 219; *Pdl,* 247), which is also a test and trial of time—and of crime. This crime is the result not so much of the infraction of a law as of the law itself: for the law of undecidability is aporetic, implementing itself only through the violation of self: the law of the double bind. The relation to the other, to which Derrida returns again and again, in this text and elsewhere, entails nothing less:

> We are caught, the one and the other, in a sort of heteronomic and dissymmetrical warp of social space, and more precisely, of the relation to the other: before all organized *socius,* before all *politeia,* before all determinate "government," *before* all "law." Before and in front of it, in the sense of Kafka's "Before the Law."
>
> But let there be no mistake: before all *determinate* law, as natural or positive law, but not before the law *in general.* For the heteronomical and dissymmetrical warp of a law of originary sociality is also a law, perhaps the very essence of law. What is unfolding at this moment and what we are experiencing uncannily, is perhaps only the silent deploying of that strange violence that forever has insinuated itself at the origin of the most innocent experiences of friendship or of justice. We have begun to *respond.* (*PoF,* 231; *Pdl,* 258)

Derrida's response is marked by the -abilities we have begun to delineate here. Without being able to go into *Politics of Friendship* in further detail,[5] it will perhaps be sufficient to point to the structure of the text not just as intertextual, but even more, as intratextual. Everything begins, as he writes, with a "rumor"—with an "on dit": Diogenes Laertes attributing a remark to Aristotle—"Oh my friends, there is no friend"—that is then reinscribed successively in a series of texts that constitute a legacy and a history, but with no determinable origin or referent, not at least in the sense of an absolute beginning. There are repetitions, reinscriptions, reversions, recoils, but no authoritative text that could provide a measure of philological certitude. This is why perhaps the most powerful and most decisive chapter in Derrida's book is entitled "Replis"—"recoils" as it is translated into English. But perhaps it is not entirely out of place to also hear in the word its English cognate, "reply."

Derrida's -abilities re-ply (to) those of Benjamin, and of many others, by rewinding them in a space-time warp that challenges its readers to experience the test and trial of time and of crime, an *épreuve* for which there is no passing grade.

PART TWO

Legibilities

CHAPTER TEN

Genealogy of Modernity

History, Myth, and Allegory in Benjamin's
Origin of the German Mourning Play

History is the shock of tradition and political organization.
—Walter Benjamin

One of the most pressing questions opened, or reopened, by the Poststructuralist problematization of representation concerns the concept of history. Ever since Claude Lévi-Strauss first gave prominence to Structuralism as a movement of thought by attacking Sartre's notion of historicity as uncritically ethnocentric and teleological, the status of history—whether as object, discipline, or method of investigation—has been a primary focus of attention, debate, and controversy. The temper of this controversy is reflected in the title of one of the first articles purporting to give a general theoretical assessment of the movement of thought: Alfred Schmidt's "The Structuralist Attack upon History." If Schmidt's study, published in 1968,[1] articulated the position of the "first" Frankfurt School, its self-proclaimed successor, the "second" Frankfurt School of Jürgen Habermas, has added some nuances to this position, but in the end hardly altered it. In his lectures on *The Philosophical Discourse of Modernity*, Habermas charges that "Poststructuralism has to pay a high price" for its "radical critique of reason," namely, the inability "to account for its own situation."[2] "Negative Dialectics, Genealogy and Deconstruction evade in a similar manner those categories according to which modern knowledge has not by accident differentiated itself, and upon which we base our understanding of texts today."[3] One of these "categories" is, of course, history, and Habermas's account of what he calls Foucault's "transcendental Historicism" indicates how he construes the poststructuralist evasion of history:

> The space of history . . . is filled with the utterly contingent advent of new discursive formations, which burst upon the scene [*Aufblitzen*] and disappear without any order; in this chaotic multiplicity of ephemeral universes of discourse there is no place left for any sort of overriding meaning [*übergreifenden Sinn*]. The transcendental Historicist looks as though into a kaleidoscope . . . Under the stoical glance of the archaeologist, history freezes [*erstarrt*] into an iceberg, laced with the crystalline forms of arbitrary discursive formations.[4]

What worries Habermas in Foucault's archaeological and genealogical reading of History is the disappearance of a place from which the whole can be taken in, from which the "übergreifende(r) Sinn" that he finds missing in Foucault can be constructed. What is striking, however, is the extent to which Habermas's characterization of Foucault's "transcendental historicism" gravitates, in its metaphors, toward the language of Walter Benjamin: the manner in which these singular forms appear is that of an *Aufblitzen*, a sudden bursting-forth of light, which just as abruptly disappears: one is reminded of Benjamin's fascination with the shooting star, which he elevates to the status of an allegorical emblem in his reading of Goethe's *Elective Affinities*.[5] Similarly, the kaleidoscope attracted Benjamin's attention for precisely the reasons that elicit Habermas's critique: the radical discontinuity of the successive configurations.[6] And yet perhaps above all it is the figure of "freezing," of an *Erstarren* of phenomena that both recalls Benjamin's insistence on the necessity of arresting the flow of events, and at the same time underscores the divergent direction in which such a necessity takes him. Whereas for Habermas the consequence of such petrification is the emergence of an "autonomy" that is moribund and abstract, because "without origin [ursprungslos],"[7] for Benjamin it suggests the "discontinuous finitude" that defines the object of what he calls "historical-philosophical" interpretation as an idea.[8] And as the title of his study of the *Origin of the Mourning Play* indicates, such "monadic" discontinuity of the "idea," far from establishing an "autonomy" that would deny origination, leads Benjamin to rethink the notion of "origin" itself, and with it, the concepts of history, tradition, and all they entail.

To be sure, such rethinking is not just cognitive: it implies a perspective that does not take epistemology or theory of science for granted, which is why the preface to Benjamin's study of the German baroque theater bears the somewhat unusual title "epistemo-critical," and not the more familiar term, "epistemological." For what Benjamin seeks to articulate in that preface is not simply another type of cognitive investigation, but rather a form of interpretation that does not take cognition for granted. Benjamin thus seeks to distinguish such interpretation both from literary and art history or criticism on the one hand, and from philosophical aesthetics on the other. Instead, he employs to describe his interpretive perspective the term *geschichtsphilosophisch,* "historical-philosophical," a word that is familiar enough but whose particular significance at the hands of Benjamin here turns out to be anything but self-evident or familiar.[9] Despite its obvious indebtedness to a certain Hegelianism—mediated for Benjamin by the writings of the young Georg Lukács—the conception of history to which he resorts here and in other writings of this period is incompatible with at least one prominent aspect of Hegelian thought: the dialectical resolution entailed in the notion of "reconciliation": *Versöhnung.*[10] This holds even if Benjamin employs the term "dialectic" in describing his notion of origin: "The guidelines for philosophical investigation [*Betrachtung*] are inscribed in the dialectic that accompanies [*beiwohnt*] origin. It demonstrates that in all essentials uniqueness and repetition [*Einmaligkeit und Wiederholung*] mutually condition one another. The category of origin is therefore not a purely logical one, as Cohen holds, but rather historical" (GS1, 226; *Origin,* 46). Although Benjamin calls the "category" of origin historical, his discussion of it in the "Epistemo-critical Preface" suggests that it is far more than just one historical category among others. We have already discussed Benjamin's notion of origin in relation to the process of translation (see Chapter 6). But origin can also be seen as the decisive category for his concept of history in general—and not just in *The Origin of the German Mourning Play.* For the sake of convenience, we re-cite the passage from the book's preface:

Origin, although an historical category through and through, has nevertheless nothing in common with emergence [*Entstehen*]. In Origin what is meant is not the becoming of something that has sprung forth [*Entsprungenen*], but rather that which springs forth out of coming-to-be and passing-away [*dem Werden und Vergehen Entspringendes*]. Origin stands in the flow of becoming as a maelstrom [*Strudel*] that irresistibly draws [*reißt*] the stuff of emergence into its rhythm. In the bare manifestation of the factual the original is never discernible, and its rhythm is accessible only to a dual insight. It is recognizable on the one hand as restoration, as reinstatement, and precisely in this as on the other hand incomplete, unfinished. (ibid.)

I interrupt the citation here to make a few comments. Although Benjamin will develop explicitly his notion of the "dialectical image" only some ten years later, this description of origin is itself as good an instance of such an image as one is liable to find. It is also an exemplary instance of Benjamin's writing style. The general pattern is to take one step forward and the next step back, but slightly to the side, slightly skewed. Origin is thus introduced as "an historical category through and through," a clear enough beginning, except—except that the very next turn of phrase bars the way to determining "historical" in the most familiar manner: in terms of genesis, a process of emergence, or coming-into-being (in German: *Entstehen*). The following sentence begins by continuing and amplifying the negative aspects of the description: origin is neither a kind of birth (as one might have thought), nor is it a mode of growth; it is not the *Werden,* or becoming, of something that has already emerged or 'sprung forth' *(Entsprungenen).* Rather, it is the offspring *(Entspringendes)* of coming-to-be and going-away, *Werden und Vergehen.* Grammatically, *Ursprung* is determined with reference to the present participle, *entspringend,* rather than to the past participle, *entsprungen.* The action of becoming is not "governed" by a substantive or a subject *(kein Werden des Entsprungenen),* but is instead the result of a complementary if conflictual interplay of becoming and passing-away. The conflictual configuration of coming and going, appearing and vanishing, development and decay, only underscores another aspect of the conflict, implicitly articulated at the lexical level. The root of "origin" in German is, of course *Sprung,* cognate with the English "spring" or "leap." Benjamin's discussion of the *Ursprung* here begins by establishing a negative relationship between the "sprungness" of the *Ur-sprung* (one thinks of Hopkins's use of "sprung rhythm") and the more sedate and more stable stance implied in the German word translated as "emergence": *Entstehen* (literally: arising, in the sense of taking a stand, assuming a stance). Origin, in short, qua *Ursprung,* has nothing to do with taking a stand, going upright, with acquiring a certain stature, status, or stability. Origin is springing, a leap, an offspring that springs from the alternation of becoming and passing away, of coming and going. Origin, the original leap, as it were, thereby emerges as a kind of cast-off: an *Entspringendes,* an abrupt jump away, an off-spring. Temporally, it is no more a beginning than it is an end, no more coming to be, than passing away. Its leap seems instead to be suspended between the two poles of coming and going, future and past. But how can an irreducible "leap" or "jump" be "suspended" without ever taking a stand, without relapsing into a certain constancy, without acquiring a minimal consistency? This is what the remainder of the passage proceeds to explore.

Having established that the origin proceeds by leaps and bounds, unconfined by the fixed borders of a stand or a stance, the passage immediately reverses, or suspends, its own description by nevertheless bringing the origin to a standstill and by putting it in its proper place: it "stands" *(steht),* Benjamin writes, in the flow or flux of becoming, from which it has just been demarcated but which now reveals itself to be the medium of *origination* after all. Origin is origination. It does not merely leap, it is not merely cast off as the offspring of becoming and passing away: it stands squarely in the flow. And yet, here again, reversal is followed immediately by reversal, peripeteia by peripeteia: having been assigned to its proper place and hence treated almost as though it were a physically visible thing, origin turns in upon itself, as it were, in being designated as a *Strudel,* for which the published translation of "eddy" hardly seems adequate. For if the origin has been put in its proper place, its situation turns out to be a violent perpetual motion. And moreover, it is one that develops considerable power: as a vortex or maelstrom, it draws (literally: tears, rips: *reißt*) the raw materials of emergence *(Entstehung)* into its force field. Or, as Benjamin puts it, preferring a temporal figure: into its "rhythm." Origin is however neither primarily temporal nor spatial but rather a movement in which the one turns into the other and vice versa: what "stands" its ground, as it were, in and against the flow of time, is not a stable entity or essence: rather, it is something that turns in upon itself, and that, in so turning, tears asunder the "material" out of which entities emerge, arise, and decay, drawing them into its rhythm. Origin, which "stands" firm in the flow of time as though it were a thing or an entity, is neither: it is, above all a rhythm of origination, recurring regularly with a force capable of drawing the materials out of which entities and things are composed into its movement.

This is why origin cannot be perceived at the level of mere fact: it organizes the "material" of facticity according to its rhythms, but these cannot be reduced to their material components. Like the "Idea," from which it is inseparable, Origin for Benjamin entails the relations that elements entertain with each other, rather than their simple factual subsistence. Which is another way of indicating that "origin" is itself nothing simple: as rhythm, it is double, at least. It is in his articulation of this duality that Benjamin's notion of origin once again undoes the expectations it has in part encouraged, by distancing itself from the more familiar uses of the word. The duality or duplicity of origin consists in an internal fracture: an effort of restoring and reinstating that never reaches its goal. Origin is thus not merely distinguished from becoming or from coming-to-be *(Werden, Entstehen):* it is directed simultaneously toward the future and toward the past. Its effort is not simply to bring something radically new and different into being, but rather to "restore," to "reproduce" *(Wiederherstellung).* Origin, as Benjamin describes it here, is conservative and repetitive in the most literal sense. At the same time, its project of restoration and reinstatement is inevitably destined to be "incomplete, unfinished" and it is this unfulfillment that determines the future from the perspective of origin. In origin, the goal ends up as interruption.

Mindful of this, and also of Benjamin's remark about the reciprocity of "uniqueness and repetition" in determining the historicity of origin, we can return to the passage under consideration and follow it, if not to a conclusion, then at least to a certain culmination: "In every originary phenomenon the form [*Gestalt*] is determined, in which again and again an idea confronts and struggles [*sich auseinandersetzt*] with the historical world, until it lies there in the totality of its history. Consequently, origin does not rise above the findings of fact, but rather concerns their pre- and post-history" (GS1, 226; *Origin,* 46). The passage elaborates the remarks already quoted concerning the "dialectic" of "uniqueness and repetition" that inheres in origin and that makes it a historical rather than a logical category. What emerges here, however, is that the effort of origin to "restore" and "reproduce"—which already implies a certain repetition—is destined to lead to a more manifest form of repetition by virtue of the aporetical character of its effort to reproduce or restore the unique. Hence the "totality" of which Benjamin speaks does not signify the overcoming of originary incompleteness, but rather the deployment of the possibilities of differential relations that define the idea. The latter, as Benjamin has already explained, shortly after the beginning of his "Epistemo-critical Preface," can be described, or rather, "circumscribed"—that is, described by circumlocution—as the forming or shaping *(Gestaltung)* of the context *(Zusammenhang)* in which the unique and extreme *(das Einmalig-Extreme)* stands in relation to its counterparts.[11] As usual, one should not read too quickly over the paradox that such "circumscribing" entails. For how can what is unique and singular relate to its *Gleichartigen,* to its homologues: that is, to other singularities? How can the "singular" be similar, *"gleichartig,"* except through the difference that simultaneously singularizes and separates it, rendering it unique, *einmalig?* In short, what is articulated in the Idea is a relation of singularities to one another, in which they are not subsumed under a general concept—the idea is not a concept, Benjamin states repeatedly, although it presupposes conceptual discrimination—but rather an assemblage of singularizing differences that are irreducible to each another. This is why Benjamin places such importance on what he calls the "extremes": the "unique" *(Einmalig)* is also extreme, he insists, because the extreme resists subsumption and normativization. What singularities have in common is their incommensurability.

With this in mind, we can paraphrase Benjamin's description of the relation of origin and history as follows: an originary phenomenon may be defined as the form in which an idea, as the configuration of singular extremes, sets itself apart *(sich auseinandersetzt)* in and with the historical world, until it has exhausted its recombinatorial possibilities. The origin sets itself apart, is intrinsically split, since its movement is that of an ever incomplete attempt at restoring and reproducing. Originary phenomena are therefore not absolutely original in the sense of an absolute beginning. They are a function of repetition: extreme, unique, and yet paradoxically inseparable from a movement of restoration and reinstatement that in turn can never be reduced to a present moment. Instead, the origin constitutes the present by splitting it into a pre- and a post-history and this split is what constitutes its originating historicity. The historicity of origination splits history, both empirically and in its idea. If the latter evolves in the mode of the present-to-hand (facticity), or of the presence-to-itself (ideality), the origin can be properly construed only if we are mindful that the German root-word *Sprung* also means crack. The *Ur-Sprung* is the irremediable split or crack that marks the movement of restoration and reinstatement by which singular beings seek to totalize themselves in their extremity.

It is this irreparable fissure or crack that impairs the possibility of history ever being written or thought of in a full and authentic manner, but that at the same time constitutes the historicity of the origin—and above all the origin of historicity itself. This distinction between history and historicity is not made explicitly by Benjamin, neither in this text nor elsewhere. It imposes itself, however, if one wishes to articulate the difference that distinguishes origin from history, in either the Hegelian dialectical or the historicist positivist sense. Since in the perspective of Benjamin's theory of origin history can be construed neither as the unfolding of conceptual discourse, nor as a positive concatenation of facts, nor finally as any sort of historicist amalgamation of the two, another term is helpful if not indispensable in order to maintain this distinction. Benjamin himself speaks of "natural history" to designate the specific splitting and suspension of history that we have already described as that of "pre-" and "post-history" *(Vor- und Nachgeschichte)*:[12] "The pre- and post-history of such [originary] beings is, as a sign of their being saved or gathered into the shelter of ideas, not pure but rather natural history" (*GS1,* 227; *Origin,* 47). What Benjamin calls here, in the most oxymoronic sense imaginable, "natural history"—not the history of nature but history *as* nature—is precisely the discrete, discontinuous, un-genetic aspect of the origin, the split coherence of that which articulates itself in a manner entirely incompatible with any sort of linear or even dialectical development. In the preface, Benjamin will seek to elaborate the "natural" history of originary phenomena: works, forms, and above all ideas, through a reference to the Leibnizian notion of "monad," which he uses less to explain the relation of immanence, totality, and isolation that marks the idea of origin (and the origin of the idea) than to underscore the enigma of their convergence. The following passage suggests certain practical consequences that result from this enigma:

> The deepening of historical perspective in [philosophically oriented] investigations . . . renders the idea total. Its structure, shaped as it is by this totality, and in contrast to its inalienable isolation, is monadological. The idea is a monad. The being that its pre- and post-history brings to it, offers, in its own hidden [history], the abbreviated and obscured figure of

the rest of the world of ideas . . . Each idea contains the image of the world. Its staging [*Darstellung*] amounts to nothing less than the task of delineating [*zeichnen*] this image of the world in its very abbreviation [*Verkürzung*]. (*GS1*, 228; *Origin*, 47–48)

To present or "stage" an idea is to "delineate" the "image of the world" contained in the tension of its isolated, and yet monadological, being. "Historical perspective," deepened by philosophical interest, renders the intrinsically isolated idea "total," in the sense of a monad. But if this monadological totality can be said to condense "the rest of the world of ideas" into its own obscure and foreshortened "figure," it is because the latter, qua idea, has in turn "its own hidden history" that awaits deciphering. It is this history that hides in the crack that splits it, internally as it were, into "pre- and post-history." It is this crack, this *Sprung,* that constitutes the chance of history to be something more than the mere registration and reproduction of what has been. In a note written a decade later, Benjamin recalls the significance of this *Sprung*: "From what are the phenomena to be saved? Not only, and not so much from the disrepute and contempt into which they have fallen as from the catastrophe that a certain kind of tradition, their "valorization as heritage," very often entails. They are saved through the disclosure [*Aufweisung*] of the breach [*Sprung*: leap, crack] in them" (*GS5,* 591; *AP,* 473). The *Origin of the German Mourning Play* seeks precisely to save German baroque theater by staging its idea, deciphering its hidden history, and disclosing the breach in which it originates: that is, becomes historical. In the process, it also uncovers the hidden history of modernity, but only by encrypting it.

The "Epistemo-critical Preface" establishes the following sequence: (1) The German baroque theater, and in particular, its form as "Mourning (or Sorrow) Play," is an idea, that is, a "staging of phenomena." (2) This staging *(Darstellung)* in the idea is monadic: that is, the phenomena represented in one idea reflect, in a discontinuous, abbreviated, and obscure manner or "figure," other ideas, which together constitute a "world." This notion of the idea as monad therefore establishes a paradox, or at least a tension, between the discrete and discontinuous singularity of the individual idea, and the "world" of ideas that it figures.

The notion of the idea as monad thus implies the task of articulating, if not simply bridging this gap between singularity and totality, specificity and world, a task that Benjamin assigns to "interpretation": "The idea is a monad—the representation of phenomena rests prestabilized in it as in their objective interpretation" (*GS1*, 228; *Origin*, 47). Interpretation is not something added to the idea: it is its mode of "staging" a world of phenomena selectively and tendentiously. This Nietzschean notion is powerfully at work in Benjamin's theory of the idea, and his approach to the German mourning play is marked by it.

The sequence in which this approach gets under way is worth attending to. Having completed his discussion of the interpretive character of the idea, Benjamin turns, rather abruptly, to what today would be called the history of its "reception." The history of this reception is "paradoxical," and this in turn, Benjamin argues, is tied to the peculiar nature of baroque theater. The reasons for this lack of "historical resonance" can be retraced to two major motifs, which were to find little sympathy in the Romantic and post-Romantic spirit that determined modern German philology and literary studies: first, the political disposition of the "officials" *(Beamtentum)* who wrote baroque plays, which Benjamin sums up in the motto: "Everything for, nothing by the people" (*GS1*, 229; *Origin*, 48). In short, the subject of history for the German baroque is in no way identical with its object. Its subject matter does not emphasize national tradition: it treats neither popular myths nor monumental events. Second, and related to this first factor, is the obvious imperfection of the individual plays themselves: nowhere do they achieve the formal versatility of a Calderon or the grandeur of a Shakespeare. Instead of testifying to artistic mastery and freedom of spirit, German baroque plays "emerged out of an extremely violent effort [*in einer höchst gewalttätigen Anstrengung*] and this alone testifies that their form was not shaped by any sovereign spirit" (*GS1*, 229–230; *Origin*, 49). Summing up: the lack of historical resonance accorded the baroque drama is a result first of its lack of artistic accomplishment, as evidenced in individual works, and second, of its lack of freedom, as evidenced by the absence of autonomous, sovereign subjects. The concept of a people producing its history through its works—the concept, in short, of a self-generating subject-object and ultimately, in the Hegelian sense, the concept of the concept—are not just absent from baroque drama: they are challenged radically by it. It is this challenge that Benjamin takes up and elaborates into one of the most compelling genealogies of modernity that we have been given—a genealogy that begins with a challenge directed at the Romantic-Idealist notion of history as the activity of a constitutive subject realizing itself through meaningful works.

The "body" of Benjamin's book is divided into three major sections: the first deals with the "political anthropology and typology" of the mourning play, the understanding of which is said to be "the precondition for escaping from the predicaments of an historicism that does away with its object [by treating it] as a necessary but inessential [*wesenlose*] transitional phenomenon. In the context of these realities the particular significance of baroque Aristotelianism, designed as it is to divert superficial observation, takes on its full significance" (*GS1*, 278; *Origin*, 100). Thus, already in 1924, the primary obstacle to an understanding of the German baroque, according to Benjamin, who addresses it in the first third of his study, is the genetic-teleological thinking of "historicism," which effaces the distinctive essence of its object by reducing it to a link in a developmental process.[13] And yet, paradoxically enough, although such a reduction tends to efface the essence of its object, the latter itself precisely lends a certain support to such effacement. The "particular significance of baroque Aristotelianism" lies precisely in the way it aids "and abets a certain self-effacement" (ibid.). It is, Benjamin suggests, something of a diversionary movement, designed to lead observers astray. Astray from what? And why?

The first section of Benjamin's book that thus concludes has already provided at least the initial elements of a response: the baroque mourning play takes place in a world that sees itself as fallen nature without any visible sign of grace.[14] It is a world without stable authority: the sovereign partakes of a creation in which ubiquitous guilt drives those who rule to become first tyrants, and then, often, martyrs. Power changes character: it detaches itself from rulers and devolves upon those who know how to exploit the weakness of others, whether strong or weak; which is why perhaps the most characteristic figure of the baroque, who completes the triad of its "political typology," alongside the tyrant and martyr, is the intriguer, schemer, or perhaps better: plotter. For the plotter—*der Intrigant*—is related to the plot *(die Intrige)* not just lexically, but semantically and etymologically, as Benjamin's argument makes clear. If the term "intrigue" derives from the Latin *intrigare*, "confuse, confound," such confusion is inseparable from a tendency of the baroque to which Benjamin attaches considerable importance: its "projection of temporal process into space," and in particular into that particular space known as the "court" (*GS1*, 271; *Origin*, 92). The intriguer is the "exponent of [this] showplace," the exemplary courtier, in that he has no proper place, no "home" outside of it (*GS1*, 275; *Origin*, 97). Inside, however, his function is to in-trigue, to confuse, and the condition of such confusion is precisely the particular spatialization and localization of processes that are usually considered to be temporal or historical in character. As, for instance, political processes: "The course of political events [*Geschehen*] is frozen and fixed by the plot [*die Intrigue*], which strikes the seconds [*schlägt den Sekundentakt*]" (ibid.). The plot beats time, as it were, by em-plotting it, confining and con-fusing it within the narrow and local space of the court. And if the plotter, the intriguer, is not the master of this space, he remains the one who best knows how to move in it. His "power, knowledge and will" are endowed with a "demonic" quality, associated by Benjamin with the fact that he has "access to the office of the Prince, where the assaults of high politics are devised" (ibid.).[15]

What also makes the schemer such an exemplary figure is that "Baroque drama knows historical activity only as the depraved doings of schemers" (*GS1*, 267; *Origin*, 88). And yet, no less relevant in this context is that the age itself, in a certain sense, schemes.[16] Not that it does this with full awareness, much less with calculating deliberateness. Here as elsewhere Benjamin's observation is valid, that no age was ever less transparent to itself than the baroque.[17] And yet, in seeking to authorize itself by appealing to Aristotle, baroque theoreticians both obscured the novelty of their theater and at the same time helped to prepare its rejection, since they encouraged its evaluation in terms of criteria to which it could never conform (which, as Benjamin points out, it never even tried to). "Through a gesture of submission" to classical models and standards, the baroque in its novelty sought "to secure for itself the most binding authority," that of ancient Greece (*GS1*, 278; *Origin*, 100). Baroque authors, scholars, and critics thus all worked to institute the most misleading, if also highly strategic, conception of their drama as one to be measured by the models of classical tragedy.

The analysis and dismantling of this association is the major concern of the second, central part of Benjamin's book. It is to this part that we now turn.

There is perhaps no better indication of the tenacity of the problem that Benjamin confronts in this section of his study than the English translation of its title: *Origin of the German Tragic Drama*. The translator notes that his "difficulties begin with the word *Trauerspiel* (literally = mourning play)" but the gloss he then supplies implicitly justifies the departure from literality in the title; the word, he adds, "is used to refer to modern, baroque tragedy as distinct from classical tragedy."[18] If the referent can be described as "modern, baroque tragedy," then there can be little harm, it would seem, in translating *Trauerspiel* as tragic drama, no matter what the German word may mean, literally or otherwise. That the translator is not entirely at ease with this decision, however, is indicated by the fact that the German word is retained in the body of the text. The unstated position that presides over the English translation, in the form of its title, is that however significant the distinctions may be, they nevertheless take place within the continuity of a self-identical genre—tragedy. It is precisely this position that Benjamin begins this section by criticizing: what characterizes modern theories of tragedy, he argues, is their dismissal of all "philosophy of history." Here as elsewhere, Benjamin's use of the word *"Geschichtsphilosophie"* (or its adjective, *geschichtsphilosophisch*) is anything but self-evident. But in this context, one of its meanings, is clear enough: that of a distinction or singularity that resists subsumption under a universalizing concept, no matter whether the latter is an aesthetic genre or a self-fashioning subject.[19] As Benjamin puts it, in a somewhat antiquated German: *"Geschichtsphilosophie ward ausgeschieden,"* literally: "the philosophy of history came to be eliminated" (*GS1,* 280; *Origin,* 101–102).

This lapidary statement is remarkable for several reasons: first, because it marks the point of departure of Benjamin's effort to reintroduce a historical-philosophical perspective into the theory of tragedy. Second, because his theory of the distinctively modern character of the baroque *Trauerspiel* is developed on the basis of and in sharp distinction to a historical-philosophical conception of Greek tragedy. And finally, because the elimination of *Geschichtsphilosophie*, which both characterizes modern theories of tragedy and at the same time renders them incapable of understanding the specifically historical nature of the baroque mourning play, is itself a continuation of certain baroque conceptions, which themselves already entail a certain elimination of the "historical." The resulting implication is that this obliteration of the historical, which originates in the baroque and then continues in its modern reception, renders the historical significance of the baroque both constitutive of modernity, and at the same time inaccessible to it. The baroque mourning play thus begins to emerge as the origin of a modernity whose distinctive historicity resides, in part at least, precisely in the effacement of historical distinction. Benjamin attempts first to reconstruct just what it is that has been effaced, in order then to articulate the irreducible distance that separates it from its modern successor (mindful that succession for Benjamin is always discontinuous).

What, then, are the salient traits of Benjamin's historical-philosophical idea of tragedy? It is, first of all, a theory of the distinctly Greek nature of tragedy, a distinction based on the specific historical situation of the Greeks. Tragedy, according to Benjamin, has as its distinctive precondition the dominance of myth. It is this dominance that is decisively challenged by the defiance of the tragic hero. His death is interpreted as a sacrifice: a sacrifice of his person to the future of the community, to a people that will no longer be dominated by the (polytheistic) powers of a mythic world, which Benjamin describes with two key words: "demonic" and "ambiguous" *(zweideutig):* "The decisive confrontation [*Auseinandersetzung*] with the demonic world order gives tragic poetry its historical-philosophical signature. The tragic relates to the demonic as paradox does to ambiguity" (*GS1*, 288; *Origin*, 109). If the "ambiguity" or *Zweideutigkeit* is "demonic," it is because it is tied to the polytheism of the mythical world, in which no clear hierarchy permits an unambiguous identification of authority. What is thereby at stake in Greek tragedy, is, in the most general sense, the emergence of a principle of singular identity, of singularity as a principle that challenges the multiplicity and ambiguity of the existing, mythical order. "The old rights of the Olympians are disqualified," Benjamin writes, in the name of a "new, unknown God" (*GS1*, 285–286; *Origin*, 107). The death of the hero is a sacrifice, then, but one that heralds the advent of a new world order as well as a new social structure. Or, as Benjamin puts it, employing a word that was soon to acquire sinister notoriety, the advent of a new type of *Volksgemeinschaft* (community of the people). The defiance and death of the tragic hero thus constitutes "a preliminary stage of prophecy" (*GS1*, 297; *Origin*, 118), and its prophecy is paradoxical for at least two reasons. First, it announces the advent of a new order through the refusal of the tragic hero to speak the language of a world he no longer accepts. And second, it is paradoxical because the new order that is thus prophesied, which involves the common destiny of an entire people, is announced by a hero whose stubborn silence confirms "the icy solitude of the self" in the words of Rosenzweig, whom Benjamin cites (*GS1*, 286; *Origin*, 108).[20]

Tragedy is thus first of all bound to a hero whose silence is prophetic, and whose demise announces the triumph of the self: not so much as an individual but rather in general, as Man and God, and as a People that embodies both in its Community. This paradoxical process involves four interrelated aspects on which Benjamin insists: it is agonistic, it is juridical, it is theatrical, and above all—for this is common to all the others—it is linguistic. It is agonistic, in the defiance and challenge of the established mythical order by the emerging isolated self. It is juridical insofar as this challenge takes the form of a trial and even more, of an appeal to judicial review: for if the hero is put on trial by the established order, by myth, the latter's verdict is both "portrayed and subjected to appeal and revision" in tragedy. The hero thus is engaged "in an as it were contractual process of atonement" *(in einem gleichsam verträglichen Sühneverfahren)* that is doubly significant: it entails not only the "reestablishment but also the undermining of an older legal order in the linguistic consciousness of a renewed community" (*GS1*, 294; *Origin*, 115). In entering into something like a "contractual" relationship with the gods, the hero demonstrates that he is on a similar level with them and thereby subverts the difference required to sustain their claim to divine authority. And yet the language of the hero is not that of the lawyer or the judge: for he does not accept the law, and therefore has nothing to say. Indeed, like Orestes in the *Eumenides*, he says nothing: this is the literal meaning of the German word on which Benjamin's account of the tragic so greatly depends, and which is weakly translated into English as "silence." For "silence" is a condition, a state: in English, one is silent, or at best, "falls" silent.

The *Schweigen* of the hero, by contrast, is performative; it is an act of defiance even if it is not fully understood as such by the hero. It entails a positive decision not to speak a language whose authority is thereby rejected or negated. Unlike "silence," *Schweigen* is not a state into which the tragic hero falls—it is a refusal to speak. "The affinity of trial and tragedy" on which Benjamin insists also serves to underscore their distinction: in both, "the Logos breaks through the Ordeal in Freedom" (*GS1*, 295; *Origin*, 116), but the freedom is different in each. In the trial such a breakthrough presupposes the existing juridical structure; in tragedy, the refusal of the hero to speak announces a new kind of language and of assemblage. This assembly takes place not simply in the court, however much this remains its model: it takes place in the "amphitheater," an open theater in which the community, as spectators, also assumes the role of judge. The spectators function as the "controlling instance." And yet this very fact transforms the nature of their control: the verdict of spectators in the theater cannot claim the same status as that of judges in a court. For what is at stake is also the law itself. In this sense the theatrical trial does not replace one law, that of mythical ambiguity, with another, that of monotheistic univocity; rather, in a strange way it "appeals" and reviews the verdict of myth by repeating it, and replacing it with what Benjamin calls a *non liquet*: "The community attends this appeals trial as controlling instance, even as judge . . . But a *non liquet* always resounds in the conclusion of tragedy. The solution [*Lösung*] to be sure is always resolution or redemption [*Erlösung*], but it is only ad hoc [*jeweilige*], problematic, limited" (*GS1*, 296; *Origin*, 116–117). Redemption is limited, because it is tied to the isolated individual. It has not yet found a common language that would allow it durably to transcend the death of the hero. That step is taken by the dialogues of Socrates, which therefore mark both the "irrevocable epilogue of tragedy" and its ineluctable consequence. For the silent prophesy of the self implies an echo that it, as individual, cannot supply, and it is the function of Socratic irony to make that echo audible and meaningful. With the raising of this self-consciously ironic voice, death loses the definitiveness that constitutes its specificity in tragedy. "In place of the sacrificial death of the hero, Socrates provides the example of the pedagogue" (*GS1*, 297; *Origin*, 118).

But this is by no means the end of the story; the didactic epilogue has in turn an aftermath, although a more enigmatic one: the self-consciously ironic and pedagogic use of silence by Socrates is replaced by the "purely dramatic language" of the Platonic dialogues, which for Benjamin are situated "this side of the tragic and the comic, of their dialectic. Their purely dramatic [quality] brings the Mysterium, which had gradually been secularized [*verweltlicht*] through the forms of Greek drama, back and reinstates it: its language, as that of the new drama, is above all that of the mourning play" (ibid.).

This then is how Benjamin determines and situates tragedy, in order then to demarcate it definitively from his primary concern: the baroque mourning play. Before going on to examine this demarcation in some detail, it may be useful to reflect for a moment on the rather subtle turn that Benjamin gives, at the end, to the story that he is telling here. The story line itself is familiar enough, and it is no accident if Benjamin relies in part on the most academically respectable sources in reconstructing it. In support of his reliance on the theory of the "agonistic" nature of tragedy, immediately inspired by his friend Florens Christian Rang, he cites not Nietzsche, whose text on the Greek *agon* he seems not to know, but rather Jacob Burckhardt (*GS1*, 294n; *Origin*, 115n). Indeed, although Benjamin concedes a certain merit to Nietzsche for detaching the question of the tragic from that of ethos and for recognizing its link to myth (*Sage*) (*GS1*, 280; *Origin*, 102), it is Wilamowitz whom he cites in order to elaborate that relationship.[21] But his major source remains Franz Rosenzweig's *Star of Redemption*, from which he borrows the notion of the sacrificial and prophetic silence of the tragic hero. The story that Benjamin pieces together from Rang and Rosenzweig, Wilamowitz, Nietzsche, and Lukács seems at first sight straightforward enough: the mythic order of pagan polytheism, characterized above all by its "demonic duplicity" *(dämonische Zweideutigkeit)*, by destiny and guilt, is "broken through" in tragedy. This is summed up in a citation from an essay that Benjamin had published in 1914, "Destiny and Character": "In tragedy demonic destiny is broken through. Not however through the pagan vicious circle of guilt and atonement being resolved and supplanted [*abgelöst*] by the purity of an expiated mankind, reconciled with the pure God. Rather, in tragedy the pagan senses [*besinnt sich*] that he is better than his gods, but this awareness leaves him speechless . . . The paradox of the birth of genius in moral speechlessness, moral infantility, constitutes the sublime in tragedy" (*GS1*, 288–289; *Origin*, 109–110). The story is familiar for several reasons.

First, because it seems to follow a linear pattern: there is first the mythic order, then its challenge through tragedy, which announces the coming of a new order, that of Man and God, Community and Freedom. And second, because it recounts the progress of self-consciousness: the defiant speechlessness of the individual self, its refusal to speak and its inability to comprehend, finally is replaced and supplanted by its parody—the self-conscious martyrdom of Socrates, which sounds the knell of tragedy precisely by no longer accepting the finality of death: "Socrates looks death in the eyes as a mortal . . . but in it he recognizes something alien, beyond which, in immortality, he expects to find himself. Not so the tragic hero, who draws back in horror from the force of death as from something familiar, that belongs to him and to which he belongs. His life derives from death, which is not its end, but its form. For tragic existence [*Dasein*] finds its task only because the borders, those of linguistic as well as physical life, are given with it from the very beginning, postulated in it" (*GS1*, 293; *Origin*, 114). This story-line is reassuringly dialectical: the defiant silence of the tragic hero announces the coming of other voices: "Out of enormous emptiness reverberates inwardly the distant new commands of the gods, and through this echo coming generations learn their language" (ibid.). The tragic hero, by providing an example, is thus "pedagogical" long before Socrates arrives on the scene to assume silence and death and thereby transform them into the constituents of an ironic martyrdom. Benjamin agrees with Nietzsche in seeing this act as related to Christianity. Socrates thus both achieves tragedy and at the same time finishes it off, and in so doing prepares the way for Christian redemption. Or so it would seem.

So it would seem, that is, if one does not stumble onto the limits of this story in its closing chapter, as it were, which is so brief and elliptic that one would be inclined to pay it little attention were it not for at least three factors. First the German baroque mourning play turns out to be not simply the "other" of, or entirely distinct from, Greek tragedy, but also to be related to it in a far more intimate manner than Benjamin's explicit and massive rhetoric of demarcation would tend to suggest. Second, the movement of the text itself enacts, as it were, precisely the rhythm of origination, that of "restoration" and at the same time incompleteness. And finally, this very rhythm turns out to be a salient trait of what Benjamin describes as *"Darstellung,"* which alone is capable of articulating or staging the "idea." Such exposition,

Benjamin insists, "is an independent [*ebenbürtig*] form of prose" (*GS1*, 209; *Origin*, 29); it resembles not so much speech, which appeals to word and gesture in order to establish its continuity and unity, as writing, which "with every new phrase stops anew and starts all over again." As the "authentic method of the philosophical tractatus" (ibid.), such writing, which Benjamin also calls "philosophical style," has four "postulates": "The art of setting apart [*Absetzens*] as opposed to the chain of deduction; the persistence of the treatment [*Abhandlung:* treatise] as opposed to the gesture of the fragment; the repetition of motifs as opposed to shallow universalism; the fullness of concentrated positivity as opposed to polemical negation" (*GS1*, 212; *Origin*, 32). What makes "setting off" or "apart," *Absetzen* (a term that returns with a certain regularity throughout this book), an "art" rather than a science or element of a scientific method, is that it is bound up, within the "philosophical style," with a movement that pulls in a somewhat different direction: that of "repetition" or of "restoration." Setting apart is not usually considered to be compatible with repeating or restoring. It is the tension engendered by their association that perhaps explains how and why the movement of origin can and must be both restorative and unfulfilled.

In a passage that provides a remarkable instance of just such a tension, both within its own movement and in its ramifications, the death of tragedy converges with the death of Socrates: "In place of the sacrificial death of the hero, Socrates offers the example of the pedagogue. The war, however, declared by his rationalism upon tragic art, is decided by Plato's work with a superiority that ultimately strikes the challenger more decisively than the challenged, against tragedy. For this occurs not in the rational spirit of Socrates, but rather in the spirit of the dialogue itself" (*GS1*, 297; *Origin*, 118). This is the "passage" that operates the decisive transition from tragedy to *Trauerspiel:* for the "spirit of the dialogue itself" is neither tragic nor rational but rather "purely dramatic language, this side of tragic and comic, of their dialectic." The purely dramatic language of the Platonic dialogue, which comes after tragedy, comedy, and their (Socratic) dialectic, is at the same time "this side," *diesseits* of them. This language thus functions in a way very different from the infantile, mute prophecy of the tragic hero: far from announcing the coming of God, Man, and Community through the silent self-negation of the Self, it prepares the way for something that has already been: for the "Mysterium" that the forms of Greek drama had "gradually secularized" but that returns in this "purely dramatic language." Past, present, and future are thus no longer the clearly demarcated dimensions of a dialectic of self-realization: rather, they are facets of a repetitive process in which decisions, far from being decisive, turn abruptly against the deciders. The syntax and sequence of Benjamin's phrase dramatizes this turn: "The war, declared by [Socratic] rationalism upon tragic art is decided by Plato's work with a superiority . . ." So far, so good, it would seem: the pupil Plato brings to fruition what the teacher, Socrates, initiated: the rational verdict or decision against tragic art. Except—except that the rest of the sentence comes full circle, arresting the reader through the inversion of expectation: ". . .with a superiority that ultimately strikes the challenger more decisively than the challenged, against tragedy." The "superiority" of the judge—here, Plato—turns against the "challenger": the language is that of the *agon*, appropriately enough, for we are still close to the world of tragedy. But the "decision" of the struggle turns against itself: its consequences do not permit a "decision," if we take the word in its etymological sense of "separating" or setting apart. For if the decision goes against the challenger—here, Socrates—that does not mean that it goes *for* tragedy. Which is why I have kept, in my literal translation, the rather inelegant conclusion of Benjamin's phrase, which in German is no less startling than in English: "with a superiority that ultimately struck the challenger more decisively than the challenged [*als die Geforderte*], against tragedy." The clumsy conclusion offers an example of that "literal rendering of syntax" that Benjamin elsewhere proposes as the principle of all translation.[22] What an argument seeks explicitly to deny or to obliterate nonetheless imposes itself through an irrepressible repetition that concludes the phrase only by exploding it, leaving the addressee as a monstrous excrescence at the end. The leftover *non liquet* that startles our expectation of a well-rounded conclusion suggests that the "decision" goes against both challenger and challenged, against both Socrates and tragedy. "Against tragedy," since what it mysteriously suggests is not the "victory of God and of Man" over the forces of myth, but the return of Man as a Mysterium that challenges the triumph over death, whether tragic or philosophic. The return of this Mysterium occurs in a language that is neither tragic nor rational and yet that is inconceivable without both: a "purely dramatic language" accompanies the "origin of the German mourning play" and marks it as far from over.

> For there is an irretrievable image of the past that threatens to disappear with every present which does not recognize itself as intended in it.

This observation, which concludes the fifth of Benjamin's remarks in "On the Concept of History," one of his last writings, would hardly seem to be applicable to the relation of the baroque mourning play to Greek tragedy (GS1.2, 695; SW4, 391). In the section of the text just discussed, we have seen how Benjamin invests enormous energy in laying the groundwork for that "art of setting apart" that he saw as the first condition of an authentically "philosophical style." His entire effort to introduce a "historical-philosophical" perspective into the analysis of the baroque mourning play requires him to establish its radical difference from the genre of tragedy, which he argues is specific to the Greeks. His argument, as we have seen, goes against the testimony not just of the scholarly tradition of his time, but also of theories of the baroque itself, which, in its quest for legitimacy, gladly draped itself in the mantle of an Aristotelianism that knew nothing of "sorrow" or "mourning," but rather of terror and pity (GS1, 297; Origin, 119). After reading Benjamin, one would be tempted to conclude that all that tragedy and *Trauerspiel* have in common are the first three letters of their names (in German, that is). If tragedy originates in its challenge to the mythical order that has hitherto defined the being of a people, the mourning play—and the allegorical attitude from which it is inseparable—"has its origin in the confrontation [*Auseinandersetzung*] of a guilt-ridden nature [*physis*] with a purer *natura deorum*, embodied in the Pantheon" (GS1, 400; Origin, 226). The mourning play is thus not merely different from tragedy; it appears in essential ways to be diametrically opposed to it. For the defiant silence of the tragic hero constitutes an act that announces a radical break with the vicious cycle of guilt and atonement rather than a confirmation of its ineluctability. The thrust of the tragic sacrifice is to point beyond the existing order to something radically different, to point beyond myth toward history. In the baroque mourning play, this perspective is closed off: history has been secularized as "nature," with the latter being understood as fallen:

"In terms of the martyr-drama it is not moral transgression but the very estate of man as creature that provides the grounds for the catastrophe. This typical downfall so different from the extraordinary [situation] of the tragic hero, is what the dramatists had in mind when . . . they described a work as a *Trauerspiel*" (*GS1*, 268; *Origin*, 89). Undoubtedly, then, the most striking difference between tragedy and *Trauerspiel* relates to the significance of the subject: in tragedy, as we have seen, everything is centered around the fate of the tragic hero, isolated precisely as a "self." The mourning play, by contrast, "knows neither heroes nor selves, but only constellations" (*GS1*, 310–311; *Origin*, 132)—not simply of persons, but also of things. If tragedy heralds the dawn of a new age as that of a new Humanism, the sinful state of a fallen world places humans and things on the same level. Humans are treated as things, and things as human. For it is not the advent of a divine Logos, speaking through human voices, that is determining, but the emergence of inscriptions, of legends and emblems taking the place of names: "If the tragic hero in his 'immortality' saves not his life, but only his name, the characters in the mourning play lose, with death, only their named individuality but not the vital force of their role. Undiminished they revive in the world of ghosts" (*GS1*, 314–315; *Origin*, 136). As such passages accumulate in the course of Benjamin's discussion of the mourning play, the reader increasingly senses that the relation between *Trauerspiel* and tragedy, although certainly not one of identity, may also not be that of pure and simple opposition. The function of death, in the passage just quoted, is symptomatic: in a certain sense the mourning play is not just opposed to tragedy; it seems to repeat it, as a kind of parody. The death of the hero in tragedy, according to Benjamin, heralds the advent of a new age and a new life: that of a community indebted not to the demonic duplicity of mythical polytheism, but to the self-identical order of a monotheistic and humanistic world, the political expression of which is precisely a free and self-determining *Volksgemeinschaft*. In this perspective, Socrates only brings to self-consciousness what was already at work in the stubborn and infantile—that is, speechless—defiance of the hero: the affirmation and universalization of the principle of self-identity: One God, One Mankind, One People. *E pluribus unum*. It is precisely this principle, however, that recurs in the mourning play: "Death, as a figure of tragic life, is an individual fate; in the mourning play it not infrequently emerges as a collective destiny, as though it summoned the participants to appear before the highest court" (*GS1*, 314; *Origin*, 135). It is the court, however, that demonstrates just how the mourning play relates to tragedy, namely as a mode of repetition, and also as a form of origination in the Benjaminian sense. For the mourning play both repeats and transforms, restores and irremediably dislocates, the agonistic trial in which tragedy has its model. It should not, of course, be forgotten that for Benjamin tragedy itself is already a repetition. It repeats myths, sagas, and in subjecting them to review, subverts their authority. "If myth is a trial, tragedy is its depiction and revision [appeal] in one" (*GS1*, 295; *Origin*, 116). It is a repetition, but one aiming at a definitive decision that overturns the mythical verdict. The death of the tragic hero, his refusal to continue speaking, leaves the mythical order with ostensibly no recourse.[23] As Benjamin himself repeats, this time in contrast to the mourning play, "The Greek trilogy is not repeatable ostentation, but rather unique [*einmalig*] resumption or retrial [*Wiederaufnahme*]" (*GS1*, 298; *Origin*, 119). Of course, the "uniqueness" of the tragic revision of myth is always, as we have seen, accompanied by the "non liquet" that already calls its verdict into question. But the intention aimed at such a decisive verdict seems nevertheless constitutive of tragedy, as Benjamin interprets it. The case of the mourning play, by contrast, is quite different: one would be tempted to say that it overturns the tragic court of appeals and reinstates the initial verdict, were there any decision. Precisely that, however, does not take place: there is no final verdict, and the sentence is not so much suspended as indefinitely deferred:

> Whereas tragedies end in a decision—however uncertain this may be— the mourning play essentially entails the possibility of appeal as martyrs utter it . . . The legal digression may be pursued even further and, in the spirit of the medieval literature of complaint [*Klageliteratur*], one may speak of a trial brought by the creation [*der Kreatur*], whose charges [*Klage*] against death—or against whatever else they may be directed— are laid *ad acta* at the end of the mourning play after having been only half treated. Revision and retrial [*Wiederaufnahme*] of the case are thus implicit [*angelegt*] in the mourning play. (*GS1*, 315–316; *Origin*, 137)

With this indefinite suspension of sentencing, which in turn prepares the way for an equally indefinite series of repetitions, revisions, and revivals, the "court" of the mourning play reveals its true nature. It is the site not of an adjudication, but of what in French is appropriately called a *non-lieu*, a "non-place" or, less literally but more familiarly, a dismissal for lack of evidence. What is dismissed, in the baroque court, is not just the law, in the name of which sentencing could take place, but the place itself. It is literally dis-missed, set into play, divested of its function as a stabilizing site of identical bodies, and instead dislocated as the stage or showplace *(Schauplatz)* of a theatrical representation. The exemplary site of the baroque mourning play is, first of all, the court of the local ruler, and secondly, the theater of that court. What characterizes both is that they are local, hence without the cosmic claim to universality of the Greek amphitheater; and that in their limited locality, they wander: "In the entire European mourning play, the stage cannot be rigorously fixed as an authentic place, for it too is dialectically riven. Bound to the court state, it remains a wandering stage; its planks are an inauthentic representation of the earth as the created scene [showplace] of history; this theater travels with its court from place to place" (*GS1*, 298; *Origin*, 119). In its peregrinations, the "court" of Greek tragedy, which was authentically juridical, has become politicized. The particularism of the Greek city-states, which in its revolt against the "demonic" and "equivocal" order of myth led to a prophesy of a universal world order, has now come full circle: it is in the name of a universal world order, that of the fallen state of creation, that the baroque mourning play wanders from town to town, enclosed in the immanence of its particularism. And yet, with the claim of world-domination. History has been secularized as nature, but it is a nature that consists of a collection of particulars, with no possibility of its ever forming a whole. Death is no longer the line that separates finite being from itself, and thus the dialectical negation of the negation. Rather, it is what "digs most deeply the jagged line of demarcation that separates nature [*physis*] from significance [*Bedeutung*]" (*GS1*, 343; *Origin*, 166), thus engendering allegory. In allegory, things are cut off from what they seem to represent, or rather, they "signify precisely the non-being of what they represent" (*GS1*, 406; *Origin*, 233). Whatever is represented allegorically has no being apart from its being represented. Above all, its essence is inaccessible to good works, or to work of any kind. In the absence of the possibility of meaningful action, what emerges is mourning and melancholy as eminently theatrical attitudes. In this sense, allegory is eminently theatrical, since the being of what it represents can be determined only by virtue of its being placed before *(vorgestellt)* someone else: for instance, before a spectator. But neither spectator nor spectacle, neither court nor theater, add up to a self-contained whole. Benjamin describes their distinctive structure while discussing the peculiar relation of emblems to allegory:

> In its most developed form, the baroque, allegory brings with it a court; around a figural center, which, in contrast to conceptual circumlocutions, is never lacking in authentic allegories, the emblems are grouped in their profusion. They seem to be arbitrarily arranged: "The Confused 'Court'"—title of a Spanish mourning play—could be cited as the [exemplary] scheme of allegory. "Dispersion" and "collectedness" [*"Zerstreuung" und "Sammlung"*] are the law of this court. Things are brought together according to their significance; indifference to their existence [*Dasein*] disperses them once again . . . Fanaticism in assembling is balanced by slackness in arranging. (*GS1*, 364; *Origin*, 188)

In contrast to the "punctual" quality of the tragic hero, and to the unity of place in which the tragic action is held to take place, the site of the mourning play is not merely that of a particularity that cannot be fixed: it is a site that is local, but in its locality also universal. It is a "plot," but as such, one that is always highly confused. It is the site of a confusion, in which the "center" serves as the focal-point of divergent forces: those of collection and of dispersion. The site and structure, the plot of the mourning play is thus neither unified, nor chaotic. It is the site of a conflict and of a divergence. It is neither that of that isolated individual (the tragic hero), nor of the liberated community prophesied by the death of that individual. It is neither that of tragic infantilism, nor of Socratic irony. It is "this side" of tragedy and comedy, since it has not attained the unity that they propose. It is the site of the plotter, a demonic but also a comic figure. As exponents of the court, plot and plotter can also be said to be "this side" of the two major dramatic genres, tragedy and comedy, insofar as the structured confusion they entail seems to recall precisely what tragedy set out to dethrone: the equivocal, demonic multiplicity of a mythical order not (yet?) subordinated to the principle of sovereign identity, be it that of the One God, that of Universal Humanity, or that of the self-determined Community of People.

But if the mourning play recalls the myth, it recalls it from a point that is also beyond tragedy, or rather, from a place that is the result of the worlds that tragedy announces: the world of Christian monotheism, the world of renaissance humanism, the world of secularization begun with the tragic challenge to myth issued by the self and out of which the self emerges. If an ever increasing immanence of such secularization results from the revolt of the self, of which tragedy is a decisive turning-point, then it is the reformation and counter-reformation that set the scene for the return of myth, and in a certain sense, perhaps, for the return of Mystery: this time, however, in the deepest recesses of that immanence. As allegorical plot and intriguing plotter. It is in the allegorical revelation that the most complete immanence is at the same time the most enigmatic alterity that Mystery returns to plague and delight the audience of the mourning play. Neither isolated selves nor members of a "people," the assembled and soon to be dispersed spectators of the wandering court theater emerge as the "original" and distinctly modern heirs of the tragedy that they repeat and at the same time dislocate. The rhythm of that repetition, intermittent in its effort to restore and its failure to achieve, scans what can be called "modernity."

What does the German baroque mourning play mourn? According to our previous interpretation, the answer that imposes itself is: the death of tragedy. The mourning play, which is not a mournful play so much as a play about mourning, and one that gives satisfaction to mourning, plays to the mournful (*GS1*, 298; *Origin*, 119). The question remains, then, what do the mournful mourn and how does the mourning play play up to this mourning, allowing sorrow to find a certain satisfaction?

Where there is mourning, there is the sense of loss. What is it that is sensed as lost by the German baroque? First and most obviously, a certain relation to transcendence, one that would allow space for the hope of salvation, of redemption. "The religious disposition remained," remarks Benjamin of the baroque; "only the religious solution [*Lösung*] was denied it by the century, in order in its stead to demand or to impose a worldly, secular [*weltliche*] solution" (*GS1*, 258; *Origin*, 79). The century of the German baroque has a religious problem without a religious solution. The problem is guilt. But it is not a guilt that is the result of any action. Rather, it is the "adamitic guilt" of the creation. It is "destiny," *Schicksal*, which for Benjamin, far from being pagan in character, is resolutely Christian: it is "the entelechy of events [*Geschehen*] in the field of guilt" (*GS1*, 308; *Origin*, 129). In the baroque generally, and in the German baroque drama in particular, the loss of every eschatological perspective is associated with a "relapse to the condition of mere creation" (*GS1*, 260; *Origin*, 81). This "relapse" (*Rückfall*) is what annuls, or rather rolls back, the temporal dimension by transposing it "into a spatial inauthenticity and simultaneity" (ibid.). Why "inauthentic," a word that recurs frequently in Benjamin's study? Because together with the loss of a transcendent, eschatological perspective, there is also the devaluation of human action, volition, intention. Nothing one can do, in any sort of deliberate or planned manner, can alter the terrible truth that imposes itself on baroque immanence: the enigma of death. With the loss of transcendence, death both confirms the finitude of life, its "secular" aspect, and at the same time poses acutely the question of its significance. This significance is radically different from that epitomized by the death of the tragic hero. This death is rendered eloquent, paradoxically, by the refusal of the tragic hero to speak: in remaining silent, he both assumes his death and transcends it, by allowing it to bear silent witness to the future triumph of God and of Man. This prophetic refusal to speak, which Benjamin presents, paradoxically but consistently, as the speech act par excellence, is no longer available to the baroque: "Whereas the middle ages place the frailty of worldly events and the transience of creation on display as way-stations on the path to salvation, the German mourning play buries itself entirely in the hopelessness of the earthly order. If it knows any solution whatsoever, it lies more in the depth of this predicament [*Verhängnisse*] than in the accomplishment of a divine plan of salvation" (ibid.). In a certain sense, then, what the baroque mourns is not just the death of tragedy, but also the significance of death for tragedy. The baroque mourns the loss of a notion of death that entailed the promise of a New Order, that of self-identical subjectivity: the One God, the universality of Man, determining itself as a People, and gathering itself into the totality of a Community. Not the least of the paradoxes that mark this period, Benjamin remarks, is that "of all the profoundly torn and ambivalent [*zerrissenen und zwiespältigen*] times of European history, the Baroque is the only one that falls in a period of undivided Christian rule" (*GS1*, 258; *Origin*, 79). With the loss of a subjectively transparent relation to transcendence, which initially emerges with Greek tragedy, which finds a continuation in the "rationalism" installed by Socratic irony, and which persists, in different forms to be sure, in medieval Catholicism and renaissance humanism— with this loss of transcendence, what becomes equally problematic is its constitutive other: immanence. Death, instead of defining the contours of the Self and establishing a bridge, by dialectical mediation, between the self-destroying individual (the tragic hero), and the self-determining community that his death prepares—now leads nowhere, and least of all toward any sort of (transcendent) beyond. Death remains, as it were, trapped in the world of immanence: the dead do not depart, or if they do, it is only to return as revenants, as ghosts. Instead of defining identity, death returns as the shadow that splits life into a life that consists largely in passing-away, and a death that, like Kafka's Hunter Gracchus, has nowhere to go but back to the living. Living and dying tend to overlap. Mourning, *Trauer,* responds to this confusion with the theatrical reanimation of a world emptied of meaning. Baroque mourning is not just sorrow and regret; far from it. It originates in the horror *vacui* that death in a thoroughly secularized world cannot fail to inspire. But here, as always, the origin involves a split, a pre- and a post-history: "Those who looked deeper saw themselves set into an existence consisting of the rubble of halfhearted, inauthentic acts. Life itself struck out against this . . . the idea of death fills it with profound horror. Mourning is the state of mind [*Gesinnung*] in which feeling revives the emptied world as masquerade, so as to derive an enigmatic satisfaction from its appearance" (*GS1,* 318; *Origin,* 139). Mourning resurrects the fallen world as theater—but as allegorical theater. Allegory signifies "precisely the non-being of that which it represents [*vorstellt*]" (*GS1,* 406; *Origin,* 233). It can always signify something other than what it ostensibly designates. The line that both separates and relates the allegorical *signans* to the allegorical *signatum* is "death," and this "line of demarcation" is, as we have seen, "jagged." It separates what it delineates not simply from others, but also from itself. And yet, this space of separation, which precisely limits the efficacy of intention in the face of death, also makes way for it within the shadow that the face— *facies hippocratica*—casts. Mourning, Benjamin writes, is determined "through the astonishing tenacity of intention, which among the feelings is found, apart from here, perhaps only in love (and there not playfully)" (ibid.). Since there is no place for this intention to go, and certainly not upward, toward a transcendent heaven, it has no choice but to become profound: "Profundity is characteristic above all of the mournful. On the road to the object—no: on the way in the object itself—this intention progresses as slowly and solemnly as the marches of the rulers" (ibid.). Intention is in no hurry to reach its *goal*, which here would mark its *end*. The result is an inclination to profundity, to grave and solemn manifestations out of which Benjamin derives the "affinity of mourning and ostentation" (*GS1*, 319; *Origin*, 140) so characteristic of baroque theater and of its sensibility.

Trauer, then, is a feeling, a sentiment, but above all it is an *emotion*: a *movement* provoked by a world-structure to which it responds and which in its own way it tries to alter. The trouble, of course, is that in the ruthlessly secularized, spatialized world of the baroque, the "motoric activity" that is mourning, according to Benjamin (*GS1*, 318; *Origin*, 139), has literally no place to go. No place, that is, except to the place itself, as such—that is, as a locality that, while not the whole, remains all there is, *das gesamte Dasein*. It is the peculiar quality of this space—that it is all there is, and that there is nowhere else—that makes the world a stage, and the stage a world.

But it is not quite true to say that this is a world that is going nowhere: the world is going somewhere, which is, literally, nowhere: it is going toward its demise. The secularized world of the baroque is going toward its end, not as a goal that would give it meaning but as a destination separating it from itself, and in this separation, joining it to itself.[24] In the most literal, straightforward sense possible—which is at once the most equivocal, the most "demonically ambiguous," the most mythical—the baroque mourning play is going nowhere. "Natural History," *Naturgeschichte*, expresses this strange movement that—like that "Passante" of Baudelaire who will fascinate Benjamin a decade later—takes place only in passing away. As Natural History "nature" is no longer the realm of birth and of growth, of nativity and naturalness, but of coming-to-pass as passing-away, as *Vergängnis*. It is this throwaway that is picked up by Allegory.

The allegorist picks up where death leaves off with a nature that is historical in passing away, and natural in its endurance and recurrence. Death is at work in allegory, however, not just as decline and decay, but more intimately as that which separates each thing from itself: from its essence, from its significance, and above all, from its name. In the world of allegory, the name, Benjamin writes, has become a mere "label" *(Schild)* with which a vulnerable *physis* seeks to shield and protect itself. The possibility that "each person, every thing, each relation can signify any other, arbitrarily" *(ein beliebig anderes)* pronounces a verdict on the profane world that Benjamin describes as "annihilating, yet just: it is designated as a world in which details no longer matter very much" (*GS1,* 350; *Origin,* 175). But the "name-tags" *(Namensschilder)* of things and persons in the natural-historical world of the baroque also make them easy game for the allegorist and for his melancholic, but also often sadistic and even vampiristic, inclinations. "If the object becomes allegorical when submitted to the glance of melancholy, which drains the life from it, if it remains dead, albeit secured for all eternity, it is all the more at the mercy of the allegorist . . . It acquires the significance that the allegorist gives it. He inserts it and subverts it: this must be understood not psychologically, but ontologically. In his hand the thing becomes something else" (*GS1,* 359; *Origin,* 184).

In short, the natural history, or theater, of German baroque allegory assumes the emptiness of the world in which it finds itself by reenacting it as a violent parody. For the allegorist does not simply empty things of their intrinsic substance and essence; he also invests them with new life and meaning, albeit as part of a masquerade, a spectacle. The world is no longer simply empty of meaning: it is, simultaneously, and hence, inauthentically overflowing with meaning.

In this sense, the argument can be made, and I have been trying to make it, that the emergence of the German baroque allegory, and of the mourning play, mark the return of precisely that mythical ambiguity and ambivalence that the death of tragedy was supposed to overcome, although it is a return that takes place in a resolutely Christian culture. What could be more mythical—in the sense of that demonic equivocation—than the baroque world that emerges in Germany as a result of and in reaction to the Protestant Reformation? Whether it be in the return of pagan gods, such as Saturn, god of melancholy (and also of extremes), or the resurgence of astrology, or finally in the crucial figure of the "plotter" (the intriguer), the "court official, whose power, knowledge and will is raised to [the level of] the demonic" (*GS1,* 276; *Origin,* 97–98)—baroque allegory and the mourning that it stages reinstate mythical ambiguity in all of its originating power: that is, as restoration and incompletion. The originality of this origin, however, is the extent to which it both enacts and resists the totalization that Benjamin ascribes to the historical articulation *(Auseinandersetzung)* of the idea. It enacts it in its fascination with world domination, in the uncontested sway of Christianity in Europe. It resists it in its inability to exercise that domination other than as self-destruction, a self-destruction that calls into question the very process of construction itself: of configuration, and constellation. Or rather, it confuses them. Thus if Benjamin can assert that the "mourning play knows no heroes" in contrast to tragedy, "but only constellations" (*GS1,* 310–311; *Origin,* 132), he will also go on to insist that baroque allegory resists precisely such constellations and that this in turn allows the world of things to elude the control of the melancholy allegorist.[25] Indeed, the allegorist's "absolute knowledge" is ultimately a knowledge of nothing, for it has no *fundamentum in re,* no foundation, since things, without ever ceasing to "lie at his feet as dust," nevertheless "in the simplicity of their being elude him, as enigmatic allegorical pointers" (*GS1,* 403; *Origin,* 229). Allegory has the Midas touch: whatever comes into contact with its melancholy hand is "transformed into something significant. Transformations of all kinds were its element, and its scheme was allegory" (ibid.). But those transformations also exclude a universal equivalent—except for death and destruction. The death-bound natural history of the baroque knows no gold standard: all it knows is the power to effect transformations, if not to resist them.

Transformations of all kinds: it is precisely this that sets the scene for the concluding scene of Benjamin's story. Schematically, it can be retold as follows: With the elimination of deliberate action as a means for helping a fallen, guilty world toward grace, knowledge becomes the most powerful mode of being available to the baroque. But the knowledge of allegory is ultimately suspended over a "precipice of bottomless profundity [*Abgrund des bodenlosen Tiefsinns*]" (*GS1,* 404; *Origin,* 231), since all that it knows could just as well be different. And indeed, what it knows is ultimately "the non-being of what it represents." "Transformation"—in German, *Verwandlung* (the title of Kafka's story, translated into English as "Metamorphosis")—thus designates this move from one particular form of non-being to another. Again, we see how and why the two exemplary figures of subjectivity in the German baroque are the melancholy allegorist and the plotter. The plotter, or intriguer, like the allegorist, is the "master of meanings" (*GS1*, 384; *Origin*, 210) and past master of intrigue, of transformation. But the transformations in which the baroque in its specifically German form is engaged are distinguished precisely by their resistance to being emplotted, or rather "transfigured" into a totalizing tale:

> But the transfigured apotheosis, as it is familiar from Calderon, can not be set up with the banal reserves [*Fundus*] of the theater . . . It develops compellingly only out of a meaningful constellation of the whole, which it only emphasizes all the more, albeit less enduringly. The deficient development of the plot, which does not even remotely approach that of the Spaniard, constitutes the insufficiency of the German mourning play. Only the plot would have been capable of conducting the organization of the scenes to that allegorical totality with which, in the image of the apotheosis, something of a radically different order from the images of the development emerges and gives mourning its cue both for its entry and its exit. The powerful design of this form must be thought out to its end. (*GS1*, 408–409; *Origin*, 235)

What can it mean, in the context of what Benjamin has been describing for some two hundred and fifty pages, to end by asserting—or rather, demanding—that "the powerful design [*der gewaltige Entwurf*] of this form must be thought out to the end, *ist zu Ende zu denken*: what kind of an "end" can there be for this "powerful design" that never entirely succeeds in forming a form? What Benjamin has just done, and which this injunction presumably both resumes and interprets, is precisely to intervene as a deus ex machina, which is to say, in the language of the baroque, as both a plotter and an allegorist. He has described the "transfigured apotheosis" of Calderon, or rather brought it to bear on the subject of allegory itself. This subjectivity, which has to do with "the nonbeing of what it represents," is itself ultimately null and void. "Subjectivity, which plunges like an angel into the depths, is overtaken by allegories and held fast in heaven, in God through 'ponderacion misteriosa'" (ibid.). Except—except that this is precisely what cannot be and is not accomplished by the German baroque mourning play. It cannot be accomplished by it because of a deficiency in the intrigue, in the plot, which "alone would have the capacity to organize the scenes into the allegorical totality" that would finally delimit—usher in and escort away—mourning. What Benjamin gives us both confirms and repeats this lack: as at the end of the "Critique of Violence," he speaks in the name of that divine intervention that alone could delimit allegory, but he does it in precisely the allegorical manner that he has spent pages describing: by treating allegory as the "plunge" of subjectivity, he is able to employ its non-being dialectically, making it the generating force of a new transcendence. But what he gives us is just another typical image of allegory at work: the personification of the empty world as the work of the allegorist, feigning to forget that this person is a persona and that the face that it hides is above all the *facies hippocratica* of natural history as the bearer of corpses. "The powerful design of this form must be thought through to the end; only under this condition can the idea of the German mourning play be treated [*gehandelt werden*]" (*GS1*, 409; *Origin*, 235). Benjamin lays a hand here on the "idea of the German mourning play," with the same gesture that the allegorist lays a hand on the things he handles. In these hands, the "idea" becomes a "form," in which "the image of the beautiful" is "held fast" on the final day. The vertiginous maelstrom of the *Origin of the German Mourning Play* can be arrested only by this double gesture of holding up and holding fast, of *Festhalten*, transitive and intransitive: holding the falling and fallen subject of allegory, in God, and of the "image of the beautiful" by its form. This allegorical gesture par excellence is what makes Benjamin's *ponderacion misteriosa* no less "demonically equivocal" than the fallen subjectivity whose salvation it promises. Benjamin's "end" is itself "overtaken" *(eingeholt)* and held fast by an allegory that knows no end but only endings, significant, but without sense.[26]

CHAPTER ELEVEN

Awakening

The Meaning of Immediacy

In a programmatic text written in 1916, "On the Program of the Coming Philosophy," Walter Benjamin sketches the outlines of an intellectual project that will inform his writing until its premature end. In this early essay, Benjamin seeks to rethink the relationship between "a certitude of knowledge that is lasting" and "the dignity of an experience that passes."[1] The continuing importance of this relationship he explains as follows: "The philosophical interest in universals always strives to attain both the timeless validity of knowledge and the certitude of temporal experience. What philosophers thereby are unaware of is that such experience, in its entire structure, is *singularly temporally limited* [singuläre zeitlich beschränkte]" (*GS2*, 158; *SW1*, 100–101). The question of how experience would have to be construed in order to take this "singularly temporal" limitation into account is one that never ceased to agitate Benjamin. But the various responses it provoked also transformed the question itself. In his early discussion of this problem, five points deserve to be retained, since they indicate the direction his future work was to take. First, the singular temporality to which he refers cannot be conceived strictly in a Kantian perspective, which for him was based on the "sublimated idea [representation: *Vorstellung*] of an individual, mind-body ego that receives sensations by means of the senses and forms its representations on this basis" (*GS2*, 161; *SW1*, 103). Temporal singularity cannot therefore be conceived in terms of the individual. Second, from this results the necessity of reconstruing the relationship between experience and knowledge otherwise than has previously been done, which is to say, "independent of the subject-object terminology" (*GS2*, 167; *SW1*, 103). Benjamin thus seeks to elaborate an alternative not only to the dominant subjectivism but also to the subject-object dualism as such. How might such an alternative be construed? This question brings us to the third point: "The large-scale revamping and correction of the one-sidedly mathematically and mechanistically oriented concept of knowledge can only be attained by relating cognition to language . . . A concept of knowledge that is developed out of a reflection upon its linguistic nature will lead to a corresponding concept of experience" (*GS2*, 168; *SW1*, 107–108).

This turn toward language as a medium of reflection on philosophical knowledge—which repeats the move made in the eighteenth century by Johann Hamann in his critique of Kant—is conceived of by Benjamin precisely as a way of averting formalism. Language is construed as the medium not just of knowledge, but also of an experience that takes into account its own singularity and temporality. In its resistance to thorough-going formalization, language emerges as the medium through which Benjamin's fourth consideration will be articulated, one that once again is developed in critical continuation of Kant: "The formalistic dialectic of post-Kantian systems, however, is not based upon the definition of the thesis as categorical relation, the antithesis as hypothetical relation, and of the synthesis as disjunctive relation. Nevertheless, in addition to the concept of synthesis, that of a certain non-synthesis of two concepts in another is bound to take on great systematic significance, since in addition to synthesis there is the possibility of another kind of relationship between thesis and antithesis" (*GS2*, 166; *SW1*, 106). The Kantian notion of a "disjunctive synthesis" thus becomes a point of departure for Benjamin, who here emphasizes the possibility and necessity of conceiving a different, non-synthetic relationship between concepts, which alone will be capable of relating the "temporal singularity" of experience to the "timeless certitude" of the concept.

All of these four points are tentatively combined by Benjamin in an

appendix to his essay, in which he attempts to draw out the consequences of the previous argument in terms of the relationship of philosophy to religion. This appendix, which Benjamin himself describes as a
"sketchy allusion," is too complex to be succinctly summarized. Perhaps the following passage, however, can help to indicate the direction
that Benjamin envisaged the argument taking: "It must be said that
philosophy overall in its questioning never stumbles upon the unity of
being-there [*Daseinseinheit*], but rather only upon new unities of lawful tendencies [*neue Einheiten von Gesetzlichkeiten*] of which "being
there" [*Dasein*] is the integrating factor [*Integral*]" (*GS2*, 170; *SW1*,
108). This concept of "Dasein"—"existence" or more literally, "being-
there"—exemplifies Benjamin's approach to what a "non-synthetic"
relation of concepts might involve. The notion of "existence" or "being-there" implies a "unity of experience" that can in no way be understood as the sum of experiences, to which the concept of knowledge as
teaching or instruction [*Lehre*] in its continuous unfolding *immediately*
relates: . . ." This in turn involves "religion, which however is given to
philosophy at first only as *instruction* . . . From a *purely* metaphysical
viewpoint the root-concept of experience turns into its totality in an
entirely different way from that of its individual specifications, the sciences: namely immediately, whereby the meaning of such immediacy in
respect to that mediacy remains to be determined" (*GS2*, 170; *SW1*,
109). This last remark announces the task that will occupy Benjamin's
subsequent writing as a whole: the attempt to recover, uncover, and
articulate the way being-there is immediately linked to experience
through transforming the notion of knowledge into that of instruction,
which acknowledges its temporal character in its "continuous unfolding." The "continuous unfolding" of knowledge as *Lehre,* instruction
and teaching, thus implicates writing and language in general in the
process that sustains the immediate experience of being-there.

Benjamin will never fully abandon this notion of written *Lehre* as the
medium in which being-there is experienced immediately in its entirety.
What he will question is the "continuity" of this unfolding, and hence
of the writing that is its materialization.

The Immediacy of Meaning

"Might awakening be the synthesis resulting from the thesis of dream-
consciousness and the antithesis of the consciousness of being-awake?

In this case, the moment of awakening would be identical with the 'now of knowability,' in which things put on their true—surrealist—face. Thus, what is important in Proust is the engagement [*Einsatz*] of life in its entirety at those supremely dialectical breaking points [*Bruchstelle des Lebens*], awakening. Proust begins with a depiction of the space of someone waking up [*des Erwachenden*]" (*GS5*, 579; *AP*, 463–464). This passage, from Convolute N of the "Paris Passages" (N 3a,3), introduces what is arguably the most important concept of Benjamin's theoretical effort in this complex of texts. "Awakening"—*Erwachen*—is his final attempt to meet the challenge he had outlined in the early programmatic essay: articulating the "non-synthesis" between concepts that would bring together "thesis and antithesis" in a relation that would not be subsumptive or reductive of their constitutive differences. This means, in turn, that what Benjamin refers to as the "supremely dialectical breaking-points of life" are not to be understood from a Hegelian standpoint, which is always one that privileges, however subtly, the totalizing unity of the synthesis over the particular differences of its component parts. A "breaking point"—or more precisely, as Benjamin writes in German, a *Bruchstelle,* is to be distinguished from the power of the negative that informs the Hegelian dialectic, precisely insofar as it is *and remains* a "place," which is to say, a spatial-temporal determination that is not *"aufgehoben"*: negated and absorbed by the movement of the concept. As with the baroque allegory studied and construed by Benjamin, the tendency of such *Bruchstellen,* breaking points or places, is to bring to a halt, at least temporarily, the progress of time by fixing it into, and as, a place (however "broken"). The "break" in the place—the break as a place—is what results when the destructive course of time is temporarily brought to a halt.

Such breaks, however, are for Benjamin not primarily negative or privative in character. They constitute privileged moments of what, in the following note, he describes as a "constellation of awakening": "Demarcation of the tendency of this work against Aragon: Whereas Aragon remains stuck in the realm of dreams, the task here is to discover the constellation of awakening . . . Whereas there remains in Aragon an impressionist element—'mythology'—. . . here the effort is to dissolve 'mythology' into the space of history. That, however, can of course only happen through the awakening of an as yet unconscious knowledge of what has been [*des Gewesenen*]" (*GS5*, 571–572; *AP*,

458). On the one hand, Benjamin insists on the difference that separates his notion of awakening from that associated with Aragon and the Surrealists, who remain too caught up in the "dream" and not sufficiently in "history." On the other hand, however, such a separation can also become the object of his criticism, as in the following note directed against Carl Jung: "[Jung] wants to keep awakening too far apart from the dream" (N 18,4). What Benjamin seems to be arguing for, therefore, involves a relationship of awakening to the dream in which separation itself becomes the constitutive factor: awakening relates to the dream precisely in being separated from it. It is this *relating through separation* or as separation that characterizes what he calls the "constellation." This could indicate how a certain "non-synthesis" could nevertheless relate concepts to one another while preserving their differences and without subordinating them to a totalizing continuity or unity.

Out of such a non-synthetic "constellation" results not knowledge, but rather what Benjamin, very precisely, calls "knowability": *Erkennbarkeit*. Not "knowability" as an abstract, general principle, but knowability as a temporal possibility that always exists *now*: the "now of knowability," *Jetzt der Erkennbarkeit*. This "now of knowability" is not however simply *here* and now: since it is always situated in a place that can never be fully actualized, it is always "there," *da* (as in "Da-sein," being-*there*), rather than simply "here," in the place defined by the presence or proximity of a subject to itself: its self-consciousness. The "now of knowability" can never be entirely reduced to the "here" of self-consciousness.

Such a now is an *Augenblick*, the *glance* of an *eye* whose sight is always split between what it is and what it sees. In such an instant, what becomes possible is not simply knowledge as reality, but knowability as ever-present possibility, a virtuality that has more in common with the Kierkegaardian or Nietzschean instant *(Augenblick)* than with the Hegelian "moment" as the self-negating component of a dialectical totalization.

Such "knowability" is not, for Benjamin at least, simply a preface to its realization as full-fledged knowledge. It has its own dignity, precisely as potentiality, and above all, it has its distinctive structure. It is this structure alone—which is that of *awakening* as distinguished both from consciousness and from unconsciousness—that explains how and why knowability, whose manifestation is inseparable from its vanishing, cannot be reduced to the positive knowledge it both makes possible and relativizes.

Awakening must therefore be investigated on its own terms, as a distinctive experience, and not simply as a transition from the dream to being-awake, from unconsciousness to self-consciousness. Similarly— but the one is perhaps the paradigm for the other—"passages" in Benjamin's writing are never just transitions, ways leading from one point to another. Given this caveat, however, it is not easy to determine just how such a distinctive experience is to be described. For normally we identify things either as being self-contained or as being means, as being either independent or dependent. This kind of alternative or opposition, however, is not adequate to describe the singular movement of "awakening," which involves transformation or alteration and yet is not simply a movement toward a goal. How such a transformation might be conceived I want to suggest, not by reading Benjamin directly, but by going to the text he repeatedly cites—but rarely interprets—as being exemplary of "awakening."

"Just as Proust begins his life-story with awakening, so every historical presentation should begin with awakening, indeed, should be concerned with nothing else. Thus, this one is concerned with awakening from the nineteenth century" (N 4,3). The experience of awakening— awakening *as* experience—thus stands at the beginning "of every historical presentation," whether of the life-history of a singular being or that of an epoch. But that which stands at the outset is not a limited event that is experienced once and for all and then left behind. Otherwise, how could Benjamin assert that each historical presentation should not only "begin" with such an "awakening" but in fact deal with nothing else? Awakening is thus an origin in the double sense that Benjamin, in the "Epistemo-critical Preface" to the *Origin of the German Mourning Play,* gave to the term: a movement striving for "restoration and reestablishment on the one hand, and precisely therein incomplete and unfinished on the other . . . The orientation for a philosophical consideration [of it] are prescribed by the dialectic that accompanies the origin. Out of it emerges the fact that uniqueness [*Einmaligkeit*] and repetition condition one another" (GS1, 226).[2]

In its restorative, repetitive, never-fulfilled movement the "origin" is, Benjamin concludes, a thoroughly "historical" phenomenon. But the motor of that history is not the fulfillment of the individual, but rather the *emergence of the singular* through iterations that are *transformative* rather than simply recursive. The singular emerges through iteration as that which precisely is not the same, which does not "fit in." Singularity, far from being self-contained, is thus a function of repetition and therein far removed from individuality, in the sense of indivisibility.

Awakening involves this kind of singularity. Benjamin associates it repetitively—once again Proust is no doubt his model—with childhood, but with a childhood that, as in the Freudian perspective, does not simply vanish into the past but determines the future. Benjamin's reasoning, however, is not strictly psychoanalytical, at least not explicitly. In the early drafts of the "Passages" there are two places that suggest how he construes the singular staying-power of awakening, which, although bound to an instant, nevertheless exercises lasting temporal effects:

> Awakening is the exemplary case of remembering. Through it we succeed in remembering what is closest to us (closest to the Ego). It entails what Proust means when he writes of the experimental relocation of furniture, what Bloch means when he writes of the obscurity of the lived instant.(h° 3; (*GS5,* 1058; *AP,* 883)

> Awakening is namely the dialectical, Copernican turn of commemoration. It is the preeminently and thoroughly composed revolution that turns the world of the dreamer into the world of those who are awake. (h° 4; ibid.)

Awakening is "thoroughly composed," operates "with cunning" (ibid.), and perhaps somewhat surprisingly, allows us—our "I" or Ego—to remember what is closest to us, not what is furthest away. To acquire an idea of what is "closest" to us—so close, indeed, that it becomes harder to "see" than what is further away—we need only reread the pages from the opening of *Combray.* "Proust begins," Benjamin writes, "with a description (*Darstellung:* presentation, staging) of the space of someone waking up *(Raum des Erwachenden)."* We should note that Benjamin emphasizes on the one hand the "space," and on the other, the situation of *"des Erwachenden,"* the person "waking up." Two of the essential traits of awakening are thereby highlighted: first, its spatial dimension, and second, its distinctive temporality. As we will see, the one conditions the other. Awakening is essentially spatial because of its distinctive temporality. Before we elucidate this point, we should note that the emphasis on spatiality already foregrounds what Benjamin describes as the "physiological" (h° 4) dimension of awakening instead of approaching it as primarily a mental event. Awakening is thus considered in relationship to the body rather than to consciousness. Or rather, consciousness will be shown as determined by the body, rather than the other way around. And because the process is tied to the body, it is also essentially spatial in nature. Hence the exemplary significance that Proust, and Benjamin, attach to the "experimental" rearrangement of furniture, which serve as spatial orientation markers.

But this spatiality of awakening, tied to the body, is in turn determined by its distinctive temporal mode, which is articulated in the use of the gerund to determine the subject of the action: *des Erwachenden*, "the awakening (person)." Why the gerund? Because the gerund, and the present participle from which it is derived (as its nominal form), entail a form of "presence" that involves both participation and partiality. Like Benjamin's origin, the present participle is never complete, always returning, but forever unfinished. And it is "present" only with respect to the instance of its enunciation: the "subject" that awakens is "present" only with respect to the process of "awakening." It is the intrinsically interminable sequence of discontinuous repetitions entailed in the present participle that implies and requires *localization* in order to "take place." In this sense, the (person) awakening never wakes up in general, but always in and with respect to a determinate place. The locality in turn is never closed upon itself or self-contained, but opened to further relationships by the iterations that take place "in" it. To be sure, such iterations are never infinite, they will always *stop*, but that stopping will never amount to a conclusion or a closure. Rather, it will be more like an interruption or a suspension. A cut.

All of this is described with infinite complexity at the beginning of *Combray*, even if the present participle is not to be found in that description, but rather the imperfect. *Du côté de chez Swann* begins with the reflection of the narrator on past moments of awakening, which in turn are not to be separated from moments of falling asleep: "For a long time, I went to bed early. Sometimes, my candle scarcely out, my eyes would close so quickly that I did not have time to say to myself: 'I'm falling asleep.' And, half an hour later, the thought that it was time to try to sleep would wake me."[3] Whether falling asleep or waking up, the common denominator lies in the way in which consciousness lags behind its "own" activity—or perhaps more precisely, how it is overtaken by that activity. One never quite does what one (subsequently) thinks one is doing. But even more important perhaps is the fact that this being out-of-sync with one's "own" activity is, already in Proust, no longer articulated within the parameters of the subject-object discourse that Benjamin in his early writings diagnosed as inadequate. Rather, what emerges is precisely what the subject-object duality seeks to subordinate: the singularity of spatial-temporal positioning, significantly depicted here as the *disarticulation* of bodily members. It is the experience of the dislocated arm, shoulder, or other bodily joint that distinguishes awakening from other experiences:

> A sleeping man holds in a circle around him the sequence of the hours, the order of the years and worlds. He consults them instinctively as he wakes and reads in them in a second the point on earth that he occupies, the time that has elapsed up to his waking; but their ranks can be mixed up, broken. If towards morning, after a bout of insomnia, sleep overcomes him as he is reading, in a position too different from the one in which he usually sleeps, his raised arm alone is enough to stop the sun and make it retreat, and, in the first minute of his waking, he will no longer know what time it is, he will think he has only just gone to bed. If he dozes off in a position still more displaced and divergent, for instance after dinner sitting in an armchair, then the confusion among the disordered worlds will be complete, the magic armchair will send him traveling at top speed through time and space, and, at the moment of opening his eyelids, he will believe he went to bed several months earlier in another country.[4]

In contrast to the usual opposition between sleeping and waking, here it is their affinity that is emphasized. In both conditions, time is divided into hours, years, and moons, which form a circle around the sleeper. But this well-formed circle can at times break apart and when this happens, the *position* of the sleeper—that "point on earth that he occupies" ("*point de la terre qu'il occupe*")—is no longer certain or assured. This is what happens in those breaks or turns of time, for instance, when after a sleepless night one finally dozes off, but "in a posture too different from that in which he usually sleeps" ("*dans une posture trop différente de celle où il dort habituellement*").

Position, "posture [*posture*]"—this defines the situation in which awakening takes place—dislocation as the power that establishes relationships in and through separation: separation from the habitual positions of the body and its members, for instance. Such dislocations *can* be human, but do not have to be: they take place at that border where the body "remembers" that it is not necessarily human. For instance, the narrator remembers "the organic creaking of the woodwork [*les craquements organiques des boiseries*]" while falling asleep. Other times he recalls a woman being born "from a false position of my thigh."[5] Pleasure itself goes together with bodily disarticulation: "My body twisted by the weight of her stature [*mon corps courbaturé par le poids de sa taille*]."[6] Important is the fact that if he collapses into a position even more displaced and divergent, for example after dinner in an armchair, then the upheaval will be complete in worlds out of orbit.[7]

The "setting" here—and what we have are not simply recollections, but scenes, with particular attention paid to their setting—seems hardly insignificant. "After dinner in an armchair"—what could be more comforting and more comfortable? But any belief in the durability of such a situation is immediately unsettled by an "upheaval" that "completes" its overturning in a "world out of orbit"—a world gone wild.

Just such a belief—Marcel calls it explicitly a *"croyance"*—shatters both in waking-up and falling-asleep.[8] It shatters insofar as the position of the body can, in such transitional experiences, no longer be taken for granted. In being dislocated, wrenched out of joint, the body remembers that it is not simply the container of an autonomous subject but independent in its own right. And yet that independence is very different from the self-contained sovereignty to which the subject aspires. For it is constituted out of a situatedness that is both spatial and relational, and as such is precisely never self-contained, never "organic." "Spatiality" here designates precisely what Hegel, interpreting the notion of "extension," described as *"Auseinandersein"*: "being beside—or outside of—oneself."[9] Space as extension strives to move away from itself and in this striving it becomes time, which in turn becomes the measure of movement, in the sense of change-of-place, that is, "locomotion." But there are other kinds of movement, "emotions" for instance, but also dislocations, movements that go nowhere and yet do not stay in the same place. The following passage from Proust's text, which describes the unexpected emergence of a mirror and its effects, demonstrates just such a movement, going nowhere and yet not standing still:

"I had been mentally poisoned by the unfamiliar odour of the vetiver, convinced of the hostility of the violet curtains and the insolent indifference of the clock chattering loudly as though I were not there; where a strange and pitiless quadrangular cheval-glass, barring obliquely one of the corners of the room, carved from deep inside the soft fullness of my usual field of vision a site for itself which I had not expected; where my mind, struggling for hours to dislodge itself, to stretch upwards so as to take the exact shape of the room."[10] Again and again Marcel emphasizes how it is only through the position of his body that he can orient himself while awakening. He thereby demonstrates to what degree the perception of the self depends on the perception of a relation to others via the perception of one's body, which however includes sensations that are not directly defined as visual representations. Perception of one's body entails necessarily, explicitly or implicitly—more explicit than implicit in the process of awakening—awareness of its relation to what it is not: its setting, its surroundings, in space but also in time. And what surrounds in time is, even more obviously than in space, never simply present or presentable, never exhaustible, and hence never simply in conformity with one's conscious expectations. In this disruption (bouleversement) of expectations, memory, forgetting, and fantasy, but perhaps also anticipation (memory projected into the future) all intermingle and are difficult to distinguish, clearly and distinctly, from one another.

In the passage just cited such intermingling is more concretely depicted: namely, as the unexpected emergence of that "emplacement," that emplacement or position, almost in a military sense, which in a certain way articulates something like the dislocation of the locality, of place itself. This unexpected emplacement, which brutally traverses the familiar field of vision, "barrant obliquement un des angles de la pièce," precisely by concealing that corner, reveals the space itself to be a pièce, a "room" but also a play, staged in a theater whose borders are never definitively set.

It is to this singular movement of awakening that Marcel responds through his attempt to dislocate his thoughts: "Ma pensée, s'efforçant pendant des heures de se disloquer" ("my thought, struggling for hours to dislocate itself"), in order to take on the dimensions of the room ("s'étirer en hauteur pour prendre exactement la forme de la chamber"). But the movement of dislocation—here: of stretching to fit the

room—which not merely accompanies awakening but constitutes it—
this movement does not stop at "forms," even at the form of form itself: which is to say, the form of a room as *container*. For this room
does not merely contain. It is a stage for a play that is a fragment rather
than a complete work: a stage where something comes to pass, a pas-
sage-way, perhaps, but one that is not going anywhere. It is on such a
stage, or rather, *as such a stage,* that the Paris Passages take (their)
place. Retracing their movement, in a manner that combines synthesis
with non-synthesis without subordinating either to the other, is perhaps
what could be called *reading.*

CHAPTER TWELVE

Taking Exception to Decision

Walter Benjamin and Carl Schmitt

> Epigrammatically [inscribed] on an engraving that depicts a
> stage, showing on the left a jester and on the right a prince, the
> following: When the stage is left empty, there's no difference
> any longer between a fool and a king (*Wann die Bühne nu wird
> leer / Gilt kein Narr und König mehr*).
>
> —Walter Benjamin

In December 1930, Walter Benjamin sends the following letter to Carl
Schmitt:

> Distinguished Herr Professor,
>
> You will be receiving in a few days from the publisher my book, *Origin
> of the German Mourning Play*. With these lines I would like not simply to
> announce its arrival, but also express my joy at being able to send it to
> you, at the suggestion of Mr. Albert Salomon. You will quickly see how
> much the book owes you in its presentation of the seventeenth-century
> doctrine of sovereignty. Perhaps I may go even further and say that in
> your later works as well, above all in "Dictatorship," your mode of re-
> search in the realm of political philosophy has confirmed my own mode
> of research in matters concerning the philosophy of art. If in reading my
> book this feeling seems comprehensible to you, the purpose of my sending
> it will have been fulfilled.
>
> With the expression of particular esteem,
> Your very devoted
> Walter Benjamin[1]

This letter is not to be found in the first two-volume edition of
Benjamin's *Correspondence,* published in 1966.[2] The esteem that
Benjamin expressed for the eminent political thinker who, just a few
years later, was to publish texts such as "The Führer Protects the Law
[*Der Fuhrer schützt das Recht*]" (1934) and "German Jurisprudence

Battles the Jewish Spirit [*Die deutsche Rechtswissenschaft im Kampf gegen den jüdischen Geist*]" (1936) hardly fits the picture that Benjamin's initial editors and former friends, Gershom Scholem and Theodor Adorno, wished to present to a broad audience. As understandable as their decision to exclude this letter may have been at the time, it nonetheless reflects a malaise related to the way in which Benjamin tends to resist any attempt at univocal classification or straightforward evaluation, political or otherwise. It is as though the fact that he had been able to admire and draw inspiration from the work of a prominent Catholic conservative who was later to become a conspicuous member of the Nazi party could only muddy and compromise the significance of an oeuvre that both Adorno and Scholem, whatever their other differences might be, agreed was of exemplary significance. It is as though the acknowledgment of a debt amounted to a moral contamination of Benjamin by Schmitt.

Such a malaise is palpable in the remark of Rolf Tiedemann, who is to be credited with publishing the letter to Schmitt in the critical apparatus he assembled for the German edition of Benjamin's *Collected Writings* that he edited. The letter, he remarks, is *denkwürdig,* although he does not say just what sort of thoughts it might be worthy of (*GS1,* 887). One response that is often encountered in this context traces Benjamin's interest in Schmitt back to the critique of liberal, parliamentary democracy shared by both. But this explanation, as evident and as accurate as it may be, hardly suffices to account either for the debt mentioned by Benjamin in his letter, or for the manner in which it manifests itself in his book. Rather, the work of Schmitt figures in Benjamin's study of German baroque theater for at least two related but very distinct reasons. First of all, the mourning play *(Trauerspiel)* and above all the dynamics of its *origin,* both imply a certain relationship to history and to politics. Second, and more specifically, Benjamin encounters the question of sovereignty not simply as a *theme* of German baroque theater, but as a methodological and theoretical *problem:* as we shall see, according to Benjamin every attempt to interpret the German baroque risks succumbing to a certain lack of sovereignty.

The German baroque mourning play has as its true object and substance historical life as represented by its age (*GS1,* 242–243; *Origin,* 62). But the relationship between *Trauerspiel* and history is far from a one-way street: if German baroque theater is concerned primarily with history, this history is in turn construed as a kind of *Trauerspiel*. This is why Benjamin's formulation, here as elsewhere, must be read as rigorously as possible: the true object of baroque drama is not just historical life as such, but rather historical life *as imagined by its age ("das geschichtliche Leben wie es jene Epoche sich darstellte")* (*GS1*, 262; *Origin*, 62). The primary representation and representative of history, however, in the baroque age is the sovereign: "The sovereign is the representative of history. He holds the course of history in his hand like a scepter [Der Souverän repräsentiert die Geschichte. Er hält das historische Geschehen in der Hand wie ein Szepter]" (*GS1*, 245; *Origin*, 65).

Benjamin's insistence on the historical subject matter of the *Trauerspiel* thus leads him necessarily to the question of political sovereignty and its relation to history. But it is not merely the thematic aspect of his subject that moves Benjamin to examine the question of sovereignty, and hence to consult the theories of Schmitt. In his letter, Benjamin writes that he has found in Schmitt's works a confirmation of his own styles of research, *meine[n] eigenen Forschungsweisen*. Just what Benjamin might be referring to becomes clearer if we turn to the beginning of the first chapter of his book, dealing with *Trauerspiel* and tragedy. Benjamin begins his study proper by announcing that his interpretation of the German baroque mourning play will be directed toward the *extreme (die notwendige Richtung aufs Extreme)*, and not the average or shared traits of the plays he is investigating (*GS1*, 238; *Origin*, 57).

In thus foregrounding the constitutive importance of a concern with extremes in pursuing his philosophical investigation, Benjamin places himself squarely in a tradition that goes back at least to Kierkegaard's essay on *Repetition*. But the text in which this mode of thinking probably impressed itself most profoundly on Benjamin was Schmitt's *Politische Theologie*, the first chapter of which concludes by insisting on the significance of the extreme case:

> Precisely a philosophy of concrete life must not draw back before the exception and before the extreme case, but rather must harbor the greatest interest in them. For it the exception can be more important than the rule, not from any sort of Romantic irony for the paradoxical, but with the entire seriousness of an insight that reaches deeper than the clear generaliza-

tions of that which repeats itself as an average. The exception is more interesting than the normal case. The normal proves nothing, the exception proves everything; it confirms not only the rule: the rule lives only from the exception.[3]

In the "Epistemo-critical Preface" to the *Trauerspiel* book, where Benjamin seeks to elaborate the premises and implications of his reading of German baroque theater as an idea, it is precisely to the extreme that he appeals in order to indicate just how the idea distinguishes itself from the subsumptive generality of the concept: "As the shaping of the complex in which the singularly extreme stands with its like, the idea is circumscribed. Therefore it is false to understand the most general indications of language as concepts, instead of recognizing them to be ideas. To want to depict the universal as an average is perverse. The universal is the idea. The more precisely the empirical is investigated as an extreme, the more profoundly it will be penetrated. The concept takes its point of departure in the extreme" (*GS1*, 215; *Origin*, 35).[4] As Schmitt explicitly states, what is characteristic of the *Einmalig-Extreme* is that it is a borderline notion: it is situated at the extremity of what is familiar, identically repeatable, classifiable; it is the point where the generally familiar is on the verge of changing into something else, the point at which it encounters the other, the exterior, the alien. To think of the idea as a configuration of singular extremes *(Einmalig-Extreme)* is to construe its being as a function of that which it is not.

Such passages indicate how Benjamin's mode of investigation, his *Forschungsweise,* is indebted to that of Schmitt: both share a certain *methodological extremism* for which the formation of a concept is paradoxically but necessarily dependent on a contact or an encounter with a singularity that exceeds or eludes the concept. This singular encounter takes place in and as the extreme and it is the readiness to engage in this encounter, according to Benjamin, that distinguishes philosophical history from art history, literary history, or any other form of history that presupposes the givenness of a general concept under which the phenomena it addresses are to be subsumed: "Philosophical History as the science of origin is the form that allows the configuration of the idea to emerge out of remote extremes and ostensible excesses as a totality marked by the possibility of the meaningful juxtaposition of such oppositions. The exposition of an idea can under no circum-

stances be considered successful as long as virtually the circle of its potential extremes has not been fully traversed. Such traversing remains
virtual" (*GS1,* 227; *Origin,* 47).[5] The circle of extremes can be traversed only virtually not simply because the extremes themselves are
never fully present or realized as such. Rather, it is organized, elliptically as it were, around a double center: around a *Vor- und a
Nachgeschichte.* This pre- and post-history of the singular idea constitutes the "abbreviated and darkened figure of the rest of the world
of ideas" ("verkürzte und verdunkelte Figur der übrigen Ideenwelt";
ibid.), a figure that is to be deciphered, read: *abzulesen.* And it is here,
precisely, that Benjamin finds himself faced with a problem that seems
to bear a particular relation to the German baroque and its interpretation: "Again and again in the improvised attempts to present the meaning of this epoch, one encounters that characteristic dizziness provoked
by the view of its spirituality circling in contradictions . . . Only an
observation come from afar, refusing the temptation to take in the
whole, at least at first, can, in an as it were ascetic schooling, lead the
spirit to the kind of stability that allows it to remain in control of itself
while viewing the panoramic sight" (*GS1,* 237; *Origin,* 56).[6] In the baroque, the circle of potential extremes to be traversed in the staging of
an idea has become an encirclement of contradictions and antitheses
from which there seems no escape, but only the giddiness, the vertigo
that its spectacle elicits.

What sorts of contradictions and antitheses encircle the German baroque? Not the least of these appears to be a singular discrepancy
between its artistic intentions and the aesthetic means at its disposal.
And it is here that Benjamin encounters the problem of sovereignty in
a guise that seems to be peculiar to the German theater of the time:
"The German drama of the counter-reformation never attained that
flexible kind of form that offers itself to every virtuoso grip, such as
that Calderon gave to Spanish drama. It was formed in a highly violent
effort and this, all by itself, would indicate that its form did not bear the
imprint of any sovereign gesture. Nevertheless, the center of gravity of
the Baroque mourning play lies there . . . This insight is a precondition
of investigation" (*GS1,* 229–230; *Origin,* 49).[7] What is modern, topi-
cal, *aktuell* about the baroque in general and about the German baroque in particular is thus tied on the one hand to a certain lack of sovereignty, to a certain incapacity to produce consummate artistic forms,

and on the other, to an effort of the will that strives to compensate for this lack but threatens instead to overwhelm all those who seek to interpret it: "Confronted with a literature that sought, as it were, to silence the existing world and the world to come through the munificence of its technique, the uniform plenitude of its productions and the violence of its value-judgments, the necessity of the sovereign attitude, as it is imposed by the idea of a form, must be emphasized. The danger of plunging from the summits of knowledge to the enormous depths of baroque mood remains even then hardly trivial" (*GS1*, 237; *Origin*, 56).[8] The lack of sovereignty of German baroque theater, as well as the power of its will seeking to compensate for that lack, render a sovereign attitude all the more imperative and all the more difficult for those who seek to interpret it. This is at least one explanation for why Benjamin is led to look for a confirmation of his style of research in the *Lehre* of Schmitt concerning, precisely, the question of sovereignty.[9]

If the primary object of the German *Trauerspiel* is history as represented in the figure of the sovereign, the destiny of the ruler in baroque theater manifests a regularity that suggests the inevitability of a natural occurrence: "The constantly repeated spectacle of princely rise and fall . . . stood before the poets' eyes not so much as a morality play but by virtue of its persistence as the natural side of the historical process" (*GS1*, 267; *Origin*, 88).[10] History as a repetitive and ineluctable process of rise and fall is identified with the nature of a fallen creation lacking any discernible, representable possibility of either grace or salvation. It is the loss of a redemptive perspective that marks the baroque conception of history and renders it inauthentic and akin to a fallen state of nature.

Such a conception or confusion of history with nature entails at least two fundamental consequences for a theater whose primary concern is, as we have seen, precisely the spectacle of this history. First, the loss of the redemptive dimension results in a radical transformation of the dramatic element of the theater, insofar as it had been tied to a narrative-teleological conception of history. The traditional Aristotelian analysis of the plot in terms of unity of action resulting from the exposition, development, and resolution of conflict is no longer applicable. History, as Benjamin puts it, wanders onto the stage ("Die Geschichte wandert in den Schauplatz hinein") (*GS1*, 271; *Origin*, 92). Second, the baroque naturalization of history profoundly affects the figure of the sovereign, the primary exponent, we remember, of history. The naturalistic destiny of the prince does not merely imply the rise and fall of an individual figure, but more importantly the dislocation of sovereignty as such. Out of this dislocation Benjamin develops what he calls the typology and political anthropology of the baroque. The reason that this typology must be elucidated at the outset is because it arises out of the articulation, or rather disarticulation, of sovereignty, and hence of history, the primary object of the German baroque *Trauerspiel*.

Benjamin's reconstruction of the political anthropology of the baroque consists of three figures of varying stature and status, each of which is unthinkable without the others. This trio consists of the tyrant, the martyr, and the plotter *(der Intrigant)*. It is the first and the last that will be of particular interest to us here.

The point of departure for this typology is, of course, the figure of the prince. It is here that Benjamin makes explicit reference to Carl Schmitt's theory of sovereignty. To grasp the significance of Benjamin's use of Schmitt, it will be helpful if we first review certain aspects of Schmitt's discussion of sovereignty, starting with the famous passage at the beginning of *Political Theology* in which the notion is first defined: "Sovereign is he who decides on the state of exception. This definition alone can do justice to the concept of sovereignty as a borderline concept. For borderline concept signifies not a confused concept, as in the murky terminology of popular literature, but rather a concept of the most extreme sort" *(Politische Theologie,* 11; *PT,* 5).[11] Despite the apparent and seductive clarity of this definition, it leaves a number of problems unresolved, above all regarding the notion of the state of exception. First of all, the state of exception, Schmitt insists, is not simply equivalent, in German, to a state of emergency or of siege: not every danger or threat constitutes an *Ausnahmezustand* in Schmitt's sense, since not every exception per se represents a threat to the norm. The state of exception that constitutes the object and product of the sovereign decision is one that threatens or calls into question the existence and survival of the state itself as hitherto constituted. Sovereignty consists in the power to decide on or about the state of exception and thus in turn includes two moments: first, a decision determining that a state of exception indeed exists, and second, the effective suspension of the state of law previously in force so that the state may meet and surmount the challenge of the exception. In thus deciding on—and thus *determining*—the *state* of exception, the sovereign also effectively determines the limits of the state itself. It is this act of delimitation that constitutes political sovereignty according to Schmitt.

This is why the translation of *Ausnahmezustand* by state of exception is not quite accurate, or rather, why it obscures the delicate balance of similarity and distinction that determine the relationship of the State as *Staat* and the exception as *Zustand*. The *Ausnahmezustand* is a state in the sense of having a relatively determinate status; as a *Zustand*, it is "always something other . . . than an anarchy and a chaos [and therefore] in a juristical sense there still exists an order, even if not a legal order. The existence of the state conserves here an undoubted superiority over the validity of the legal norm. The decision frees itself of every normative restriction and becomes in an authentic sense absolute. *In the exceptional case the state suspends law by virtue of its drive to self-preservation, as one says*" (*Politische Theologie*, 18–19; *PT,* 12, my emphasis).[12] The paradox or aporia of Schmitt's position is suggested here by the conclusion of the passage just quoted. For if the decision is as radically independent of the norm as Schmitt claims, it is difficult to see how the decision of the state to suspend its laws can be justified at all, since all justification involves precisely the appeal to a norm. This is why, in appealing to a right of self-preservation, Schmitt acknowledges that the term is more a way of speaking than a rigorous concept: "In the exceptional case the state suspends law, by virtue of a drive to self-preservation, as one says." In one sense then, the sovereign decision marks the relationship of the order of the general—the law, the norm, the concept—to that which is radically heterogeneous to all such generality. In this sense, the decision as such is sovereign, that is, independent of all possible derivation from or subsumption to a more general norm. It is a pure act, somewhat akin to the act of creation except that what it does is not so much create as interrupt and suspend. If such interruption and suspension can never be predicted or determined in advance, it is nonetheless not arbitrary insofar as it is understood to be necessary in order to preserve the state as the indispensable condition of all durable law and order.

And yet, precisely insofar as it is situated in this temporality of repetition and reproduction, the decision cannot be considered, Schmitt notwithstanding, to be entirely absolute. Rather, it constitutes itself in and as *a break with* . . . , an interruption or suspension of a norm. In separating what belongs to the norm from what does not—and in this sense *every* authentic decision, as Schmitt asserts, has to do with an exception—the decision distinguishes itself from the simple negation of order, from chaos and anarchy as Schmitt writes, and can indeed lay claim to having some sort of legal status. The problem, however, is that such a claim can only be evaluated and judged after the fact, as it were, which is to say from a point of view that is once again situated within a system of norms.

For Schmitt, this paradox is articulated in the fact that the State, which is the condition of all law and order, is itself constituted by a decision that is prior to and independent of all such considerations: "The Authority proves that in order to produce law it need not be based on law" (*Politische Theologie*, 20; *PT*, 13).[13] Yet the non-legal or a-legal status of the sovereign and exceptional decision is justifiable and indeed identifiable only insofar as it provides the conditions for the reappropriation of the exception by the norm. The State has thus the first and the last word in Schmitt's theory of sovereignty.

This brings us to a second aspect of Schmitt's thought. Up to now, we have been considering it in terms of a relatively abstract, general, and quasi-logical theory of decision; but Schmitt's thinking is also historical, as the very title of the book, *Political Theology*, suggests and as the following passage makes explicit:

> All pregnant concepts of the modern theory of the state are secularized theological notions. Not only in their historical development, because they were transposed into political theory from theology, for instance insofar as the omnipotent God became the omnipotent legislator, but also in their systematic structure, the knowledge of which is required by a sociological consideration of these concepts. The state of exception has for jurisprudence a significance similar to that of the miracle in theology. Only when this analogous position becomes conscious can the development that the ideas concerning the philosophy of the state have followed over the past centuries be recognized. (*Politische Theologie*, 36; *PT*, 49)[14]

To be sure, in the analogy that Schmitt is here constructing, historical development is subordinated to systematic considerations. At the same time, it is only in a reflection or recall of the historical transfer, or rather transformation of theological categories into political ones, that the systematic structure of political discourse is fully revealed. The salient trait of that structure is, as we have already seen, its dependence on a transcendence that exceeds its self-identity and that thus harbors an irreducible alterity and exteriority, just as the miracle—the example cited by Schmitt himself—in Augustinian doctrine both exceeds and explains the created world. If historical reflection on the development of political discourse reveals its theological origins and hence its dependence on a certain transcendence, the actual historical development of political theory and of theology has moved in an opposite direction: "To the concept of God of the seventeenth and eighteenth centuries belongs the transcendence of God as opposed to the world, as the transcendence of the sovereign vis-à-vis the state belongs to the philosophy of the state. In the nineteenth century ideas of immanence extend their domination increasingly" (*Politische Theologie*, 49; *PT*, 63).[15] To these representations of immanence belong the identification of ruler and ruled, and above all that of the state with the state of law (the "identity of the state with the legal order," ibid.). But if the development of modern thought has thus tended to efface the originating and constitutive relationship of the political to transcendence in the name of notions of autonomy and self-identity, Schmitt's own approach itself is not entirely free of such tendencies. This can be seen in the manner in which he construes the relationship between political and theological categories that for him is the key to an authentically historical and systematical understanding of modern politics. For what emerges in Schmitt's discussion of the relation of politics and theology is the common basis, indeed underlying identity, of the two. For instance, he finds confirmation of his theological-political thesis in the position of Alger, for whom "the monarch in state doctrine of the seventeenth century is identified with God and has the same position in the state as has the God of the Cartesian system in the world" (*Politische Theologie*, 46; *PT*, 60).[16] The method that Schmitt advances in *Political Theology*, which he calls the sociology of concepts, thus employs the notion of analogy in order to reduce difference to identity, as the following programmatic declaration clearly demonstrates: "The metaphysical image that a particular epoch forges of the world has the same structure as the form of political organization it considers self-evident. The determination of such an identity constitutes the sociology of the concept of sovereignty" (*Politische Theologie*, 59–60; *PT*, 46, my emphasis).[17] One would be tempted to say that Schmitt's critique seeks to replace the ideas of immanence *(Immanenzvorstellungen)* of modern political theory with ideas of identity *(Identitätsvorstellungen),* in a move meant to recall the heterogeneity of political concepts out of the oblivion into which it has fallen, but that only succeeds in once again reducing alterity to the same: to "dieselbe Struktur" and to "die Feststellung einer . . . Identität."

With the ambivalence of Schmitt's approach to the political in mind, let us now turn to the manner in which the question of sovereignty emerges in Benjamin's study of the *Origins of German Baroque Theater:*

> The sovereign represents history. He holds historical happening in his hand like a scepter. This attitude is anything but a privilege of the theater. Considerations of political theory underly it. In a final confrontation with the legal lessons of the middle ages a new concept of sovereignty was formed . . . If the modern concept of sovereignty amounts ultimately to a supreme, princely executive power, the Baroque develops out of a discussion of the state of exception and makes the most important function of the prince that of excluding it. (GS1, 245; *Origin,* 65; my emphasis)[18]

A note at the end of this passage refers to *Political Theology.* And yet the very words that seem only to paraphrase Schmitt constitute in fact a slight but decisive modification of his theory. Schmitt, we remember, defines sovereignty as constituted by the power to make a decision that consists of two moments: first, the determination that a state of exception exists, and second, the effective suspension of the state of law with the end of preserving the state as such. For Schmitt, then, the state of exception must be removed, *beseitigt,*[19] done away with, but only in each particular case, never as such: that is precisely what Schmitt criticizes modern political theory for trying to accomplish by excluding consideration of the state of exception from the determination of sovereignty.[20] Benjamin, by contrast, describes the task of the sovereign in the very terms that Schmitt rejects: the sovereign is charged with the task of *excluding* the state of exception, "den auszuschließen." In short, that which is already exterior, the *Ausnahmezustand,* is to be exteriorized once again, *ausgeschlossen,* and this applies not only to the state of exception as an individual, determinate threat to the state—the position of Schmitt—but to the state of exception as such, that is, as that which transcends the state in general.

In short, the function assigned to the sovereign by the baroque, according to Benjamin, is that of transcending transcendence by making it immanent, an internal part of the state and of the world, of the state of the world. And the reason why the baroque is so attached to the state of the world Benjamin explains as follows:

> The religious man of the Baroque clings so to the world because he feels himself, together with it, driven towards a cataract. There is no (a?) Baroque eschatology, and precisely for that reason a mechanism that heaps up and exalts everything born on earth, before it delivers it over to the end. The beyond is emptied of everything wherein even the slightest breath of world weaves and from it the Baroque extracts a plenitude of things that tend to avoid all shaping and reveals it at its height in a drastic form, in order to evacuate a last heaven and as a vacuum to put him into service, to annihilate the world with catastrophic force. (GS1, 246; Origin, 66)[21]

What the baroque consequently rejects is any admission of the limitation of immanence and it does so by emptying transcendence of all possible representable content. Far from doing away with transcendence, however, such emptying only endows it with an all the more powerful force: that of the vacuum, of the absolute and unbounded other, which, since it is no longer representable, is also no longer localizable out there or as a beyond. The otherness that is no longer allowed to remain transcendent therefore reappears this side of the horizon, represented as a cataract, abyss, or fall. Or, even more radically, as *allegory*.

In this perspective, the function of the sovereign to exclude the state of exception conforms fully to the attempt of the German baroque to exclude transcendence *by incorporating it*. But the very same desire to exclude transcendence also condemns the function of the sovereign to malfunction. For unlike the political-theological *analogy* of Schmitt, the baroque sovereign, and particularly the German baroque sovereign, is defined precisely by his *difference* and distance from God, just as baroque immanence sets itself up in contradistinction to theological transcendence. At the very point in time when the political sovereign successfully gains his independence vis-à-vis the Church, the difference between worldly power and that of the divine can no longer be ignored. The result, as Benjamin formulates it, turns out to contradict directly the conclusion of Schmitt: "The level of the state of creation, the ground on which the Mourning Play unfolds, determines unmistakably the sovereign as well. However high above subject and state he may reign, his rank includes him in the world of creation: he is the Lord of creatures, but he remains a creature" (GS1, 263–264; Origin, 85).[22] Schmitt, we recall, had construed the theological-political analogy in terms of a relationship of fundamental similarity: the sovereign transcends the state as God transcends the creation. By contrast, Benjamin's notion of secularization stresses precisely the incommensurability of the change it entails.

Such incommensurability becomes even clearer in the specific case of German baroque theater: "The turn away from the eschatology of the spiritual plays characterizes the new drama in all of Europe; nevertheless the insensate flight into a nature without grace is specifically German" (GS1, 260; Origin, 81).[23] The German baroque theater flees desperately to nature—which we remember is for it the other face of history—only to discover that there is no grace or consolation to be had there either. The undoing of the sovereign results from the sense that in a creation left entirely to its own devices, without any other place to go, the state of exception has become the rule.[24]

The result is that the sovereign finds himself in a situation in which a decision is as imperative as it is impossible: "The antithesis between the might of the ruler and his capacity to rule led, insofar as the Mourning Play goes, to a distinctive trait that is only apparently generic, and whose illumination is only possible against the background of the theory of the sovereign. This is the incapacity of the tyrant to decide. The Prince, in whose hands the decision on the state of exception reposes, shows himself at the earliest opportunity to be unequal to his task: a decision is practically impossible for him" (GS1, 250; Origin, 70–71).[25] The sovereign is incapable of making a decision, because a decision, in the strict sense, is not possible in a world that leaves no place for heterogeneity: the inauthentic, natural history of the baroque allows for no interruption or radical suspension of its endemic and perennial interruptions. The sovereign reacts by seeking to gather all power and thus becomes a tyrant; and yet the more power he has, the more he demonstrates his incapacity to arrive at an effective decision. Faced with this situation, the tyrant can easily turn into a martyr. Both figures, Benjamin observes, are for the baroque only two sides of the same coin, "The Janusheads of the Crowned . . . the necessarily extreme marks of the princely essence" (GS1, 249; Origin, 69).[26] In emphasizing the dictatorial tendency of the sovereign, Benjamin follows Schmitt here practically to the letter.[27] And yet in so doing, he arrives at a result that is almost diametrically opposed to that of Schmitt: the very notion of sovereignty itself is put radically into question. One extreme illustration of this is the figure of Herod, King of the Jews, "a mad autocrat and a symbol of disordered creation [der als wahnwitziger Selbstherrscher ein Emblem der verstörten Schöpfung wurde]," and as such also an exemplary illustration of the fate of the sovereign for the seventeenth century: "The apex of creation, erupting into madness like a volcano and destroying himself and his entire court . . . He falls victim to the disproportion [eines Mißverhältnisses] between the unlimited hierarchical dignity, with which he is divinely invested and the humble estate of his humanity" (GS1, 250; Origin, 70).[28] The key to the secularization of which the German baroque is the result is thus for Benjamin not so much an analogy based on proportion, and hence on identity, as a relation based on disproportion, on a Mißverhältnis.

The effects of this disproportion, as Benjamin elaborates them, do not stop at the dismantling of the sovereign, who splits into an ultimately ineffective if bloody tyrant, and a no less ineffective martyr; neither does it come to rest at any of the compromises possible between these two poles, such as the stoic ostentation that often marks baroque representations of the prince. Rather, the splitting of the sovereign is accompanied by the emergence of a third figure who stands in radical dissymmetry to the other two. This third figure—figure of a certain third (tertium datur)—who completes Benjamin's baroque political anthropology and typology—is the plotter, the Intrigant: and it is he who turns out to hold the key to the fate of sovereignty in the German baroque mourning play.

To understand what distinguishes the plotter from the two other figures in the baroque political triad, it must be understood that the incapacity of the sovereign to decide involves the transformation not merely of an individual character-type, but also of the manner in which history itself is represented in the Trauerspiel. And this in turn determines the way in which representation takes place. With the split of the sovereign into tyrant and martyr, what is dislocated is not just the unity of a character, but the unity of character as such. This disarticulation is of particular importance for baroque theater.

If the Aristotelian theory of tragedy assigns primary importance to the unity and wholeness of action, and requires to this end consistency of character,[29] precisely this consistency and unity are undermined together with the status of the sovereign. Nothing demonstrates the distance of the *Trauerspiel* from the Aristotelian theory of tragedy more emphatically than this disaggregation of the sovereign and hence of the action, which in turn contributes to the peculiar *theatricality* of baroque drama:

> Just as compositions with restful lighting are totally unknown in Mannerist painting, so it is that the theatrical figures of the epoch stand in the harsh glare of their changing resolve. In them it is not so much sovereignty that strives to emerge, placed on display by the stoical turns of phrase, but rather the abrupt arbitrariness of ever-changing emotional storms, in which Lohenstein's figures in particular billow and flutter like tattered flags flapping in the wind. Through the smallness of their heads—if this expression may be understood figuratively—they are not unlike Greco figures, driven not by thoughts but by unstable physical impulses. (*GS1*, 251; *Origin*, 71; my emphasis)[30]

From this account it is clear that the dilemma of the sovereign in baroque drama is also and above all that of the subject as such: it is no longer determined by its head—that is, by its consciousness, its intentions—but by forces that act independently of conscious volition, that buffet and drive it from one extreme to another. A powerful dynamic is thus unleashed that, however, does not really go anywhere. Instead, like torn flags whipped about in the wind,[31] baroque figures are driven by tempestuous affects over which they have little control. What results is a rhythm of abrupt and unpredictable twists and turns and it is this rhythm that determines the structure of plot in the *Trauerspiel*. Moreover, since neither plot nor character is sufficiently unified or consistent to provide a comprehensive framework for the play, this framework must be sought elsewhere. That elsewhere turns out to be the theater itself as stage, artifice, and apparatus. This is implicit in the passage cited, which describes how the theatrical figures of the age appear *im grellen Scheine*, in the "harsh glare of their changing resolve." The dismantling of decision as a definitive, ultimate, and absolute *act* opens the way to a different kind of *acting*: that which takes place on a stage lit up by spotlights, bathed in that "harsh glare [*grellen Scheine*]," a phrase that recurs frequently in Benjamin's text and that recalls the *Scheinwerfer* of the theater.

In the theatrical space thus opened by the dislocation of action and of the subject, and above all in the confusion that results, the sovereignty of the tyrant is replaced by the mastery of the plotter: "In contrast to the temporal and spasmodic progression, represented in tragedy, the Mourning Play plays itself out in a spatial continuum that could be called choreographic. The organizer of its imbroglio, predecessor of the ballet director, is the plotter" (GS1, 274; Origin, 95).[32] The discontinuous temporality of decision, here associated with tragedy, is replaced—that is, resituated—within a spatial continuum in which exceptional interruptions are no longer possible because they have become the rule. The regular nature of the interruption paradoxically becomes programmable and the programmer, or choreographer, is the intriguer. The etymology of the word in-trigare, discussed earlier—namely, to con-found and confuse—turns out to be all the more appropriate in a world in which the clear-cut separation of a decision is no longer effective.

The intrigue or plot is thus designated by Benjamin as a Verwicklung: an imbroglio or entanglement, but one that is organized. Baroque drama thus entails a plot that is based not on a sovereign subject as "hero" but on a masterful organizer or promoter (Veranstalter). It is precisely the calculating nature of this mastery that fascinates the baroque audience: "His depraved calculations awaken in the observer of the Haupt- und Staatsaktionen (Political Action Plays) all the more interest insofar as he recognizes not just a mastery of the political apparatus, but an anthropological, even physiological knowledge that fascinated him. The superiority of the plotter consists entirely in understanding and will" (ibid.).[33] The amoral calculatedness of the plotter contrasts radically with the attitudes of both the tyrant and the martyr. Only the intriguer confronts a state of the world in which the exception has become the rule, and therefore in which universal principles—including the principle of the interruption of principle qua decision—can no longer be counted on. The intriguer exploits mechanisms of human action as the result of forces over which there can be no ultimate control, but which precisely for that reason can be made the subject of probabilistic calculations.

The contingency of such calculations turns the intrigue into something closer to a game or exhibition of virtuosity, rather than into the expression of a cosmic strategy for the good of all or of the State. Thus not only the subject matter of the Trauerspiel—historical action—changes, but its dramaturgical structure as well. Plot is replaced by plotting. As Benjamin puts it: "Baroque drama knows historical activity only as the depraved goings-on of schemers" (*Das Drama des Barock kennt die historische Aktivität nicht anders denn als verworfene Betriebsamkeit von Ränkeschmieden*) (*GS1*, 267; *Origin*, 88). At the same time, however, the structure of the plot changes: "It differs from the so-called counter-plot of classical tragedy through isolation of motifs, scenes and types . . . Baroque drama [also loves to] set adversaries in harshly illuminated, specially arranged scenes, in which motivation plays the smallest role. Baroque intrigue unfolds, one can say, like a change of decoration on an open stage, so little is illusion intended in it" (*GS1*, 254; *Origin*, 75).[34] The utter indifference to psychological or moral motivation, combined with the encapsulation of conflicting figures through "harshly illuminated specially arranged scenes," precludes any sort of resolution in a totalizing dénouement. What interests the baroque is not so much the dramatic resolution of conflict as its representation through a mechanism that acknowledges and even flaunts its own artifice. "The privileged site and scene of such emphatically theatrical artifice is the court: The image of the stage, more exactly: of the court, becomes the key to historical understanding. For the court is the innermost stage . . . In the court the Mourning Play sees the eternal, natural décor of the course of history" (*GS1*, 271; *Origin*, 92–93).[35] The eternal, natural character attributed to the court in the baroque testifies to the situation of a unique historical period, in which "Christianity or Europe is divided into a series of European Christendoms, whose historical actions no longer claim to take place in the flight and flow of a redemptive process" (*GS1*, 257; *Origin*, 78).[36] Thus, with the traditional Christian eschatological perspective blocked, the irreducible partiality and provinciality of the local court renders it the exemplary site and stage of a movement of history that has been reduced to conspiratorial plotting, the aim of which is the destabilization of power rather than its consolidation. This is why the structural dynamics of the plotter cause him to resemble comic figures or the fool rather than the prince who would be sovereign. If the plotter is most at home in the court, it is only insofar as he knows that there can be for him no proper home, "*keine eigene Heimstätte.*" (*GS1*, 275; *Origin*, 97). In this sense the plotter can be said to be the *exponent of the stage (Schauplatzes)* as that place in which no one, including the Sovereign, can be at home.

Unlike the sovereign, however, the plotter knows that the court is a theater of actions that can never be totalized but only staged with more or less virtuosity. By thus heeding only the rules of the game without seeking to reach ultimate principles, the plotter begins where the sovereign hopes to end: with the exclusion of the state of exception. The state of exception is excluded as theater. What characterizes this theater is that in it nothing can ever authentically take place, least of all the stage itself: "In the entire European mourning play the stage is never strictly fixable, an actual place, but rather like everything else, dialectically riven. Bound to the court it remains a wandering theater; inauthentically its boards represent the earth as the created showplace of history; it moves with its court from city to city" (*GS1*, 298; *Origin*, 119).[37] If the stage of baroque theater is never fixed but rather dialectically riven and thus inauthentic, what distinguishes the German baroque is the impossibility of a dialectical *Aufhebung* that would reconstitute its fissures into a totality: "Only the plot (intrigue) would have been capable of forming the organization of scenes into an allegorical totality, with which the image of the apotheosis elevates itself above the elapsed images and gives mourning at one and the same time the cue for its entry and exit" (*GS1*, 268; *Origin*, 235).[38] It is precisely the inability to even approach such an apotheosis that characterizes the *German* baroque theater in contrast to its Spanish counterpart in Calderon. Yet if this limits its aesthetic value with respect to Spanish or English playwrights such as Calderon and Shakespeare, it is also what gives it its distinctive historical-philosophical significance. For even in Calderon, what is presented is not the "image of apotheosis" but rather the lesson that the "transfigured apotheosis is not to be attained with the banal reserves of the theater" alone (ibid.). In this sense, the failure of the German baroque mourning play is more authentically theatrical than are the successes of its Spanish counterpart. What the German baroque mourning play leaves as the originality of its heritage is its "demand for interpretation [*Anspruch auf Deutung*]" (*GS1*, 409; *Origin*, 235)—to which Benjamin's *Origin of the German Mourning Play* has provided the exemplary response. Like the baroque mourning play, it ends with an "appeal" rather than a decision—or a command (*GS1*, 315; *Origin*, 137).

Such an appeal can find no place in Schmitt's theory of sovereignty and of the decision that could be said to muffle it. For the theater of the

German baroque diverges both from classical tragedy and from the Schmittian theory of sovereignty in that it leaves no place for anything resembling a definitive decision. Rather, it is precisely the absence of such a decisive verdict and the ensuing perspective of unending *appeal* that mark the *Trauerspiel:* "One can drive the excursion into the juristic realm even further and in the spirit of the medieval literature of lament speak of a trial of the creation, whose complaint and accusation—*Klage*—against death—or against whomever else it may be directed—at the end of the mourning play is tabled in a semi-finished state. Its review and resumption are implicit in the mourning play" (*GS1*, 315–316; *Origin*, 137, my emphasis).[39] Nothing could demonstrate more clearly the distance between this eternal process of review, adjourned in a half-finished state, and the notion of an absolute, absolutely definitive and ultimate decision. It is the distance between Schmitt and Kafka. Here as there, the question of decision, of its power and its status, is tied to a certain determination of space. Whereas in Benjamin this determination is revealed to be the errant stage of an inauthentic and unlocalizable place, decision for Schmitt can be situated in terms of an unequivocal point and thus put in its proper place, once and for all: "The legal force of the decision is something other than the result of an argument. It is not calculated by means of a norm, but rather inversely: only from a point of ascription can it be determined what a norm and normative correctness is. Starting from the norm no point of ascription can be produced, but only a quality of a content" (*Politische Theologie,* 42–43; *PT,* 32; my emphasis).[40] If Schmitt asserts here that the norm presupposes a point of ascription, a *Zurechnungspunkt* on which one must be able to rely, but which the norm as such cannot provide, the unmistakable conclusion for him is that decision alone can provide such a point. In his reinscription of Schmitt, Benjamin takes exception to this point, ascribing its effects not to decision but to interpretation. In so doing, he reveals that what is at stake is perhaps not a point at all but a *stage,* in all the senses of that word—one around and on which anything can happen, even the appeal for a miracle.

CHAPTER THIRTEEN

Violence and Gesture

Agamben Reading Benjamin
Reading Kafka Reading Cervantes . . .

In a book published in French and Italian in 2003 and translated into English as *State of Exception,* Giorgio Agamben, as in many of his other writings, refers to the work of Walter Benjamin at particularly decisive points in his argument. In this book, whose title indicates an indebtedness to Carl Schmitt that Agamben shares with Benjamin, the author elaborates a theory of the "state of exception" as the notion through which a certain Western tradition of "bio-politics" seeks to assimilate the heterogeneity on which it depends and thereby to treat it as the integrating element of its own "death machine" (*EE,* 145).[1] The "state of exception" thus serves as the pretext of a violence bent on justifying and reproducing a political-legal system that presents itself as the indispensable condition of that "minimal order" (Schmitt) required in order for life to be livable. One particularly emphatic reference to Benjamin by Agamben in this book occurs in chapter four, "Gigantomachy around a Void," in which he contrasts Benjamin's "Critique of Violence" with Schmitt's theory of the "state of exception" as that which both defines and legitimates the Sovereign as the power that can suspend the reign of positive law—of the constitution— in order, allegedly, to restore the minimum order required for legality to function. Benjamin, by contrast, in his essay "The Critique of Violence," develops a notion of violence as radically distinct from all "law" *(Recht, droit)*; this form of violence is defined as "pure means"—which is to say, as "mediality without end" that serves no purpose and therefore has to be "considered independently of the ends it pursues" *(EE,* 105). Agamben, always an incisive and suggestive reader of Benjamin, cites a passage from a letter written in 1919 to Ernst Schoen, which argues for a notion of "purity"—*Reinheit*—that is *conditional* rather than absolute: "The purity of a being is *never* unconditional or absolute; it is always subjected to a condition. This condition always differs depending on the being at issue; *never* however does this condition reside *in the being itself*. In other words: the purity of each (finite) being never depends upon it itself [*ist nicht von ihm selbst abhängig*]. The two beings to which we attribute purity above all are nature and children. For nature the external condition is human language."[2] To be finite, according to Benjamin, is to depend on something other than itself, on extraneous conditions. "Purity" thus is not a characteristic of immanence, not an unadulterated property that is no more or no less than just itself, but, as Agamben notes, "relational." In the case of violence, he continues, "purity" should be sought not in "violence itself" *(pas dans la violence même),* but "in its relation to something external." Anything that defines its "purity" or identity in terms of its relation to something else can, of course, be considered to relate to that something else as a "means" to an "end." But in the *Critique of Violence,* Benjamin explicitly excludes this traditional and teleological conception of "means," a move that for Agamben is of the greatest significance: "Here appears the theme—which shines only for an instant, and yet long enough to illuminate the text in its entirety—of violence as 'pure means,' which is to say, as the figure of a paradoxical 'mediality without end': i.e. a means that, while remaining such, is considered independently of the ends it pursues" *(EE,* 105). For the Benjamin of the *Critique of Violence,* it is easy to identify the "end" that must be excluded in order to arrive at a critique of violence—of its conditions of possibility (and perhaps also of impossibility): it is *Recht:* "right" or Law (with a capital L) as that which informs the realm of positive laws (small l) and the reign of legality. But it is far more difficult to describe in positive terms the alternative relationship that would comprise the condition of violence as a means without end, a "pure" means. Agamben takes up Benjamin's suggestion at the end of the passage quoted earlier, in which language is described as the other of nature—"For nature the external condition is language." In his 1916 essay "On Language as Such and on the Language of Man," Benjamin defines the purity of language as consisting in its ability to communicate nothing other than "communicability pure and simple," which Agamben then applies to pure violence as well: "Just as, in his essay on language, language is pure when it is not an instrument serving the end of communication but rather communicates itself immediately, i.e. communicates a communicability pure and simple; so too violence is pure when it does not find itself in a relation of means to end but rather maintains itself in relation to its very mediality [*avec sa médialité même*]" (*EE*, 106). The "paradoxical figure" that Agamben associates with a "mediality without end" recurs in his paraphrase of Benjamin's notion of "pure language" just quoted, but in a slightly different guise, when he describes the mediality of language as that through which language communicates immediately its own communicability.

At this point, however, it is necessary to reflect for a moment on the precise formulation used here by Benjamin: The two German words used in this context by Benjamin is first, *"Mitteilbarkeit,"* usually translated as "communicability," which in the case of language as such he then qualifies as being "immediate" *(unmittelbar)*.[3] To translate "Mitteilbarkeit" into English as "communicability," however, is to efface one of its decisive connotations. A more precise if less idiomatic translation that has on occasion been employed is "impartibility."[4] But there is perhaps an even better possibility in English, one that is both more literal and more idiomatic although it resists nominalization and thus cannot be used everywhere. This option is: *parting with* ("teilen" = to part, "mit-" = with). The mediality of language would thus consist in a movement that separates *from* itself, and yet—here the paradox, of what Benjamin himself in that early essay calls the "magic" of language—in so doing establishes a relation to itself as *other*. In relating (to) itself as other, it stays "with" that from which it simultaneously departs. The "purity" of language as medium would thus consist in the constitutive immediacy of its "-ability" to stay *with* that from which it parts. As a medium it would be a "means without end" only insofar as the word "without" defines a relation not of simple exclusion or negation, but of participation "with" the "out"-side of an irreducible and yet constitutive exteriority.[5]

With respect to violence, Agamben formulates its analogical relation to the mediality of language as follows:

> And just as pure language is not another language, does not occupy any place other than that of natural, communicating languages, showing itself in them by exposing them as such, in the same manner pure violence reveals itself only as the *exposing and deposing* of the relation between violence and right. This is what Benjamin suggests immediately following [the passages quoted], by evoking the theme of violence which, as anger, is never a means but only a manifestation *(Manifestation)* . . . Pure violence *exposes and cuts* the bond between right and violence, and can thus appear not as violence that governs or executes *(schaltende),* but as violence that purely acts and manifests itself *(waltende).* (*EE,* 106)

In this elaboration of Benjamin's notions of "purity" and "mediality" as they operate in his conceptions both of "language" and of "violence," Agamben deploys a series of conceptual couples that are as suggestive as they are enigmatic: "exposing and deposing," "exposes and cuts," "executes and acts (or manifests)." From the last pair, however, it is clear that these concepts only reproduce the paradox of a "mediality without end," or as Benjamin formulates it, of a mediality that would be "immediate," *un-medi-able (un-mittel-bar),* by defining the latter ultimately as a function of the self, as a kind of self-reflexivity: as a "violence that *purely* acts and manifests *itself.*" If, however, the Benjaminian notion of purity is "not substantial but relational" (*EE,* 104), then how can the purity of violence consist in an action that manifests violence "itself" or "as such," apart from every exteriority, from everything other than itself? Or is there a kind of manifestation, a kind of act that is defined precisely through just such a relation to something other than itself? What, in short, is involved in a violence that is *waltend* but not *schaltend?* Can the two be as clearly separated or distinguished as Agamben, following Benjamin, seems to believe?[6]

It is in the perspective of such unresolved questions that Agamben turns briefly to Benjamin's reading of Kafka to indicate a possible alternative to the bio-political "death-machine" sustained by a "state of exception" that suspends the rule of law only to totalize it in and as *its other.* Agamben focuses on two passages in Benjamin's Kafka interpretation. The first is contained in a letter to Scholem, in which Benjamin distinguishes his own reading of Kafka from that of his correspondent: "Your point of departure is the . . . redemptive [*heilsgeschichtlichen*] perspective opened by the trial proceeding; mine is the tiny absurd hope, as well as the creatures who on the one hand are concerned by this hope, but in whom on the other its absurdity is mirrored."[7] The second passage quoted by Agamben is from another letter written by Benjamin to Scholem and concerns the relation of the text to those who study it: "Whether the text [*die Schrift:* scripture] has been lost by the students, or whether they cannot decipher it, amounts to the same since without its key, the text is not text but life. Life as it is conducted [*geführt*] in the village at the foot of the castle."[8] Agamben does not cite another remark of Benjamin's in the same letter, which however lends further support to his general interpretation and thesis. It concerns the status of the "law" in Kafka's work: "Kafka's own insistence upon the law I consider to be the dead point [*Totenpunkt*] of his work, by which I mean only that it cannot serve interpretation as a fulcrum from which to set the work into motion."[9] It is worth noting that Benjamin's notion of "interpretation" here involves not reproducing the essence or meaning of the work as is, but rather setting it into motion. As such, interpretation seems akin to the relational notion of "purity" previously discussed. Thus, Benjamin's reading of Kafka does not seek to elucidate the religious doctrine that might be implicit in the work, but rather to bring out those aspects that call for change and transformation, for a certain "movement." The category Benjamin invokes has a Hölderlinian resonance: *Umkehr,* "inversion," reversal or also, turnabout.[10] And he glosses this in a passage that Agamben does not cite: "Kafka's messianic category is '*reversal*' or study."[11] Agamben, who does not dwell here on the notion of reversal, places the motif of "study" at the center of his reading of Benjamin's reading of Kafka:

> To the baring [*mise à nu*] of mythical-juridical violence effectuated by pure violence corresponds, in the essay on Kafka, as a kind of vestige, the enigmatic image of a legality [*d'un droit*] that is no longer practiced but only studied . . . a legality without force or application, like that into whose study the "new lawyer" [reference is Kafka's story of that name] plunges in leafing through "our old codes" . . . What could be the sense of a law that were thus to survive its deposing [*sa déposition*]? The difficulty encountered here by Benjamin corresponds to a problem that can be formulated . . . in the following terms: what happens to the law after its messianic fulfillment [*son accomplissement messianique*]? (This is precisely the controversy that opposes Paul to his Jewish contemporaries). And what happens to the law in a classless society? (This is precisely the de-

bate between Vychinski and Pasukanis) . . . What is important here is that the law—not practiced but studied—is not justice but only the gate that leads to it. What opens a passage toward justice is not the annulling of law, but its deactivation and dereliction [*la désactivation et le désœuvrement*]—which is to say, another use of it. (*EE,* 109)

In the studies of Kafka's students as Benjamin reads them, Agamben finds the suggestion of an alternative "use" of law, one that would no longer be "contaminated" by application and enforcement and hence would be "liberated from its own value" as use-value: "This liberation is the task of study—or of play," he concludes, inasmuch as such an activity can relate to the world as something "absolutely unappropriable" and therefore incommensurate with any judicial order (*EE,* 109).

From what however would such "study" or "play"—and we will shortly try to examine their possible relationship—liberate? Agamben's response conflates Schmitt and Derrida, for it points to the *spectrality* of a "law" maintaining itself in and through the state of exception. "Study" and "play" would thus presumably provide a liberating alternative to "the process of an infinite deconstruction, which, by virtue of maintaining law in a spectral life, is no longer capable of ever getting to the end of it [in the sense of finishing up with it: in French, *ne parvient plus à en venir à bout*]" (*EE,* 108). Thus whereas according to Agamben deconstruction interminably maintains the rule of law in a spectral state of suspended animation, the suspension of the practice of law in its study, or in play, opens the way to a "definitive liberation" (109).

Agamben's powerful and challenging reading of Benjamin on Kafka thus provides him with a glimpse of a positive alternative both to the Schmittian state of exception and to Derridean spectrality. It rests on an interpretation not of Kafka's characters' engaging and suspending the rule of law, but of the auto-suspension and spectral reproduction of the rule of law in the state of exception. Since such engagement and suspension are tied, by Agamben, reading Benjamin reading Kafka, to the figures of the "students," let us take a closer look at the role they play in the texts of Benjamin and Kafka.

Benjamin introduces his discussion of the students with a brief story. In a Chassidic village one Saturday evening, after the end of the Sabbath, a group of Jews are sitting in a tavern discussing what they would choose if each were granted a single wish. One opts for money, the next for a son-in-law, yet another for a work bench, and so on. At the end only the village beggar is left and after some hesitation, this is the wish he relates:

> "I wish I were a powerful king ruling in a distant land and lay asleep at night in my palace and from the outermost border [of the country] the enemy attacks and before dawn cavalry reaches my castle without meeting any resistance and I awake in a panic without any time even to get dressed and have to flee with only a shirt to my name and am pursued through mountains and valleys, forests and hills and without rest day and night until I land safe here on the bench in your corner. That's what I would wish." The others stare at him clueless. "And what would this wish get you?" "A shirt" was the answer. (GS2, 433; SW2, 812)

"This story," Benjamin comments, "leads deep into the household of Kafka's world." And he elaborates with a messianic allusion that can be found frequently in his writings, although here it seems to raise as many questions as it answers: "After all, no one says that the distortions [*die Entstellungen*] that the coming of the Messiah will one day set right [*zurechtzurücken: straighten out*] concern only our space. They also certainly affect our time" (GS2, 433; SW2, 812). In this perspective, the beggar's wish is not to rule forever, to *walten*, but rather more modestly simply to survive *for a while,* if only with a "shirt" on his back—and to his name.[12] Without bothering to give the slightest commentary or gloss on this story he has just recounted, Benjamin then goes on to recite a short text from Kafka's collection *The Country Doctor,* entitled "The Next Village." In it a grandfather expresses the following concern: "Life is so astonishingly short. Now in memory it seems so compressed that for example I can barely comprehend how a young man can decide to ride to the next village without fearing that—not even considering unlucky accidents—even the time of our usual, happily passing life will never be sufficient for such a ride" (ibid.). It is necessary to keep in mind this sense of urgency in order to situate Benjamin's reading of Kafka's students. For, Benjamin continues, there is one group among Kafka's creatures that "in a very peculiar manner reckons with the brevity of life." This group includes "fools" and "apprentices" (*Narren* and *Gehilfen*), but its true "spokesmen and ruler" are the students. Benjamin introduces them through this short dialogue, from Kafka's novel *Der Verschollener,* formerly translated as

Amerika and more recently as *The Man Who Disappeared:* "'But when do you sleep?' Karl asked and stared at the student in amazement.— 'Yes, sleep!' said the student. 'I'll sleep when I'm finished with my studies'" (*GS2, 434; SW2, 813*). To study is, among other things, to learn by rote, to remember, and perhaps above all, to repeat. But in listening and observing the student, it becomes clear that there will never be enough time to get to the *end* of it all—*d'en venir à bout*—before it is time to *stop*. However, the response to this dilemma is to repeat it. And yet, or because of this situation, the student responds to Karl's question—"But when do you sleep?"—not by answering it but by repeating its final word in what could almost be an affirmation: "Ja, schlafen!," which would perhaps best be rendered in English as "Sleep . . . yes!"[13] But far from being a sign of agreement, the student's affirmative iteration only echoes the question. And what follows—"I'll sleep when I've finished my studies"—puts off the response indefinitely. If, as Benjamin suggests, the students are the *Wortführer,* the spokesmen of that "tribe" *(Sippe)* "that in the most peculiar way reckons with the brevity of life," then this response affirms only that the question has arrived, has been heard, even understood, but nothing more.

Benjamin comments this passage as follows: "In their studies the students keep watch [*wachen die Studenten*]. The hunger artist fasts, the doorkeeper keeps silent and the students keep watch [*wachen*]" (*GS2, 434; SW2, 813*).[14] The *Wachen* of the students is not watchful *waiting* as much as it is watchful waking: that of the insomniac. For there is nothing to wait for; these studies lead to nothing, least of all to fresh knowledge. And yet they are still far from worthless, as Benjamin makes clear: "Perhaps these studies amounted to nothing [*sind ein Nichts gewesen*]. But if so, they stand in close proximity to that nothing, which alone makes anything useful [*brauchbar*]—namely, the Tao" (*GS2, 435; SW2, 813*).[15] Benjamin's reference here to the dependence of everything *useful*—*brauchbar*—upon a certain "nothingness" (*Nichts*) recalls Agamben's arguments in *State of Exception*. But when Benjamin elucidates Kafka's Tao by citing a passage from *The Chinese Wall*, it becomes evident that his way leads in a different direction from that envisaged by Agamben. For it goes in the direction not of "play" but rather of a certain kind of *handwork* such as that involved in the following passage from Kafka, cited by Benjamin: "Hammering a table together with such excruciatingly precise skill [*peinlich ordentliche*]

Handwerksmäßigkeit] that one could not say, 'For him such hammering is nothing at all,' but rather 'For him such hammering is real hammering [*ein wirkliches Hämmern*] and at the same time nothing at all
[*auch ein Nichts*]'; with the result that the hammering would become
even bolder, more determined, more real and, if you like, more insane"
(*GS2*, 435; *SW2*, 813–814). The specificity of the kind of "use" or
practice involved in such "real hammering," which at the same time is
"nothing at all," involves a factor that does not seem to play a significant role in Agamben's considerations, although one might expect it
to, given its importance in the complex relation of "law" to "life" that
is the dominant concern of *State of Exception*. That factor is *repetition*.[16] Thus, the appropriation of "life" by "law" through the state of
exception can also be seen as the effort to install and impose a certain
repetitiveness on a singularity that is no less involved in repetition, but
in a different way. For the *singular* (as distinct from the *individual*) can
only appear—and indeed is only conceivable—as the vestigial or spectral *after-effect of a repetition,* as that which does not disappear in the
reproduction of the identical and yet which by itself is "nothing at all."
Like the "pure," the "singular" is "purely" *relational*.

It is this dimension of repetition that constitutes the medium of the
student's studying, as it is described in Kafka's text.[17] In other words,
if, according to Benjamin's remark cited by Agamben, the students
no longer possess the "key" to the texts over which they pore, and if
this observation is tantamount to equating those texts with "life," then
this transformation of text into life can also be described as the transformation of repetition from a process aimed at reproducing identity to
one that allows for the *aporetical resurgence of the singular:* aporetical,
because the singular as such is not identically repeatable, reproducible,
unique—but its uniqueness is also not separable from a certain repetition. Such repetition "produces" the uniqueness of the unrepeatable
in the form of those unexpected, often uncontrolled movements that
Benjamin designates as "gestures" (*Gebärde, Gestus, GS2*, 435; *SW2*,
814). And it is precisely in a certain kind of repetitive "gesture" that
Benjamin sees the similarity between the studying of the students and
that "hammering" which at the same time is "real" and yet also "nothing at all": "It is just such a decisive, fanatical gesture [*Gebärde*] that
the students [*die Studierenden*] have in their studies [*bei ihrem
Studium*]. Nothing could conceivably be more bizarre. The scribes, the

students are out of breath. They are always chasing off after something [*Sie jagen nur so dahin*]" (*GS2*, 435; *SW2*, 814). It is in such unpredictably spasmodic and interruptive "gestures" that the students, in their own peculiar way—"*auf eigentümlicher Weise*"—"reckon with" a time that is always in danger of running out. The gestures of the students combine the most extreme concentration with the most hectic exertion bordering on loss of control. The student whom Karl encounters one evening on the balcony of the building in which they both rent rooms spends most of his time reading, "accompanied by rapid lip-movements," a rapidity that Karl finds repeated, again and again: "He watched silently as the [student] read his book, turned the pages, now and then looked something up in another book that he grasped with lightning-like rapidity [*mit Blitzesschnelle ergriff*], and often jotted down notes in a notebook, whereby surprisingly he always sank his face deep into the notebook."[18] "Gesture," which here renders the student faceless, is according to Benjamin the decisive medium of Kafka's writing. Although he does not dwell on this point in his discussion of Benjamin's reading of Kafka in the *State of Exception*, Agamben does deal with the subject briefly, but again very suggestively, in his "Notes on Gesture" published originally in book form in 1978, and first translated into English in *Infancy and History*.[19] Although he is not mentioned by name in them, these "Notes" owe much to Walter Benjamin, whose shadow looms large over an argument that looks to cinema for the reintroduction of gestures into the image: "Cinema leads images back into the realm of gesture . . . Bringing the element of awakening into this dream is the task of the film maker."[20] Strangely and significantly it is not in the more obvious allusions to Benjamin that the most pertinent part of these notes is contained, at least insofar as the essay on Kafka is concerned. Rather, it is in a concluding quote from Varro, which situates gesture "in the sphere of action," while distinguishing "it clearly from acting *(agere)* and doing *(facere)*":

> A person can make [*facere*] something and not enact [*agere*] it, as when a poet makes a play, but does not act it [*agere* in the sense of playing a part]; on the other hand, the actor acts the play but does not make it. So the play is made [*fit*] by the poet, but not acted [*agitur*] by him; it is acted by the actor, but not made by him. Whereas the *imperator* (the magistrate in

whom supreme power is invested) of whom the expression *res gerere* is used (to carry something out, in the sense of taking it upon oneself, assuming total responsibility for it), neither makes nor acts, but takes charge, in other words bears the burden of it *(sustinet)*.[21]

Varro's distinction between the poet who makes the play, the actor who acts in it, and the *imperator,* who "neither makes nor acts but takes charge" and assumes the burden of carrying out the act, is illuminating with respect to the peculiar status of Kafka's students as read by Benjamin. For it is above all in the *acting of actors on a stage* that Benjamin finds the most telling confirmation of the gestures of the student, both in their suddenness and in their repetitive mixture of reality and nothingness: "Actors must be quick as lightning in catching their cues. And also in other respects they resemble these assiduous students [*diesen Beflissenen*]. For them in fact "hammering [is] real hammering and at the same time nothing at all"—namely, when it is part of their role. They study these roles; only a bad actor would forget any of its words or gestures" (*GS2,* 435; *SW2,* 814). The actor, like the student, is a reader, and above all, a reader whose reading involves memory, attention, speed, and surprise. And the sense or purpose of his acting cannot be separated from its execution, its performance: in that sense it is like that "hammering" that is both "real hammering and at the same time nothing at all," since it accomplishes nothing that can be separated from its own repetition. At the same time, Varro's reference to the *imperator* is no less illuminating, since it highlights, by contrast, what is particularly *"eigentümlich"*—distinctively peculiar—about the students and actors. Neither of the latter "carry through" or "take charge" in the way Varro attributes to the *imperator.* They do not "bear" the same "burden." A remark of Agamben's from the final chapter of the *State of Exception* helps clarify this complex relationship. In that chapter, in a section discussing precisely a passage from the *Res Gestae* of Augustus, Agamben cites the latter's distinction between the *impersonal power* of governing officials *(magistrat)* and the notion of "authority" usually associated with the Emperor, which is held to be inseparable from his person *(EE,* 136). Agamben thus insists on the *"incarnation* of an Auctoritas" in "the physical person" of the sovereign such that the death of that person creates a problem that does not exist with respect to "magistrates." In this he sees a forerunner of the

"charismatic" *Führer* or Leader of modern fascism, which belongs "to
the bio-political tradition of *auctoritas* and not to the juridical tradition
of *potestas*" (140). It is this tradition that foresees a convergence of
law and life in the "exceptional" figure of the individual Sovereign or
Leader that marks the transformation of "the juridical-political system
into a [bio-political] death machine" (145).

It is this convergence that is powerfully disrupted and interrupted by
the gestures of students and actors, whose studying and acting is both
real and nothing at all, which is to say, *leads* to nothing separable from
its own repetitive and spectral reenactment. Such repetitive and spectral reenactment subverts the very notion of "act" as "actualization":
acting is not *action* but *reaction* and *response,* which is why the "actor" is as far removed from the man of action as the stage is from the
sage. Or as far removed as are the student's "gestures" from any form
of self-expression.[22] The student's face is hidden by the gesture with
which his head sinks into his books. The gestures of actors or students
do not express their selves but rather expose and undo those selves irremediably. Which is to say also, for Benjamin at least, *theatrically.* The
great "chance" of theater, its sole chance to survive the challenge of
the new media, he situated in its *Exponierung des Anwesenden:* which
is to say, in its age-old capacity to "expose the present" in the double
sense of that word, including both *those present,* the "audience" or
Publikum—a word Benjamin never cared for—and the "present," insofar as it entails a temporal moment considered to be self-contained and
self-enclosed. Benjamin's notion of gesture entails the interruption and
the disruption of all such self-containment, and it does this by staging
finitude. In his essay "What Is Epic Theater?" Benjamin provides the
following account of gesture: "In opposition to the actions and undertakings of people [gesture] has a determinable beginning and a determinable end [*einen fixierbaren Anfang und ein fixierbares Ende*]. This
strict frame-like closure of each element of a posture [*Haltung: bearing*], which nevertheless as a whole is situated within the flow of life, is
even one of the dialectical foundations [*Grundpositionen*] of gesture.
From this an important conclusion follows: gestures are all the more
prevalent where an acting subject [*einen Handelnden*] is interrupted"
(GS2, 521). Gesture thus interrupts not just the "flow of life" in which
it is situated, but also its two most essential constituents: the goal-
directed action of a subject, "*eine[s] Handelnden,*" and the end-

directed movement of a *Handlung,* a plot or story, but also an action: "For epic theater therefore the interruption of the plot—*der Handlung*—is paramount" (521). In thus interrupting the "flow of life" and the flow of intentional activity, gestures ex-pose and deface those that "make" them far less than that they are unmade and undone by them. Just such a gesture accompanies the end of the scene in which Karl encounters the student. Karl has asked him for advice as to whether he should leave his current position in which he feels badly exploited. The answer he receives takes him by surprise: the student tells him to stay where he is.

> "You advise me, then, to stay with Delamarche?" Karl asked.
>
> "Absolutely [*unbedingt*]," said the student, his head already sinking into his books. It seemed as if it were not he who had said the word [*das Wort*]; as though spoken by a voice that was deeper than that of the student, it resonated long after in Karl's ears. Slowly he went to the curtain, glanced back a last time at the student, who now sat utterly immobile in the light of the lamp, surrounded by profound darkness, and then slipped back into his room.[23]

The voice responding to Karl's uncertainty about what to do echoes in his memory as though it had been disembodied, separated from the person ostensibly uttering it; its authority is one of disincarnation, and yet is in no way detached from the body; it is the voice of a specter rather than of a spirit, its "deeper" tone suggesting a person far older than the presumably still relatively young student. The voice removes itself from the person to whom it is supposed to belong and resounds in memory before fading away into the silent image of the student sitting motionless in the spotlight of the lamp, surrounded by darkness. This echoing and fading away of the voice—its *Verschallen*—is what defines the *"Verschollener."*

"The gate to justice is study," remarks Benjamin, and the study of the law, Agamben adds, when it comes to replace and supplant its practice, can prepare the way to "liberate" things from their "proper value," rendering them "absolutely unappropriable" (*EE,* 109) and perhaps also absolutely *inappropriate.* Study, for Benjamin no less than for Kafka, is inseparable from *reading,* even and perhaps especially where the text or script or key has been lost: "To read what never was written" was a phrase of Hofmannsthal that Benjamin was fond of quoting. At the end of his essay that is not just "on" or "about" Kafka, but is also dated and dedicated to the "tenth anniversary of his death,"[24] Benjamin provides an instance of just what such a reading—which repeats that which never was, and thereby sets Kafka into motion—might entail. In a short piece, he suggests, Kafka may have "found the law of his journey" and succeeded, "at least once" in "bringing its breathtaking speed in line with that epically measured step that he no doubt spent his entire life searching for. He entrusted it to a text [*Niederschrift*] that became his most consummate not merely because it is an interpretation:

> Sancho Pansa, who moreover never boasted about it, succeeded over the years, by amassing lots of chivalry and adventure novels for the evening and night hours, in so distracting from him his devil, to whom he subsequently gave the name Don Quixote, that the latter flamboyantly carried out [*aufführte*] the craziest deeds, which however for lack of a predetermined object, which should have been Sancho Pansa, did no one any harm. Sancho Pansa, a free man, perhaps out of a certain sense of responsibility, followed Don Quixote on his crusades, with an even temper, and gleaned from them great and useful entertainment until his end. (*GS2*, 438; *SW2*, 816–817)

Benjamin glosses this briefly but conclusively: "Sober fool and hapless assistant, Sancho Pansa sent his rider before him. Bucephalus outlived his. Whether man or horse no longer matters so much as long as the burden is lifted from one's back" (*GS2*, 438; *SW2*, 817). Sancho Pansa's gesture, which follows rather than leads, has little in common with the Imperial *res gestae,* for its "thing" is not action but acting, or rather *restaging* a spectacle and following it out. Or, as Benjamin puts it in the already quoted letter to Scholem of August 11, 1934: "Sancho Pansa's existence [*Dasein*] is exemplary [*musterhaft*] because it consists essentially in *rereading his own* [*im Nachlesen des eigenen*], however foolish and quixotic."[25] And if *we follow and reread* Kafka's short account and Benjamin's even shorter gloss, we may discover that in *interpreting (Auslegung), rereading and restaging one's own life,* a repetition takes place that *lifts the burden* from the subject who would be sovereign, granting him a certain freedom—that of divesting himself of his rider and simply going along for the ride.

"Going along for the ride" is not quite as simple or straightforward as it might seem. Following one's master as a "free man" may seem a far cry from a certain messianic pathos of salvation and redemption that can be found in the writings of both Agamben and Benjamin. But perhaps it is not as unrelated to that pathos as it might appear.

This at least is what begins to emerge from the short concluding chapter of Agamben's recent book, *Profanations*.[26] There, Agamben returns to Sancho Pansa, whom he now follows into a movie theater, somewhere in the provinces. Sancho is looking for Don Quixote, whom he finds in the theater, seated on the side of the screen. But because the theater is full of children, Sancho cannot get through to him. Sancho is forced to take a seat in the back, and finds himself next to a young girl—"(Dulcinea?)" conjectures the text parenthetically—who offers him a candy. Then, the film begins and shows a lady in distress: Don Quixote draws his sword and proceeds to demolish the screen, leaving only its empty wooden framework to receive, and efface, the images projected. All this meets with the wholehearted approval of the audience of children—with one exception. The little girl, "alone in the hall," fixes Don Quixote with a disapproving stare.

Of the moral of the story, which Agamben, unlike Kafka and Benjamin, does not hesitate to conclude,[27] I will retain here and now only the following: it is simply that "Dulcinea, whom we saved, cannot love us." The little girl next door, as it were, could not approve of Don Quixote's spectacular demolitions, however laudable their intention. And the narrator must confess that the price of those demolitions is high: "Dulcinea, whom *we saved*, cannot love us."[28] But who is this "we" who "saved Dulcinea" and who now realizes that he will not be loved in return? Is it Don Quixote? Sancho? The Author?

One of the most insistent motifs of *Profanations* stresses the imperative need of restoring or reinventing a certain *separation*—akin to that through which the opposition of the sacred and the profane was constituted and maintained. For it is just this separation, so Agamben asserts, that is in danger of extinction today by what Benjamin, in "Capitalism as Religion," described as the "cult religion of capitalism." This cult, Agamben argues, has both universalized and abolished separation—and with it, the possibility of profanation as well.[29] In the light of this critique, it is noteworthy that Agamben's restaging of Benjamin reading Kafka reading Cervantes seems in turn to suspend, if not abolish, the separation—and with it the distinction—that was so decisive in the previous scenarios from which he draws: that between Sancho Pansa and Don Quixote. In Agamben's version, Sancho, in the foreground at first, is suddenly and definitively eclipsed once Don Quixote springs into action, so that at the end of the story, the narrator appears to speak in the name of both. Moreover, this speaking is couched in the first person plural, providing the book with a resounding conclusion—echoing the first-person-plural discourse that dominates not just this book but most of Agamben's other writings as well. It is the "we" of a (not only grammatical) subject, which precisely by virtue of its *redemptive* ambition seems justified in assuming the first person *plural,* however ironic, *disabused,* and melancholy its tone may be.

And yet, what Agamben has noted elsewhere with respect to "Kafka's allegories"—namely "that at their very end they contain a possibility of an about-face that completely upsets their meaning,"[30] seems to apply here to his own "allegory" as well. All that is required to upset the reading just given, for instance, is to focus on the invisible, just as Benjamin, citing Hofmannsthal and quoted by Agamben, sought to "read what had never been written."[31] The reader need only recall the figure of Sancho Pansa, who in the meanwhile has vanished from the scene, in order to imagine another scenario that might follow upon the antics of Don Quixote in that remote provincial movie theater: one beginning perhaps with an exchange of glances between Sancho and his disgruntled neighbor and which continues with the gift of another lollypop.

Such a sequel would only demonstrate the trait that for Benjamin distinguishes the genuine story from other epic forms: the fact that once it is over one is always justified in asking, "What happened next? [*Wie ging es weiter?*]" (*GS2,* 455; *SW3,* 155).

To be continued...

CHAPTER FOURTEEN

Song and Glance

Walter Benjamin's Secret Names
(zugewandt—unverwandt)

> When I was born, the idea came to my parents that I might possibly be-
> come a writer. In that case, they thought it would be a good idea if it were
> not immediately obvious that I was Jewish. Therefore, in addition to my
> first name, they gave me two other, very unusual ones. Suffice it to say
> that parents forty years ago could hardly have been more prescient. What
> they held to be remotely possible has come to pass. Their efforts to con-
> front this fate, however, were stymied by the person concerned. Instead of
> making the two thoughtfully provided names public with his writings, he
> shut them up in himself. He watched over them as the Jews used to do
> over the secret names they gave to each of their children. The children
> themselves learned about these names only on the day of their coming-to-
> manhood [Mannbarwerdens]. Since however this can happen more than
> once in a lifetime, and perhaps not every secret name always remains self-
> same and unchanged, its transformation can easily reveal a new coming-
> of-age. And yet, notwithstanding, it is this name that collects the forces of
> life in itself, allowing them to be called upon and protecting them against
> those who are uncalled for.[1]

These words were written by Walter Benjamin on August 12, 1933,
some eight months after the National Socialists came to power, but
they were published only in 1972 by Gershom Scholem, who had discovered the text among Benjamin's papers and devoted an article to its
interpretation.[2] Scholem at first believed that the anecdote with which
Benjamin began the essay was fictitious. Later, however, he learned
from Werner Fuld, the author of a biography of Benjamin,[3] and who
had seen his Gestapo file, that he had indeed been given two additional
names besides his first one, "Benedix" and "Schönflies." The latter was
his mother's family name; the former, the first name of his paternal
grandfather.[4] As Scholem observes, however, if these names were in fact
destined to serve as a protective, literary cover, they were badly chosen,
since "every Jew at the time would have immediately known that only
a Jew could be called Benedix Schönflies. The masquerade would have
been entirely insufficient. Benjamin, however, did not know very much
about things Jewish [*Benjamin kannte sich in jüdischen Verhältnissen*

nicht sehr gut aus]."[5] Scholem's remarks here point up a number of curious problems both in Benjamin's short text, and in his own reading of it. First of all, if these two "secret" names were found in a Gestapo file, they were presumably officially given, and hardly therefore "secret." Nor could they be secret if they were to fulfill the function of obscuring Benjamin's Jewish origins. So much for Benjamin's introduction of this text. The second curiosity pertains to Scholem's own commentary. If as he asserts "every Jew at the time would have immediately known" that the names in question could only be those of a Jew, how could Scholem suppose that Benjamin for his part would not have known this as well, no matter how little he knew "about things Jewish"?

A possible response is that Benjamin, despite appearances to the contrary, is not in this text primarily concerned with his empirical autobiography, with the "real names" he may have been given, at least according to the Gestapo file. It is not just the fact that these names are nowhere mentioned in this text—that would be consistent with Benjamin's keeping them "secret"—but rather that his concern here lies more with the vicissitudes that the secret undergoes than with the names it thereby affects. Two of these vicissitudes stand out. First, Benjamin is fascinated with the idea of names being kept secret *from* the persons they name. He is so taken by this idea that, according to Scholem, he attributes a custom to Jewish tradition that it never entertained. In this tradition, Scholem asserts, parents give their children not "secret" names but Hebrew names, to be used in ritual prayers. These names remain "secret" only to those families who do not practice the traditional rites: in short, to "assimilated families" of the type to which Benjamin belonged. This is how Scholem sums up the situation: "In a certain sense one can designate Benjamin's description as accurate insofar as assimilated families are concerned. For there, the Hebrew names that are given, without exception, at circumcision, remain unknown until the Bar Mitzvah . . . because no one uses them . . . In pious families, on the other hand, every child knows his Hebrew name very well long before then, and this name remains unchanged throughout his entire life, providing he observes Jewish law (and its sexual prescriptions)."[6] What Scholem implies, here, is that Benjamin's invention of, or rather, interest in the "secret" dimension of "proper names" has as its precondition a certain non-observance of Jewish tradition and ritual. The "secret," from this point of view, would emerge only to the extent that this tradition was no longer viable. If this is so, it becomes even more significant that Benjamin insists on "inventing" a "Jewish" tradition that never existed. What Benjamin invents is a tradition of the "secret": a "secret tradition." It is the tradition apparently of a collective, a community, but as Scholem suggests in his essay, it is a collective that departs from the established traditions of that community; in place of a collective bound together by ritual practice, there emerges a dimension that is more individual, an erotic dimension.[7] The name becomes "secret" when it loses its relation to ritual and enters into a relation with the erotic.[8] This shift can be gauged in what Scholem describes as the "decisive" turning-point of this short text, which gives a new meaning to the notion of "attaining manhood," in German: *Mannbarwerden*.[9] In Jewish tradition, this does not designate a primarily biological or sexual event, but a ritual one: the coming to "manhood" marks the age when the child becomes a "man" in the sense of being permitted to read the Torah in religious services, and assuming responsibility for following all its prescriptions. Thus, becoming a "man" entails assuming an active role in ritual practices, and therefore qualifying to count as part of the minimum of ten adult males required to constitute a public community of prayer.[10] In short, becoming a "man" means, first and foremost, assuming a full role in the religious community. For Benjamin, however, it is precisely the gendered dimension that seems to replace the liturgical one: becoming a "man"—and this is not the same as just coming to "maturity," which is how the published English translation of this text reads—for Benjamin is defined in a way that separates one from this kind of community, but also from one's (previous) self. For the event is no longer one that takes place once and for all, but rather one that can repeat itself, each time reestablishing and changing the identity of whomever it affects.

Scholem, invoking convincing biographical evidence, sees the grounds of such separation in Benjamin's eroticism, which caused him to violate the monogamous precept of Jewish Law: "Being a man [*die Mannbarkeit*], which, in the Jewish tradition is only marginally sexual, is now related to the awakening of love, something that can happen in life more than once, namely with each new real love. To the pious person, which is to say, one who is true to the law, his 'secret name' remains unchanged throughout his life, because beyond his lawful marriage he has no sexual relations with other women."[11] Benjamin, as

Scholem does not fail to point out—and indeed elsewhere Benjamin himself does—could not be counted among such pious persons.[12]

Thus, according once again to Scholem, Benjamin's relation to the Jewish tradition was profoundly ambivalent: "It is entirely consistent with Walter Benjamin's convoluted essence that, although he was fully aware that Jewishness [*das Jüdische*] constituted both the foundation of his being and the goal of his thinking, it should have been perceptible almost exclusively in the 'overtones' of his work, albeit in very conspicuous places."[13] The assertion that "Jewishness" constituted for Benjamin "both the foundation of his being and the goal of his thinking" is however hardly self-evident. As we have already begun to see, and as Scholem himself insists, Benjamin knew very little about that tradition, and much of what he knew he rejected, at least insofar as it concerned ritual practice. But Scholem's claim is problematic not just in respect to Benjamin's autobiographical, empirical practice. It appears to presuppose that *"das Jüdische,"* as Scholem puts it—"Jewishness" or the "Jewish element"—can be identified as constituting both the "foundation" of his "being" and the "goal" of his "thinking." In order to evaluate fully such an assertion, it would be necessary first to read and analyze virtually all of Benjamin's texts from this point of view. And given the indisputable fact that, if there is such a relationship, it must be sought in the "overtones" of his writing, as Scholem puts it, rather than in its direct themes or statements, the interpretation would have to be as microscopic as it was extensive. Even the very short but very dense and difficult text we are discussing will prove far too complex to be exhaustively analyzed in the limited space available here.

Such complexity, however, makes it difficult to accept the kinds of generalizations to which Scholem all too often succumbs, as for instance, when he remarks that "Benjamin's 'theological thinking,' which in his earlier years was very pronounced, was . . . informed by Jewish concepts. Christian ideas never had the power of fascinating him."[14] For someone whose thought was developed in constant dialogue with Kant, the early Jena Romantics, Goethe, and above all, Hölderlin, this seems a rather difficult statement to uphold. That Benjamin's thought *also* developed in *Auseinandersetzung*—that is, critical confrontation—with certain aspects of the Jewish tradition is beyond all doubt and Benjamin is quite explicit about this. That such an *Auseinandersetzung* precluded the kind of exclusive and exclusionary perspective expressed in the passage just cited from Scholem, however, is no less certain. The rule in approaching such a complex and ambivalent relationship is surely closer to that stated, succinctly, by Elisabeth Weber in her preface to the remarkable series of interviews she conducted and published under the title *Questions au judaisme* (Questions asked of Judaism): "Questions concerning Judaism, Jewish tradition and history, always also concern other traditions."[15] A brief example from Benjamin's work will have to serve as an index. In his essay on Kafka, in which he emphasizes the author's relation to certain Jewish traditions, Benjamin highlights the importance of "studying," highly valued in the Jewish tradition, before introducing a somewhat surprising reference: "Perhaps such studies were worth nothing. But they stand very close to that Nothing, which alone can make Anything useful: that is to say, the Tao."[16]

Perhaps these few remarks will suffice to suggest how complex a role "religion" or "religions" play in Benjamin's writing, and why only a process of prolonged and minute reading, one that is not entirely in the throes of a priori convictions, can possibly hope to arrive at an arguable interpretation of a writer as convoluted as Walter Benjamin.[17] Alternatively, paraphrases, summaries, and facile generalizations that leapfrog over textual difficulties to arrive directly and quickly at clear-cut conclusions almost inevitably have to leapfrog as well over precisely what is most specific and distinctive in his writing and thinking.

The passage cited at the outset, the first of four paragraphs that compose this text, exemplifies the ambivalence of Benjamin's relation to the Jewish tradition to which Scholem refers, without however at the same time in any way confirming the conclusion he draws from it. Benjamin never names the two "very unusual names" to which he refers, and this for cause, since he goes on to describe how he kept these names "shut up in himself" in order to hide behind them, as his parents had intended. Scholem, however, is convinced that these names can be named, deciphered from the title Benjamin gives to this text: "Agesilaus Santander." In the text itself, Benjamin nowhere refers to this title explicitly. In Scholem's reading of it, however, it becomes an anagram of "Der Angelus Satanas," "The Angel Satan" (with one "i" left over). There is no doubt, as Scholem argues, that Benjamin was fascinated with such language games, in which he himself frequently indulged. It is also certain that such games were for him not simply entertaining exercises, but rather significant experiments exploring the relation of identity and symbolization. The problem is that the mere identification of such an anagrammatic possibility, however suggestive, does not in and of itself obviate the need for further reading and interpretation of this text. For what, after all, can it mean for Benjamin to employ two very different names: one, that of a Theban King ("Agesilaus"), and the other, the name of a city in Northern Spain, as a title, even and especially if they are intended as an anagram of the more abstract and ostensibly more transparent notion of "The Angel Satanas"? Is Benjamin thereby suggesting that the "New Angel" that accompanies him physically and spiritually since his purchase of Paul Klee's *Angelus Novus* watercolor in 1921, is in fact a "Satanic Angel"? And if so, what would that signify? The answer cannot be sought in this text alone, of course, but rather in other texts, such as his earlier study of German baroque theater, in which Satan plays an explicit and important role.

Toward the end of his book on the *Origin of the German Mourning Play* (1924), Benjamin places the figure of Satan at the very center not just of baroque allegory, but of modernity itself. Satan, he writes (or rather cites), is "the 'original allegorical figure'" insofar as he appears as the great tempter of man, specifically by offering him "initiation into knowledge."[18] Such knowledge, Benjamin argues, must be sharply distinguished from "truth": "The intention that underlies allegory is so opposed to that which is concerned with the discovery of truth that it reveals more clearly than anything else the identity of the pure curiosity that is aimed at mere knowledge with the proud isolation of man" (*GS2*, 403; *Origin*, 229). This motif of isolation traverses all of Benjamin's writing and is in part responsible for its complex relation to anything communitarian, be it "Jewish" or "Revolutionary." There is, however, another aspect of Benjamin's discussion of "Satanic temptation" in the *Trauerspiel* book that is relevant for our considerations. Out of the mood of "mourning" that dominates the German baroque "mourning play,"

> three original satanic promises are born. They are spiritual in kind. The *Trauerspiel* continually shows them at work, now in the figure of the tyrant, now in that of the intriguer. What tempts is the illusion of freedom—in the exploration of what is forbidden; the illusion of independence—in the secession from the community of the pious; the illusion of

infinity—in the empty abyss of evil . . . Absolute spirituality [*Geistigkeit*], which is what Satan means, destroys itself in its emancipation from the sacred. Materiality—but here soulless materiality—becomes its home. The purely material and the absolutely spiritual are the poles of the satanic realm and consciousness is their illusory synthesis. (*GS2*, 403–404; *Origin*, 230)

Freedom, independence of the individual, infinity—these notions, which served Kant as instances of what he called "regulative ideas" and thus constituents of "reason," are portrayed by Benjamin here as the quintessence of a certain modernity, and in particular of its conception of a subject that is free, autonomous, and infinite, which is to say, fully self-conscious. Such a conception, which at first takes the form of "absolute spirituality," must for Benjamin lead ultimately to self-destruction, since it misconstrues the finite, material, interdependent nature of human existence. Such self-destruction does not, however, cause it simply to disappear but rather to alter its mode of being. From "absolute spirituality," it becomes a no less pure if "soulless materiality." These two "poles": "the purely material . . . and the absolutely spiritual" constitute the satanic realm, which in turn is held together only by the "illusory synthesis of consciousness." The name of this illusory synthesis is the "self," and the emergence of this illusion *as illusion* constitutes what Benjamin designates as "allegory," in which matter and spirit, expression and meaning are linked only by an unbridgeable chasm: the chasm of "signification."

Although there is no space here to delve further into the baroque "background" of Benjamin's short text, the brief passage just discussed will, I hope, indicate that wherever it is a question of "names," "secret" or not, these names must be read as allegories, rather than as symbolic or direct presentations of what they designate. "Agesilaus," King of Sparta, who vanquished Persians, Thebans, and Athenians successively before finally suffering defeat at Mantinea, could be read as a figure whose life exemplifies both the drive for infinite power and the inescapable destiny of finite beings. "Santander," a town not very far from the island of Ibiza, where Benjamin was when he wrote this text, localizes in a European, Catholic country, what might otherwise seem to be a metaphysical or mythical figure: Agesilaus at Santander suggests allegorically Benjamin on Ibiza. However powerful the claims to freedom, autonomy, and infinitude may be, their fate is already prefigured in the fact that those claims have to be made from a site whose locality belies the infinitude of those claims.

That "Agesilaus (at) Santander" could *also,* as Scholem suggests, be an anagram of "Der Angelus Satanas," "The Angel Satan," takes on a certain plausibility in view of the role played by the figure of Satan in what for Benjamin was a distinctively modern, and indeed distinctively Christian, crisis. Christianity brought with it the Good Tidings of freedom, autonomy, and infinitude. But it therefore had to answer for doubts and uncertainties that never entirely disappeared, and indeed intensified at particular historical periods. The fall of Satan, and the fall induced by Satan, were for him symptoms of the doubt that rose to challenge the promise of redemption through knowledge. The figure that perhaps most emphatically was identified with this challenge for Benjamin was that of Martin Luther. This is why Luther, the Reformation and Counter-Reformation, together with their theatrical offspring, Hamlet, occupy such a central position in his discussion of the German baroque mourning play. It is not, however, the dogmatic Luther who is important to Benjamin, but rather the melancholy figure whose radical antinomianism threatens *all* dogma, including his own: that of *sola fides,* grace by faith alone.

Benjamin's attitude toward the Jewish past and its traditions is marked by the same sort of radical antinomianism, and this calls into question Scholem's assertion that an *exclusively* "Jewish" element provided the "foundation" of his being and the "goal" of his thought. To examine a concrete instance of this, let us return to the initial paragraph of *Agesilaus Santander.* Its discursive mode at first is retrospective and narrative, but then shifts gradually to what might be described as a dramatic-theatrical style of writing. The text begins with what is apparently a recollection, that of having been given two names by his parents for a very special reason. That reason refers to the particular situation in which Benjamin found himself at the time he was writing: that of a Jewish refugee from Nazism eking out a living in Catholic countries such as France and Spain. That situation defined part of what it meant for him to be "Jewish," but from outside, negatively, in terms of dangers and hardships. Benjamin's anecdote, however, describes not the keeping of a ritual—with which, as we have seen, it has little in common—but rather an individual gesture on the part of his parents, seeking in advance to protect their child: "It might be a good idea if it were not immediately obvious that I was Jewish." Benjamin acknowledges that his parents were uncommonly prescient in taking such a measure. But he immediately adds that his response to their concern condemned their efforts to naught. Instead of using the names—which would only be "secret" in hiding his "real" name and identity—Benjamin "shut them up in himself." In so doing, he both allowed his Jewishness to appear to the world through his writing, and at the same time participated in a ritual that he designates as Jewish, but which, as Scholem argues, applies more to the *abandonment* of religious practices by "assimilated" Jews rather than to their adherence to traditional ritual or beliefs.

Instead of allowing his parents, through the device of the secret names, to "watch over" their child, Benjamin, by shutting up the names in himself, replaced his parents' concern, which he fantasmatically attributes to a nonexistent religious practice, with an introspective one. This "shutting up" of the names in himself is one form of that "separation" that Benjamin, in the history of European religions, associates with the Lutheran Reformation and the modernity to which it gave rise. At the same time, the reference to the supposed but fictitious "Jewish" tradition of "secret names" allows Benjamin to display his own, highly distinctive version of this kind of naming. In traditional Jewish ritual, the constancy of the name and of the person named is guaranteed by observation of the Law. Benjamin's shutting up of the secret names results in a very different situation. His version of naming, secret or not, involves not the establishment of continuity and constancy, but rather insistence on repetition and change. "Coming to manhood" is no longer a single, unrepeatable event marking the assumption of responsibility by adult Jewish males. Instead, it becomes an event that "can occur more than once in a lifetime." A corollary of this repeatability and multiplicity is the fact that "every secret name" that reveals itself at such moments "need not remain the same and unchanged." The name can change, and with it, the identity of the person it names, whose "life-forces" it nevertheless gathers and protects.

But protects against whom or what? Despite the obvious external danger that Benjamin begins by acknowledging, this mutability of the name, through the multiple possibilities, erotic or not, of "becoming a man," introduces a different sort of struggle and dynamic. It is one that no longer plays itself out *between* the "self" and its external "others," between Jews on the one hand and non-Jews on the other, but rather *within* the relationship of the self to its name or names. In this sort of conflict-situation, there can be no hiding behind "secret names." Indeed, the "secret" itself begins to change its nature. The name is no longer a secret to *others,* but to the one who bears it. And since it changes, it can also be described as a *secret to itself,* as it were. Hence, a different sort of response to this metamorphosing secret is called for, and it is this response that Benjamin's text goes on to describe.

Or rather: to *stage.* The difference between a description and a staging lies primarily in the shift in the position of the writer. If a description and a narration presuppose a position that is essentially detached from what is being described or narrated, a staging acknowledges the involvement of the subject in the space of recounting. This involvement is marked, from the second paragraph on, by a series of unexpected turns, *peripeteia,* that endow the text with an increasingly dramatic, and indeed theatrical, cast.[19]

It is no accident therefore that the first *coup de théâtre* concerns the status of the name itself. For if, as Scholem elsewhere asserts, Benjamin's relation to Jewish motifs turns on his conception of the "name,"[20] from the very beginning of the text this conception reveals a significance that is at variance with that found in most organized religions, whether Jewish or other. The name no longer functions to guarantee the constancy and continuity of the named, in the image of its Creator, understood to be one and the same. Rather, it becomes a differential mark of that which distinguishes the human from the divine and singularizes it: its *mutability.* "Perhaps not every secret name remains self-same and unchanged" is the way this idea is introduced in the opening paragraph. But after concluding that paragraph by ostensibly returning to a more familiar and more reassuring notion of the name as that which unifies and protects the "self" from external threats, the second paragraph, or scene, of the text begins with yet another surprising twist: "But in no way is this name an enrichment of the one who bears it. It deprives him of many things, but most of all, of the gift of appearing to be the same old person [*ganz der Alte zu erscheinen*]."[21] Not only does the name not stay the same—the person named is overtaken by this destiny of change. And contrary to what one generally expects or thinks, it is the name that is responsible for this change, rather than operating as a mark of permanence. This conception of the "name" diverges radically from that which is familiar and on which we tend to rely, in our everyday affairs perhaps even more than in our intellectual endeavors. Benjamin was fond of quoting Karl Kraus's dictum "the closer we look at a word, the more distantly it looks back,"[22] and in this text, something similar happens to one's secret name or names. They do not stay the same, and that is perhaps their greatest and most enigmatic "secret."

As Scholem suggests, this conception of a changing name is anything but traditionally Jewish—nor, I would surmise, would it be at home in any monotheistic orthodoxy.[23] The question of whether or not one of the defining functions of organized monotheistic religions is to promise a certain constancy of self, tied to the immutability of the religious institution itself, and ultimately to the Creator and His Name (or Names), is one I will leave here in abeyance. For this text, at any rate, the mutability of the name and the named, the repeatability of the process of "coming to manhood" introduces a series of transformations that endow the remainder of this text, as indicated, with a distinctly scenic and theatrical quality. The narrative-retrospective moment does not vanish but is reinscribed in a series of allegorical transformations that allow no simple or univocal identification. The lines just quoted, describing how the mutability of the name prevents one from "appearing to be the same" as one was, are followed by an instance of just what happens to someone who can no longer appear to be *ganz der Alte:* "In the room where I last lived, that other [*jener*], before stepping forth, armed and polished, out of the old name and into the light, hung up his picture in my home: New Angel. The Cabbala recounts that in each instant [*Nu*] God creates innumerable new angels, all of whom are destined, before they dissolve into nothing, to sing his praises for a single moment before his throne. In the process, mine had been interrupted: his features had nothing human [*nichts Menschenähnliches*] about them."[24] The "old one" who no longer appears to be the same, now "steps forth" out of the old name, which he discards as a kind of cocoon, into the light, reborn but in radically different guise. No longer as a person, nor even as a name, but rather as a *picture*, provided with a new name or rather, with a title: "New Angel." Given the biographical and textual background, one cannot but think of the "Angelus Novus" of Klee's watercolor, to whose interpretation he returned repeatedly throughout the rest of his life. No straightforward *Bilderverbot* can be found in Benjamin's work, which, as here, is fascinated by images. And yet, there is a kind of prohibition at work in the images inscribed in his texts. For they bear no manifest resemblance to what one expects—here, for instance, to human beings. That which steps out of the "old name" into the light, reveals itself to be an image, a picture—a *Bild*—that vexes as much as it satisfies (one of Benjamin's favorite words, in this context, was *Vexierbild:* a picture-riddle that "vexes" by puzzling and demands to be deciphered). The "new angel," who "hangs up his picture" on the wall of Benjamin's room, is one such *Vexierbild.*

What such images entail in his writing is never the prohibition of images pure and simple, but rather the dislocation of the logic of representation with which images are generally viewed, at least in the "West." This little vignette, however, condenses in remarkable fashion just what is involved in the dislocation. However much Benjamin may have been fascinated by the Cabbala, the legend he quotes from it here—like the Jewish custom of giving Hebrew names—serves only as a point of departure, not of arrival, as do his other references to elements of Jewish tradition: the giving of Hebrew names, or the tradition of "angelology" in general. Benjamin's "new angel," who emerges out of the old names to sing the praises of the Lord for a brief instant, is *interrupted*, prevented from fulfilling its destiny, but also . . . from *disappearing.*[25] The form this frozen, arrested, interrupted trajectory assumes is that of an image, and more precisely, of a figure. But far from being a figure that reveals, manifests, represents—a meaningful image—this figure is enigmatic, the result of a violent intervention and interruption. The interruption of a *work.* The work of the angel has been interrupted, but its suspension holds out another possibility: that of a certain kind of survival. The angel that survives as "interrupted" image, however, differs from the traditional notion of angels insofar as its image displays no resemblance to the human form and figure, created, as the Bible says, in the image of God.

What does this image, which is not like anything human, resemble? First, and perhaps foremost: an artifact. The *Angelus Novus* is not just "an image," but a picture hung on the wall of a room by the "old one" whom the narrator of this text no longer entirely resembles. This image, in its dissimilarity to anything human, is what remains when one no longer appears to be entirely the same as before. It is an image of change, of time, of aging. In that, its original mission has left traces. At the same time, as a picture it is quite literally, but also metaphorically, forced to "hang around" for a while. The image of what one once was is replaced by this painting, hung up in the room where the narrator "last lived." Just as he cannot hope to stay the same by virtue of his secret names, so this picture does not remain a simple picture but rather splits, doubles itself and sends out its emissary, its angel—who is no longer simply a picture hanging on a wall—down to earth in pursuit of the narrator: "Moreover, he paid me back for being disturbed in his work. By taking advantage of the circumstance that I came to the world under the sign of Saturn—the slowly revolving planet, the heavenly body of hesitating and delaying—he sent his female figure to follow the masculine one in the picture, but by way of the slowest, most ominous detour, although both had been such close neighbors."[26] If this angel is descended from those described in the Cabbala, it is already a very distant relative. Not only does it fail to carry out its heavenly mission, it takes its revenge by sending down a "female figure" to punish the one it holds responsible for interrupting its work.[27]

Rightly or wrongly, this angel is an avenging angel. It has been interrupted in its "work," holds the narrator responsible, and seeks to pay him back. It does so by both remaining itself, a picture hung on a wall, and at the same time becoming something else, sending its mirror image as an avenging angel to pursue Benjamin. It is as though the picture, by becoming other than what it is, acquires an allegorical character: its "meaning" detaches itself from its initial source and starts to move.

This new "mission" ushers in the third major section or scene of the text, one in which the author-narrator splits in a way not entirely unlike the splitting or doubling of the angel (or of the secret names). The narrator, who up to now has written of himself in the first person, now splits into an I and an "it":

Perhaps he [the Angel] did not realize that he thereby mobilized the strength of the one against whom he moved. For my patience yields to nothing. It beats [its wings] in a way not unlike the Angel's, since very few strokes are required to render it unmovable in face of the one it has decided to await. It, however, with claws like the Angel's and beating wings sharp as knives, gives no sign of pouncing upon the one it has in its sights. It learns from the way the Angel embraces his partner with a glance, before fitfully and irresistibly withdrawing. He draws him in his wake, fleeing into a future out of which he has emerged [*aus der er vorgestoßen ist*]. From it [the flight], he expects nothing new any more, only the glance of the person toward whom he is turned.

And so—having just seen you for the first time—I went back with you to the place from where I had come.[28]

Until the third paragraph, the text has been limited to a description of a relatively static situation. First, the memory of the secret names. Then, the more dynamic but still relatively stable emergence of the picture from the old name, as well as the unfolding of the picture's contents, the angel interrupted in its work. Out of this interruption comes the sending of a second, avenging angel. And then, in this third paragraph or scene, comes the response. It is surprisingly anti-climactic and un-dramatic. In a certain sense, nothing happens. But as Benjamin says of the Taoist element in Kafka: it is that nothing upon which everything depends (*GS2*, 435; *SW2*, 813). It is the response not of an action, or even of a reaction, but of "patience"—a feature that appears to resemble the angel, from whom it in any case "learns." This "patience" has claws, and wings that cut through the air, "not unlike [those] of the angel." But unlike the angel, the wings of Benjamin's patience seem to have no mission other than to mark time: that is, to *stay put*, "immovable in face of the one they have decided to await." There is, in a sense, a double doubling: the angel duplicates itself in its feminine counterpart; and Benjamin's "patience" mirrors the claws and beating of the angel. A series of repetitions or duplications are deployed, but each time with a significant alteration: the emissary of the angel is feminine, not masculine; the wings of Benjamin's patience beat in order to stay put and in so doing anticipate the angel described in thesis 9 of one of his last writings, "On the Concept of History": "He [the angel] would like to stay, awaken the dead and piece together what has been smashed. But a storm blowing from paradise has caught itself in his wings and is so strong that the angel can no longer close them" (*GS4*, 697–698; *SW4*, 389–400). When the wind that blows from Paradise blows toward catastrophe—as in the baroque period that Benjamin saw as the origin not just of the German mourning play, but of Western modernity in general—then the best one can hope for is to hold one's ground. Here, in the text of 1933, the context is less sinister, and less manifestly historical. But the gesture is the same: holding off the thrust of time and history with a few "beats" of the wings of patience, making "interruption" into the possibility of salvation, however slim. This is "patience" in the literal, as well as the figurative, sense. It does not undertake any *action*: its sole activity is marking time, as it were. In such "marking" of time resides, perhaps, that "weak messianic power" of which Benjamin writes elsewhere,[29] and which in his "Theological-Political Fragment" he associates with the "eternally passing [*ewig vergehende*]" nature of the world (*GS1*, 204; *SW3*, 305–306). This is very different from the mission of the angel, which was to sing the praises of the Lord and then to disappear. Benjamin's angel is the result of the interruption of its song and its replacement by a glance.

As a conclusion, it is something of an anticlimax. Benjamin's patience holds its ground, neither more nor less. It learns from the angel neither to destroy its partner nor to succumb to it. Like the angel, it draws back and with it, draws the other after it, fleeing into a future out of which it has come. The two, angel and partner, patience and partner, withdraw in a movement that is both spasmodic *(stossweise)* and irresistible, in a kind of dance that replaces the song that had been interrupted. And yet that substitution is not definitive: the angel withdraws slowly but surely into the future, "out of which it has emerged." It should not be forgotten that the "future" of this angel was nothing other than its disappearance. It is only here inasmuch as this future has been interrupted. But while the future can be interrupted, it cannot be abolished. The angel, which has "emerged" out of this future, proceeds to draw its partner back into it: back into a future in which there will be nothing more to see. In thus withdrawing, all it can hope for is the glance of the person toward whom it is turned, a glance that follows and mirrors its departure.

From this flight, however, the angel—or is it the narrator's patience—has little to hope for, "only the glance of the person towards whom he is turned [*dem er zugewandt bleibt*]."[30]

But toward whom is this Angel turned, *zugewandt?* In what direction is his glance directed? Every interpretation I have read of Klee's famous *Angelus Novus,* including those of Benjamin himself, has simply assumed that the angel is facing the spectator. For instance, Scholem, when he attempts to identify the referent of the final apostrophe: "The final formulation contains both the possible relation to the face of the beloved, whom he had decided never to forsake even though he had never possessed her, as well as a statement about the angel itself, who maintains itself facing Benjamin [*im Angesicht Benjamins*], at whom his wide-open eyes, whose glance seems never to be empty, are directed and from whom, as the human being he had chosen, he was determined never to waver."[31] But in his effort to distinguish "angel" from "beloved"—as though the two could be as clearly separated as if they were two distinct persons—Scholem, like almost all others who have commented on this picture, seems never to have looked at it closely. For even a fairly summary glance should allow one to notice that the glance of Klee's *Angelus Novus* may be directed in the general direction of the viewer, but that his eyes are riveted *elsewhere:* off to one side. The eyes of the angel are "fixed," but not on the beholder. They look past him or her, glancing off into the space they share, but without having any discernible object.

This strange kind of glance recalls the description given by Scholem, in another essay, of the unforgettable impression left by Walter Benjamin upon Scholem the first time he saw him, speaking at a meeting of students on the eve of World War I: "I don't remember any more what he said, but I remember vividly his appearance as a speaker. It left an indelible impression insofar as *he never looked at the audience* and instead spoke freely while *staring impassively* [*unverwandt*] *at a remote corner of the auditorium ceiling,* to which he spoke with great intensity and, as far as I can remember, in perfectly formed phrases [*druckreif*]."[32] Such *impassiveness* is a quality that Benjamin cultivated, quite deliberately, in his writing, and apparently also in his speaking. It is to be confused neither with indifference nor with passivity. It emerged from the double gesture of being turned toward—*zugewandt*—and yet in the process glancing off that toward which it is turned, and thus remaining detached, separate, impassive: *unverwandt*.

The New Angel glances at us and yet past us, the way Walter Benjamin looks at and past his past, which involves a certain Jewish tradition, including the separation of, and from, that tradition. It includes this, but not this alone. In thus looking past the past, such a glance perhaps leaves room for a different kind of future, one that would not lead "back" simply to the place from where we have come. For if this text, and Benjamin's writing in general, suggest anything, it is that such a place can never be found, because it never stays where it was.

CHAPTER FIFTEEN

"Streets, Squares, Theaters"

A City on the Move—Walter Benjamin's Paris

It is anything but self-evident that the writings of Walter Benjamin, and most recently the accumulation of notes and excerpts devoted to the Parisian Passages, should continue to enjoy such wide popularity. For Benjamin's criticism, as distinct from much cultural criticism today, never forgets that whatever his subject-matter may be, its distinctive specificity always entails a certain structure of language, and hence, of its interpretation. Never does Benjamin appeal to a "materiality" of objects that would not simultaneously involve a signifying structure. And nowhere is that more evident than in his approach to the city, and in particular, to the Paris through which his Passages pass, or—if I can coin a phrase: *impasse*. This city, perhaps more than any other, emerges in Benjamin's writing as itself a *text*. To be sure, to understand the kind of textuality that constitutes Paris for Benjamin, it is imperative that the notion of "text" be taken in the larger sense assigned to it some thirty-five years ago by Jacques Derrida, who, in his programmatic essay "Of Grammatology" argued for a notion of a "generalized text," to be distinguished from the more familiar notion of book, or from the more restricted phenomenon of words actually written or printed on a page.

This notion of a "generalized text"—one that would accommodate a "city" no less than an exclusively verbal structure—has had a somewhat checkered history, and in part for understandable reasons. For it has seemed to many, and not just at first sight, that this attempt to "generalize" the notion of text had something imperialistic about it, extending the realm of script, and with it the rule of scribes, to all aspects of human existence, and perhaps of existence in general.[1] But this suspicion in most cases was based on a misreading so evident that it had to be driven by a desire to retain precisely what the notion of "generalized textuality" was designed to challenge: the priority of a certain notion of self-presence, identity, and meaning with respect to their mode of articulation. The misreading to which I refer quite simply ignored the fact that what allows the notion of textuality to be "generalized" in the way indicated by Derrida—and before him, by Benjamin—was not its discursivity, nor its substance, but rather its *mode of signifying*.[2] Building on Saussure's notion of signification as a process distinct from and structurally prior to representation, a process constituted by differential relations rather than by the representation of a self-identical referent, Derrida's notion of a general and generative textuality argued that any process of articulation, whether discursive, using words and language, or non-discursive, using images, sounds, or any other "sense impressions," operates in the manner of a text insofar as meaning determines itself through the differential relations in which it is engaged. What distinguished Derrida's approach from that of orthodox structuralists such as Saussure—and what even today makes the term "poststructuralist" a usable and viable designation—is the way it construes the operation of these differential relations. Unlike Saussure, *différance* for Derrida was invariably caught in a double bind: that of "binding" itself. Which is to say, the differential process entailed the deferring of a meaning that therefore could never be self-contained or complete. Any semantic determination inevitably depended on what it could never fully assimilate or integrate. An illustrative example is looking up a word in the dictionary: each new reference opens up new possibilities, ad infinitum. The existence of conventions generally serves to short-circuit what would otherwise be a *regressus ad infinitum*. But only at a cost, for the implications and connotations always exceed whatever definition or determination we decide, or convention decides, to make.

The notion of a generalized—or perhaps better, *generative*—textuality, then, never implied the servile recourse to an authoritative and irresponsible "pedagogy," but rather the acknowledgment of an inevitable involvement in a network of responses and appeals, readings and definitions that cannot legitimate itself *in its own terms*. Such involvement is therefore inevitably *exposed* to a future that will never be entirely predictable, or fathomable.

It is the burden and challenge of such *exposure* that marks the writings of Walter Benjamin, and perhaps none more than those gathered in, and as, the *Passages*. What they expose is nothing more or less than the *allegorical cast* of apparently material reality. Such allegorical exposure takes responsibility for the unknowable that sits at the heart of all efforts to decipher and decode, interpret and communicate. To take responsibility, in other words, for something that cannot be controlled, but that nevertheless calls insistently for a response.

This is perhaps the secret fascination of Benjamin's writings: in exposing the allegorical cast of their subjects, they *demand a response* that goes beyond the conventional notion of reading as the rendering of meaning.[3] Benjamin never forgot that reading, far from being simply the reassuring recognition of the familiar, involved the taking of risks and the exposure to danger. Nowhere was he more concerned with this than in his *Passages,* as the following passage, from Notebook "N," suggests:

What distinguishes images from the "essences" of Phenomenology, is their historical index . . . The historical index of images indicates not merely that they belong to a particular time, it indicates that only in a particular time do they come to be readable [*zur Lesbarkeit kommen*]. And this coming to be readable defines a critical point in their innermost movement. Every present is determined through those images that are synchronic with it: every now is the now of a determinate knowability.[4] In it truth is charged with time to the breaking point. (This breaking, nothing else, is the death of intention, which thus coincides with the birth of genuine historical time, the time of truth.) It is not so much that what has gone by [*das Vergangene*] casts its light upon the present, or that the present casts its light upon what is gone; rather, the image is the constellation that ensues when what has been [*das Gewesene*] converges with the Now in a flash. In other words: image is dialectics at a standstill. For while the relation of the present to the past is purely temporal, that of what has been to the Now is dialectical: not temporal in nature but rather imagistic. Only dialectical images are genuinely historical, i.e. not archaic images. The image that has been read [*das gelesene Bild*], which is to say, the image in the now of Knowability, bears to the highest degree the stamp of the critical, dangerous moment that underlies all reading. (N 3,1)[5]

The "historical image" that Benjamin describes here is not something that can simply be seen, but something that must be *read*. Its "readability" or legibility—its *Lesbarkeit*—is what results from the highly conflictual kind of relations that produce it. This is why Benjamin takes pains to emphasize that the historicity of an image does not result simply from its belonging to a particular epoch, but rather, from what he designates as its "synchronic" relation to it. Such synchronicity is constituted as much by separation as by convergence. It is precisely this simultaneity, involving both proximity and distance, that is the condition of any possible "knowledge" of images, their "knowability." Such "knowability" is situated not in the interval between two fixed points, for instance between the Past shedding light on the Present, or the Present shedding light on the Past, but rather in a different sort of space: that of a convergence that does not result in simple identity. What it produces is articulated through two very different and yet complementary figures in Benjamin's writing: the *Blitz,* the lightening flash, and the *constellation,* the more or less stable agglomeration of stars.

One might be tempted here to try and relativize the tension of these two figures so dear to Benjamin by ascribing the "flash" to the manner in which "what has been," in coming together with the "Now," acquires a certain stability as the "constellation." And that would not be entirely wrong. The point, however, is that this constellation in and of itself remains marked by the abrupt and instantaneous process out of which it emerges. It is defined by the *potentiality* of *Zerspringen,* of breaking apart, which Benjamin describes as the "genuinely historical time, the time of truth." Truth then, with Benjamin as with Heidegger, entails not the correspondence of an intention with an intended object: it is not the fulfillment, and hence, confirmation, of a temporal movement, tending toward a goal, but rather "the death of *intentio*" which is simultaneously the "birth" of another kind of time, not that of the subject, but of "history" and of "truth."

Only in this sense can the dialectical image be said to be both "knowable" and "legible." "Knowable" because "legible." But "knowledge" here is as unstable as is truth, and "reading" is the articulation of the two. Articulation, here as elsewhere, designates not simply identity or synthesis, but a disjunctive bringing-together and keeping-apart, for instance of the most extreme movement—that of the lightning bolt *(blitzhaft)*—and the most extreme stasis, that of the constellation.

This indicates just why Benjamin should have been interested in questions that seem as much spatial as temporal, and above all in their disjunctive convergence, as for instance, in "Paris" designated "as Capital of the nineteenth Century." For such "localizations" interrupt and suspend the goal-governed, teleological temporality of self-conscious "intentionality," in which all movement is construed from the perspective of an ultimately static, detached, and unquestioned fix-point, one that reflects, more or less unconsciously and uncritically, the point of view of the observer. It is this notion of "time" that is "exploded" by the spatiality of a text that must be read, that is "readable," *lesbar,* but that can never be wrapped up in a definitive or conclusive meaning. This is why the "critical" moment that underlies all reading is also designated by Benjamin as being a "dangerous" one. For it inevitably poses a threat to its own identity by acknowledging its involvement in a movement whose end can be neither fully foreseen nor entirely controlled. The *danger* that underlies this kind of critical reading would thus be of the same sort as the danger that haunts human life itself, and this might ultimately explain much of the resistance to reading and to its correlatives, textuality and writing. In this case, however, the "generality" of the text and of reading would be tied not to the universality of the concept or that of "theory," but to the critical moment of *singularity* that marks the *disjunctive convergence* of the two: of the general and the particular, the theoretical and the practical.

This is why the kind of textually oriented reading called for here by Benjamin, or practiced by Derrida, distinguishes itself both from traditional theoretical and from traditional critical discourse precisely in the way it responds to this singularity. Its involvement in texts—which are always singular structures even when they are non-discursive, as here, where they concern "readable images"—does not lead to general conclusions that can be extrapolated from their singular occurrences and made into the elements of a universally valid system of knowledge or even of a methodology. Benjamin has no methodology, no more than does Derrida. His writings, however, can be read as tracing lines of force that lead in certain directions. In the remarks that follow, I want to explore a few of these directions.

I will begin with a passage that is inscribed in Notebook P of the Paris Project, to which the editor of the German edition assigned the title "The Streets of Paris." But as we shall see in an instant, what

Benjamin is concerned with here is not simply "the streets" of Paris, but rather their relation to their "names." Here, as always, language for Benjamin marks a certain movement of convergence, of simultaneity, transforming what otherwise might be taken as being *self-contained* into a dynamic and elusive relationship to be read, which is to say, into a text:

> Paris has been spoken of as the *ville qui remue,* the city that is always on the move [*die sich dauernd bewegt*]. But no less significant than the life of this city's layout [*Stadtplans*] is here the unconquerable power of the names of streets, squares or theaters, a power that endures [*dauer(t)*] notwithstanding all topographical displacement. How often were those individual little stages, which, in the days of Louis-Philippe still lined the Boulevard du Temple, torn down only to see them resurface newly constituted in some other *quartier* (I refuse to speak of "city districts" [*Stadtteile*]); how many street names, even today, preserve the name of a landed proprietor who, centuries earlier, had his property on their ground? The name, "Château d'Eau," referring to a long vanished fountain, still haunts various *arrondissements* today. (P 1,1)[6]

"Streets, Squares, Theaters"—the triad that I have chosen for the title of this chapter leaves out, as you have just heard, a fourth element that stands apart from the other three, and yet is inseparable from them: the "names" assigned to each of these urban sites. And yet each relates to its name differently. In what follows, I want to explore some of those relationships. But first, we must recall that Benjamin is speaking not just about the city in general, or even of the European city during a particular period, but of one very singular city and a very precise time: nineteenth-century Paris. Paris during this period was, for Benjamin, distinguished by a characteristic that he described, typically enough, by using a spatial category that turns out to be surprisingly difficult to render into English. In German, Benjamin called it a *"Schwelle,"* usually translated as "threshold." But this latter term does not begin to do justice to what Benjamin means by the term. He explains this significance by precisely demarcating the word from what "threshold" would generally be taken to imply, and then elucidating its meaning by referring to the verb, *schwellen,* cognate with the English, *swell:* "The *Schwelle* must be radically distinguished from the limit or border [*Grenze*]. *Schwelle* is a zone. Change [*Wandel*], passage, flooding lie in the word 'swelling' [*schwellen*]" (O 2a,1).[7] Benjamin's insistence on distinguishing "threshold" from "limit" or "border," from *Grenze,* is significant of the manner in which he rethinks the notion of place more generally. No longer defined, as has been the tendency ever since Aristotle, primarily through its function of delimitation or containment, in what was an essentially linear manner, place, as *Schwelle,* entails the breakdown of the clear-cut opposition between inside and outside. Swelling indicates a crisis in the function of containment. The container no longer serves as a fixed place to define movement as change of place, but instead is itself caught up in a movement, a tension, but itself becoming over-extended. Such a "swelling" is thus always both more and less than what it appears; not just an extended but a distended *res intensa*. In this respect it is profoundly related to the notion of "allegory" initially elaborated by Benjamin with respect to German seventeenth-century theater, but to which he returns in his analyses of the nineteenth century as well, albeit in a different, more interiorized form. It is this kind of distended, inflated place that will render the topography of nineteenth-century Paris legible as a text, albeit as an allegorical one.

Allegories have a particular relationship to names and to naming. If an allegory always entails the potential of meaning something other than what it seems, at first sight, to represent or to designate, then it is clear that whatever name it bears will be subject to a similar instability. This is not, however, what the passage just quoted seems to say, or to start off by saying. It not only *seems* to say, but actually *does* say, that the dynamics of change and movement so widely associated with Paris, as the city said to be constantly in motion, *la ville qui remue*—that this movement of change seems to be held in check by "the irresistible force in the *names* of streets, squares or theaters," names which, all topographical displacements notwithstanding, seem to "last." But as we will see, they last or endure in very different ways. For the three urban sites cited here by Benjamin as instances of the "topographical displacement" of a city "on the move" are quite different from one another. Streets and Squares are structural designations of urban localities, but what about "theaters"? Their relation to the city seems quite different. A theater is first of all an edifice, a building of sorts, not an organization of urban space in the sense of "streets and places." And yet Benjamin appears to place the three in a series, implying some sort of commensurability or at least connection between them. Although he does not comment directly on this connection, in the sentence that follows Benjamin goes on to develop the theatrical aspect of the city by referring to "those small stages" *(jene[r] kleinen Bühnen)* located on the *Boulevard du Temple,* which, despite being torn up again and again during the reign of Louis-Philippe, reappeared regularly elsewhere in the city—whether with the same names Benjamin does not say.

Without discussing explicitly the notion of theater or theatricality here, with respect to the city, Benjamin's example strongly suggests that the power of the city to resist the passage of time and space relates as much to theatricality as to language. And this power in turn is related to the particular ability of the stage to survive its own demise. For a stage is a place that can be destroyed, displaced, dislocated, but that still can reappear elsewhere with what is apparently an irrepressible force. What is constant, then, in the constant transformation of the city, is neither the physical existence of individual locations, nor even the ideal existence of their names, but rather the recurrence of theatrical stages in different places. The stage, unlike the traditional, Aristotelian notion of place, is movable, returning as both different and the same. The survival-power of such "stages" thus both runs parallel to and diverges from the ostensible longevity of place-names. For when we look more closely—that is, reread—the way Benjamin describes the function of those names, we discover a far less unified and coherent account that one might have expected: "How many street names, even today, preserve the name of a landed proprietor who, centuries earlier, had his property on their ground? The name, 'Château d'Eau,' referring to a long vanished fountain, still haunts various *arrondissements* today." (P 1,1). The first instance seems clear enough and conforms to our expectations: the name of the owner of a certain property is preserved in the name of the street that is located on that property. Human finitude finds a certain survival in the persistence of the name. But the very next example diverges radically from this familiar scheme. To be sure, the name is no longer that of a person, a land-owner, for instance, but a thing, an artifact: *Château d'Eau,* which formerly referred to a singular, "long vanished fountain," returns in the place-name, but as a ghost, to "haunt" not simply the place of its origin but places in which that particular tower may never have existed. In this case, then, the survival of the name does not preserve the memory of its bearer but rather underscores the ever-present possibility of an uncanny proliferation, which

Benjamin goes on to develop in his third and concluding example of the power of Parisian place-names:

> In their own way even the famous restaurants [*Lokale*]—to say nothing of the great literary cafés—secured their small-scale communal immortality [*ihre kleine kommunale Unsterblichkeit*], as with the Rocher de Cancall, the Véfour, the Trois Frères Provinçaux. For hardly has a name imposed itself in the field of gastronomy, hardly does a Vatel or Riche become famous, than all of Paris, out to the suburbs, is teeming with Petits Vatels and Petits Riches: such is the movement of the streets, the movement of names, which often enough run at cross purposes to one another. (P 1,1)

It should be noted that in German the generic term for bars, bistros, and restaurants is *Lokal*. For what Benjamin is describing in this passage is precisely the fate of the *local*, of *localization* in the "topographical dislocation" that marks the Paris as a City on the Move, but moving in the sense of "swelling" already discussed. How do "localities," *Lokale*, survive this land-swell? They secure a "small scale communal immortality" precisely through the reiteration of great and famous names that thereby return as diminutives. But the abrupt shift in this third and final example, from ordinary proper names to *famous* place-names, introduces an element that sheds light on the role of the theatrical in Benjamin's discussion of the city. A certain *fame* is perpetuated and associated with more or less proper names, with making a name. Such famous names are then transported and reproduced in other areas, for instance, as "Petit Vatel," thereby acquiring a certain "communal immortality." But the claim to such immortality presupposes precisely the dimension that defines theatricality: the *interplay* with spectators, listeners, audience. The "little stages" are not just constructed places, but *places that play to a crowd*, to others who are their addressees and witnesses at once. The space of the theater, of the stage, of the theatrical scene, is defined not just by its physical perimeter but rather by the far less definable, heterogeneous others to which it appeals, and which through their responsiveness retroactively make places into theatrical stages. What Benjamin seems to be suggesting in this paragraph is that the characteristic Parisian locality is theatrical in this precise sense of being other-directed or, if you will, heterogeneous. It is therefore a *Schwelle*, not in the sense of a transition or interval situated between two fixed points or places, but as a zone of indefinite expansion and inflation reaching out to others on whose response it depends. This zone is theatrical in being internally split, divided into spectacle and spectators, stage and audience, inseparable and yet distinct. Such an audience marks the intrusion of the outside on the ostensibly self-contained interior of the place, "swelling" it, as it were, inflating it, making it larger than life, and yet also dislocating it in principle by rendering it dependent on a perimeter that is essentially displaceable, involving not just other places but also other times. For a theater is always also a place of memory and of anticipation, where what *has been* is rehearsed and repeated as what is *to come.*

We have had a slight glimpse, perhaps, of how a theater and a stage might function in this urban configuration. But what about streets and places? In another passage from the same notebook, Benjamin indicates what a "street" means for him:

> "Street," to be understood, must be contrasted to the older notion of "way." Both are, in their mythological nature, entirely different from one another. The way connotes the terrors of going astray [*des Irrgangs*]. The leaders of wandering peoples must have benefited from their afterglow. In the incalculable turns and decisive dividing of ways the solitary wanderer even today can feel the power of ancient indications [*Weisungen*]. By contrast, whoever walks on a street apparently does not need any such indicators or a leading hand. He succumbs to its power not in going-astray but in the monotonous fascination of the unfurling band of asphalt. The synthesis of these two terrors, however, going astray in monotony, is to be found in the labyrinth [*stellt das Labyrinth dar*]. (P 2,1)

The labyrinth is a figure to which Benjamin returns frequently in his description of the city in general, and nineteenth-century Paris in particular. It shows that the relatively simple opposition between "street" and "way" is not sufficient to characterize urban space. To be sure, the unpredictable meanderings of the "way" require guides in a manner that the urban streets apparently do not. But the city is not just a conglomeration of streets and an absence of ways. Rather, the unpredictability and sudden surprises of the traditionally rural way changes shape and character in the city: it becomes less linear and more repetitive: one can go astray not simply by losing one's way, but by the reiterative "monotony" of streets that seem to duplicate one another and yet as repetitions are still different from each other. In their very recurrence they create a trancelike monotony that finds its visible epitome in the hypnotic unfurling of the "asphalt band." The reiteration of this unfurling in its (hypnotic?) monotony is what Benjamin calls the experience of the "labyrinth." Like those names and stages that return with a difference, losing their ostensible propriety and coming to designate something other than their original "owners" and locations, the paths that come together in the interlocking network of the labyrinth entice one to move ever further into the maze without disclosing a way out. The result is a certain *amazement,* not just "in" the city—which, we have begun to see, has no stable interior—but rather, far beneath its imperial surface, in what in Paris is called, appropriately enough, the *Métro:* "But names only reveal their true power when they surface [*auftauchen*] in the labyrinthine halls of the Métro. Troglodytic imperial lands—thus emerge Solférino, Italie and Rome, Concorde and Nation. Hard to believe, that all of these run together up above, converging under the bright (blue) sky [*unterm hellem Himmel*]" (P 2,3). Names of self-glorifying, victorious historical battles, of ancient cities and deities, all "surface" far under the earth of the imperial capital, where they acquire an archaic resonance as the names of subway stations. The old, rural way returns in nineteenth-century Paris in subterranean form, as its sub-ways. Its name is that of the generic city itself. In this labyrinthine city under the city, Benjamin's version of the Platonic Cave, the cave-dwelling subway riders can hardly fathom that these archaic names "come together" up above to form a coherent system of the Capital, urban and historico-political at once. And for Benjamin at least, the amazement of these sub-urban cave dwellers is not merely an indication of how deluded they are. Perhaps their subterranean amazement is closer to the kind of experience that alone, for Benjamin, can disclose the most profound reality of the city. It is the experience of that "zone" he calls the *Schwelle,* and it is an experience that is becoming increasingly rare: "We are very poor in threshold experiences. Falling asleep is perhaps the only one that is left for us. (But this would also include awakening)" (O 2a,1). Awakening is an experience of the *Schwelle* insofar as it is inseparable from falling asleep—and vice versa. It is not a linear transition *from* one state to another, from a state of sleep *to* a state of wakefulness, but rather an *experience* that *traverses* a zone no longer bounded by the familiar oppositions of sleep and wakefulness, which are no longer mutually exclusive but rather overlap.

It is this experience of the *Schwelle* as overlapping and as superimposition that characterizes the final scene of this chapter, after those of Streets, Theaters, and Stages: that of the Square or Place. Benjamin's description of it seems to contradict everything we have said up to now about the function of names and language in the city:

> And then those timeless tiny squares, which are there before you know it and on which names do not stick, which have not been planned long in advance like the Place Vendôme or the Place des Grèves, placed under the protection of World History, but which are houses that slowly, half asleep [*unausgeschlafen*] belatedly assemble before the wake-up call [the reveille] of the Century. In such squares it is the trees that have the word, even the smallest give thick shade. Later, however, their leaves stand like dark-green milky glass before the gas lanterns and their earliest green glowing at night gives spring a green light to enter the City. (P 1,2)

Benjamin's description here recalls Marvell's "green thought in a grade shade," which William Empson analyzed as the highest, most complex form of the *Seven Types of Ambiguity* that, he argued, distinguish the language of poetry from the logic of communicative speech.[8] Such ambiguity is all the more striking here insofar as these little places or squares entertain a rather tenuous relation to discursive language. Unlike the great and celebrated Plazas and Places, these little squares have no permanent names; they seem so small, so erratic that names will not "stick" to them, but only houses and trees. Nevertheless, however material they may appear, these houses and trees are anything but nonlinguistic, even if the language they speak is very different from what we are most familiar with. In his rendition of these little squares, the houses that inhabit them present themselves belatedly, still half asleep, before what Benjamin calls the reveille of the Century, a rag-tag and motley army sharply distinct from the great Historical Monuments that stand smartly under the patronage of World History. These little houses play a role situated somewhere between that of an unheroic protagonist and a simple, inanimate stage-property.[9] They are decor and actor at once. And yet it is not they who have the last word. Rather, the action of the play—and this description of the little square is in fact an elaborate and complex scenario—is tied to the least active, least human, least dynamic, in the traditional sense at least, element of the scene: to those trees, of which "even the smallest give thick shade."

With this mention of the trees, something very strange happens to this scene. As Benjamin might have said in his book on the German baroque theater, time wanders onto the stage.[10] But it is a curious, ambiguous time, marked by adverbs and adjectives such as "later" and "earliest": "Later, however, their leaves stand like dark-green milky glass before the gas lanterns and their earliest green glowing at night gives Spring a green light to enter the city" (P 1,2). "Later"—presumably after the *reveille* of the little houses before the call of the Century—the waking light of day is mitigated by "the dark-green milky glass" shed by the shade of even the "smallest" trees. Is the tiny square a place of awakening, or of falling asleep, or of the superimposition of the one on the other, its divergence and convergence at once? At any rate, it is a place where nature and technics come together in the "earliest green glowing" of leaves lit up at night, not by the moon, but by "gas lanterns." And their reply is to give a green light as a "signal" that is no less paradoxically technical: in German, *ein automatisches Einfahrtssignal* [an automatic entry-signal], one of those words that resemble the verbal monstrosities periodically used to caricature German to non-German speakers. Yet it is precisely this convergence of nature and technics, light and dark, signal and change, in the color of a shadow and a glow, which marks the irreducibly relational language of the tiny square, with its little houses and smaller trees.

The automatic signal that they give opens the square, and with it the gates of Paris to the advent of spring. But at the same time it also gives the allegorical reader the green light to enter the city as a text composed not just of words and of images, of sounds and of shocks, but also of silent lanterns and shadows glowing green in the dark.

CHAPTER SIXTEEN

God and the Devil—in Detail

What is the relation between *detail* and *knowledge?* Between the proverb dear to Abby Warburg, to Adorno, but also to Flaubert and doubtless many others, which states that "God is in the detail," and the formulation that suggests a possible explanation for this divinity attributed to the detail, by "detailing" it in terms of a "microstructure of knowledge"? If "God" is in the "detail," then it is because the latter can be considered to be not just a source of "knowledge," but its very infrastructure. At the same time, this only tells half of the story, at most. For it is not just God that inhabits the detail, but also—and this is the far more widespread popular idiom—the Devil. "Der Teufel steckt im Detail." And this devil, one can assume, is far less friendly—less "lieb"—than his divine counterpart. What is it that has allowed the *detail* to become both a divine residence and a diabolical hiding place? Could this peculiar destiny have something to do with its relation to "knowledge," and to the "microcosm"? With the advent of nanotechnologies, these questions are no longer simply academic.

To help set the stage on which we will explore these questions, two passages may be useful. The first is taken from Walter Benjamin's description of the "antinomies of (baroque) allegory," from his book on the *Origin of the German Mourning Play:* "This leads us to the antinomies of the allegorical, the dialectical treatment of which cannot be avoided if the image of the mourning plays is to be evoked. Each person, every single thing, each relation can signify an arbitrary other [*ein beliebiges anderes*]. This possibility pronounces upon the profane world a verdict that is devastating but just: that world is designated as one in which things do not depend so strictly upon details."[1] To stop the quotation here, in order to highlight the transformation of the "detail" in Benjamin's account of allegory, is however highly misleading. For what he is describing is precisely named as an "antinomy."

Since this book is written throughout at the interface of German and English, it may not be inappropriate to use a difficulty in translation as a way of entering into the changed function of the "detail" as Benjamin here describes it. In the passage just quoted, I have modified the published English translation, which is both simpler and more categorical than Benjamin's German text. John Osborne, the English translator, renders the last phrase as follows: "It is characterized as a world in which the detail is of no great importance" (175). The German text, by contrast, reads: "sie wird gekennzeichnet als eine Welt, in der es aufs Detail so streng nicht ankommt" (350). To translate "so streng nicht ankommt" as "of no great importance" may seem at first glance to be well within the bounds of the permissible. But the nuance here—or should one say, the *detail?*—turns out to be anything but insignificant. What Benjamin is pointing out here is not the pure and simple devalorization of detail by baroque allegory, but rather the *transformation* of its function. What changes is above all a certain *Strenge*—a certain *stringency* or *rigor*—be it that of the detail itself, or be it (as idiomatic English would suggest) that of the *attention paid it*. That strict attention to detail is no longer favored in the world of the German baroque, however, does not mean that details themselves have lost all meaning; indeed, precisely the opposite is the case. It is the coexistence of such opposites—the loss of stringency accompanied by a different sort of gain—that constitutes what Benjamin refers to as the *antinomies* of the Allegorical, from which the "detail" is not at all excluded. We need only continue the interrupted citation to discover the other side of the antinomy: "But it is impossible to ignore—especially for anyone familiar with allegorical textual exegesis—that those indispensable props of signification [*Requisiten des Bedeutens*] by virtue of their very pointing at something else, acquire a potency [*Mächtigkeit*] that makes them appear incommensurable with profane things and raises them to a higher level, indeed even sanctifies them" (*GS1*, 351; *Origin*, 175). Details are thus anything but insignificant or superfluous: they are *required* by baroque allegory, but as *Requisiten des Bedeutens*, indispensable theatrical props of signification. Such properties are not just "antinomian," as Benjamin states of allegory in general, but *theatrical*. These two characteristics are quite revealing for the transformed role of detail, as Benjamin is describing it. As *signifying property*, the "detail" is devalorized with respect to a criterion of value modeled on an ideal of identity as essentially self-contained or self-present. In this perspective, the value of a detail derives from its organic relation to that from which it has in some way *detached* itself but of which it still remains an integral part. Here the French and Latin etymology of the word comes into play: the "detail" is something that has literally "cut itself off from" the whole to which however it still in some sense "belongs." One type of such "belonging" is indicated by the "commercial" sense the word assumes first in French, and then, as a borrowed word, in German, where "détail" comes in the eighteenth century to signify not just small-scale retail commerce but, by implication, the circulation of commodities attached to it. In other words, that which is "cut loose" and "into pieces" is thereby given the ability to *circulate* as a commodity and in the process to acquire an exchange-value very different from its intrinsic "use-value." A somewhat similar use of the term in English would be in the military sense, where a "detail" is a small group assigned a mission that separates it from the main body as in the film *The Last Detail*.

What Benjamin describes as the "antinomies of the allegorical"— and which plays itself out in the transformed significance of the *detail*—is an earlier, non-commercial, non-economic, non-military version of the metamorphosis of *detail* into *detail*—or, to stick with English, of *detail* into *retail* as an effect of expanded commodity production. But the term "version" is misleading here. It would be precipitous to regard the baroque allegorical detail as merely a predecessor of its bourgeois successor. It deserves to be considered in its own right—even and especially if what distinguishes it calls all such "ownership" and "rights" profoundly into question.

What distinguishes Benjamin's interpretation of the baroque detail is that its spatial dimension becomes distinctively *theatrical*. In other words, to understand the transformation of detail under the pressure of baroque allegory, into a *Requisit des Bedeutens,* one must first understand the nature of the "theater" that thus becomes its indispensable "staging area."

In order to better situate the distinctive quality of this theatricality, it will be useful to go back to an early text that plays an important role in Benjamin's book on the Mourning Play, since he invokes it as a model in his elaboration of his own methodology in his "Epistemo-critical Preface." The same text, however, is also not unrelated to the framing of our topic, namely, the detail as a "microstructure" of knowledge. I am referring to Leibniz's *Principles of Philosophy,* better known as the *Monadology.* This text, written in 1714, is perhaps the first text of modern philosophy that assigns a central role to the *detail,* and it is one that demonstrates the ambiguous, ambivalent, and "antinomian" position that will be assigned to this notion in the centuries that follow—up to and including the present. It will also enable us to indicate just what is remarkable about Benjamin's emphasis on the theatricality of the detail as stage-property, as *Requisit.* For whatever else may be said about Leibniz—and here I can only touch on one or two points that are particularly pertinent—his notion of the "monad" is paradigmatic for the conception that most informs and distinguishes much of modern thinking: the striving toward *self-contained immanence.* Monads, the building blocks of being, are "simple substances . . . without parts."[2] Having thus defined the monad, Leibniz is immediately confronted with the problem of differentiating it, and thus saving it from imploding into the tautology of pure self-identity: Despite their simplicity, self-containment, and imperviousness to outside interference—"Monads have no windows through which something can enter or leave" (§7)—monads "must have some qualities, otherwise they would not even be beings" (§8). Monads must thus "be different from one another" and this difference cannot stem from external sources. There must therefore be a principle of "internal difference" or "internal principle" that distinguishes one monad from another and also is responsible for change. This principle Leibniz calls *appétition,* "appetite"—not in the sense of bodily hunger, of course, but as a principle of *internal striving.* The problem, however, still remains: how is one to think change, differentiation, appetite as an internal function of a being that is purely and perfectly *simple*—that is, that contains no *parts?* Here is Leibniz's answer, introduced in the most discontinuous and groping manner possible, a fact worth remarking in a thinker who places so much importance on continuity and self-containment:

§11. But it is also necessary that, besides the principle of change, there should be a *detail* of that which changes, which would constitute, so to speak, the specification and variety of simple substances.

§12. This detail must envelop a multitude in the unity or in the simple; for natural change only producing itself by degrees, something changes and something remains, and consequently it is necessary that in the simple substance there should be a plurality of affections and relations, although it has no parts. (My emphasis and modified translation.)

Without being able to delve very far here into the subtleties of Leibniz's interpretation, let me single out the following points. First, the *detail* is distinguished from a "part": its relation to the monad is not that of part to whole, for the simple reason that the monad is conceived as essentially simple and unified, indivisible into elements or parts. The *detail* thus entails a modification of this simplicity, but one that is contained within the homogeneity of the monad. As Leibniz puts it, the detail "should envelop *(doit envelopper)* a multitude *in the unity*" or simplicity that constitutes the monad. How is it supposed to do this? In two ways: first, by providing precisely something like an "envelope"—an internal envelope to *contain* multiplicity within the simplicity of the monad. And second, by giving rise to what Leibniz calls a "perception," which he defines as a "passing state that envelops and represents a multitude in unity or simple substance" (§14). Thus, the *detail* is that aspect of the monad that makes *perception* possible and with it, differentiation. But the "perception" to which the detail is linked is one that Leibniz emphatically, and in opposition to Descartes, distinguishes from "apperception or consciousness." For it is here that "the Cartesians have failed badly, taking no account of perceptions that are not apperceived" (§14). For Leibniz, by contrast, "perceptions" can be either apperceived or not apperceived. Consequently the *detail* marks that aspect of the monad where consciousness converges with the unconscious. Although the latter is a term that Leibniz does not employ, his description of the unapperceivable anticipates, in certain non-trivial ways, what two centuries later Freud will come to call the unconscious. "When there are a great multitude of small perceptions where nothing is distinguished, one is stupefied [*étourdi*]. As when one turns continually in the same direction several times in succession, whence arises a dizziness that can cause us to faint and does not allow us to distinguish anything" (§21). The detail thus demonstrates a highly ambiguous, if not ambivalent, structure. On the one hand it marks the aspect of diversity that is necessary both to change and to differentiation of the monad. On the other, it must conform to the overall principle of the monad, which is that of self-containment, immanence, "autarchy" as Leibniz writes (§18). It does this by "enveloping" the "multitude" within the "unity or simplicity" of the monad. In short, the *detail* is the principle by which diversity is reconciled with immanence. At the same time, however, there is never just *one* detail within a single monad, but rather many. And although each single detail is understood as the unifying envelope of multiplicity, together they reintroduce a certain multiplicity "back" into the monad. It is the plurality of details within the monad that explains what Leibniz calls the possibility of its being "*étourdi*," "stunned" or "stupefied"—or, perhaps, *unconscious*. Why "unconscious"? Because the description of the way in which the detail produces *étourdissement*—which is a certain absence of consciousness—recalls salient features of the Freudian Unconscious. First, there is the excess of multiplicity over unity, or at least over differentiated unity: there is "a great multitude of small perceptions where nothing is distinguished"—corresponding to what Freud will call "over-determination," a structural characteristic of the unconscious. Second, there is something like a repetition-compulsion, "as when one turns continually in the same direction several times in succession." Thirdly, Leibniz associates this type of undifferentiated (or over-determined) repetition of the same with dizziness and with death. And although Freud insists that the unconscious knows nothing of death,[3] he nevertheless reemphasizes the latter's link to the unconscious in his speculations on the *death-drive*.

Although such anticipations and affinities doubtless serve to highlight the contemporaneity of Leibniz's thought and in particular his notion of the *detail*, they should not be allowed to obscure the singular motif to which that notion, together with that of the monad, responds: a conception of being in terms of immanence, self-containment, autarchy. Such a conception is the result of two interrelated movements: one of *separation* and one of *self-containment*. The monad is separate, and it is self-contained. This does not mean that it is self-created, which it is not. But as a created being, it is self-regulating, automatic, autarchic. In this respect, it is a "mirror" of the universe, but from a limited "perspective" or "point of view." What however enables it to "mirror" the universe from which it is both detached, and as detached, also connected, is the *detail*—the detail is that which detaches itself from what would otherwise be the pure self-sufficiency of the simple and unitary monad, and what, as detached, becomes capable of "mirroring" or "representing" that from which the monad has separated itself: other monads and the more complex substances they compose. The internal detachment of the *detail* thus introduces into the windowless monad the possibility of its representing the diversity "outside" it. It does this, as already indicated, through the process of *perception*.

The detail thus manifests a double nature: it is the vehicle of multiplicity, variety, diversity, exteriority, but only insofar as it *integrates* their alterity into the *immanence* of the monad, which is to say, into a being construed on the basis of *self-containment*. This is why the *detail* is a necessary but not sufficient component of the monad. It is necessary in order to open up that *internal* space required if the monad is to be capable of entertaining "relations" with the outside world without abandoning its principle of autarchy and entelechy (§56). But it is not *sufficient* since the very diversity with which it is associated also perturbs the simplicity and unity of the monad. Left to its own devices, the detail would dissolve into an infinite regress: "And since all this *detail* only envelops other contingencies that are prior to it or more detailed, each of which requiring a similar analysis for reason to be rendered, no advance is made and it is necessary that a sufficient or ultimate reason be sought outside of the sequence or *series* of this detail of contingencies, however infinite it might be" (§37). Left to its own devices, then, the detail would introduce an infinite series or sequence of "envelopes" that would ultimately engulf the microcosmic unity, simplicity, and order of the monad, and of the world it represents. Against this diabolical perspective there can be only one protection:

§38. Thus, the ultimate reason of things must be (sought) in a necessary substance, in which the detail of changes is only eminent [*ne soit qu'éminemment*], as in the spring, and this is what we call God.

§39. And, this substance being a sufficient reason of all this detail, which is everywhere connected, *there is only one God and this God is sufficient*.

"God is in the detail," but only insofar as the detail is in God. The principle of being of the monad—that of self-containment—can only be secured from the proliferation of details (on which it nevertheless depends)—insofar as this proliferation itself is ultimately and originarily *contained* in a being that ultimately *comprehends* all detail without being affected by it: "There is in God the *power,* which is the source of everything, then the *knowledge, which contains the detail of the ideas,* and finally the *volition,* which effects the changes or productions according to the principle of the best" (§48). God thus emerges as the principle of a creative power that *comprehends* and thus *contains* what is necessary for the singularization of monads and yet what also threatens its self-containment: the *detail.* "Detail" here—as in the military expression—both designates what we commonly think of as the singular component of a larger complex and signifies the result of a process of *detailing:* of detaching, separating, cutting out of a segment, as well as the result of that process, which, despite its singularity and separateness, still entails a composite.

The *detail* thus becomes one of the paradigms for thinking about the composition of that composite under the specific conditions of Western modernity. Those conditions, Benjamin suggests—to return in conclusion to his study of the German baroque theater—are very much tied to the events known as the Reformation, and to the reaction it produces, the Counter-Reformation. Although I cannot go into detail here, it is this dual analysis: of the separation and isolation implicit in the Lutheran challenge to established Christian orthodoxy, and of the response, in "both confessions" (*GS1,* 258; *Origin,* 79), as Benjamin writes, to this radical antinomianism that leads to the "antinomies of allegory" and to its apparent devalorization of the "detail." But as already suggested, that devalorization only tells half of the story. The other is that the detail takes on new and unpredictable significance, and in so doing becomes paradigmatic for the situation of the singular, solitary individual confronting God without the mediation of established rites and stable conventions to serve as guide.

The result is a proliferation of details without a unifying or informing point of view. There are "properties" but without assured owners or sites: in short, props—stage-properties, *Requisiten.* As in Leibniz's account, there are perceptions, points of view, appetites, but no unifying, overriding guarantee of order or organization. Instead there are "combinations," "intrigues," manipulations of all sorts. To be allegorical, a property must give rise to certain *knowledge:* but it is a knowledge that is Satanic rather than Sacred:

> Satan tempts. He initiates men in knowledge, which forms the basis of culpable behavior . . . This confirms the significance of baroque polymathy for the Mourning Play. For something can take on allegorical form only for the man who has knowledge. But on the other hand, if contemplation is not so much patiently devoted to truth as unconditionally and compulsively, in direct meditation, bent on absolute knowledge, then it is eluded by things, in the simplicity of their essence, and they lie before it as enigmatic allegorical references; they continue to be dust. (*GS1,* 402; *Origin,* 229)

What Benjamin is describing here is the fate of monads whose *details* can no longer be derived from a divine origin: when it is no longer God but the Devil that is in the detail. When that happens, however, the detail is no longer itself "in" anything at all: rather it lies exposed, like "dust," signifying "enigmatically" on the theatrical stage. In place of the monad—instead of the monad as self-contained place—there is a stage, which is a place, but one that is no longer fixed or defined. It is a *Wanderbühne,* a traveling stage that characterizes the German baroque theaters, which followed their Courts in an ambient "confusion" that was simultaneously the principle of their own structure: "The profusion of emblems is grouped around the figural center, which is never absent from genuine allegories, as opposed to periphrases of concepts. They seem to be arranged in an arbitrary way: *The Confused 'Court'*— title of a Spanish Mourning Play—could be adopted as the model of allegory. This court is subject to the law of 'dispersal' and 'collectedness.' Things are assembled according to their significance; indifference to their existence allows them to be dispersed again" (*GS1,* 364; *Origin,* 188). But not only "indifference to their existence" allows such assemblages "to be dispersed again": their "significance" itself prescribes such scattering, since it is as arbitrary and fragile as any convention in a world where there are so many details that "strict attention" is no longer either possible or plausible.

In lieu of a conclusion, let me end with an anecdote. In the production of a film, as is well known, the narrative sequence of the story rarely corresponds to the sequence in which the scenes are actually shot. As a result, one of the tasks of the production crew is to assure a certain "continuity" between scenes that are supposed to follow one another in the story but may have been filmed weeks or months apart. An acquaintance of mine, while working on the production of a film, warned the director that the lighting of a scene did not fit with the scene that preceded it in the story-line. The director replied that the audience would not notice, but that if they did, it would be a sign that the film had failed. The director was undoubtedly right. Attention to detail can never be separated from that from which it is constitutively detached. Which is why, "strict" or not, the detail remains, even today, the uneasy residence that God is condemned by language to share with the Devil— and perhaps with some others as well.

CHAPTER SEVENTEEN

Closing the Net

"Capitalism as Religion" (Benjamin)

Ein Zustand, der so ausweglos ist, ist verschuldend. (A
situation that is inextricable is guilt-producing.)
——Walter Benjamin

Was geschiehet, es sei alles gelegen Dir! (Whatever happens,
let everything be laid out for you.)
——Friedrich Hölderlin

"We cannot draw closed the net in which we stand"—thus Walter
Benjamin explains why he will not write an essay entitled "Capitalism
as Religion." The text that bears this title, written in 1921, will remain
a fragment, like Benjamin's "oeuvre" itself: a series of texts that never
quite come together to form a work, but at most a "constellation" in
which *empty spaces* are at least as significant as the "stars" they serve
to situate.

Benjamin's predilection for "Eternity by the Stars"—the title of
memoirs written in prison by the revolutionary Blanqui—in which he
saw a precursor of Nietzsche's teaching of the "eternal return," did not
exclude a certain fascination with more earthly structures and stric-
tures: which is to say, with the knots and nodes, links and interstices
that make up "the net in which we stand." Curious, this notion of
standing "in" a net. So curious indeed that the English translation prefers to replace "standing" with the more plausible, more familiar notion of being "caught": "We cannot draw closed the net in which we
are caught."[1] What could be more convincing than being "caught" in a
net? And yet; despite the fact that Benjamin *could* easily have written as
much in German, where the word *Verstrickung* stood ready and waiting to render the notion of being inextricably trapped, he chose instead
to use the verb *stand: "Wir können das Netz in dem wir* stehen *nicht*

zuziehen." We cannot draw closed—draw to a close—the net, not because we are trapped in it, but because, more precisely, we are standing in it. We take our stand in the net. And not just in any net, of course, but in a particular one, the one for instance in which Benjamin sets out to assert, and argue, not just that capitalism is "conditioned" by religion, but that it *is a religion,* or rather, "an essentially religious phenomenon." Standing *in this* net, and at the same time *standing in for it,* Benjamin undertakes to develop an argument that the context, the "net," in which he and his readers stand, does not allow itself to be demonstrated.

The argument is simply, or not so simply, that capitalism must be considered a religion insofar as it "serves essentially the satisfaction of the same concerns, torments and troubles [*Sorgen, Qualen, Unruhen*] to which what is called religion formerly proposed answers."[2] Just what these concerns, torments, and troubles in turn respond to or address will never be stated, not at least in this fragment. And perhaps for the very reason that Benjamin advances here at the outset of this text, and which explains why, in a certain sense, the text will never be written, or at least, never completely: "The demonstration [*Nachweis*] of this religious structure of capitalism, not only as [Max] Weber believes, as a religiously conditioned phenomenon, would even today lead astray [*auf den Abweg*] into immeasurable, uncontrolled [*maßlosen*] universal polemics" (*GS6,* 100; *SW1,* 288). In one of the very few references in his writings to Max Weber, Benjamin asserts the need to go further than the author of the *Protestant Ethic and the Spirit of Capitalism* in determining the significance of religion, and in particular of Christianity, for the socioeconomic system that dominates the modern period. At the same time, however, he also asserts the impossibility, or rather the *inopportuneness,* of taking this very step, or at least, of *demonstrating* its necessity. Such a demonstration, the *Nachweis* that Capitalism is not just the result of a religious upheaval, but that it itself assumes the functions of a religion, would, Benjamin asserts, lead only to an incalculable and uncontrollable polemic. To provide a full-fledged demonstration that Capitalism "is" a religion, rather than being merely the result of one, would thus lead astray, along an *Abweg* that is precisely *off-target* by virtue of presenting *too many* targets. In a *Universalpolemik* everyone and everything is fair game, without limits or measure: *maßlos.*

The accomplishment of the project announced by the title of this short text, then, is rendered impossible, or inopportune, by "the net in which we stand"—we being the writer as well as his readers. Both stand in the net of a capitalism that, Benjamin asserts, *is* a religion, at least as hitherto understood, but which, if it were named and above all shown to be such, would unleash a wave of aggression that, in its very limitlessness, could encompass the world: a second world war.

The chilling and unusual word *Universalpolemik* echoes the more familiar *Universalgeschichte: universal history.* Except that what comes into view is not the culmination of world history, but the limitless perspective of a world at war with itself: a Hobbesian *bellum omnium contre omnes,* but on a global scale. It is this prospect, by virtue of its lack of all measure, its *Maßlosigkeit,* that stops Benjamin in his tracks, as it were, here at the very outset of his argument. And yet, this most curious of all introductions still has one more unforeseen turn in reserve. After explaining why it is not opportune to offer a demonstration of what therefore will have to be restricted to mere assertions, he concludes his opening paragraph, or gambit, with the following rather cryptic prediction: "We cannot draw closed the net in which we stand. Later however this will be seen through [*überblickt*]" (GS6, 100; SW1, 288). Does this mean that the "net in which we stand" will "later" be drawn sufficiently to a close to allow us to look it over, taking it all in with our own two eyes? Where will those eyes be positioned? And just what will they see: what exactly is the "this"—*dies*—that is "later" to be seen through? Is it the net? Our situation standing in it? The impossibility of drawing it to a close? The universal polemics its naming and exhibition would produce? All of these? Some of them? None? Something else?

As if this were not complicated enough, there is a second conundrum. Where are we to place this "later" that will bring the solution to which Benjamin refers? Is it simply further on in his text? Is it in a text written later by Benjamin (for instance, the *Passages*)? Or is it after Benjamin's texts as a whole, part of their "afterlife," perhaps including a situation in which "we" no longer "stand" in the same "net," or at least not in the same way? Could that *later* be today? Tomorrow? Yesterday?

Let us leave these questions in suspense, at least for now, in order to turn to another one that constitutes their common point of departure: Why should the demonstration that capitalism is a religion risk unleashing a global polemics defying all measure? A possible response is indicated by Benjamin's unusual choice of words. As already suggested, it is neither easy nor convenient to stand "in a net," especially when that net consists in "the same cares, torments and troubles" to which religion formerly provided answers, and to which today capitalism seeks to respond.[3] What are those "cares, torments and troubles" and how does capitalism seek to respond to them?

Paradoxically, but significantly, it is the answer to the latter question that will allow Benjamin to approach, if not respond to, the former. It is paradoxical, since it amounts to inverting the usual, expected relation between response and that to which it is responding: stimulus, question, challenge, threat. It is no accident, however, that Benjamin takes the reverse route: he will first examine the nature of the response, in order then to approach, carefully, that to which it is responding.

Thus, after warning that he will not be able to demonstrate or bring proof of his assertion that Capitalism *is* a religion, and not just an effect of one, he goes on to describe what this assertion entails. Capitalism is a religion that displays four interrelated traits, all linked to the notions of *cult* and *guilt (Debt-as-guilt)*. These traits are, in the order followed by Benjamin:

1. Capitalism is a cult-religion, and indeed, perhaps "the most extreme that ever existed."
2. The cult of capitalism is extreme because it never pauses. It is characterized by "permanent duration."
3. The incessant cult of capitalism is *verschuldend,* which, according to the dual meaning of *Schuld* itself, must be translated both as "guilt-producing" or "culpabilizing," and as "debt-producing" or "indebting." In what follows, I will therefore translate *Schuld* as *debt-as-guilt.* And finally,
4. The God of this religion, far from redeeming from guilt, is drawn into it. As a result, this God "must be kept secret and addressed only at the zenith of its (his) culpability-indebtedness" *(erst im Zenith seiner Verschuldung).*" (GS6, 101; SW1, 289)

Needless to add, these four traits, which are intricately intertwined, demand discussion. To begin with, the relation of Capitalism to its cult is, as we have seen, for Benjamin unique. If it is the "most extreme that ever existed," this is not to be understood just quantitatively. Capitalism carries the cult to the extreme in a number of ways. First, it frees the cult from its traditional service of theological dogma, understood as a series of ideas that would be exemplified or realized through the celebration of rites. Rather, in Capitalism everything becomes meaningful only by standing in direct, "unmediated relation to the cult." It is worth paying particular attention in this phrase to the word "unmediated" or "immediate"—*unmittelbar*—especially since it disappears in the English translation.[4] And yet, as is often the case with Benjamin, a certain notion of "immediacy" is decisive in articulating what is distinctive in his argumentation.[5] Indeed, the entire question or problem of "Capitalism as Religion" hangs on this nuance, namely, that it is not just a cult-religion, but a religion whose cult is *immediately* meaningful. This *immediacy of the cult* marks the first in a series of aspects that will distinguish Benjamin's notion of "cult" from the concept as traditionally understood. Capitalism takes the cult to the extreme, Benjamin's argument implies, by allowing it to become its own source of meaning, that is, by endowing it with a certain autonomy. As we shall see shortly, this radically transforms its relation to the divine: instead of drawing its meaning from the latter, or from ideas associated with it, the capitalist cult is itself the locus and source of all meaning. But to attribute such autonomy to the cult is at the very least to complicate the meaning of "cult" itself. Benjamin refers to "Utilitarianism" in this context, suggesting that its "religious coloration" can be illuminated through the notion of a cult that is itself the immediate source of all meaning. Although he does not elaborate, one can surmise that the immanence of the capitalist cult is related to a certain quantification, or even a certain deification, of number and of quantity ("the greatest good of the greatest number" being the phrase most commonly associated with "utilitarianism").

This suspicion could explain the transition from the first to the second trait of the capitalist cult: "With this concretion of the cult is connected a second trait of capitalism: the permanent duration of the cult" (*GS6*, 100; *SW1*, 288). Since the cult no longer draws its meaning from something radically separate from it, but only from itself, that self consequently becomes its own measure. And the measure of a self is its ability to endure, which is to say, to withstand the transformative effects of time. This leads Benjamin to one of the most enigmatic lines in this text, if not in all of his writing: "Capitalism is the celebration of a cult sans rêve et sans merci" (*GS6*, 100; *SW1*, 288). Benjamin was, as is well known, fascinated with dreams. But his formulation here is startling all the same. For not only does it not seem to fit very well with what follows: it also echoes a French expression that means something quite different. The expression is, "sans trêve ni merci," "without *truce or grace.*"[6] It is a phrase Benjamin would have read in Baudelaire's poem "Le crépuscule du soir," one of the *Tableaux Parisiens* that he had been translating for years and that he completed in the same year he wrote "Capitalism as Religion." The phrase is decisive for the poem, which recounts how the evening twilight in Paris no longer functions as a refuge and consolation from the burdens of a day that for most is a work-day; for no sooner has the sun begun to set, then other figures begin to emerge to prey upon the unsuspecting. Those figures include

Les voleurs, qui n'ont ni trêve ni merci,
Vont bientôt commencer leur travail, eux aussi,
Et forcer doucement les portes et les caisses
Pour vivre quelques jours et vêtir leurs maîtresses.[7]

Thieves, for whom there is neither rest [*trêve:* truce] nor mercy
Will soon begin their work, they too,
And force softly open doors and chests
To live a few days with their mistresses.

Although as Benjamin will demonstrate in his writings on the nineteenth century, dreams abound in capitalism and indeed are essential to it, what he here argues is that there is no "truce" or "pardon" in the capitalist work-day, which includes the night as well. Much later, in his notebooks for the *Passages*, Benjamin will observe that there is also no real "twilight" in Paris, because once the sun goes down the electric lights go on.[8] Even the natural alternation of day and night, then, tends to be suspended by the "progress" of technology. But in the text of 1921, it is above all the "cult" of capitalism with which Benjamin is concerned, and it is as "permanent" as it is revolutionary. But what it revolutionizes is above all the notion of cult itself. A cult is traditionally bound up with a spatial-temporally organized practice. As such it must be delimitable in space and time. That however is precisely what no longer holds of the cult of capitalism: it never stops, never pauses, never leaves room for "truce" or for "grace." It is, in short, permanent struggle and conflict that gives no quarter: "sans trêve ni merci." All that remains is "Schuld": debt-as-guilt. And, of course, the cult itself.

But if a cult is no longer consecrated to the worship of a deity that is by definition radically distinct from it, as infinite as the cult is finite, then just what sort of a "cult" is capitalism? And indeed, why call it a "cult" at all?

We have to remember that this text of Benjamin's dates from 1921, some fifteen years before he will invoke the notion of "cult" to distinguish traditional art from art in the age of its technological reproducibility. But as we shall see, the two "cults" have much in common.

The "celebration of the cult" in capitalism "knows no weekday" and hence, no *holidays* either. All days are equally holy: "No day that would not be a festive day [*Festtag*]," but precisely because of this, the "unfolding of its sacral pomp" takes on a "fearful meaning [*einen fürchterlichen Sinne*]," one involving "the most extreme exertion of the worshipper [*der äußersten Anspannung des Verehrenden*]" (*GS6*, 100; *SW1*, 288).

Why is this pompous celebration of the cult so *fürchterlich*, so horrendously fearful? After all, a demonstration of pomp is characteristic of traditional religious rituals, as is the "exertion" demanded of the worshippers. What is so fearful about the capitalist cult? "Wie wenn es keinen Feiertag mehr gibt?"

What is so fearful, quite simply, is that the cult consists in a war without pause or end, *sans trêve ni merci,* a life-consuming exertion without truce or grace.[9] But if the war itself is without end, this is not true for the singular beings caught up in it, as the end of "Le crépuscule du soir" makes clear:

C'est l'heure où les douleurs des malades s'aigrissent!
La sombre Nuit les prend à la gorge; ils finissent
Leur destinée et vont vers le gouffre commun;
[. . .] Encore la plupart n'ont-ils jamais connu
La douceur du foyer et n'ont jamais vécu!

It's the hour where the suffering of sickness mounts!
Somber night takes them by the throat; they end
Their destiny and go toward the common grave;
[. . .] Most of them never having known
The softness of the hearth and never having lived!

"Sans trêve ni merci," all there is at the end is "le gouffre commun," the common fate of singular mortals, many of whom will have never known the comforts of home and indeed, have scarcely lived.

But this grim ending in turn only poses a new question: how effective can the cult of capitalism be if this "gouffre commun" is all the "good news" it can bring in response to the "cares, torments and troubles" formerly answered by religion?

It is in answer to this implicit question that Benjamin abruptly, without explicit transition, moves to the third trait, which will turn out to be that which explains all the others: "This cult is thirdly culpabilizing. Capitalism is presumably the first case of a religion that does not atone but produces guilt. In so doing, this system of religion stands in the collapse [*steht . . . im Sturz*] of an enormous movement. An enormously guilty conscience, which does not know how to atone, seizes on the cult, in order not to atone for its guilt but to make it universal, hammering it into consciousness until finally and above all God Himself is included in this guilt, so as finally to interest him in atonement" (*GS6,* 100–101; *SW1,* 288). We begin to see why Benjamin began by noting that any "demonstration"—any *Nachweis*—of his argument would be extremely *inopportune* and would provoke a "universal polemic" with incalculable consequences. For it is never opportune to call attention to the fact that the net in which we are standing is suspended over the void. If this net cannot be drawn to a close, we now see why: the place "in" which we are standing is not just a net but also a "collapse" or a "plunge"—a *Sturz.* Its "*enormous* movement" *(ungeheure Bewegung)* finds its equal and measure only in the "*enormously* guilty conscience" *(ungeheures Schuldbewusstsein)* that echoes it, but also momentarily suspends it as well. The "plunge" is a movement down to the earth and down into it, and as such is *ungeheuer*: excessively unfamiliar and yet all too familiar. Everyone takes this plunge because everyone is caught up in debt-as-guilt, *Schuld.* For the cult of capitalism, guilt is no longer limited to those who, like the ailing figures in "Le crépuscule du soir," reach nightfall without ever having known daylight, but is extended to the universe at large, including its Creator.

It is here that the power and fascination of the capitalist cult begin to emerge. Its aim is not to secure Divine forgiveness or grace, but rather, in including God among the guilty, to "last until the end": "It inheres in the essence of this religious movement, which is capitalism, to hold out until the end, until the final and full culpabilizing of God, consummating the state of the world as despair [*Verzweiflung*] which precisely had been *hoped for*" (GS6, 102; SW1, 288; Benjamin's emphasis). The only thing that presents itself as eternal in this world is the cult of capitalism itself, which now takes over the role formerly assigned to the Creator, who has now become part and parcel of the Creation. As a result, the Creation is no longer the product and image of a transcendent divine essence—"God's transcendence has fallen," it has taken the "plunge"—but rather of an exclusive and ongoing process that brooks no alternatives and allows no way out. The formula for this achievement is quite simply that of "the extension of despair into a global religious system": *die Ausweitung der Verzweiflung zum religiösen Weltzustand*. The Creator is caught up in the headlong plunge of the Creation toward the abyss. There is no limit any more to despair, no escape from it.

In this process, the dimension of "globalization" is crucial. For it affirms the elimination of transcendence as the closing down of alternatives. "God is not dead, he has been given a human destiny" (GS6, 101; SW1, 288). But that "destiny" only confirms a world in which there is no longer any way out. And it is this that seals the production of guilt: "a situation that leaves no way out is guilt-producing. 'Cares' are the index of this guilty consciousness of entrapment [*Ausweglosigkeit*]" (GS6, 102; SW1, 289). The cult of capitalism thus does not merely *respond* to "cares, torment and troubles": it produces them, or rather reproduces and intensifies them through its elimination of alternatives, whether it be the transcendence of the divine or an alternative social system. And what gives the cult its fearful efficacy is that it does not impose this reproduction from without, but rather from within, through the consciousness of guilt, experienced not just as individual guilt, but as a shared destiny of the community, *un gouffre commun*. In this way, the consciousness of being guilty responds to, but also confirms, those "cares, torments and troubles" to which religions have traditionally sought to provide answers. If, as Benjamin writes, "'Cares' arise in the anxiety of communal, not individual-material entrapment [*Ausweglosigkeit*]," then the guilty consciousness fostered by the permanent cult of capitalism becomes the basis of this communal experience, and of the alleviation it presumably affords.

But there is another aspect to Benjamin's discussion of capitalism as the practice of a relentless, guilt-producing cult, an aspect that we have hitherto neglected, but that is indispensable to his argument. It has to do with the fourth point, one that apparently occurred to him in the process of writing, since at the outset he wrote of only three "traits" or features of capitalism as religion. The fourth, as we have seen, has to do with the fate of God. It also involves Benjamin in a discussion, on the border of criticism and polemics, with two thinkers he cites by name: Freud and Nietzsche.

The point of departure, then, is that fourth unforeseen and therefore supplementary "trait" *(Zug)* that defines Capitalism as Religion and as cult: the relation to its God. In a passage that is strongly reminiscent of the memoirs of Judge Daniel Paul Schreber, but also of Nietzsche, Benjamin describes how the cult of capitalism, far from seeking atonement from guilt, is guilt-producing to the point where God Himself is overtaken by it. "God is not dead," he observes, but lives on as part and parcel of "human destiny," *Menschenschicksal.* The notion of "Schicksal"—fate or destiny—had been a constant object of reflection for Benjamin in the preceding years, culminating in an essay published the same year that "Capitalism as Religion" was written: "Destiny and Character" *(Schicksal und Charakter).* In that essay Benjamin sought to draw a sharp distinction between the notion of destiny, which he associated with a system of law and order *(Recht)* derived from pagan myth and sustained by "misfortune and guilt" *(Unglück und Schuld)* and character, which he associated with comedy and theater as a response of singularity to the generalizing verdicts of law, guilt, and destiny.[10] Far from breaking with the order of destiny, then, the legal system sustains and confirms it. And it does so by addressing human beings as strictly natural, as "bare life": "The judge can see destiny wherever he wants to: in every punishment he must blindly include destiny. The human being is never struck by this, but rather the bare life in him, which takes part in natural guilt and misfortune by virtue of phenomenality [*kraft des Scheins*]" (GS2, 175; SW1, 204). The "phenomenality" or "semblance"—*Schein*—to which Benjamin here refers is a result of the conception of human being as "bare" or "mere" life, which is to say, considered in terms of pure immanence. Only when human being—*der Mensch*—is reduced to its purely natural and biological dimension does it become *subject* to *destiny,* and hence to *guilt.* The paradox here is that by treating human life as though it were autonomous and self-contained, it is inscribed in a nexus or network of guilt, a *Schuldzusammenhang*. What "holds together" the network is the refusal to accept a certain indebtedness qua relationality—a refusal implied in the "naturalization" of human being as "mere" or "bare life." Cut off from its constitutive relation to others, the only alternative left to life is death. The hypostasis of life thus inevitably implies the same of death. Life that is understood as merely natural, that is, as "bare life," is rendered incapable of accounting for its constitutive condition, which is to say, for its finitude. The indebtedness to others thus is "internalized," rendered immanent, for instance as "original sin," understood as the intrinsic cause of death. Death is thus interpreted as a product of life, of the Living, rather than as its enabling limit. *Schuld as indebtedness* is thus reinterpreted as moral culpability, as a *property* rather than as a *trait*. A property "belongs" to a subject and thereby stabilizes it; a *trait* tends to *draw* it *elsewhere*. As "guilt," *Schuld* seeks to define "bare life" in terms of itself: its actions and intentions, thus incorporating its "end" in its beginning. In so doing, however, it transforms the heterogeneity of human being into its absolute other and seeks to appropriate it as such. "Destiny" is one name of this appropriation, and the guilt-nexus is its medium. "Bare life" is thus inextricably linked to bare death. As *semblance*, "bare life" is thus inevitably haunted by its other, the shadow of a death that both *defines and exposes* its "bareness," its *Blöße*.

This is why something as little natural, as social and technical as a system of jurisprudence could become the institutional condition under which the semblance of "bare life" would perpetuate itself beyond the demise of the pagan religious system that initially supported it. It is in this context that Benjamin observes that "Law [*Das Recht*] condemns not to punishment but to guilt. Destiny is the guilt-nexus [*Schuldzusammenhang*] of the living" (*GS2*, 175; *SW1*, 204). When, therefore, Benjamin writes in *Capitalism as Religion* that God has been involved *(einbezogen)* in "human destiny," this is another way of saying that the divine is now enmeshed in the network of guilt that marks the medium of the living, as "bare life." But this introduces an enormous problem. For the destiny of "bare life," in being guilty, is to be punished by death. In this sense, the guilt of the living confirms death as the penalty for human existence. Death becomes a sentence punishing the living for the guilt of "bare life," that is, of life construed in terms of the immanence of nature. In a note jotted down several years earlier, in the summer of 1918, Benjamin formulated the thought underlying this argument succinctly:

> Wherever there are pagan religions, there are concepts of natural guilt. Life is somehow always guilty, its punishment: death.
>
> One form of natural guilt that of sexuality, involving enjoyment and the generation of life.
>
> Another that of money, involving the mere possibility [*bloße Möglichkeit*] of existing. (*GS6*, 56)

These three assertions help circumscribe the very complex situation in which the divine finds itself in the cultic religion of capitalism. First, the divine, by becoming human, has also become guilty of that "bare life" which is punishable by death. The only thing that survives unscathed is the guilt- and debt-producing cult of capitalism itself. But this cult in turn requires at the very least agents of appropriation and exchange: exchange of commodities, appropriation of value. Benjamin does not refer to this here, although he will much later, in his notebooks of the 1930s, the "Arcades Project." But he does already insist on the need for a certain figure of the human in order for the cultic system to function. It is a human figure that is deified precisely to the extent that the traditional religious deity has been humanized. Since this humanization of the deity also deprives the latter of its transcendence, however, the figure must be "hidden," but at the same time elevated above the level of mere mortals. I quote Benjamin once again, describing this fourth trait of capitalism as religious cult: "Its fourth trait is, that its God must be kept secret [*verheimlicht*], and only addressed [*angesprochen*] at the zenith of its culpabilization [*Verschuldung*: also indebtedness]. The cult is celebrated before an immature [*ungereiften*] deity, each representation, each thought of it violates [*verletzt*] the mystery [*Geheimnis*] of its maturity [*Reife*]" (*GS6*, 100; *SW1*, 288). To describe the deity worshipped by the cult of capitalism in terms of "ripeness" or "maturity" is to underscore what results when the transcendence of the divine has been naturalized and humanized. As human, the God is incomplete, but its incompleteness can be construed only in terms of the living as "mere life," which is to say, as a lack of "maturation," as *Unreife*. This is why the naturalized-humanized God has to be kept secret, *verheimlicht*. But at the same time, given its integration into human destiny, the process of divine maturation can be construed only as the culmination of the guilty indebtedness of "bare life" to and in death. It is this that constitutes the "zenith" at which point alone it can be addressed, *angesprochen*.

The result is a cult that is highly ambivalent and ambiguous. It is designed to cultivate nothing other than *itself,* which is to say, its own ability to "hold out until the end." This cult, in short, cultivates the end as it own. It seeks to appropriate the end, but does this insofar as it assumes the appearance of the "bare" and barren "life" it both presupposes and seeks to outlast. The deity must therefore be hidden, and yet still be accessible—*ansprechbar*—so that the semblance *(Schein)* of "bare life" can be sustained. Life can be construed as bare only in the shadow of a semblance that cannot be seen and that in this concealment serves as an invisible object of adoration.

One way of worshiping such a concealed God consists in reenacting the process of concealment. Such reenactment can take the form of *targeting*: an object (person, figure, idea) is evoked, named, described, but only in order then to be done away with, sidelined, *beseitigt*. Perhaps this is why, immediately following his unforeseen description of the fourth trait of capitalism, the concealment of an unripe, indebted, and guilty God, Benjamin takes aim at two targets, two proper names. The first is that of Freud: "Freudian theory also belongs to the priestly domination of this cult. It is conceived in a thoroughly capitalist manner. The repressed, the sinful representation, is—by virtue of a profound analogy, yet to be thought through—capital, which pays interest on the hell of the unconscious" (*GS6,* 101; *SW1,* 289). Benjamin takes aim at "Freudian theory," which he sees as participating in "the priestly domination of this cult" of capitalism. If psychoanalysts are priests of this cult, it is by virtue of a "profound analogy" linking "the repressed" to "capital." Although he does not develop this analogy, he associates it with the interest-bearing function of capital, which he assimilates to the repression of a "sinful representation." It is thus the theological, and for Benjamin essentially Christian notion of "sin" that provides the *tertium comparationis,* or as Marx might have said, the "universal equivalent" for the "profound analogy" between capital and repression. Without being able to "think through" this "profound analogy" here, two points in Benjamin's account of it can be noted. First, he correctly describes the object of repression as a *representation (Vorstellung),* and second, he characterizes it as "sinful"—*sündig*. The representation is not "sinful," however, insofar as it is "an idea of sin," the curiously Puritanical interpretation of the English translation. For the representation is "sinful" not because of its object, but because it claims to represent something that cannot be represented. Whether this is construed in Marxian (and Ricardian) terms as the socially necessary labor-time that constitutes the measure of "value," or whether it is conceived in religious terms, as a deity whose transcendent alterity defies representation, Benjamin's text does not say. By comparing the destiny of the repressed representation in the unconscious with that of capital, producing interest out of "the hell of the unconscious," Benjamin seems to imply that the debt- and guilt-producing "sin" of both—repression and capital—resides in the process of *self-production* that allows only quantitative and incremental distinctions. In the following paragraphs, where he is no longer criticizing Freud but rather Nietzsche, he will define the "function of guilt/debt" in its "demonic ambiguity" as that of *returning* "interest upon compound interest" *(Zins und Zinseszins)*. The interest in a profitable *return of interest* is what transforms *Schuld* as *debt* into *Schuld* as *guilt*.

It is this self-consistency and continuity that also mark the second "target of opportunity" that Benjamin will cite, or take aim at in order to instantiate or exemplify "capitalist religious thinking"—Nietzsche. The name Nietzsche enters Benjamin's text explicitly only to be negated: God is *not* dead, Benjamin writes, but rather lives on in human, natural form. Benjamin thus seeks to distance himself from Nietzsche at the same time that he acknowledges implicitly his indebtedness to Nietzsche's pioneering analysis of the "demonic distinction" between *Schuld* as *debt* and as *guilt*. Benjamin's naming of Nietzsche is thus no less ambivalent than that analyzed by Nietzsche in the word *Schuld*. Nietzsche is addressed, as it were, *angesprochen* by Benjamin at the zenith of a certain *Verschuldung*, although it is not at all clear whether this *Verschuldung* is that of Nietzsche, as Benjamin suggests, or also and above all that of Benjamin himself with respect to Nietzsche.[11]

To explore this ambiguity, let us reread the manner in which Benjamin mobilizes Nietzsche in the service of his argument (which is not, we recall, a demonstration). Following the assertion that God is not dead but has assumed a human destiny, Benjamin continues: "This passage [*Durchgang*] of the planet man through the house of despair in the absolute solitude [*Einsamkeit*] of its course is the *ethos* defined by

Nietzsche. This man is the overman, the first that, recognizing the capitalist religion, begins to fulfill it. Its fourth trait is that its God must be kept secret" (*GS6*, 101; *SW1*, 289). The trait of modern man that Benjamin cites as defining the trajectory of "the planet man through the house of despair"—a trajectory that is deliberately couched in pagan, astrological terms[12]—is that of a certain *solitude, Einsamkeit*. Everything depends on just how this solitude is construed. By being associated here with the astrological movement of "the planet man through the house of despair," Benjamin emphasizes its *relationality:* this is not the isolated individual, but a being whose solitude is defined in terms of a complex constellation that is neither purely natural (that is, astronomical), nor purely human. Least of all is it defined as "bare life," although it is determined by a "despair" that results from the "fall" of "transcendence." Benjamin's fascination with astrology, patent here, has at least two dimensions. First, it involves a relation to a cosmos that is neither immanently meaningful nor divinely symbolic: a move away from the religions of the Book, be they Christian or Judaic. Second, nature appears as a textual network to be read rather than as an image to be seen. This is why astrology and allegory are generally linked in his writing.

In "falling" then, the transcendence of the divine does not simply disappear: it lands squarely in the "destiny" of the "human": that is, in the net of guilt, whose strands are held together by the sentence of death as penalty and punishment. The problem, for Benjamin, is the way in which Nietzsche responds to the "fall": "The thought of the *Übermensch* transposes the apocalyptic 'leap' [*Sprung*] not into over-turning [*Umkehr*], atonement [*Sühne*], purification, penance [*Büsse*], but rather into an ostensibly continuous, although ultimately explosive, discontinuous elevation [*Steigerung*] . . . The *Übermensch* is the historical man who has arrived at and outgrown heaven without *turning around [ohne Umkehr]*" (*GS6*, 101; *SW1*, 289; my emphasis). Here, as always with Benjamin, but perhaps even more than usual, we have to be attentive to details. Note first that the "fall" of transcendence—"God's transcendence has fallen"—has now become an "apocalyptic *leap*"—a *Sprung*. Benjamin does not take issue with this shift or translation, nor with its "apocalyptic" character. What he criticizes is that for Nietzsche this "leap" retains the character of the *leaper,* God, without subjecting it to a radical "turn-about," an *Umkehr,* a

word that immediately recalls Hölderlin. The words that follow, however, are far more orthodox and Christian: atonement, purification,
penance *(Sühne, Reinigung, Büsse)*. Thus, while Benjamin is ostensibly reproaching Nietzsche—as Heidegger will do in his lectures of the
1930s—for remaining within the parameters of traditional Christian
humanism and its conception of history, the language he himself uses is
far closer to this conception than that of Nietzsche. At the same time,
while criticizing it, Benjamin attributes a quality to Nietzsche's "ethos"
that he himself will increasingly endorse in the years to come, namely,
that of being "explosive" *(sprengend)*: "This exploding of the heavens
[*Die Sprengung des Himmels*] through heightened humanity, which, religiously (even for Nietzsche) is and remains culpabilization-indebted-
ness [*Verschuldung*], was pre-judged [*präjudiziert*] by Nietzsche. And
similarly by Marx: capitalism that does not overturn itself becomes,
with simple and compound interest [*mit Zins und Zinseszins*], which
are functions of *Schuld* (see the demonic ambiguity of this concept), socialism" (*GS6*, 101–102; *SW1*, 289). Benjamin's move here, in thus targeting Nietzsche, is no less "ambiguous" than that which he attributes
to the word *Schuld*. For it was Nietzsche, of course, who extensively
discussed this ambiguity and its implications in the second book of the
Genealogy of Morals. Benjamin seems obliged to forget or to ignore
this fact, and with it his own indebtedness toward Nietzsche, in order
to take full credit for the argument expounded in *Capitalism as Religion*, which depends entirely on this ambiguity.

It is only by thus targeting Nietzsche, flanked and framed by Marx
and Freud, that Benjamin is able to give his argument the semblance
of a conclusion, by asserting not just that capitalism (and socialism
as well) are religions, but more distinctively, that they are parasitic off-
shoots of Christianity: "Capitalism developed itself—as could be
shown not just with Calvinism, but with the other orthodox Christian
tendencies—parasitically from Christianity in the west, so that *in the
end* [*zuletzt*] its history is essentially that of a parasite, that of capitalism . . . The Christianity of the Reformation period did not simply
favor the emergence of capitalism—it transformed itself into capitalism" (*GS6*, 102; *SW1*, 289; my emphasis). Capitalism thus emerges
here not just as a religion, but as the parasitic byproduct of a particular
religion, Christianity, which in taking over the host, takes control over
Western history as well. In what way is the religion of capitalism the

parasite of Christianity? Precisely by exploiting the "demonic ambiguity" of its culpabilizing *and* indebting power. How does it accomplish this? Although Benjamin's text begins to dissolve at this point into bibliographical notes, significantly right after targeting Nietzsche, Marx, and Freud, it still manages to provide several hints of a possible response to this question. Here is the first, jotted down in a kind of telegraphic shorthand: "Comparison between the images of saints of different religions on the one hand, and the banknotes of different states on the other. The Spirit that speaks out of the ornamentality [*Ornamentik*] of banknotes" (*GS6*, 102; *SW1*, 290). The "spirit" that speaks out of the *ornamentality* of banknotes is not the same spirit that speaks through the depictions of saints. But it is spirit nevertheless. The spirit of capitalism, however, in contrast to the spirit of Christianity, does not take as its point of departure depiction at all, for instance that of the human body martyred and/or transfigured in faces of suffering and hope. Rather, Benjamin contrasts such holy pictures with the baroque ornamentation on banknotes. What previously would have supplied a framework for a manifestation now takes on its own value as frame while at the same time separating itself from any possible "content." For what it "signifies" is not individual suffering and the promise of its transcendence, but the numeric measure of value as a social relation of force. At the same time, however, Ornamentality is appropriate to a manifestation that is fully cut off from that which it manifests, value, while at the same time fulfilling the indispensable function of differentiating, measuring, and manifesting that value. But the "good news" that such banknotes bring with them is that of their own capacity to circulate and be exchanged. To that circulation and exchange they tolerate no alternative and it is this exclusivity that provokes "cares: a spiritual malady that is peculiar to the capitalist period" (*GS6*, 102; *SW1*, 290). Cares, of course, are what call for religions in the first place, and as such are not limited to capitalism. The particular bond that links cares to capitalism is that of *debt-as-guilt*, the sense of being the author and owner of one's cares and torments: cares as the private property of those they concern. This sense of proprietorship, and hence of debt-as-guilt, is reinforced by the immanence and lack of alternative that distinguish the world of capitalism. "Spiritual (not material) impasse [*Ausweglosigkeit*] [leads to] poverty, vagrant, beggarly monasticism. A situation so devoid of any way out produces guilt and debt [*ist verschuldend*]" (*GS6*, 102; *SW1*, 290). In short, the religion of Capitalism, like the religions that preceded it—above all, Christianity, but also what Benjamin often refers to as a mythical (that is, polytheistic) Paganism that he conceives as its predecessor—promotes *debt-as-guilt* as the *officially sanctioned response* to distress. This promotion of debt-as-guilt in turn reproduces and strengthens the sense of distress: "Cares are the index of the guilty consciousness of the impasse [*Ausweglosigkeit*]" and thus aid the "cult" to cultivate itself, without "truce or grace." But at the same time that care and guilt confirm that there is no way out (of the cult), they offer the only way "in": into the community. "Cares result from the anxiety of a communal, not an individual-material impasse." Cares, concerns, troubles, and above all the sense of debt-as-guilt hold together this new community, this church without dogma but also without end or limit. And yet how is such an incessant und unlimited cult to be construed? It seems to have something to do with the ornaments on banknotes, with that in money that distinguishes it, as a sign of value, without representing that value in the way the sacred pictures of saints sought to represent the relation of suffering to beatitude. Such iconography has been supplanted by a certain ornamentality in capitalism, but this still does not tell us just how or why capitalism should be considered the "parasite" of Christianity. The problem is even more complex in view of the fact that the distinctive quality of the capitalist religious cult, its relentless exercise and durability, stands in contrast to if not contradiction with the necessity of a cult to be celebrated at specific times and places, and thus, not to be perennial and ongoing but rather discreet, limited, localizable, and repeatable. How could a cult be at the same time both localizable and ubiquitous, incessant and yet also clearly delimited and defined?

It is not in the fragmentary jottings of 1921 that elements of an answer to this question are to be found, but rather in other fragments, written some fifteen years later, and now collected in the volume on the "Paris Passages." I am thinking in particular of the notebook "B," dealing with "Fashion." For although he no longer refers directly to the earlier fragment, Benjamin's notes on *Mode* provide us with at least a partial instantiation of the cult he had announced but could not demonstrate in the text of 1921. In between the two writings he had articulated a notion that would enable him to negotiate the contradictions of capitalism as religion and as a cult of *Verschuldung:* the notion of "alle-gory" elaborated in his 1924 study *Origin of the German Mourning Play.* Allegory both intensifies and undermines the function of guilt: *intensifies,* insofar as it responds to a situation in which the possibility of redemption and grace being no longer a given, care and anxiety are all the greater and thus, the need for "guilt" all the stronger; *under-mines,* insofar as there is no clear-cut authority or standard by which "guilt" could be determined.

Much of this ambivalence can be felt in Benjamin's discussions of fashion. The two mottos he places at the head of his considerations sum up the two poles of the ambivalence. First, Leopardi: "Fashion: Lord Death, Lord Death!" Then, Balzac: *"Rien ne meurt, tout se trans-forme":* Nothing dies, everything changes. Benjamin cites the phrase from Leopardi's "Dialogue of Fashion with Death" to suggest how fashion establishes a link between the religions of the past, in particu-lar, Christianity, and the new religion of Capitalism. Benjamin adds a new scene to the encounter of fashion and death, which in his version is less of a dialogue and more of a pantomime:[13]

> Here fashion has introduced the dialectical turning-point [*Umschlageplatz*] between the female and the commodity—between lust and the corpse. Her tall and crude assistant [*flegelhafter Kommis*], death, measures the century with a yardstick, serves as model himself to save money and orga-nizes single-handedly the liquidation, the fire-sale that in French is called "revolution." For fashion was never anything else but the parody of the colorful corpse, provocation of death through the female, and between shrill laughter learned by rote, the bitterly whispered dialogue with decay. That is fashion. Therefore it changes so rapidly; tickles death and is al-ready someone else again, someone new, when he finally turns around to strike her. For a hundred years she owed him nothing [*ist ihm . . . nichts schuldig geblieben*]. Now finally she is about to abandon the field to him. He however, on the banks of a new Lethe that carries the asphalt stream through passages—he donates [*stiftet*] the armature of the whore as a tro-phy. Revolution. Love. (*GS5,* 111; *AP,* 62–63)

Fashion, for Benjamin, defines itself through its parodic if also bitter di-alogue with death, which is also one with decay. Death and fashion are joined together by their shared interest in the human body and its rela-tion to time. Time, the medium of change, can be that of constant re-newal or steady decline. With the Reformation, the pendulum inclined toward decline rather than renewal, at least from the perspective of

Benjamin's *Origin of the German Mourning Play.* Mourning the loss of a transparent relation to transcendence, *Trauer,* Benjamin writes, "reanimates with masks [*maskenhaft neubelebt*] the emptied world" (*GS1*, 318; *Origin*, 139), a world in which action and "good works" are no longer the guarantee of grace. Out of this theatrical turn of mourning toward the *mask* in order to produce at least the semblance of a reanimation that according to Luther otherwise had become accessible to "faith alone"—out of this theatrical turn of the baroque emerges "fashion," which seeks to outwit death at its own game: that of mastering time. Time itself has shifted from serving as a *narrative* medium—a medium of Christian soteriology—to becoming a *theatrical* one: that of the *Trauerspiel* in the German baroque, but also that of fashion in nineteenth-century Paris. This shift in the medial function of time also entails a certain spatialization: that of the stage, the scene, and the theater. The absence of what Benjamin, using a term borrowed from Erich Unger, often refers to as the "force of the frame (or of framing)" *(Gewalt des Rahmens),*[14] ushers in the necessity of an audience, spectators, addressees, called on to take the place of an authority that is no longer authorized. With the weakening of the Christian narrative that hitherto comprehended and contained the passage of time, this passage must be dealt with otherwise, and it is here that fashion—and death—intervene. Death thus assists fashion in the effort to cover up, if not overcome, the disastrous effects of time. But the spread of commodity-production and consumption assigns a new role to death by placing it at the center of a system of production based on the consumption of the producers. Already in the seventeenth century, Benjamin argued, this altered sense of time and history placed death, and the corpse, at the center of its preoccupations: "From the viewpoint of death, life is the production of corpses" (*GS1*, 392; *Origin*, 218) and corpses, in turn, the epitome and paradigm of the "allegorizing of the phusis" (*GS1, 391; Origin*, 217). Fashion continues this allegorizing in the nineteenth (and following) centuries and at the same time ritualizes it. The predominance of the commodity, which Benjamin investigates throughout the *Passages*, provides fashion with both its condition of possibility and its components: condition of possibility, in that by investing things with new life-like allegories, commodities signify independently of what appears to be their spontaneous, inherent existence; and components, since the elements of fashion consist of the body exposed to time, coupled with the concealment of its most devastating effects. Each time death looks around in order to "strike" *(um sie zu schlagen),* fashion is already elsewhere, having changed its guise and its place in order to implement the motto of Balzac, "Nothing dies, everything changes." At the same time—and it really is at the same time—nothing dies, because everything, qua commodity, is already dying, which is to say, functioning in the absence of itself, insofar as "self" names the unity of that which stays the same over time. And yet, paradoxically, fashion underscores the paradox that everything stays the same even while searching to be new and different. But the sameness of fashion is precisely a *sameness without self.*[15]

It is this that perhaps explains the place that replaces the field of battle that Fashion has now abandoned: "the banks of a new Lethe" that "rolls through the passages in the stream of asphalt." The Passages are organized to encourage both the forgetting of death and its commemoration. Both converge in the commodity as an object of desire, especially when that commodity is inseparable from a human body: that of the whore. But it is not the whore as such, her face or her body, that death "donates" as "trophy" marking the defeat, or at least the retreat, of Fashion: it is "the armature" *(die Armature),* a word that returns frequently in Benjamin's writings on the passages, and that points toward the hidden framework that allows things to be seen, displayed, exhibited, desired, purchased, and consumed—but which itself remains generally unnoticed. One could say that one of the primary tendencies of Benjamin's work on the Passages is to call attention to the invisible *armature,* its necessity and its ramifications.

The word is, like so many others, itself a network of significations. Coming from "arms," it suggests shields and struggles, defense and assault, but also bodily members, although not necessarily human ones. In this particular case, the "armature" also names the frame of the brassiere and of clothing generally, the hidden construct that gives form to that which conceals in exhibiting and exhibits in concealing: in short, the ideal object of desire. The armature both delimits bodies, desire, and commodities and at the same time allows them to circulate. On the banks of the new Lethe, the Passages, it becomes a "trophy" commemorating a previous victory while also facilitating the desire to forget the "Lord" or "Mistress" who now commands the scene: "Herr" or "Madama Morte."

Fashion is back in fashion, today, almost a century after Benjamin wrote that it combined a sense of "coming things" with an aversion to the immediate past. At a time when one of the most popular slogans, in politics as in business, is the exhortation to "move forward," and to do so without looking back, Benjamin's observation is more suggestive than ever:

> A definitive perspective on fashion emerges only from the observation that to each generation that which has just gone by [*die gerade verflossene*] appears as the most thorough-going anti-aphrodisiac. (B 1a,4)

> A thoroughly related problem emerged concerning the new velocities, which brought a changed rhythm into life. This too was at first tried out playfully. Roller coasters appeared and the Parisians adopted this entertainment as though obsessed . . . Fashion provided satisfaction from the beginning for this enigmatic need for the sensational. Only a theological approach, however, can get to the bottom of this need, since out of it speaks a profound, affective human attitude toward the course of history. (B 2,1)

The drive to "move forward" is of course, as Nietzsche again had analyzed, always also and perhaps above all the drive to move away from the past—from a past that is at the same time a harbinger of the future. Speed only accelerates this process, with all of its ambivalence. Fashion participates in this acceleration, producing the semblance of a move forward and away from the past while at the same time staying the same; in so doing, it offers consolation and hope to a self that also hopes to stay the same, to survive as self-same. But instead of the self, what is left is the armature of a *sameness without self.* Which is not to say that the self disappears. On the contrary, it remains the motor of a more general "acceleration of traffic, the tempo with which information is transmitted, with which newspaper editions relay and relieve one another [*sich ablösen*]—this all amounts to the attempt to eliminate all breaking off [*alles Abbrechen*], all rough ends and abrupt endings [*jähe Enden*] and [the insight into] how death as severance [*Einschnitt*] hangs together with all the straight lines of the divine course of time [*mit allen Geraden des göttlichen Zeitverlaufes zusammenhängt*]" (B 2,4). What Benjamin describes, however, is not quite what he asserts, as developments since he wrote this have made abundantly clear. What he describes is not simply the "elimination" of "all breaking off" (*alles Abbrechen*) through the rapid succession of information, but rather the integration of the *break* into the "news"—as "breaking news" that fills in the gaps between the true "breaks," which of course are commercial: "Stay with us, we'll be right back after the break." After the break—back to breaking news, designed, as with fashion, to break but also channel the forward rush of time toward a more definitive break that defies the staying-power of the "self." Fashion, and the "news," which has adopted its rhythm, can be said to "mimic" and "parody" death insofar as they stage the break with the aim of covering it over, as it covers and exposes the bodies of its "models." These bodies are exhibited as "models" in that they seem to have already absorbed and survived the break, rendering it survivable to the spectator.

The same could be said of the "ending," which remains "abrupt," but which the acceleration of tempo strives to integrate into a spectacle that can be seen in its entirety and thus survived. "Abruptness" frames this sight according to a principle that Benjamin, writing on epic theater, was one of the first to formulate: that of the formative power of *interruption*.[16] The "abruptness of endings" is thus integrated as interruption into a network—which is to say, into a net of relations that only works, only becomes a *work*, insofar as its mortal openness is framed, formed and rendered meaningful by a *linear narrative* that Benjamin does not hesitate to designate as *divine (göttlich)*. Such a narrative is implied in his surmise that "death as severance [*Einschnitt*] hangs together with all the straight-lines of the divine course of time [*Zeitverlaufes*]" (B 2,4).

Such "hanging together," however—which ties dispersed strands together and makes them into a network—always presupposes the exercise of a certain legitimating force, if not of violence: a *Gewalt*. Benjamin, who shortly after this passage writes of the "force of fashion [*Gewalt der Mode*] over the city of Paris," concludes his observations on the interruptive force of fashion with the following questions: "Were there fashions in Antiquity? Or were they prohibited by the 'force of the frame' [*Gewalt des Rahmens*]?" (B 2,4). The second question suggests that where the frame has sufficient force to enforce closure, there is neither room nor need for fashion. The necessity of fashion, consequently, arises only where the "force of the frame" is too weak to impose its authority—where the frame has gone underground, as it were, and become an *armature*. This is the situation in which Fashion emerges to take the place and assume the function of a linear eschatological narrative by giving meaning to interruption, severance, and abrupt endings. With fashion, the armature is what transforms the net into a network.

All of this is itself hidden away in the banality of a word that is difficult to translate into English. It occurs in a passage that describes the speed with which information is transmitted, in particular by "newspaper editions [that] *replace and relay* one another." The German word, which I translate here, inadequately, as "replace and relay," is *sich ablösen*. The root of the verb, *ablösen*, is cognate with the English "loose" or "loosen" and designates the *loosening of bonds or ties*. Acceleration, epitomized in fashion but by no means limited to it, diminishes the significance of the single, isolated self-contained place, held together by its armature, by increasing the power of moving from place to place, thereby decreasing the time required to traverse distance. The goal of acceleration is thus that of being able to be here and elsewhere at one and the same time. The time of this simultaneity has to be "one and the same" if that which takes place in it is to be considered *similar*, indeed, *identical to itself*. By thus reducing the time of traversal, the self seeks absolute mobility while remaining itself: hence, the worship of everything that is or appears to be "auto-mobile," including the speed with which information is processed and circulates. The cult of speed is thus a cult of power, that of appropriating time and space for a Self that thereby hopes to extricate itself from the heterogeneous net of relations by transforming it into a network, whether of transmission, automobiles, computers, persons, or things. Such a project, however, also implies that individuals cease operating as static, isolated, and self-contained elements and instead begin to function as *components*, always in the process of being relieved and replaced *(abgelöst)*, extricated from fixed positions in the net in order to circulate in the network. Acceleration, by seeking to eliminate or integrate all "breaks and abrupt endings," thus entails a *consecration* of time, since "death as interruption hangs together with all the straight lines of the divine course of time." Acceleration and its interruption—whether in fashion, production, or circulation—are what results when the "straightaway of the divine course of time" extends and descends to earth as the hidden deity of the capitalist cult.

If acceleration thus entails a certain process of dissolution, of *lösen*, this word suggests another connection *(Zusammenhang)* between death and the divine described in the penultimate paragraph of "Capitalism as Religion": "Connection [*Zusammenhang*] between the dogma of the dissolving [*auflösenden*]—for us in this capacity a both redeeming and lethal [*erlösenden und tötenden*] nature of knowledge—with capitalism: the bottom-line [*die Bilanz*] as the redeeming and disposing [*erlösende und erledigende*] knowledge" (*GS6*, 103; *SW1*, 290). The "straightaway of the divine course of history" that is presupposed by the experience of death as severance, as *Einschnitt*, has come down to earth in and as the *bottom-line* of capitalist double bookkeeping. If Benjamin had begun by asserting that "capitalism is a religion consisting of mere cult, without dogma" (*GS6*, 102; *SW1*, 288), then we see here that the "without" in this affirmation does not maintain itself as simple exclusion. It marks a connection, a *Zusammenhang*: the cult of capitalism may be *without* dogma, but as such it still stands *in relation to* dogma. Not however to the manifest dogma of revealed religion, but to a dogma that is as hidden as the God it worships. Death as interruption, as final cut *(Einschnitt)*, joins with the infinite straightaway it negates to produce the discrete but incessant bottom line of profit and loss. This bottom line "dissolves" everything leading up, or down, to it, in producing a final result that ostensibly offers a ground on which one can stand, on which one can ostensibly *count*.

But the result of this accounting—a certain conception of "knowledge"—"solves" the problem only by dissolving it: it "redeems" *(erlöst)* from debt-as-guilt only by "killing" *(tötend)*. Such knowledge as bottom line absolves the "living" from "destiny" only by putting an end to their lives, inscribing their lives in an actuarial table that would frame all that has been and will be. In this sense, it is not just the past that is "absolved" but also the future: or at least, this is the dogma of the bottom-line that is hidden behind the "fearful pomp" of a cult ostensibly without dogma. Instead, there is the cult of knowledge as information whose circulation is no longer separable from the cult itself. Knowledge as information is its medium. This knowledge as information follows the binary logic of the capitalist balance sheet, with truth and untruth, good and evil modeled after profit and loss. Just as the bottom line marks the caesura of that which alone is held to *count*, so the dogma of knowledge aims at producing a result that can absolve itself of all that has come before and will come after. Knowledge becomes dogmatic when it is absolved of all relation and liberated, redeemed, detached—*erlöst*—from all *obligations* to past and future. Past and future themselves are absorbed and forgotten, time ostensibly overcome in the eternal presence of a bottom line that is no longer static, no longer stays put, but *moves forward*, annexing the future for the present and thus mimicking eternal life.

As a dynamic, progressive network, knowledge is designed to accomplish the work of redeeming from debt-as-guilt by absolving, dissolving, and resolving it into a profitable bottom line. But in so doing, it is also death-bringing, *tötend*, in its search to impose an end that would be ultimate and definitive. This struggle to impose an end is however itself endless, giving rise to a "universal" and unending "polemic," just as the cult it celebrates strives to be "permanent." It is also all-inclusive. In the final paragraph of his text, Benjamin suggests that much could be learned about capitalism as a religion by recalling how an "original paganism" did not construe of religion as something "higher" or "moral," but rather as something "immediately practical"; and that in so doing, it was no more clear on its "ideal" or "transcendent" nature than capitalism is today. "Rather it saw in the individual of its community who was irreligious or of another faith precisely for that reason a full-fledged member, as today's bourgeoisie sees in those of its members who are not gainfully employed [*in seinen nicht erwerbenden Angehörigen*]" (GS6, 103; SW1, 290). If capitalism is a religion that recognizes and accepts as its own even those who do not share its "faith" or who "are not gainfully employed," it is because its cult requires neither faith nor gainful employment *(Erwerb)*. All it requires to be sustained is the "bare life" of the living. Or rather, what it requires is the consciousness of self as bare life. And as bottom line. For the bottom line is what remains of the fallen transcendence, of a God who has assumed the human destiny of debt-as-guilt, and who therefore has gone into hiding. This God can be addressed only "at the zenith of his indebtedness," a zenith that appears, paradoxically, only as the letterhead at the top of the balance sheet: unripe because never definitive, always only a stage in the ongoing descent toward the bottom line. It is this descent that describes the trajectory of the cult "sans trêve et sans merci."

The divine straight-away thus cut off by the bottom line could thus be seen as a development of precisely the dilemma announced by Benjamin at the outset of this text, which he did not publish and which he suggested could never really be written: "We cannot draw closed the net in which we stand. Later however there will be an overview" (*GS6*, 100; *SW1*, 288). What can be "looked over," seen through—*überblickt*—is the balance sheet. In it, the net comes together into a network, with a bottom line exercising the "force of the frame." To draw up the net in which one stands, however, is hardly an image of emancipation from debt-as-guilt, but rather its perpetuation: a perpetuation rife with "universal polemics." But from where, then, is this overview possible: where does it take its stand? And in so targeting the bottom line, does it *overlook* the net?

A hint of an answer can perhaps be found in a text written by Benjamin some seven years earlier, a text he called "his first major work": a reading of two poems of Hölderlin, "Dichtermut" (Poet's courage) and "Blödigkeit" (Timidity). Benjamin wrote this essay in 1914 following the death of his friend, the poet Fritz Heinle. Not surprisingly, therefore, the central problem around which Benjamin's reading turns involves the relation of the poet to death, and through this, that of "the living," des *Lebendigen*, a Hölderlinian turn of phrase, to the *Divine*. It is Benjamin's interpretation of this term, which he takes over from Hölderlin and which is the marker of an enormous debt, that is of particular interest in the context of our previous discussion. For as we have seen, the notion of the *Lebendigen* is, implicitly at least, at the hidden heart of *Capitalism as Religion*, insofar as the cult that defines this religion is based on *Schuld*: debt-as-guilt, which in turn is inseparable from the *living, den Lebendigen*. Inseparable, but not univocal, and Benjamin's reading of Hölderlin opens a *space* in which an alternative notion of *Schuld*, and of its relation to nets and networks, begins to emerge. Similarly the space opened by Benjamin in this text relates to his surprising interpretation of the "living" in Hölderlin's "world" precisely *as a certain kind of space,* or rather, as a kind of *stretching*:

The living are always clearly, in this world of Hölderlin, the *stretching* [*Erstreckung*] of space, the map or surface [*Plan*] spread out, within which, (as will become visible) destiny extends [*sich das Schicksal erstreckt*] . . . Much, much more about Hölderlin's cosmos is said in the following words, which—alien as though from an Eastern world and nevertheless how much more original than the Greek Parca—confer majesty upon the poet. "Does not your foot tread upon the true as upon carpets?" ["*Geht auf Wahrem dein Fuß nicht, wie auf Teppichen?*"] (*GS2*, 114; *SW1*, 26)

It is no doubt quite a "stretch" from this gloss on "the living" to the debt-and-guilt-ridden cult of capitalism—as much as between the "carpets" on which the poet's foot *treads* to the "net in which we *stand*." And yet in the very extremities of this stretch can be read the outlines of a medium through which an alternative to the cult of capitalism becomes thinkable. The determination of "the living" as *Erstreckung* appeals to a notion of space that is quite different from the traditional conception of extension (which is how it is translated in the English edition). Rather, *Erstreckung*, a favorite word of Benjamin, is one he will later use to describe Brecht's epic theater, where it is designed, he writes, to "expunge all traces of the sensational."[17] *Sensation*, a notion he also develops with respect to the speed of the capitalist cults of fashion and information, involves the lust for "breaking news" in order to break up the lethal monotony of the self-same. "Stretching," by contrast, carries something other, although not necessarily new, into the space of the living, or rather into the living room as *Raum*. The German word *Raum*, which is generally translated as space, would be better translated as "room," with which it is cognate. *Raum*, in contrast to "space," can imply delimitation, as it does when Benjamin uses it to define "the living." It is not just space as abstract extension, but a very distinctive form of "stretching" related to situated bodies: to "stretch" is to presuppose a predetermined "room" rather than an indeterminate "space." Benjamin's effort therefore is always directed toward exploring the nature of this "room" and what happens when it begins to "stretch" (or swell). This is why the figure of the *carpet* is so important: it is that to which "the true," on which the poet *treads*, is likened. What interests Benjamin most of all in this Hölderlinian carpet is its *Musterhaftigkeit*, that is, its *patterning*. This patterning is also exemplary, since, as the English translator notes, the German word *musterhaft* can mean both exemplary and patterning. Unfortunately, in retaining *only* "exemplary" in the body of the translation, the translator makes the wrong choice, since precisely what is exemplary about the *Muster* is its *patterning*, not its specific *content*. The true on which the poet treads is a plurality of *carpets* whose singular magic resides in their distinctive patterning. Benjamin makes this unmistakably clear when he interprets the patterning as "ornament": "Just as in the image of the carpet (posited as a level for an entire system), what must be remembered is its *Musterhaftigkeit*, its patterning, the spiritual arbitrariness [*geistige Willkür*] of the ornament—and ornament therefore constitutes a true determination of layout [*Lage*], rendering it *absolute*—there thus resides within the traversable [*beschreitbar*] order of truth itself the intensive activity of the gait [*des Ganges*] as inner, plastic, temporal form" (GS2, 115; SW1, 27). This emphasis on ornamental patterning as that which makes layout absolute anticipates Benjamin's remark on the "ornamentality" of the effigies on bank-notes that replaces the iconography of sacred figures in traditional (above all, Christian) religion. But whereas the iconic figurality of revealed religion is inscribed within, and framed by an eschatological and soteriological narrative—here, in Benjamin's reading of Hölderlin, time is taken up into the figure of the carpet as that on which the poet must *tread*. *The poet treads, but does not stand.* And what he treads on is not a stable place but a *stretched layout*, one that by any stretch of the imagination is difficult to conceive. This *Lage*, layout, is rendered "absolute" by the exemplariness of its patterning. *Lage*, which is usually rendered in English as "situation," is misleading precisely insofar as the word here does *not* imply the self-contained stability of a *situs*, but rather the unstable dynamics of an ongoing relation: the lay of the land. The *layout* is always temporally determined as that which has been *laid down, gelegen*:[18] "Room can be grasped as the identity of *Lage* and *Gelegenem*: of layout and laid-out." As with the carpet, such an "identity of layout and laid-out" invites and indeed enjoins a traversal: it must be *tread on* without there ever being an assured exit or ending: "This region of the spirit is traversable [*beschreitbar*] and necessarily leaves those who traverse it [*den Schreitenden*] with each arbitrary step [*Willkürschritte*] in the realm of the true" (GS2, 115; SW1, 27). In other words, "the temporal existence" of the Living is caught up in an "infinite stretching," with respect to which "identity" can be defined as the coincidence of the layout with the laid-out, the *Lage* with the *Gelegenen*. What is "laid out"—*gelegen*—however, can never be predicted. And it is here that the admonition of Hölderlin's poem assumes its full force: "*Was geschieht, es sei alles gelegen dir!*" (Whatever happens let it all be laid out for you!). "Laid out for you"—*dir gelegen*—should not be read as suggesting that everything has been intended or designed with the poet in mind, but rather something quite different: that the poet, and with him the Living, remain true to what has been laid out as their layout, which means true to a stretching of space by time that supports a movement, a treading going nowhere, except perhaps toward a *sameness without self.* This formula, which is not to be found in Benjamin, to be sure, nevertheless perhaps begins to approximate what in this essay he designates as a "relation" that would be "*of* Genius" but not "*to* it."

This "*Gelegenheit*" or *opportunity* to which the genius of the poet *responds* is not one that can be *targeted,* however, for a layout can never be put in its place, least of all through the virtuality of a figure *(Gestalt).* The layout that has been laid out cannot be put in its place because its "identity" consists in the outreach of place itself, the *Erstreckung des Raumes.* Nothing can simply be put in its place when the place itself is being stretched and laid out—nothing except what Benjamin here calls "imagistic dissonance" *(Bilddissonanz),* which, like that of rhyme, which it echoes, involves sameness without self, repetition without equality. In this sense, opportunity, "Gelegenheit," can be said to signify "the spiritual-temporal identity (the truth) of the layout" (*GS2,* 117; *SW1,* 29). It is an event and as such cannot be made an object of cognition or appropriation. It is the event of a net-without-work: a *netting* without net profit or loss.

A serious reading of this essay would have to explore and elaborate the ways in which the "dissonance of the image" does not simply abolish targeting and figuration, to be sure, but alters their *course:* "Precisely after all the extremes of imagery [*Bildhaftigkeit*], a path and apt goal [*schickliches Ziel*] must be visible differently now" (*GS2,* 117; *SW1,* 29). Benjamin will go on to describe this difference in terms of "a peculiar doubling of the figure" in the second poem studied in the essay, "Timidity" (*GS2,* 119; *SW1,* 30). But for the purposes of the present discussion, it will be sufficient to recall the manner in which his reading draws to a close, draws a bottom line but without drawing up the net in which it stands, and indeed by suggesting the inappropriateness of any definitive conclusion: "In the end it cannot be a matter of the investigation of ultimate elements, for the last word of this world is just that of solidarity and obligation, of *Verbundenheit:* as the unity of the function of binding and bound" (*GS2*, 122; *SW1*, 32). The term *Verbundenheit* is much stronger than the English "connection," used in the published translation, would suggest. To be *verbunden* is not merely to be *connected*, but to be *bound up with, obliged, bonded*, and therefore not always separable from a certain *bondage*. It does not *extricate* the Living from the net in which they stand, but rather redefines *Schuld* as an effect not of *standing* but of *going: treading* on and in an irreducible net of *relations* that defines the room not only of poetry but of all *patterning*, and defines it as something that is never fixed and to which one must respond: as Benjamin in this essay responds to what he calls the *Gedichtete*, the "poetized," but also, more etymologically, the "dictated." To affirm such *Verbundenheit* is to acknowledge the *obligation to respond*, not just to persons, things, or subjects, but to the "sole rule of relation" that for Benjamin is the "principle of the poetized."

The adjectival-noun, *das Gedichtete*, suggests that the net of relations that constitute it should not be confused with a work, an accomplished and meaningful whole. To be sure, there will always be, will always have been, targeting, and the net will always have been put to work. But the affirmation of *Verbundenheit* makes its way on a carpet whose exemplary pattern will never be reducible to a bottom line, any more than its opportunity reduced to a target. For what is laid down opportunely *(gelegen)* will always be just another knot or node in the net through which we tread.

CHAPTER EIGHTEEN

The *Ring* as *Trauerspiel*

Reading Wagner with Benjamin and Derrida

At the outset of these reflections stand two questions. First: to what degree can the *Ring* be considered a deconstruction of "modernity" in terms of musical theater? And second: assuming this is the case, what are the consequences?

In order for these questions to unfold, the terms they bring into play require clarification; for the meaning of concepts such as "modernity" or "deconstruction" is anything but self-evident. Let us begin with *de-construction*. *De-construction* and *construction* need not be mutually exclusive. A deconstruction of modernity does not necessarily mean abolishing or destroying modernity. The distinction of deconstruction from mere destruction is part of the history of the concept, which does not begin with Derrida, who popularized the word in French during the late 1960s.[1] Already in the opening pages of *Sein und Zeit (To Be and Time)*[2] Heidegger describes his project as an attempt to "dismantle" *(Destruieren)* traditional ontology—not in order to destroy it, but rather in order that "this hardened tradition [might] be loosened up" and that "the concealments which it has brought about [might] be dissolved." On this point, Heidegger writes:

> But this destruction is just as far from having the *negative* sense of shaking off the ontological tradition. We must, on the contrary, stake out the positive possibilities of that tradition, and this always means keeping it

within its *limits* . . . On its negative side, the destruction does not relate only toward the past; its criticism is aimed at 'today' and at the prevalent way of treating the history of ontology . . . But to bury the past in nullity [*Nichtigkeit*] is not the purpose of this destruction; its aim is *positive;* its negative function remains unexpressed and indirect.[3]

No matter how much Derrida distances himself from Heidegger in various important aspects, this description also applies to deconstruction. As already with Heidegger, by re-marking and de-limiting consecrated or conventional boundaries, possibilities are released from the "hidebound tradition" in which they are otherwise largely trapped. In other words, propositions and artifacts that claim to constitute a comprehensive system are reinscribed with respect to their enabling limits, thus making way for something else to emerge.

For our purposes, these brief and highly schematic definitions should suffice to shield deconstruction against the crudest misunderstandings, such as its equation with nihilism. Things already become more difficult, however, as soon as one attempts to define the second term mentioned: modernity. Here no sharp delineation is possible. It is not that the designation "modernity" is entirely vague; but the direction in which its various meanings point cannot be as clearly determined as can the distinction between deconstruction on the one hand, and destruction on the other. If the word "deconstruction" signified nothing but "destruction" it would never have been able to exercise the fascination to which its widespread acceptance and usage today attest. Why bother to speak of "deconstruction" when "destruction" would do?

Turning to the concept of modernity, the situation is markedly different. Here there are so many different usages and interpretations that one is forced to choose among them. To simplify matters as much as possible, I will limit my discussion of the term to the dictionary. Dictionary definitions have two great advantages: they are relatively concise, and they need not worry much about conceptual consistency. They simply reflect the way a word is generally used at a given point in time, or rather, the way many people *think* that a word is used. A glance at the practical application of words is sometimes more productive than the attempt to cull doggedly a meaning from them. The following are two definitions of "modern" taken from a current (German) dictionary.[4]

modern (adj.) 1. in accordance with fashion, current taste, up to date; the dress is no longer modern; all the rooms are modernly furnished 1.1. contemporary; modern art. 2. a modern person open to the problems of the present.

So far, so good. Yet the second definition contains a surprise:

mo-dern (v.) to molder, rot; the wet leaves moldered on the ground; moldering wood.

Naturally, this is a coincidence, simply homonyms. For the adjective *modern* of course has nothing to do with the German verb *modern*, at least not lexically or etymologically. Yet can we be sure that this non-relationship is absent from the thing itself? Can we exclude the possibility that there might exist a curious—or as Heidegger might have said, a *questionable*—connection between the process of moldering and the nature of the modern?

I am not the first to arrive at this speculation. It haunts the writings of one of the most influential thinkers of modernity, namely Walter Benjamin. He always insisted on thinking of modernity in relation not only to the archaic, but also to processes of decay. The text in which Benjamin most fully fleshes out this view of modernity is his *Ursprung des deutschen Trauerspiels* (The Origin of the German Mourning Play). The historical context of his study is seventeenth-century Germany, yet his analysis of this period is undertaken from a perspective that implicitly incorporates the entirety of developments thereafter. In the German *Trauerspiel* of the baroque, Benjamin does not merely view an individual genre during a particular period of German history; rather, in addition and foremost, he discerns therein the very origin of modernity itself. And because origin is not just a single occurrence for Benjamin, but rather a discontinuous process changing in each iteration, he identifies a particular historical phenomenon, the baroque *Trauerspiel,* as the origin of modernity. According to Benjamin, this modernity is distinguished by two main characteristics: on the one hand it presents itself as a nightmare; on the other, as its staging *(Inszenierung)*. It is precisely these two characteristics that also mark the notion of myth at the root of Wagner's tetralogy.

In order to more closely examine whether more than a merely pessimistic notion of modernity links Benjamin's *Trauerspiel* and Wagner's *Bühnenfestspiel,* the following analysis will proceed in three steps. First, Benjamin's theory of modernity will be briefly outlined, using as basis his treatment of the *Trauerspiel*. Second, the perspective this opens up will be used as a lens through which to re-read various passages from the Tetralogy as well as Wagner's aesthetic writings, in order then, third, to re-pose the question of the deconstruction of modernity in a new light as a question of theater.

To begin, Benjamin's notion of modernity: this is somewhat difficult to outline, because nowhere is it systematically explicated; yet there are some important clues in *Ursprung des deutschen Trauerspiels* that will be referenced here.

According to Benjamin, modernity consists essentially in two moments. The first is a traumatic shock, which not coincidentally coincides with the *origin* of the German *Trauerspiel*. Benjamin links this shock to the Reformation, and to Luther in particular. He describes the relation between Reformation and *Trauerspiel* as follows:

> The great German dramatists of the baroque were Lutherans. Whereas in the decades of the Counter-Reformation, Catholicism had penetrated secular life with all the power of its discipline, the relationship of Lutheranism to the everyday had always been antinomic. The rigorous morality of its teachings in respect of civic conduct stood in sharp contrast to its renunciation of "good works." By denying the latter any special miraculous spiritual effect, making the soul dependent on grace through faith . . . it did, it is true, instill into the people a strict sense of obedience to duty, but in its great men, it produced melancholy. Even in Luther himself, the last two decades of whose life are filled with an increasing heaviness of soul, there are signs of a reaction against the storming of good works . . . Human actions were deprived of all value. Something new arose: an empty world.[5]

The modern emerges from this violent "reaction" *(Rückschlag),* namely as a counter-movement that Benjamin in his work on the baroque associates with the "Counter-Reformation" (although a decade later he will identify its return in the nineteenth century with post-Napoleonic "Restoration"). The possibility of such a return, however, is already anticipated in his initial determination of the origin, in his "Epistemo-critical Preface" to the book on the mourning play. The originary phenomenon, he writes there, consists precisely in a movement of return, one that can never complete itself and therefore never repeats itself *identically.* Like the origin itself, modernity determines its course through a certain striving: "On the one hand, it needs to be recognized as a process of restoration and reestablishment, but on the other, and

precisely because of this, as something imperfect and incomplete"
(*GS1*, 226; *Origin*, 45). Accordingly, it is the ever-incomplete attempt
at "restoration" that is "originary." In the age of the baroque, this
origin consists in a reaction—one that is directed primarily at the
"storming of the work" that Benjamin relates to Luther's emphasis on
faith as the sole path to grace. In the seventeenth century resistance to
the storming of the work takes the form of the Counter-Reformation,
which, however, is not limited to one of the two Christian denomina-
tions, but pervades both.[6] It reacts to the radically antinomian questioning of *all established authority* by Luther, by attempting to bolster
the institutions shaken by it. Viewed as such, this movement, which
would later shape all of modernity, can be understood as fundamentally reactionary and restorative.

Yet Benjamin's interest in his speculative construction of a philosophy of history does not lie solely in the interpretation of the Counter-
Reformation as a decisive movement of modernity, but rather in the
manner in which this counter-movement is represented in the seventeenth century. Not until it is seen in this way does the significance of
the *Trauerspiel* become clear: "There was no answer to this except
perhaps in the morality of ordinary people—'honesty in small things,'
'upright living'—which developed at this time . . . For those who
looked deeper saw the scene of their existence as a rubbish heap
of partial, inauthentic actions . . . Mourning is the state of mind in
which feeling revives the empty world in the form of a mask, and derives an enigmatic satisfaction in contemplating it" (*GS1*, 318; *Origin*,
139). Mourning, as Benjamin describes it here, is not primarily an emotional state or a psychological bearing, but rather a theatrical practice.
Mourned is not only the horrific destruction that the Thirty-Years War
left behind, but also the near abandonment of the hope that meaning
could be found in such destruction. What is mourned are the "good
works" that no longer are seen as opening the way to salvation. Yet the
vacuum this creates is not only experienced negatively; it also becomes
the site of new possibilities. If the world exists only in order to fall, it
can still be "revived in the form of a mask." Such a masked *revival*
relates to Christian *resurrection* as the "natural history" of the
Trauerspiel does to the eschatological story of salvation. This redemptive story is challenged by Luther's storming of the work. For Benjamin,
Paul Klee's *Angelus Novus* will come to encapsulate the reaction of his-

tory to this storm. What remains implicit in his various accounts of this angel does, however, become manifest in his discussion of the German baroque: namely, that the reaction to the storming of the work can only be *theatrical*.[7]

Why must this response necessarily be theatrical? Because theater has always questioned, implicitly but practically, the status of the *work*. It deals with *pieces* or *plays (Stücke, pièces),* but never with works. Constitutive of the play is that it must be *performed.* Theatrical performances can never be completely separated from their spatial and temporal localizations: they are tied to a stage and hence can never lay claim to the kind of permanence aspired to by the "work" of *art.* To the extent that the notion of a durable work is unavailable, the medium of theater offers a more temporal, more transient alternative.

An irredeemable world in which only faith, not works, counts, requires a theater to "revive" it—on the condition, however, that this revival be staged "in the form of a mask." Its horizon remains limited to the profane stage, whose harsh lighting excludes any and all transfiguration. No resurrection takes place on its boards, apart from that of ghosts and spirits. As the living dead, these specters get along quite well with a certain moldering *(Vermodern).* For, cut off from any transcendent consolation, the strict immanence of the modern world takes the form of perpetual disintegration. Or, as Benjamin observes in regard to the German *Trauerspiel:* "From the moment in which the Christian story of salvation is no longer reliably relayed and embodied in the Church and its sacraments, the history of the living is increasingly seen "from the vantage point of death" (*GS1,* 392; *Origin,* 218).

It is this vantage-point, however, that brings the theater to the fore. How does it relate to death? It masks it and represents it as allegory, that is, in the form of things that are cut off from their "natural" significance and can therefore mean everything and nothing. The German *Trauerspiel* responds to a world emptied of (eschatological and soteriological) significance by staging it as allegorical theater. As Benjamin writes, this represents something akin to "natural history," whereby the "natural" in this history is directly tied to its transience. It appears "as the tale of woe of a world" that no longer dares to hope for redemption through good works, and therefore has to settle for "masked revival" on the stage.

For only theater offers even the most slender hope of slowing, if not reversing the fate of the empty world. Only through the incessant production of spectacle—unconnected from any claim to truth—can the equally incessant production of corpses be attenuated, if not eliminated. Only a theater that interrupts its own forward progress—its plot—can provide an at least temporary distraction from that temporal movement leading ultimately to death.[8] Death, to which a clear meaning can no longer be ascribed, is lodged in a perpetually repeatable, if not eternal, process of signification that reveals itself to be the last refuge of infinity.

An empty world, works under siege, theatrical-allegorical revival of the world in plays that are no longer works—these are, according to Benjamin, the most salient traits not only of the baroque *Trauerspiel,* but of the modernity it ushers in.

Yet there is still one last move to be recounted, which is of special significance for the *Ring.* The decay of the world affects not only the creation, but inevitably the creator as well, and this includes his various proxies, whether in church or state. Caught up in this Natural History of death and decay is the figure of the *sovereign.* Following Carl Schmitt, but also modifying and radicalizing his thought, Benjamin argues that the figure of the ruler ceases to function effectively in the German baroque insofar as it itself is caught up in the exceptional circumstances it is supposed to avert (or in Schmitt, to "decide"). In sixteenth-century Germany there emerges an irreconcilable "antithesis between the power of the ruler and his capacity to rule" (*GS1,* 250; *Origin,* 70). As a consequence, the sovereign is transformed into first a tyrant and then a martyr, of which Hamlet is only the most famous example (Herod is the preferred baroque figure). Called to action, he hesitates, condemned to indecision by the uncertainty of the circumstances and above all of its possible consequences.

With the demise of the sovereign, the dramatic hero loses significance and is replaced by another, very different kind of figure. This figure, less dramatic but far more theatrical, is charged less with saving the world than with reviving it as a "mask." This is the "plotter" or "intriguer." As a consummate manipulator, the plotter no longer seeks to seize power; he does not have any interests of his "own," for he understands that in an empty, decaying world individual interests can be asserted only conditionally. Instead of forging his own plans, he takes pleasure—a hellish, satanic, Saturnine pleasure—in the possibility of serving his lord and master unto death—the death of the master, that is. A master-slave dialectic, but without the sublating movement from servile self-awareness to freedom. What the ruler cannot accomplish on his own because it means his demise, is carried out for him by his agent, the intriguer. Every step forward, however, only brings the end that much nearer. Wotan's relationship to Loge exemplifies this tendency. Loge does what Wotan wishes, while leading him only that much more certainly toward his demise. Wotan, who seeks to create a lasting work to safeguard his domain (Walhalla), succeeds but at the same time burdens himself with debts that threaten the very survival of the clan he seeks to perpetuate. These are debts therefore that he cannot or will not pay. It is only in *Siegfried* (act 3, scene 1), that he finally poses the question that clearly shows him to be the heir of the baroque *Trauerspiel*: "How to hold back a rolling wheel?"

No answer is to be found *in* the *Ring*, if it is not the *ring* as such. What after all is a *ring*? An artifact that is self-contained. Precisely this containment, however, is threatened by all *work* that depends on *others*. As absolute sovereign, Wotan cannot acknowledge such dependency. If he did so, the ring would no longer be a ring—something closed or self-contained—and as such, it could not become an object of appropriation. The attempt to usurp it fails due to the heterogeneity of the labor process, which again entails an irreducible relation to others—which is to say, to relations as such.

In the Tetralogy, the ring names, on the one hand, the desire of creating a self-contained work and of fashioning oneself as creator; on the other, the disastrousness of this desire, insofar as it consists in the denial of the other. As the "proper name" of the Tetralogy, however, the "Ring" as *title* also refers to the *Bühnenfestspiel* itself, as *Gesamtkunstwerk*. Yet can even the *Gesamtkunstwerk* withstand the storming of the work? Perhaps only to the degree that it is broken into (four) *pieces (Stücke)* by its own theatricality?[9]

In light of Benjamin's depiction of modernity, decisively shaped by his conception of the Reformation and, above all, of the Counter-Reformation, a certain paradox of the Tetralogy can be characterized as "modern." At the center of the entire myth—or should one say at its origin? (in its treatment by Wagner at least)—is the striving of an individual to maintain and assert himself as a self-identical, sovereign subject against all that is strange and other. This striving for autarchy determines the fate of Wotan from the start, insofar as his desire for self-assertion renders him unable to accept his dependency on others and his debt to the other. In this regard he finds himself in a situation that is strangely but strongly reminiscent of the baroque sovereign, who as we have seen, is subjected to an irreconcilable "antithesis between the power of the ruler and his capacity to rule," which culminates in the "indecisiveness of the tyrant" (*GS1,* 250; *Origin,* 70–71). Driven to helplessness by fantasies of omnipotence, Wotan takes precisely this path. His wavering is akin to Benjamin's description of the instability of baroque rulers, who are buffeted to and fro by uncontrollable forces, external and internal, including "the sheer arbitrariness of a constantly shifting emotional storm in which the figures of Lohenstein especially sway about like torn and flapping banners . . . For their actions are determined not by thought, but by changing physical impulses" (*GS1,* 251; *Origin,* 71). This description applies not only to Wotan, but to Alberich as well, whose "limbs" are torn apart and churned about by a "blazing fire." Along with this dismantling of the body through passion, love cannot be distinguished from hate, or, in the words of Alberich himself, "*Wuth*" from "*Minne.*" The fate of both figures calls into question the desire for self-control and wholeness, especially as it affects bodily existence. Only such a threat explains the fascination of the Rheingold, whose glittering apparition temporarily at least dims the danger of dismemberment. From the beginning on, gold is set in opposition to "the power of love" ("der Minne Macht") and "erotic desire" ("der Liebe Lust"); only forgoing both allows for the possibility of mastering "the magic spell" and of "rounding a ring from the gold" (*Rheingold,* scene 1, line 68). But as a glittering phenomenon, gold is the first thing that makes such renunciation possible. This task, which Alberich immediately makes his own, is self-contradictory: his gestures of brutally grabbing and extracting reflect precisely the dismemberment they seek to preempt. Alberich wrests the gold from the ridge in order to get a better grip on it. Gripping is, in turn, the condition for shaping the gold in order to make it into a possession. Grabbing—shaping—possessing: the gold is made into a ringlet, a circle, a ring, but above all, into a *work* in precisely the sense that, according to Benjamin, is repeatedly called into question by and ever since the

Reformation, but also defended and reinstated time and again by the Counter-Reformation. Modernity defines itself through the permutations of this conflict.

The *Ring* stages this entire confrontation as both the desire for the self-contained work and the struggle that such desire inevitably entails. The *Ring* becomes a wringing or wrestling *(Ringen)* that ultimately consumes everything resembling a work, including the subject that sought to survive as a foreman, if not as a superman.

This wrestling *(Ringen)* for the ring comes to a head in the figure of Wotan. His sovereignty appears primarily in the form of his dream of "manhood's honor, boundless might and glory," which in turn assumes the form of a completed work, "Valhalla": "The everlasting work is ended!" *(Rheingold,* scene 2, line 70). The work must be understood as "everlasting" in order to numb the fear of time as the medium of the non-eternal, of the undoing of the work—in short, of time as a medium of transience. At "work" here is the fear of a finitude that undoes all work because its end is not consummation but consumption. The sole escape, as already in the baroque *Trauerspiel,* leads from the represented world to the world of representation, that is, to theater. Salvation is to be found not in Wotan's "eternal work," but rather in its "masked revival" as a self-consciously artificial, artefactual *Gesamtkunstwerk.* This is still a work, to be sure, but one that seeks to regain its sacred meaning by presenting itself as a *Bühnenfestspiel.* Securing the sacrality of the stage, however, demands a structure that both situates and protects it. In this way, the ties between Wotan and Walhalla mirror those of Wagner to the Bayreuth Festspielhaus—as the material and specific location of each performance. Bayreuth attempts to avoid what Wagner took to be the moribund genre of "opera," a term he never accepted. Rejecting the aesthetic tradition out of which it came, he sought to create a "work" that would be capable of producing a redemptive effect rather than being the stillborn result of a moribund genre.[10] As the site of this redemptive performance, an edifice was to be constructed where no mere operas took place, but instead "Bühnenfestspiele" such as *Der Ring des Nibelungen.* Only such ceremoniously housed performances could reconcile repetition with permanence. *In the Gesamtkunstwerk as Bühnenfestspiel the redeeming power of sacrament was to be revived as music-theatrical mask.*

Yet the *Bühnenfestspiel* can only be endowed with this ritual function if it overcomes the fatal isolation of the individual work through the collective movement of the *Gesamtkunstwerk*. Collecting presupposes a fixed location, a "mighty fortress" (in the sense of the Lutheran hymn). In order to offer an alternative to the isolation of traditional "opera," the *Gesamtkunstwerk* would have to be housed and authenticated *(verbürgt)* in a fixed, recognizable, and secure location. Only then could the event plausibly make a claim to permanence, despite its relatively exposed situation. Such exposition requires not only a special stage, but also a space in which the action can freely unfold without losing itself. This space was to be created through the construction of the *Festspielhaus:* a building that due to its location high on a "fair hill" could ensure the synoptic or panoramic overview that ever since Aristotle was deemed necessary to unify the disparate elements of a fragmented world. Thus, one of the characteristics distinguishing the *Festspielhaus* from traditional opera houses, Wagner insists, is its peculiarly protective function. The building was designed to be a "protective, monumental structure" one that endows "the ideal work [with] its solid endurance" and is able to "secure the stage," as Wagner writes in his speech at the laying of the cornerstone of the Bayreuth Festspielhaus. Only then, he tells his audience, will the "work, which we seek to found today . . . not be an illusory castle in the sky," but instead become a lasting reality.[11]

In this way Wagner conceived of the Bayreuth Festspielhaus as an enabling condition for the permanence of the work, while also being a work unto itself, which he did not hesitate to compare to Beethoven's musical masterpieces. The comparison shows that for Wagner the temporal and spatial condition of a work, of its taking place, is as important as the work itself. The inclusion of place as a constitutive moment of the *Gesamtkunstwerk* fundamentally distinguishes Wagner's approach to theater from the traditional aesthetic of the eternal and timeless *work,* held to be independent of its spatio-temporal localization. By contrast, as *Gesamtkunstwerk* the work can only gather, only fulfill its essence and mission, by *taking place* in a place that is proper to it.

Wagner thereby overturns the aesthetic rejection of place, which extends at least as far back as Aristotle. Because place has to be determined in terms of time and space, an occurrence that is essentially dependent on location cannot claim to be everlasting. Every event that *essentially* depends on its *localization,* and especially on a *stage,* is thereby determined by a web of relations that does not allow for a synoptic overview. Every stage stands in relation to a space that is constituted by a divide. This constitutive split does not just separate the audience from the actors, but also divides each of these two bodies in itself. The actors represent someone or something located somewhere else and thereby also refer the audience to something other. In order to gain control of this double split, Aristotle, in his discussion of tragedy, seeks to subordinate everything connected with *opsis* to his demand for an all-inclusive, unifying *synopsis.* The setting of a tragedy may be split, but in this perspective it should still grant the viewer the possibility of taking in the whole rather than being taken in by it. This overview is designed to close up the divide. Wagner repeats this Aristotelian gesture in his aesthetic writings whenever he emphasizes the necessity of comprehensibility as a precondition for the optical and acoustic transparency deemed essential to the *Gesamtkunstwerk.* In order to bring about such transparency, the orchestra in Bayreuth was to remain hidden in its pit. In its place—that is, in the place of a stage-like apparatus—the semblance of a "mystical gulf" was to emerge as a completely "empty space."[12] In this way the (illusion of a pure) ideality of viewing and listening was to be created. By contrast, Wagner reserves his most passionate condemnation for "the scandalous thrusting-forward of this picture so that the spectator can almost touch it."[13] Accordingly, the ideality of the stage set is held to preclude all bodily contact.[14] The body—condition for touch *par excellence*—is supposed to mark the boundary dividing the ideal interior from the real outside world. As a tactile surface, the body itself casts doubt on this divide.[15] A type of seeing and listening should be made possible that Wagner terms "clairvoyance" *(Hellsehen)* and through which the invisible precondition of all sight, brightness *(Helligkeit)* itself should become accessible to experience—by listening to music. How can such a notion become concrete? Luminescence becomes perceptible not by the eyes alone, even if it remains the precondition for all seeing, but also by the ear, which makes possible the idealization of visual phenomenality. This is supposed to occur primarily by way of the "Leitmotif." In it melodies, rhythms, timbres, and instrumentations recur in an altered yet recognizable form. Such a (varying) return of the same remains the conceptual core of the Wagnerian aesthetic.[16] Whether melodic, harmonic, rhythmic, or instrumental, each involves a varying repetition that brings forth the identical and therefore assures the comprehensibility that Wagner holds to be a crucial condition for all artistic efficacy.[17] Having an effect means that the recognizable musical motifs provide an answer to Wotan's question: they "hold back a rolling wheel."

However, those who see clearly *(Hellseher)*—or more precisely, hear clearly *(Hellhörer)*—are faced by the same dilemma that Wotan summarizes in Act II of the *Walküre*:

> How can I make that other man
> who's no longer me
> and who, of himself, achieves
> what I alone desire?—
> Oh godly distress!
> Oh hideous shame!
> To my loathing I find
> only ever myself
> in all that I encompass!
> That other self for which I yearn,
> that other self I never see;
> for the free man has to fashion himself—
> serfs are all I can shape![18]

The Wagnerian aesthetic remains trapped here in the antinomy of self and other. The self needs the other in order to be the self, but admits this other only as a tautological and specular mirror image.[19] Wotan's conjuring of a "free man" who would have to "fashion himself" serves merely to reiterate this dilemma.

The death of Brünnhilde at the conclusion of *Götterdämmerung*, though I cannot elaborate this point further here, in no way breaks through this narcissistic vicious circle, but only confirms it. The ring she throws away does not end up just anywhere: it returns to its point of departure, thereby seeming to close the circle. The artifact is returned to its original, rightful, and natural owners, the Rhine maidens. The *Gesamtkunstwerk* concludes by closing itself and its audience within an ostensibly natural circuit that allows for no way out, apart from taking one's own life.

Is there really then no escape?

Perhaps an alternative can be found in a completely different type of theatrical practice, one that abandons what Wagner could not: the desire for a work that would endure. Staging here does not however mean representing things comprehensibly or shaping representations for the benefit of an ideal transparency, but instead exposing them in their division. To whom? To others for whom there exists no proper name, least of all, *"das Volk."* Nor even that of "the audience," the "spectator," or the "listener"; it would be more apt to refer to them as witnesses. In any case, the lack of a proper name points to a heterogeneity that does not allow for an unambiguous designation. One can therefore no longer invoke the "reception" of a "work" in order to designate it definitively. The inseparability of a work from its impact cannot simply be thought of as a "quality" of the work, but rather as its "task." In that the work is received—that is, repeated, altered, and translated—it is at once disfigured and adjusted. It enters into a circulation that never again allows it to return to its point of departure.

Such circulation characterizes the theatrical medium. Aristotle registered this movement in the concepts of *metabasis* and *peripeteia* without thinking through the consequences of these transformations, twists, and turns. His insight drives Wagner further to introduce the Aristotelian term, "wonder." According to Wagner, wonder should be permitted "in the poetic work" only insofar as it "renders the nature of things . . . comprehensible."[20] This recalls the way in which Aristotle linked *peripeteia* to *anagnoresis,* to a *recognition* that oriented and channeled the unexpected turn back toward the familiar and comprehensible. Thus, the theater audience should not be left in the dark for too long. At the same time, however, even the examples that Aristotle cites from *Oedipus Tyrannos* call into question the signifying effect of such recognition.[21]

A similar tension between theatrical surprise and recognition appears to have played itself out between Brecht and Benjamin in regard to the interpretation of the "lesson" to be imparted by theater. Benjamin viewed "epic theater" not only in the political sense of Brecht, but also and even more so in relation to the writings of Kafka, which though not written for the stage, have more exactly arrived at its essence. Benjamin compared this essence to a Tao, which in Kafka takes the form of a desire "to hammer a table together with the painstaking craftsmanship and, at the same time, to do nothing—not in such a way that someone could say 'Hammering is nothing to him,' but 'To him, hammering is real hammering and at the same time nothing,' which would have made the hammering even bolder, more determined, more real, and, if you like, more insane" ("Er").[22]

One has only to compare this hammering to that of Siegfried's in order to become aware of the abyss separating Wagner's motifs from Kafka's gestures *(Gesten)*. In *Siegfried* the hammering has a purpose: the recreation of the sword that is to serve anew as the tool for reaching a goal. Here, one hammers only in order to produce a work, to bring together. Yet through the repetitions of the leitmotifs the hammering becomes at once more than a mere representative, signifying act. The music echoes the hammering in that it repeats itself and thereby transforms its identity into a surging movement that refers to something beyond itself. In this way the music catches up with the originary phenomenon that according to Benjamin can never completely succeed in its restorative striving. This lack of closure breaches the logic of representation or the economy of meaning. It calls for a different form of logic or economy on which Kafka as well as Benjamin focused: that of the paradox according to which something can be itself and something else at one and the same time—a logic of *ambivalence*, not of *oppositionality*.

This logic of ambivalence is, however, what radically distinguishes theatrical staging *(Inszenierung)* from mere instantiation *(Instanzierung)*. Staging refers here to that which Benjamin once called the "great, ancient opportunity of theater," which he described as its ability "to expose what is present."[23] Those who are present, whether audience or performers, are exposed to an other or an elsewhere that can no longer be clearly identified or localized. They are called upon not only to see or to hear, but also to *witness* that they have been, and can be, simultaneously something other or somewhere else.

Wherever such *exposure* takes place, wringing or wresting *(Ringen)* are never far away, but without a ring, a circlet *(Reif)*, or a work to hold on to.

The *Ring* as a deconstruction of modernity? If deconstruction is defined through the alternative of autonomy/autarchy versus outside control, then certainly not. The *Ring* depicts a demise that starkly exposes the narcissism of a certain modernity. At the same time it attempts to give meaningful shape to this modernity as a creative, work-producing offering and idealization. In order to demonstrate such meaningfulness convincingly, it abstains from exposing theatrically the conditions of its own operation. The task of pressing ahead with this exposition thus falls to each respective staging, without which no happenings on the stage—also no *"Bühnenfestspiel"*—could ever take place.

CHAPTER NINETEEN

Reading Benjamin

Time swings itself like a pretzel through nature. The feather
paints the landscape, and when a pause arises, it is filled up
with rain. No complaint can be heard, for there is no fooling
around.

    —An eight-year-old boy, cited by Benjamin

The task of writing on Walter Benjamin is as compelling as it is intimidating. If it were clear why this is so, that would already be a beginning. It is *compelling*, because Benjamin strips his reader of all assurance with tranquil assurance, drawing him into a dizzying whirl with a hard-headed enthusiasm that pulls out all the stops and then suddenly stops short, interrupting abruptly to demand an accounting. The promise of never granted luck shimmers through his writings, casting its glow over his name, in order then to slip from the outstretched hands of the reader. All that remains is its trace as mournful script. As empty as only allegory can be, the reader—especially one who, according to a tried and tested model, has sought to distill concepts or just to take the text at its word—leaves the stage: the contradictions and inconsistencies that result pose a formidable challenge that even the dialectic can hardly resolve in a fruitful manner. And yet the reader who has been touched by these texts knows, in the words of Beckett's Hamm, that the ball is in his court: "A moi de jouer."

And it is *intimidating*: "Gifts," Benjamin once wrote, "should move the beneficiary so profoundly that s/he is shocked."[1] After reading his writings, uninhibited discourse should no longer be possible. Neither as expression nor as emulation. Distance becomes an abyss when it no longer gapes "between" but is essential; unsurpassable is the difference not only between Benjamin and his readers, but between each and their "selves." If one attempts to respond, language congeals in one's mouth, concrete as with schizophrenics and Steinberg figures. Speaking rejects death; where the voice fails, silence presents itself at first as terrifying. Muteness is heard as the discourse of death. Mute, without soul and self, the most familiar becomes strange, the most proximate remote. Followed by sadness and mourning. And yet:

Und nicht ein Übel ists, wenn einiges
Verloren gehet und von der Rede
Verhallet der lebendige Laut.
(And not simply evil is it, if some
Gets lost and of the speech
Fades away the living sound.)[2]

Therein glimmers perhaps the possibility of escaping the fatal tautology of the speaking self, of being able to experience something else. This possibility Benjamin calls: writing. The noun should be read metaphorically, like a text whose significance is to be sought not so much in its words as in the space between the lines. Only so can texts become sacred, never in what they say.

Benjamin once cited the following: "What was never written, read" (GS2, 213; SW2, 722). He did not say it himself: he cited it. The following can be considered an attempt to summon Benjamin by citing him.

We no longer know how to read.
—Marcel Proust

How to read? In accordance with the model of *perception* least of all. The truth of a text cannot be *captured* or *seized* (-ceptum) by moving *through (per-)* something to arrive at what lies behind it. The truth of a text cannot be "taken"—*wahr-genommen*. Therein it is to be distinguished from every kind of cognition. "Cognition is a having. Its object itself is determined by its ability to be 'had inwardly' [*innegehabt*]. It retains the character of a possession."[3] The *possessibility* of the objects of cognition determines itself transcendentally as their meaning, immanently as their identity. Objects of cognition are at all times present. For the cognitive subject the task is to arrive there, where it always has been. For one who is reading the situation is different. For him too cognitions are indispensable. But they do not provide anything to hold on to. They cannot be stitched together in order to "catch truth in a net spun of cognition, as though it came flying into it from without" (GS1, 208; Origin, 28). If he waits patiently until cognitions form a totality of their own accord, however, he is liable to be like someone who stares at things until they begin to dance. But instead of disclosing their essence through their dance, they seem to "implode," collapsing into an endless interior space and becoming "secret signs" (Geheimzeichen). "Not the progress from cognition to cognition is decisive, but rather the crack and leap—the Sprung—in each one individually."[4] To negotiate the crack and take the leap is to read. Meaning provides the ground, but it is never secure: "The educated reader lies in wait for turns and words, and meaning is only the background on which the shadow rests, that they cast like figures of bas-reliefs" (GS4, 433; SW2, 726).

To read then is not to go with the flow, as one speaks—or believes that one speaks—but rather groping, stumbling, interrupting oneself, like an older person whose sight has weakened bends over a text, following its movement with her fingers, always stopping anew, but only in order to continue. Such reading goes against the grain of meaning, so that the text does not disappear into it but remains as figure: as writing-image (Schriftbild). Commentary, critique, translation would thus be less reliably distinguished from one another than in their tense interrelationship, as three forms of reading. Reading as translating would call for fidelity to the word, freedom with respect to meaning. Reading as commentary would do violence to words by extracting them from the text "as though they . . . were destined to be overpowered" (GS4, 433; SW2, 726). Reading as critique would be to ask after truth, which however is less amenable to questioning than to doing qua staging. This is why critical reading is more like the deciphering of a palimpsest, "whose faded text is covered by the traits of a more powerful script that relates to it" (GS1, 125; SW1, 298).

This is how material and truth content relate to one another: so little restrained as the script of that palimpsest, as tense as the relation between meaning and significance, discourse and writing, speaking and reading—that is, as the poles around which Benjamin's thinking and writing elliptically move. To retrace that ellipse and thereby not to deny the inevitable violence involved—to expose oneself to the dizziness without succumbing to it entirely—this would presumably be what is involved in reading Benjamin.

> Writing is perhaps somewhat the contrary of thinking.
> —Jorge Luis Borges

In the beginning, also with Benjamin, was the word. An early essay is titled, "On Language Overall and on the Language of Man" (or "On Language as Such and on the Language of Man"). The title, which aims at "language overall," reflects the intention to assert and "resolve" the "profound, incomprehensible paradox" of the Logos, as the ever-present unity of linguistic and spiritual essence and being (*GS2*, 141; *SW1*, 63). In the Logos as the creative word of God is founded the creation as in its origin. The word, *actus purus,* "creative omnipotence of language" (*GS2*, 144; *SW1*, 65), erects the creation in a strictly hierarchical fashion: at its summit the word of God, at its bottom the created but mute nature; in the middle, man, authorized by God to recognize things, give them their names, and thus translate their mute language into a higher discourse. Everywhere the unity of the Logos creates what Benjamin designates as "continua of transformation" (*GS2*, 151; *SW1*, 70).

The Fall into sin occurs accordingly as a fall out of the blessed spirit of language: "The word should communicate *something* (besides itself). That is really the Fall of the spirit of language" (*GS2*, 153; *SW1*, 71). All of a sudden language thus becomes abstract, taking leave of itself, becoming external and alien, judging others and finally falling into confusion: "Signs must become confused where things are confounded" (*GS2*, 154; *SW1*, 72).

But things become confounded not just after the fall from the blessed spirit of language. For after he has described this fall, Benjamin's own account begins to confound itself: "Human life in the pure spirit of language was blessed. Nature however is mute. It is true that in the second chapter of Genesis it can be clearly felt how the muteness of nature named by man remains blessed only to an inferior degree" (*GS2*, 154–155; *SW1*, 72). This darkens the originary blessed of the pure spirit of language, even if Benjamin still insists on the difference of language before and after its fall into communication. But his persistent emphasis on that "other muteness" of nature *after* the linguistic fall begins to sway and turns finally against itself, less in a dialectical than in an antithetical manner: "Because it is mute, nature mourns. *But what leads even more profoundly into the essence of nature is the inversion of this phrase: the sadness of nature causes it to be mute"* (GS2, 155; SW1, 73, my emphasis). It is not the muteness, then, that is originary, as the Logos would have it, but rather the sadness. The self-sufficiency of the Name is thus drawn into question in the name of the named: "There is in all mournful sadness the most profound inclination to speechlessness, and that is infinitely more than the incapacity or the aversion to communicate. The mournfully sad feels itself so thoroughly recognized by the uncognizable. *To be named—even where the namer is like unto the gods and blessed—retains perhaps always a presentiment of mournfulness"* (ibid., my emphasis). It is only in his book on the mourning play, where this passage returns verbatim, although under the secularized sign of allegory, that mournful sadness is interpreted. But already in this early text "overnaming" is presented as the "linguistic essence" of mournful sadness (ibid.). Thus, Benjamin undermines his previous attempt to oppose pure and communicative language. For already the "blessedness" of the pure spirit of language was assured only at the expense of the nature singularized through its denomination. The fall, supposed to be out of the "blessedness" of the Logos into the abstraction of judgment, thus appears as always already inscribed in and prescribed by the Logos itself: as nomination it was from the very beginning also judgment. Mournful sadness would then be not so much originary as an *expression of the origin.*

With such a radical inversion of his original argument, one might think that Benjamin had been guilty of crass inconsistency. No less conceivable, however, would be the idea that he thereby armed himself against a temptation to which precisely as a theoretician of language he threatened to succumb: the "temptation of setting the hypothesis at the beginning," which comprises "the abyss of all philosophizing" (GS2, 141; SW1, 63).

There is an originary violence of writing because language is first of all writing. Usurpation has always already begun.

—Jacques Derrida

In his early essay on language Benjamin attempts to take it directly at its word, as language "overall," freed from all instrumentalization. Nevertheless, in order to think of language as Logos its other—

physis—is required. In order to conceive language in its purity, it must at the same time be thought as being prelinguistic, as *actus purus,* as creating omnipotence, a transcendental subject that produces nature as its likeness and image. In order to set the enunciation of pure language at the beginning, what is required is its other as the muteness that follows its fall. What is required is muteness, not mutation. For enunciation, as Hegel exactly understood, demands correspondence: the "existence [*Dasein*] of the spirit as immediate self" in language, he wrote, "expects . . . that the other will contribute its part to this existence."[5] In this expectation arises, according to Benjamin, the mournful sadness of that "other." To a certain logic this relation appears to be external to the Logos, as a temporal succession, as the fall out of concreteness into abstraction, out of naming into judging, out of essential being into communication. The fall is thus supposed to be not simply external but the movement that establishes the outside itself. What is thereby ignored is that "the outside entertains a relation with the inside that as always is nothing less than simple exteriority. The sense of the outside has always resided in the inside, prisoner outside of the outside and reciprocally."[6] If this insight is merely hinted at in Benjamin's early essay on language, in that "presentiment of mournful sadness" (*GS2,* 155; *SW1,* 73), it becomes an explicit theme and motif of the *Origins of the German Mourning Play,* written some eight years later.

If Benjamin's procedure in this early treatise could be described as theoretical-constructive—if he attempts to approach language "overall" in *intentio recta* and to think of it in its originary condition, the object of his unsuccessful *Habilitation* is one that is already pregiven, historically situated and in no way "overall." The *Trauerspiel* he nevertheless designates as an "idea" to be interpreted, or more precisely, to be read (just as the mourning play itself is described as a "Lesedrama"—a play to be read and not simply seen on stage) (*GS1,* 361; *Origin,* 185). As little as Benjamin seeks to deny the Platonic inspiration for his notion of the "idea," he also makes clear that it cannot be simply assimilated to this philosophical tradition. While continuing the critique of empiricism, it is difficult to reconcile it with what is generally associated with Platonism. As "objective interpretation," the Benjaminian "idea" points in a very different direction (*GS1,* 214; *Origin,* 34); but one that will only be accessible to a reading that is open to the possibility that traditional terms and concepts are employed in his writing in a most untraditional way. Benjamin's effort to think differently does not allow the terms he uses to remain what they were. Rather, they are reinscribed and displaced. His "ideas," for instance, become "monads," which in turn are defined through their character as "presentation" or "exposition"—*Darstellung*—a term that Benjamin understands more in its chemical sense, that of *recombination,* than its traditional meaning of *representation.* What is "dargestellt" cannot therefore be assumed to exist independently of its exposition, of its reinscription in relations that constitute it. In this manner concepts come into conflict with their semantic traditions—they are "beside themselves." For these "relations" remain enclosed within a sphere of immanence, or of "intensity."[7] As "monads" ideas are immediately cut off from everything simply external; but as "constellations" they remain dependent on that with which they do not directly communicate. Benjamin associates them with the "name," but also with configurations that are less expressions than signatures. Although they are inconceivable without conceptual cognition, as truth they remain heterogeneous to the cognitive realm. As in the language essay, so here too there remains a pervasive and persistent tension between Benjamin's theoretical utterances and their use in the course of his contemplative practice, that *Darstellung* that in his study of the mourning play precisely exhibits and exposes, stages and interprets the problematic dynamic of concepts such as sound, name, and symbol. If in his "Epistemo-critical Preface" to that book Benjamin recurs explicitly to the Platonic notion of "anamnesis" as the originating apprehension of the Logos in order thereby to found the *objective* character of philosophical truth, this amounts to a rejection of the philosophy of reflection of German Idealism and of the neo-Kantian subjectivism that dominated at the time (and that in a less obvious manner continues to do so to this very day). At the same time this move marks Benjamin's affinity for a tradition, whose crisis his exposition of allegory as above all a form of writing seeks to describe and to reinscribe. If the caesura in his account of the linguistic fall could still be considered to be unintentional, and at any rate at odds with the main thrust of the argument, in the book on the mourning play it becomes the key constituent of what he calls "philosophical style," marked as it is by an "intermittent rhythm" that informs the "method" of his study (*GS1,* 212; *Origin,* 32). Such intermittence, interrupting itself, is common to Benjamin's *Darstellung,* as well as to that which it exposes: the textual (but also theatrical) structure of baroque allegory. The idea as monad thus signifies not so much self-contained immanence as the irreducibility of a certain discontinuity, of a certain *discreetness* that also involves *discretion*.

For no writer ever wrote more discreetly (and discretely) than Walter Benjamin. His writing is no less allegorical than the allegory it describes, but also reinscribes, recombines, and transforms—*darstellt*. Which is why the authority of individual statements is never the instance of last resort, never assured or definitive; and those readers who take them as such have already fallen prey to a trick that in the final analysis can only be theological. Theology is Benjamin's version of the Hegelian "cunning of reason," which has come into its own, not as freedom, self-consciousness of spirit, but as aporia. Or as Benjamin, reinscribing the discourse of Kant would call it, as *antinomy*. This consists ultimately in the fact that philosophical truth can be construed neither immanently, nor transcendently. This is why Benjamin's language tends toward antithesis, metaphor and paradox—therein as well adopting the rhythm of German baroque allegory. Like it, or rather *in it*, the Logos is thought out to its end, which is not its completion *(Vollendung)* but its interruption. There is never anything "full" about the "ending" in Benjamin. Its aporias are not transcended and surpassed—*aufgehoben*—in the "name" but rather retraced and reworked in its interpretation.

Et in arcadio ego.

If the German baroque had to be characterized through a single trait, this might be the one: for it the Fall has become a permanent decline. There is no Beyond any longer. Therefore all eschatology, at least in the Christian, redemptive sense, is excluded. And therefore its originary milieu was the "strict immanence" resulting from the Reformation (*GS1*, 259; *Origin*, 80). For mournful sadness, *Trauer*, is no longer something that has befallen it from without, but rather immanent in the creation itself, as originary as only death. In the limitless immanence of the baroque world, Greece and Christianity come into their own, but as allegory: the Logos becomes the (theatrical) script it always was. "With all its force . . . the will to allegory hauls the fading word back into its space." (*GS1*, 369; *Origin,* 192). "Back," for baroque secularization, described as the "presentation of time in space" (*GS1*, 370; *Origin,* 194), spatializes a time that was from the start spatial, which arose out of space and flows into it just as speech runs its course. For that time originates from a Logos that from the beginning was self-contained, present to itself prior to all presence and to all sense *(prä-sens)*. As transcendence it is immanent to itself, its becoming passing from being to being, from the past as having-been to the future as coming-to-be, from case to case, from fall to fall. To make that time present, to transform it "into strict presence" (ibid.), to spatialize it as simultaneity through simulation, as the baroque seeks to do, entails nothing more or less than taking it at its word. If it always was improper and inauthentic as congealed space, if history was nature from the start, then time merely comes into its own in baroque allegory as space, history as natural history. The repression of nature through the Logos emerges as originary because it was there from the beginning. The eternal presence of the Logos in time, its *parousia,* knows death only as Other, as the ultimate Other: as echo, absence, muteness, mutation. Hellenically, the Logos frees itself of Mythos in tragedy and comes into its own in the death of Socrates, in the Platonic dialogue as the "irrevocable epilogue of tragedy," as Benjamin puts it (*GS1*, 288; *Origin,* 109), but without citing Nietzsche's *Birth of Tragedy*.[8] For it is not the Dionysian element of tragedy that Benjamin holds essential, but rather its challenge to what he considers to be the mythical structure of Greek polytheism. Following Rosenzweig, it is in the silence of the tragic hero—to be radically distinguished from the muteness of the mournful creation—that he sees "the treasure of an experience of the sublimity of linguistic expression" (ibid.) which as "agonistic prophesy" (*GS1*, 286; *Origin,* 107) announces the coming of a new language, one that will no longer be based on the opacity and ambiguity of myth but rather on the immanence of the self and of life. In the death of Socrates this language comes to itself as the consciousness that recognizes its own immortality in the infinitude of the Logos and speaks this recognition ironically in the form of the dialogue.

If then in tragedy and the Platonic dialogue "the ordeal . . . is broken through the Logos in freedom" (*GS1*, 295; *Origin,* 116), the Mourning Play reveals that "breakthrough"—that "freedom" itself to be mythic, insofar as the immortality of the Logos, in which the "breakthrough" consists—shows itself to be mortally fallen from the start, while being presented as irresistible decline.

Accordingly what speaks through the creation is "not only the nature of human existence as such," as in tragedy and the Platonic dialogue, "but rather the biographical historicality of a singular being in this its most naturally decadent figure: as a significant riddle and question" (*GS1*, 343; *Origin*, 166). In the creation all life was created "according to its kind" and only by virtue of this fact—not explicitly mentioned by Benjamin however—made knowable and nameable.[9] Since only the species can be regarded as immortal, the unity of the Logos, whether Greek or Christian, comes into its own only by transcending and superseding the mortality of each singular living being.[10] It is in this act of *Aufhebung* that the Logos reveals—and dissimulates—its mythical underpinnings.

Thus, the Logos tends to revert to a certain form of Mythos. The ambiguity that characterizes the latter, according to Benjamin, returns in and as the "antinomies of the allegorical," which befall subject as well as object, humans as well as things, spirit as well as matter (*GS1*, 350; *Origin*, 174): everything becomes totally self-identical, pure presence and at the same time empty, nonidentical, absent; everything exposes "the non-being of what it represents" (*GS1*, 406; *Origin*, 233). This negation, however, is also one of the dialectic, Platonic as well as Hegelian, for it concerns the status of determination, definition, *Bestimmtheit*. Instead of concretizing itself, as with Hegel, through the figure of determinate negation, it retains a certain degree of abstraction—and isolation. For "each person, each and every thing, each relation can signify something else, arbitrarily [*kann ein beliebig anderes bedeuten*]" (*GS1*, 350; *Origin*, 175). In this parousia of arbitrary significance the demonic ambiguity of the myth makes its return. The Hegelian dialectic of being and nothing goes through its motions in baroque allegory, but without ever reaching the state of Becoming. "The truth . . . that being does not turn into nothing, and nothing into being, but instead have already turned into each other . . . this movement of immediate disappearing" that in Hegel's Logic leads above and beyond itself, does not get off the ground in baroque allegory.[11] For the singular being that goes under, such a "truth" is fateful—and fatal. For what it shows is that the singular can survive only as ruin.

In this sense Benjamin's thinking is far less indebted to the Hegelian dialectic (despite his later use of the term) than to the Kantian antithetics, closer to Kant's antinomies than to the Hegelian resolution of them in a final reconciliation. Not the progression of the universal as concept sets the rhythm, but the stalling of the singular as image and as script. Not speaking but writing remains the model and mode of Benjamin's thought.

The halting simultaneity of being and nothing however comes together as script. Allegory bears the stamp of writing and thereby sets itself apart from the meaningfulness of the symbol no less than from the "detached complacency" of the sign (*GS1*, 342; *Origin*, 165–166). For the sign, no less than the symbol, lives in the shadow of the Logos. "When designating," writes Hegel, "the intelligence demonstrates freer volition [*Willkür*] and mastery in the use of images [*Anschauungen*] than when symbolizing."[12] The sign presupposes the designated as a condition of its possibility without posing questions, and is therefore only as determinate signification truly arbitrary and volitional *(willkürlich)*. Allegory by contrast tears open an abyss precisely because it inscribes its meaning "in the sign-script of evanescence" (*GS1*, 353; *Origin*, 177).

Vertigo sets in when all sense dissolves into significance, or rather, in signifying: where what must be thought is that "the signified (is) always already in the position of signifying";[13] where the "mystical nu" of the symbol is "deformed" into the "actual now" of allegory (*GS1*, 342; *Origin*, 165); where language as living speech breaks down, as in the mourning play; and where dialogue dissolves into metaphors: "Not seldom are the speeches in dialogues directed only at the allegorical constellations in which the figures relate to one another, as magically evoked signatures. In sum: the sententious declaration, as signature, reveals the scenic image as allegorical" (*GS1*, 372; *Origin*, 196). The German baroque, which stood far from any thought of revolution, permits such only in language, which "at all times (is) shaken by the rebellion of its elements" (*GS1*, 381; *Origin*, 207), whereas "the word, the syllable and the sound, freed from all inherited meanings, parade proudly as things that can be allegorically exploited" (ibid.). Taken at its word, the syntax of language collapses, its elements liberated from the domination of semantics. If allegorical script always signifies something else, "the nonbeing of what it represents," it recalls those linguistic phonemes that for Jakobson are nothing but "mere otherness."[14] This perhaps is why both in structural linguistics and in the German baroque, metaphor plays such a decisive role: not as the combination or substitution of fixed meanings, but as the language-constituting oppositionality, which as relation is the condition of all linguistic signification.[15] There is no name or noun that would not already be a metaphor. Whereas however for structural linguistics metaphor like language in general has its primary home in speech—and writing by contrast is considered pure convention, sign, replica—language for the German baroque as read by Benjamin has always been script, by virtue of the mortality of the natural world.

Benjamin cites the Romantic Ritter: "The organ of speech itself writes in order to speak" (*GS1*, 387; *Origin*, 213) and then continues: "Right in the center of the allegorical attitude [*Anschauung*] goes this doctrine that all image is only a script-image. The image is in the context of allegory only signature, only monogram of the essential being, not the latter in its envelope. Nevertheless writing has nothing subservient about it, it does not fall away in the process of reading like dross. Rather, it penetrates what is read as its 'figure'" (*GS1*, 388; *Origin*, 214). Writing here is not to be understood "metaphorically": it is metaphoricity itself, without which literalness could not be thought. But it is not only written—it has to be read. It is absorbed into reading but does not disappear. And therein alone are those tensions to be sought that constitute what Benjamin called, in a double-entendre, *unsinnliche Ähnlichkeiten*: "non-sensual" similarities that can also be "nonsensical." Such reading, which recalls those who work with "intestines, stars or dances," commemorates a reading that is "prior to all language," indeed perhaps to all writing: "What was never written—read!" (*GS2*, 213; *SW2*, 722).

The elliptical trajectory described by Benjamin's thought can never be adequately understood as one of straightforward progression, leading for instance from theology to materialism. For the decisive tensions that drive his writing and thinking are more simultaneous than successive. In the contradiction between intention and execution emerges his profound affinity with Proust, at least as the latter is read by Gerard Genette:

> Between its conscious intentions and actual execution, Proust's writing undergoes a singular inversion: starting out to discern essences, it winds up constituting or restoring mirages; destined to rejoin, through the substantial depth of the text, the profound substance of things, it ends up with an effect of phantasmagorical superimposition in which the depths destroy themselves one after the other, where the substances devour each

other. It does indeed exceed the "superficial" level of describing appearances, but not in order to reach that of a super reality (the realism of essences), since on the contrary it uncovers a level of the real where the latter by its own momentum destroys itself.[16]

In a historical epoch when the preponderance of the presence tends to banish everything other from the world of appearances—including time, memory, and history—what links Proust and Benjamin is a certain yearning, one that strives to recover not so much what is past as time itself, which has been lost but which only can count *as lost*. For both, then, the following injunction of Benjamin could apply: namely, to regard "the real world as a task in the sense of demanding that one penetrate deep enough into the workings of the real [*in alles Wirkliche*] so that an objective interpretation of the world would be disclosed therein" (*GS1*, 228; *Origin*, 48). If praxis is not merely activity but alteration of what is present, opening it to a process of unconditional transformation, then this is impossible to conceive without an interpretation that gestures toward alternatives to the existing state of affairs. The peculiar unity of contemplation and practice that Benjamin's writing deploys is formulated as what he called, in a phrase that is difficult to translate, a *Schriftbild*: literally, a script-image, or perhaps more idiomatically, an image that calls for reading. Therefore it may be helpful, at the end of these remarks, to attempt to read Benjamin himself as, and through, such a *Schriftbild*: a script that stages its own allegorical dynamics in a moving image that could also be called a *scenario*. Benjamin, for his part, called it simply: "Seagulls."

CHAPTER TWENTY

"Seagulls"

Epistemo-Critical-Dogmatic Foreplay: *Lehre*

In the "Program of a Coming Philosophy," Benjamin identifies the task of the "coming philosophy" by linking it to the philosopher to whom he doubtless was most indebted:

> The problem of the Kantian as of every great epistemology has two sides and Kant managed to give a valid explanation of only one of them. First of all, there was the question of the certainty of knowledge that is lasting, and second, there was the question of the integrity of an experience that is ephemeral. For universal philosophical interest is continually directed both at the timeless validity of knowledge and at the certainty of a temporal experience regarded as the proximate if not only object of that knowledge. This experience, in its total structure, had simply not been made manifest to philosophers as something singularly temporal, and that holds for Kant as well.[1]

It may seem curious that Benjamin singles out the very philosopher who had installed a certain notion of time at the heart of his "transcendental aesthetic," as insufficiently attentive to the problem of temporality. But not for nothing does Benjamin insist not simply on the notion of time but on its *singularity*. It is this singularity that for Benjamin determines the quality of experience largely ignored or avoided by philosophy: its "ephemerality," which, however, also constitutes for him its "integrity." The task of the "coming philosophy" will accordingly consist, Benjamin continues, in a "reformulation of the concept of cognition" which in turn will depend on the attainment "of a new concept of experience." Benjamin seeks to determine this "new concept" first by emphasizing what the old concept neglected or ignored:

> The great restructuring [*Umbildung*] and correction to be undertaken with respect to the one-sided mathematical-mechanical oriented concept of knowledge can only be achieved by relating knowledge to language as was already attempted during Kant's lifetime by Hamann. The consciousness that philosophical knowledge should be absolutely certain and a priori, that in this respect philosophy should be the equal of mathematics, caused Kant to ignore fully the fact that all philosophical cognition finds its sole expression in language and not in formulas and numbers . . . A concept of cognition achieved through reflection on the linguistic essence of knowledge will yield a corresponding concept of experience. (*GS2*, 168; *SW1*, 107–108)

The new "concept of experience" whose development Benjamin construes as the paramount task of "the coming philosophy" will thus be the result of a "reflection" on the way knowledge is rooted in the medium of language, rather than in mathematics, understood as "formulas and numbers." For "formulas and numbers" seem to suggest a medium that would continue to neglect that *singularity* from which the "integrity" of experience, according to Benjamin, cannot be separated.

The term that Benjamin employs in this text—and which will take on ever greater significance in his writings—to designate the new relationship between experience and knowledge, is that of *Lehre,* a word that is difficult to translate, but also to understand even in its own terms. It is this notion that Benjamin suggests will provide a better response than epistemology has previously supplied in its "concealed answer to the concealed question of the coming to be of cognition" (*GS2*, 167; *SW1*, 107) and which Benjamin deems to have been unproductively tautological: "Error must no longer be explained as deriving from error, just as truth can no longer be derived from correct understanding" (ibid.). Here Benjamin offers the conjecture that "the fixation of the concept of identity, unknown to Kant, will presumably have a great role to play in transcendental logic and perhaps is truly destined to provide an autonomous foundation of the sphere of cognition beyond subject-object-terminology" (ibid.). Just how the notion of *Lehre* might lay the groundwork for rethinking the relation of cognition and experience is a question that Benjamin addresses in a short but extremely dense appendix—*Nachtrag*—to the main body of this text. This main section ends with the declaration that "experience is the unified and continuous multiplicity [*Mannigfaltigkeit*] of cognition." This "unified and continuous multiplicity" requires a rethinking of the Kantian dichotomy of epistemology and metaphysics, "or to speak with Kant of the division between a critical and a dogmatic part" of philosophy—a division that for Benjamin is "not of principal importance . . . Where the Critical stops and the Dogmatic begins is perhaps not exactly to be ascertained because the concept of the Dogmatic should designate nothing more than the transition from critique to doctrine [*Lehre*], from universal to particular fundamental concepts . . . Only in doctrine [*Lehre*] does philosophy butt up against [*stößt gegen*] an absolute, as being-there [*als Dasein*], and thus against that continuity in the essence of experience, the neglect of which presumably constitutes the deficiency of neo-Kantianism" (GS2, 170; SW1, 109). *Lehre*, religious doctrine to be sure, but also *teaching*, and also *instruction*, is thus the place where philosophy enters into contact with "an absolute"—and not, as Peter Fenves has insightfully remarked, "the" absolute.[2] For this "absolute," which is inaccessible to knowledge while making it possible, requires the indefinite rather than the definite article—"an" or "one" rather than "the." In its indefiniteness, it is inseparable from the "immediacy" of a "Dasein," a "being-there" that in its *singularity* serves as the "integral" of the many different laws *(Gesetzmässigkeiten)* produced by a philosophical cognition that is always on the side of the general or the universal.

Just *where* and *how* this "butting up against" the absolute singularity of being-there takes place in the confrontation of philosophical cognition and religious doctrine remains, Benjamin admits, in this text a "sketchy allusion" *(skizzenhafte Andeutung)*. But if we recall that the path that leads philosophy from its traditional generalizing epistemology to the singular involvement with being-there passes via a "reflection on language" as the medium and condition of all knowledge, we can venture to point to Benjamin's own practice of and with language—his practice of writing—as providing a possible response. That response involves the function of what we will provisionally call "images" or "gestures" in his writing—and in particular, his instructive practice of writing images—the *Schriftbild*. In it, *Lehre* becomes *lesbar*, doctrine legible.

Reading a *Schriftbild*: "Seagulls"

There is arguably no writer of critical essays in the twentieth century who made more thought-provoking use of what are commonly called "images" or "figures"—the German word *Bild* can be translated by both of these terms—than Walter Benjamin. And no writer reflected more on this use, explicitly and implicitly. In his "Epistemo-critical Preface" to his study of the *Origin of the German Mourning Play*, where he sought to give an account of his method, he invoked the figure of the "constellation" to describe the "idea" in contrast, and in relation to the "phenomena":

> The idea thus belongs to a fundamentally different world from that which it apprehends. The question of whether it comprehends that which it apprehends, in the way in which the concept genus includes the species, cannot be regarded as a criterion of its existence. This is not the task of the idea. Its significance can be illustrated with an analogy. Ideas are to objects as constellations are to stars. This means in the first place that they are neither their concepts nor their laws. They do not contribute to the knowledge of phenomena . . . [in them] phenomena are partitioned and at the same time redeemed. (*GS1*, 214–215; *Origin*, 34)

And yet, if ideas as constellations redeem the "objects" they bring together, they themselves require such a gathering in order to live: "Ideas come to life only when extremes are assembled around them" (*GS1*, 215; *Origin*, 35) and such "extremes," Benjamin insists, are also and above all extreme in their singularity, something they impart to the idea. "Every idea is a sun and is related to other ideas just as suns are related to each other. [Their] oft-cited multiplicity is finite," and the ideas are thus marked, to Benjamin, by "discontinuous finitude" (*GS1*, 218; *Origin*, 37).

The use of "images" or "figures" is often associated with the effort to "illustrate" or make abstract thoughts more transparent, usually understood as more visualizable or representable. But if the idea, and even more perhaps, the "name" with which Benjamin associates it in this text, is radically distinguished from its "objects," about which it conveys no knowledge, at least not in the usual sense, then it should come as no surprise that Benjamin's use of "images" will hardly have an explanatory or illustrative function.

But images cannot simply be identified with the "idea" as Benjamin elaborates it in the book on the mourning play. For the image can never claim to be as detached from the world of phenomena as Benjamin claims is the case for the idea. Indeed, what will increasingly characterize Benjamin's reflections on, and use of, imagery is their emphatic and distinctly *temporal* quality. In his well-known discussion of images in Convolute N of the *Arcades Project,* the image is described as "that in which what has been congeals in a flash with the Now to form a constellation" (N 3,1). The image thus is defined as both the medium and the result of a process by which appearances—phenomena—become readable, and thereby transform time into history. In response to his earlier critique of philosophy, and in particular Kant, as not sufficiently attentive to the question of how knowledge comes into being *(das Werden der Erkenntnis),* Benjamin here cites the image as the instance through which the Now becomes knowable *(erkennbar)* because readable *(lesbar).* And this process is described as a process of transformation that goes on within the image rather than in its relation to what is outside: "This 'coming to legibility' is a determinate critical point in their internal movement" (ibid.).

The stress on immanence here would suggest that the process Benjamin is describing might be assimilated to a movement of self-fulfillment. But his account makes clear that he has a very different kind of dynamic in mind, one in which the "death of intention" coincides with the "birth of genuine historical time, the time of truth" (ibid.). This "birth" is anything but painless: like the birth of "Alien" in Ridley Scott's movie of that name, it involves the destruction of the body out of which it comes: not embodiment, but disembodiment. Such disembodiment of the "Now" is the immediate consequence of an excess of time: in the now, "time is charged to the point of exploding. (This exploding, nothing else, is the death of intention, which thus coincides with the birth of genuine historical time, the time of truth)" (ibid.).

With respect to the image thus becoming legible, becoming textual, a *Schriftbild,* the key term to which Benjamin returns again and again, is *Blitz.* The "critical point" reached by the "internal movement" of the image is one in which it reaches a phenomenal intensity, an incandescence, that, like that of a sun, only appears by simultaneously consuming itself and blinding those who would apprehend it in *intentio recta*. Death of intention—birth of the image—is that which in becoming legible, erases and effaces itself, although not without leaving traces, out of which something called "history" is pieced together. This is why it is important not to overlook the fact that Benjamin compared the idea not just to "the" sun, but to *a* sun, emphasizing its singular relationality and multiplicity.

Given the irreducible singularity of images, the linkage of their experience with the elusive and novel cognition that they provide can only be effectuated through the reading of images that are both individual and dividual, singular and multiple, but never simply generalizable in the manner of concepts. With this in mind—*eingedenk,* as Benjamin might have put it—we turn now to one singular *set* of written images, which, given their sequential arrangement, could perhaps more properly be described as a *scenario* than simply an "image." This is the short piece entitled "Seagulls." It belongs to a five-part text that Benjamin wrote in July and August of 1930, during a three-week trip through Scandinavia that he had been planning for two years. The moment was a particularly difficult and significant one in his life: he had just gone through a very painful divorce, and although his reputation as a critic was at its height, his personal and financial situation was extremely precarious. The three-week trip was thus a welcome opportunity to escape from Berlin, but also an occasion to reflect on the critical juncture he had reached.

The result was a cycle of five short essays published in September 1930 in the *Frankfurter Zeitung,* under the overall heading *Nordic Sea,* which Benjamin introduced in a manner that even for him is especially contorted, not to say tortured: "'The time in which even [*selbst*] someone who is at home nowhere [*keine Wohnung*] can live' becomes for the traveler who has left no home behind, a palace. For three weeks its halls, filled with the sounds of waves, followed one another in sequence: seagulls and cities, flowers, furniture and statues appeared on their walls and through their window day and night there fell light" (*GS4,* 383). The traveler who has no home and thus leaves none behind, experiences his journey as a "palace" through whose halls he wanders, distant and yet perhaps more at home precisely in his wandering than he was before he left.[3] Each "hall" of the palace has its name, but what kind of a name it is—proper or improper, generic or singular—is precisely one of the questions that the "hall" entitled "seagulls" explicitly addresses.

It can be noted that the sequence in which Benjamin lists the five essays that make up "Nordic Sea" is not that in which the texts were published. "Seagulls," which leads the list in the introduction, is the penultimate in the series (*GS4*, 385–386).

The piece begins with a description of a moment that is above all that of the writer and his situation on board of a ship, moving through the sea at nightfall: "Evening, my heart heavy as lead, full of foreboding, on deck." The series of paratactic phrases describes the disjunctive mood of the voyager, which is one of melancholy apprehension: his situation is bad, but it could easily get worse. The future seems particularly uncertain. From this very unstable position, he recalls—in an epic present, somewhere between memory and description—a spectacle that confronts him with a very unusual kind of movement: "For a long time I follow the flight [*Spiel*] of the seagulls. One always sits on top of the highest mast tracing the seesaw movements with thrusts in the sky. But it is never for very long one and the same. Another one comes, with a couple of wing beats it has—invited or chased, I'm not sure which—the first one. Until all at once [*mit einem Male*] the pinnacle is empty" (*GS4*, 385–386). The time of what is being recalled and described is "long" but also indeterminate. During this indefinite period the writer, like the seagull he describes, follows the movements of the flock. The usual English translation of the German word *Spiel* will not do here: the seagulls are not "playing," or at least the word does not imply that. What it does suggest is a movement that is not linear, not goal-directed, but nevertheless also not arbitrary: patterned.

But the eyes of the observer are drawn at first not so much to the seagulls in flight as to one isolated bird, sitting "on top of the highest mast" and who, from this perch, traces "with thrusts" the back-and-forth movements of the flock. The movement of the birds is thus more circular than linear, more iterative than progressive. But for the moment all of this is described only relative to that isolated bird sitting "on top of the highest mast," not simply to get a better view, but in order to reenact, mimic, in jerks and starts—*stoßweise*—the movements of the group. The contrast here is striking: there, the birds flying in a back and forth pattern, continuous and reiterative. Here, the single bird, motionless except for his spasmodic efforts to imitate the movements of the flock from which it is separated. Below, the narrator, watching the bird watching the others.

This discontinuous, spasmodic *thrusting* movement—indeed, almost a "gesture" if such can be attributed to birds[4]—recalls the description, cited earlier, of the way in which "philosophy" and cognition more generally come into contact with religious "doctrine": "Only in doctrine [*Lehre*] does philosophy butt up against [*stößt gegen*] an absolute, as being-there [als Dasein] . . ." (*GS2*, 170). A *Stoß* always thrusts *toward* something else; but it does not always make contact with it. In the case of philosophy, its thrust seems to carry it into contact with *Lehre*; in the case of the solitary seagull, perched on the highest mast of the ship, the thrusting movements remain rooted to the spot, and as a result became rather difficult to visualize. Does the bird "thrust" with its wings? With its beak? The text does not say.

What it does say is that the single, solitary bird never remains for very long alone on its perch. Soon "another one comes" and "with a couple of wing-beats" invites the other bird to leave, or chases him away, "I'm not sure which" (*GS4*, 386). In short, the single bird, like the single sun, is only one among others—perhaps like that single, indefinite "absolute." It is one among many, albeit one provisionally separated from the others. One bird arrives; the other makes way for it. But in between there is a moment that comes abruptly, all of a sudden, in which the sequence of arrival and departure is momentarily suspended and *mit einem Male*—"all at once"—"the pinnacle is empty." The perch, but also the highest point still attached to the earth, is suddenly, presumably briefly, left empty, before it is taken by one of an unending succession of occupiers. It is this caesura in the succession of birds on that perch, totally unpredictable and yet regularly recurring, that marks the discontinuous temporality of this scene, or scenario, as it unfolds before the eyes of the beholder, who is also here the voyager, narrator, and writer. His narration retraces a "seesaw" movement that repeats itself in the exchange of birds at the perch: one comes, the other goes, and it is never one and the same, but always "all at once": *mit einem Male*.

The spectacle, however, grows more complex: "Until all at once the pinnacle is empty. But the seagulls haven't stopped following the ship. Impossible to survey [*unübersehbar*], as always, they describe their circles. Something else brings an element of order to them. The sun has long since set, in the East it is very dark. The ship sails southward. Some light is left in the West" (*GS4*, 386). The pinnacle is suddenly empty, but the seagulls continue to follow the ship. Discontinuity and continuity, emptiness and a certain plenitude butt up against one another in this evolving spectacle. But to speak of plenitude—Benjamin to be sure does not—only brings out the complexity of the movements of the birds. First of all, they are impossible to take in at once: the very phrase, "all at once," "*mit einem Male,*" which will recur a few lines later, describes a singularity that does not so much unify as interrupt. The desire of the observer to take everything in at one shot, to bring everything together in a single *Anschauung*—a single glance (or, if you will, "intuition")—is precisely not possible here. And this is not merely because of the extent of the flock or of its flight; the limit is set not by the extension of the spectacle but by its intensity. For although the movement of the birds is first described as circular, it is "something else"—that is, something other than the regularity of a geometrical figure or pattern—that "brings *an element of order* to them." Note once again the use of the indefinite article here: not "order" as such, in general, but a very singular, partial, and not fully determinate order: *one* among possible *others*.

What that order is, the text does not say at first. Instead it describes the scene, the place that alone, it seems, can introduce "an order" into the movement of the birds. In other words, it is not that movement in and of itself, not the geometrical pattern of circularity or the temporal alternation that suffices to make what is taking place significant (if not meaningful). Rather, "something else" is required and that something else has to do with the particular setting in which the spectacle is taking place. The description of that setting is that of a threshold: that marking the transition from day to night, from light to dark. At the same time, this transition also marks a certain spatial opposition between East and West: the setting sun leaves a glimmer of light in the West, while the East is already "very dark."

Most of the account up to now, and in particular this description of the setting, is narrated in the present tense. But with the passage from description of the scene to recounting of the event, the tense shifts from present to imperfect, and this shift is introduced by the word "now" (*nun*):

> What now took place with the birds—or was it with me?—happened by virtue of the place that I, so commanding, so solitary, had chosen out of melancholy in the middle of the afterdeck. All at once there were two sea-gull populations [*Völker*], one the Eastern, the other the Western, left and right, so totally different that the name "seagulls" dropped away. Against the backdrop of the moribund sky [*des erstorbenen Himmels*], the birds on the left retained something of its brightness, glittered with every turn up and down, got along or avoided each other and seemed not to stop weaving an uninterrupted, unpredictable [*unabsehbare*] series of signs, an entire, unspeakably changing, fleeting winged web—but one that was legible [*ein lesbares*]. (*GS4*, 386)

The place from which the writer views this spectacle, one that he chooses out of melancholy, but that affords him perhaps the best view—this place is what brings an element of order into the movement of the birds. But just as the place is divided into West and East, left and right, dark and light, the order that it imposes on the flight of the seagulls is a divided order, involving a division so extreme that it calls into question the very unity of what it has divided. The short piece of writing is entitled "Seagulls," but this generic name seems to "drop away" from the two groups—indeed "peoples" or "popula-tions" (*Völker*)—since they seem so different from one another that a single name can hardly apply to both. "All at once"—*mit einem Male*—there are "two" groups. Or as Benjamin entitled another of his short fragments, citing a German idiom with an erotic con-notation, "Einmal ist keinmal": roughly, "Once is nonce" (*GS4*, 433–434).

The use of the word "peoples"—*Völker*—to describe the two bird-groups, plus their association with the East (dark, absence of light) and the West (streaks of light still visible), also suggests a political allegory associated with the splitting of the birds into two groups. But as so of-ten with Benjamin's text, the meanings fail to line up neatly: here, in-stead of a parallelism, Benjamin seems to use a chiasmus, so that East and West change places in the syntax of his sentence, just as later on, the birds themselves will change places in their flight. Similarly, light is not just bright but only becomes legible through its interplay with the dark of the dying sky.

But the East is not simply the East—not one and the same. When Benjamin wrote this he was deciding whether to go to Palestine at the invitation and urging of Scholem, to learn Hebrew and deepen his knowledge of Judaism and Jewish tradition. Shortly after returning from his "Nordic" trip, it became clear that he would stay in Europe and that the turn "Eastward" would not lead him to Palestine, at least.

The allegorical quality of the description hangs therefore less on any determinate meaning that could be attached to it—Benjamin's attachment to ambiguity needs hardly to be stressed—but rather on the way in which the "observer" turns out to be far more than mere observer, just as the allegorist is more than just neutral interpreter. It is this involvement that allows the question that imposes itself on him to mark the scene as profoundly allegorical: "What now took place with the birds—or was it with me?—happened by virtue of the place that I . . . had chosen" (GS4, 386). In allegory, it is the place, not the person, that decides. That place is always one of melancholy, solitude, and command. It is as a function of this over-determined place, "in the middle of the afterdeck," that the spectacle of splitting takes place, ultimately dividing the "seagulls" and divesting them of their name.

The place and its perspective recalls that of the Angelus Novus, who sees the rubble of history piling up in front of him, as he is carried—or blown—into the future. Here, the voyager being carried south by the ship is facing its wake, and what he sees is the barely visible spectacle playing itself out against the backdrop of a sky—or heaven: the German word, Himmel, signifies both—that has "died out" (erstorben). The birds in the West, on the Right, "retained something of its brightness"—of its light after death, which is perhaps not quite the same as "life" after death. Nameless, having lost their proper name, they "swoop up and down," getting along or avoiding one another much like the humans with whom they share perhaps only—but it is hardly trivial—one thing: mortality. But the difference, perhaps, is that their movements do not seek to deny this: they do not move forward, or even back, they do not progress or regress, but merely fly high and low, "weaving an uninterrupted, unpredictable and unfathomable [the German word, used here, unabsehbar, can signify both] series of signs." Not verbal signs, and not a series that could be unified under a proper name, but signs composed of bodies in movement, in a vertical movement going nowhere and yet never simply coming home or back to its starting point. A movement that is iterative and although "unspeakably changing, still *legible*."

But what kind of reading corresponds to this legibility? The conclusion of the short text suggests a possible response:

> Except that I slipped, finding myself obliged to start all over again with the others. Here nothing awaited me, nothing spoke to me. Scarcely had I followed how those in the East, a pair of deep black beating wings flying toward a final glimmer, losing themselves in the distance and returning, when I was no longer able to describe their movement [*Zug*]. So entirely did it seize me that I myself came back from afar, black with what I had been through, a soundless flurry of wings. On the left everything had yet to be deciphered and my destiny hung on each wave, on the right it had long since taken place [*vorzeiten gewesen*] and a single soundless waving. This counter-play lasted for a long time, until I myself was nothing more than the threshold across which the unnamable [*unnennbaren*] messengers, black and white, changed places in the wind. (*GS4*, 386)

The movement of the birds is practically impossible to follow, but it is, the voyager asserts, *readable*. "*Except . . .*" Except that when he tries to read it, he "slips," loses his bearings and control, *abglitt*, slides and finds himself suddenly "with the others": on the Left, in the dark, having to start all over again, in the absence of even a glimmer of light. A dark night of the soul: "Here nothing awaited me, nothing spoke to me." The birds in the East are too obscure to be followed easily, "a pair of deep black beating wings flying toward a final glimmer." The pull and trace of their movement—their *Zug*—which he cannot follow or describe, nevertheless "seizes hold" of him "so entirely" that it moves him: he comes "back from afar," but no longer the same as he was. Rather he returns as that which he has just unfolded before him and in him, a "soundless flurry of wings" that defies proper name and identification. "On the left everything had yet to be deciphered and my destiny hung on each wave; on the right it had long since taken place, from time immemorial, *vorzeiten gewesen*" (386).

The result "of this counter-play," not just between East and West but between East and East, is that the voyager—buffeted from the one to the other, from the obscurity of what has been for time immemorial to the enigma of what is yet to come, yet to be deciphered, each side of the alternative reflected in the other—is no longer defined by his position in the center of the afterdeck, solitary and commanding; rather he becomes a "threshold" across which "*unnamable* messengers, black and white, change places in the wind."

Where legibility marks the threshold of unnamable messages and messengers, can we still be certain that the voyager bears the name of Walter Benjamin? That East is East and West, West? Or that these names are more proper than certain others: for instance, "Seagulls"?

Appendix

Notes

Acknowledgments

Index

Walter Benjamin's "Seagulls"

A Translation

Evening, my heart heavy as lead, full of foreboding, on deck. For a long time I follow the flight *(Spiel)* of the seagulls. One always sits on top of the highest mast tracing the seesaw movements *(Pendelbewegungen)* with thrusts into the sky. But it is never for very long one and the same. Another one comes, with a couple of wing beats it has—invited or chased, I'm not sure which—the first one. Until all at once the pinnacle is empty. But the seagulls haven't stopped following the ship. Impossible to survey *(unübersehbar)*, as always, they describe their circles. Something else brings an element of order to them. The sun has long since set; in the East it is very dark. The ship sails southward. Some light is left in the West. What now took place with the birds—or was it with me?—happened by virtue of the place that I, so commanding, so solitary, had chosen out of melancholy in the middle of the afterdeck. All of a sudden, with a single stroke, there were two seagull populations *(Völker)*, one the Eastern, the other the Western, left and right, so totally different that the name "seagulls" dropped off them. Against the backdrop of the moribund sky *(des erstorbenen Himmels)* the birds on the left retained something of its brightness, glittering with every swoop up and down, got along or avoided each other and seemed not to stop weaving an uninterrupted, unpredictable *(unabsehbare)* series of signs, an entire, unspeakably changing, fleeting winged web—but one that was legible *(ein lesbares)*. Except that I slipped, finding myself obliged to start all over again with the others. Here nothing stood before me, nothing spoke to me. Scarcely had I followed those in the East, a pair of deep black beating wings flying toward a final glimmer, losing themselves in the distance and returning, when I was no longer able to describe their movement *(Zug)*. So entirely did it seize me that I myself came back from afar, black with what I had been through, a soundless flurry of wings. On the left everything had yet to be deciphered, and my destiny hung on each wave; on the right it had long since taken place *(vorzeiten gewesen)* and a single soundless waving. This counter-play lasted for a long time, until I myself was nothing more than the threshold across which the unnamable *(unnennbaren)* messengers, black and white, changed places in the winds.

Notes

1. Introduction

1. "The introduction of new terminologies, as long as it does not confine itself strictly to the conceptual realm but rather aims at the ultimate objects of observation, is therefore within the philosophical realm dubious. Such terminologies—an abortive naming in which intention plays a larger part than language, are lacking in the objectivity with which history has endowed the major formulations of philosophical observation" (*GS1*, 217; *Origin*, 37).

2. Jacques Derrida, *Limited Inc.* (Evanston: Northwestern University Press, 1988), 47.

3. Ibid.

4. Ibid., 48. My emphasis.

5. Throughout much of his writing, Benjamin seeks to retain the notion of "object" or "objective" as though it could be simply opposed to and liberated from that of the "subject." This is no doubt one of the major aspects that distinguishes his thinking from that of his contemporary, Heidegger, for whom the objective always implies a subject as its reference and presupposition.

6. "Une fois pour toutes" is an expression that imposes itself on and in Derrida's later writings, precisely for the way in which it links singularity, in its uniqueness—its "one-time-ness"—to a certain generality. *Rogues* traces the trajectory that opens with a discussion of the singular occurrence (1) and concludes with the need to rethink the relation of the incommensurable to the common (Derrida, *Limited Inc.*, 111).

2. Prehistory

1. "Wer nicht in Kant *das Denken der Lehre selbst* ringen fühlt und wer daher nicht mit äußerster Ehrfurcht ihn mit seinem Buchstaben als ein tradendum, zu Überlieferndes erfaßt (wie weit man ihn auch später umbilden müsse) weiß von Philosophie gar nichts. Deshalb ist auch jede Bemänglung seines philosophischen Stils pures Banausentum und profanes Geschwätz." See Walter Benjamin to Gershom Scholem, October 22, 1917 (*GS2*, 937). The English version is in *The Correspondence of Walter Benjamin, 1910–1940*, trans. Manfred Jacobson and Evelyn Jacobson (Chicago: University of Chicago Press, 1994), 97–98. The translation here, however, is my own.

2. "In this translation, expressions like 'the power of judgment,' 'the power of thought,' 'the power of concepts,' 'the power of desire,' and so on, always refer to an ability (a 'faculty' in *that* sense). In such expressions, 'power' is never used to mean anything like *strength* or *forcefulness* (of concepts, desire, and so on.)" (*CoJ*, 3). A more recent English translation of this work, by Paul Guyer and Eric Matthews, even changes its consecrated title to stress the "power" and potentiality, rather than the actuality of the "judgment" involves. See Kant, *Critique of the Power of Judgment* (Cambridge, Eng.: Cambridge University Press, 2000). A somewhat similar move had already been made some two decades earlier by a French translator of the Third Critique, Alexis Philonenko, who entitled his translation *Critique de la faculté de juger* (Paris: Vrin, 1982).

3. "Der Verstand gibt, durch die Möglichkeit seiner Gesetze a priori für die Natur, einen Beweis davon, daß diese von uns nur als Erscheinung erkannt werde, mithin zugleich Anzeige auf ein übersinnliches Substrat derselben; aber läßt dieses gänzlich *unbestimmt*. Die Urteilskraft verschafft durch ihr Prinzip a priori der Beurteilung der Natur, nach möglichen besonderen Gesetzen derselben, ihrem übersinnlichen Substrat (in uns sowohl als außer uns) *Bestimmbarkeit durch das intellektuelle Vermögen*. Die Vernunft aber gibt eben demselben durch ihr praktisches Gesetz a priori die *Bestimmung;* und so macht die Urteilskraft den Übergang vom Gebiete des Naturbegriffs zu dem des Freiheitsbegriffs möglich" (*KdU*, 108; *CoJ*, 37).

4. Thus, in §9, Kant explains that it is not the feeling of pleasure or displeasure that grounds the communicability, but the "universal communicability of the mental state, in the given presentation, which underlines the judgment of taste as its subjective condition, and the pleasure of the object must be its consequence [allgemeine Mitteilungsfähigkeit des Gemütszustandes in der gegebenen Vorstellung, welche, als subjektive Bedingung des Geschmacksurteils, demselben zum Grunde liegen, und die Lust an dem Gegenstande zur Folge haben muß]" (ibid.).

5. In a letter to Gershom Scholem written shortly after the two essays we are about discuss, namely in 1917, Benjamin asserts that "for me questions regarding the essence of knowledge, right, [and] art are related to the question of the origin of all human intellectual manifestations [*Geistesäußerungen*] in the essence of language" (*GS2*, 932).

6. *GS2*, 157–171.

7. "To *cognize* an object, it is required that I be able to prove its possibility (whether by the testimony of experience from its actuality or a priori through reason). But I can *think* whatever I like, as long as I do not contradict myself, i.e., as long as my concept is a possible thought, even if I cannot give any assurance whether or not there is a corresponding object somewhere within the sum total of all possibilities. But in order to ascribe objective validity to such a concept (real possibility, for the first sort of possibility was merely logical) something more is required. This 'more,' however, need not be sought in theoretical sources of cognition; it may also lie in practical ones." See Immanuel Kant, *Kritik der reinen Vernunft,* vol. 26 (Hamburg: Meiner, 1960), 25–26. This English translation is from *Critique of Pure Reason,* trans. Paul Guyer and Allen W. Wood (Cambridge, Eng.: Cambridge University Press, 2000), 115.

8. "Vom Gedicht unterschieden ist es [das Gedichtete] als ein Grenzbegriff, als Begriff seiner Aufgabe, nicht schlechthin noch durch ein prinzipielles Merkmal. Vielmehr lediglich durch seine größere Bestimmbarkeit: nicht durch einen quantitativen Mangel an Bestimmungen, sondern durch das potentielle Dasein derjenigen, die im Gedicht aktuell vorhanden sind und andrer. Das Gedichtete ist eine Auflockerung der festen funktionellen Verbundenheit, die im Gedichte selbst waltet, und sie kann nicht anders entstehen als durch ein Absehen von gewissen Bestimmungen; indem hierdurch das Ineinandergreifen, die Funktionseinheit der übrigen Elemente sichtbar gemacht wird" (*GS2*, 106).

9. Such discontinuous argumentation is formalized in his account of "philosophical style" in the "Epistemo-critical Preface" to the *Trauerspiel* book: "The concept of philosophical style is free of paradox. It has its postulates. These are: the art of demarcation in contrast to the chain of deduction; the persistence of the treatise in contrast to the single gesture of the fragment; the repetition of motifs in contrast to shallow universalism; the fullness of concentrated positivity in contrast to negating polemics [Der Begriff der philosophischen Stils ist frei von Paradoxie. Er hat seine Postulate. Es sind: die Kunst des Absetzens im Gegensatz zur Kette der Deduktion; die Ausdauer der Abhandlung im Gegensatz zur Geste des Fragments; die Wiederholung der Motive im Gegensatz zum flachen Universalismus; die Fülle der gedrängten Positivität im Gegensatze zu negierender Polemik]" (*GS1*, 212; *Origin*, 32).

10. In "The Task of the Translator," Benjamin observes that the "sentence" is the "wall" before the original, whereas the "word" is the "arcade" opening passage to it (*GS1*, 18; *SW1*, 260). The adjunct here, *"und anderer,"* breaks open the walled-in meaning of the sentence, turning it into an open-ended passageway.

11. This recalls Freud's description of "isolation" as a defense mechanism that does the same work as "repression" while remaining within consciousness itself. See Sigmund Freud, "Hemmung, Symptom und Angst" in Freud, *Gesammelte Werke,* trans. James Strachey, 5th ed., 5 vols. (Frankfurt am Main: S. Fischer, 1967), 1:149–152, 196–197 (For a good English version, see Norton's 1959 edition, 45–49, 99–100). In this context it may be noted that Freud's earliest description of repression, in *The Interpretation of Dreams,*

tended to describe it as an *"Abwenden"*—a word that in German can mean both "averting" one's eyes from something, as well as "warding off" the external danger itself (See *Gesammelte Werke,* vols. 2/3, 606). "Absehen," it should also be noted, can signify looking-toward as well as looking away from, as in the noun, "Absicht," generally translated as "intention" or "design."

12. *GS1,* 212; *Origin,* 32, S. 360: "Der 'Augenaufschlag', den barocke Malerei zu einem Schema" ausbildet, "das ganz unabhängig ist von der im augenblicklichen Vorwurf bedingten Situation," verrät und entwertet die Dinge auf unaussprechliche Weise. Nicht sowohl Enthüllung als geradezu Entblößung der sinnlichen Dinge ist die Funktion der barocken Bilderschrift."

3. Criticizability—Calculability

1. *GS1,* 801.

2. Benjamin also makes use of a later series of lectures, dating from 1804, known as the "Windischmann" lectures (after the name of their editor). Although he cites these lectures to supplement his study of Schlegel's "system," he considered this source "secondary" insofar as it dated from a time when Schlegel had already renounced what Benjamin considered to be the aesthetic radicalism of his earlier period, a radicalism he deemed constitutive of the "Romantic concept of criticism" in general.

3. Peter Demetz, "Introduction," in Benjamin, *Reflections* (New York: Schocken Books, 1986), xii.

4. Benjamin is quoting a University of Munich dissertation submitted four years earlier, in 1915, by Charlotte Pingaud, entitled "Grundlinien der ästhetischen Doktrin Fr. Schlegels."

5. The literal translation of Benjamin's title into English would be: "The Concept of Art-Criticism in German Romanticism." Art criticism in English refers primarily to the plastic arts, however, whereas "Kunst," for Schlegel and Novalis (as Benjamin notes), means primarily if not exclusively what in English is known as "literature." At the same time, "literature" *(Dichtung, Poesie)* is understood by the early German Romantics to be the exemplary instance of all art, and indeed Benjamin explicitly points to the problem of this exemplification, which does not sufficiently articulate the difference between different art forms and media: "A fundamental deficiency of the Romantic theory of art," he writes, "is that 'poetry' and 'art' are not sufficiently distinguished" (*GS1,* 14; *SW1,* 118). This tendency to conflate art in general with literature in particular is also responsible for much of the current use of the terms "criticism" and "critical theory," to designate both the interpretation of literature and at the same time aesthetics and hermeneutics in general. Hence, the most economical but also accurate English translation of "Kunstkritik" today is simply "criticism."

6. Erwin Kircher, *Philosophie der Romantik* (Jena, Germany, 1906), cited by Benjamin, *Reflections,* 107.

7. "The fundamental property of symbolic form consists . . . in the purity of the form of representation, so that this becomes the exclusive expression of the self-limitation of reflection" (*GS1*, 97; *SW1*, 171–172).

4. Impart-ability

1. Karl Kraus, *Pro domo et mundo* (Munich: A. Langen, 1912), 164, cited by Walter Benjamin in "Über einige Motive bei Baudelaire," *GS1*, 647.
2. Pierre Lévy, *Sur les chemins du virtuel* (Paris: La Découverte, 1995), 10.
3. Although I cannot go into a detailed examination of it here, it should at least be mentioned that an even earlier and at least as significant philosophical rethinking of the notion of "possibility" was that undertaken by Martin Heidegger, beginning with his discussion of "being towards death" in §53 of *Being and Time* (1927). Although Heidegger does not use the term "virtual," his analysis of being-towards-death in terms of "possibility" opens the way toward rethinking the latter category as something other than a subordinate, unfulfilled mode of reality qua actuality, which is how "possibility" had been thought in the tradition emanating from Aristotle. Heidegger argues that being-towards-death can only be construed in terms of a possibility that cannot be measured in terms of realization or actualization. It is surely symptomatic that Deleuze, who calls Bergson "the most radical thinker" of the possible, does not mention Heidegger.
4. "Structure is the reality of the virtual" is from Deleuze, *Différence et répétition* (Paris: Presses Universitaires de France, 1968), 270.
5. Ibid., 273. Deleuze refers here to the Bergsonian argument that "unifies" *Creative Evolution* and *Matter and Memory* and that takes its point of departure in a "gigantic memory" that repeats itself in its differentiated segments and parts and thereby actualizes its "mnemonic virtuality." Deleuze comments: "Bergson is the author who drives the critique of the possible the furthest while at the same time insisting the most emphatically on the importance of the concept of the virtual" (274).
6. Ibid., 272.
7. Ibid. My emphasis.
8. Lévy, *Sur les chemins du virtuel*, 9.
9. *The Complete Works of Aristotle*, ed. Jonathan Barnes, vol. 1 (Princeton: Princeton University Press, 1984), 667; 419a, 15–21.
10. Pierre Sorlin, *Mass Media* (London: Routledge, 1994), 3.
11. G. W. F. Hegel, *Enzyklopädie der philosophischen Wissenschaften*, vol. 1, §12, in *Werke*, vol. 8 (Frankfurt am Main: Suhrkamp, 1971), 56.
12. The one major exception, which proves the rule, concerns the *Origin of the German Mourning Play*. Although Benjamin does not employ such a formulation in that text, one such shines in its absence: the notion of "Deutbarkeit," the ability to signify and/or to be interpreted. "Deutbarkeit" is the silent but virtual medium of "allegory."
13. "To make the symbolizing into the symbolized itself, to restore pure language

configured to the movement of language—that is the overpowering and sole aptitude of translation" (GS4, 19). It should be noted that the published English translation by Harry Zohn reverses the direction when it renders the phrase as "to regain pure language fully formed *from the linguistic flux*" (SW1, 261).

14. Jean-Luc Nancy has discussed a similar process of *"partage,"* sharing, in his book *La partage des voix* (Paris: Editions de Galilée, 1982).

15. Benjamin, GS5, 570–611.

16. This notion of "truth" as "the death of intention" takes up a line of thought that goes back at least to the essay "The Task of the Translator," where it is related to the notion of "pure language": "In this pure language, which no longer means anything and no longer expresses anything, but rather as expressionless and creative word is that which is meant in all languages, all imparting, all meaning and all intention attain a level at which they are destined to be effaced" (GS4, 19).

17. The figure of "turning inside-out"—*Umstülpens*—was previously used by Benjamin in his text *On the Image of Proust*. There the term designates the essence of an "image" that is "similar" but not identical to that which it depicts: "Children are well acquainted with an emblem [*Wahrzeichen*] of this world, the stocking, which is structured like the world of dreams when, rolled up in the linen hamper, it is "pouch" and "gift" [*"'Tasche' und 'Mitgebrachtes'"*] at one and the same time. And just as they cannot do enough to transform both of these, pouch as well as its contents, with a single grasp into yet another, third item, so was Proust insatiable in emptying the sham, the ego, with a single stroke in order again and again to introduce that third: the image that stilled his curiosity—or rather, his nostalgia" (GS2, 314). Pierre Lévy describes virtualization as a "passage from inside to outside and from outside to inside," which he also compares to a "Möbius effect." See Lévy, *Sur les chemins du virtuel*, 22.

18. Benjamin's canonical statement on this point is to be found in his "Theological-Political Fragment": "Only the Messiah completes all historical happening . . . This is why nothing historical can on its own hope to relate to anything Messianic. This is why the Kingdom of God cannot be the *telos* of the historical *dynamis;* it cannot be posed as a goal *(Ziel)*. Seen historically it is not a goal, but an end *(Ende)*" (GS2, 203).

19. Jacques Derrida, "Artefactualités," in Derrida and Bernard Stiegler, *Echographies, de la télévision* (Paris: Galilée-INA, 1996), 14.

5. Translatability I

1. Laurence Sterne, *The Life and Opinions of Tristram Shandy, Gentleman* (New York: Penguin, 1967), bk. 4, chap. 19, 326.

2. Walter Benjamin, "The Task of the Translator," in *Illuminations* (New York: Schocken Books, 1968), 73–74; the German appears in GS4, 12.

3. Immanuel Kant, *Critique of the Power of Judgment*, trans. Paul Guyer and Eric Matthews (Cambridge, Eng.: Cambridge University Press, 2000), §15, 112.

See the excellent study by Rodolphe Gasché, *The Idea of Form: Rethinking Kant's* Aesthetics (Stanford: Stanford University Press, 2003).

4. Walter Benjamin, *Illuminations*, trans. Harry Zohn (New York: Schocken, 1968), 70.

5. Jacques Derrida, *Limited Inc.* (Evanston, Ill.: Northwestern University Press, 1988), 47–49.

6. *GS1*, 140–157; *SW1*, 62–74.

7. Although Benjamin does not refer here to Kant, the latter's quite enigmatic proposal to judge the exemplary value of "genius" not in terms of imitation *(Nachahmen)* but in terms of *consequences (Nachfolge)* receives here a suggestive elaboration. Cf. Kant, *Critique of Judgment*, §49: "The product of a genius . . . is an example that is meant not to be imitated but to be followed by another genius" (trans. Werner S. Pluhar [New York: Hackett, 1987], 186–187). I follow the Pluhar translation here rather than the more recent Guyer-Matthews one previously referenced precisely because Pluhar does not efface the notion of "following" as do Guyer-Matthews (who translate Kant's "Nachfolgen" as "emulate"—thus eliminating precisely the temporal sequence that is a decisive source of what will become a distinctively contemporary concern with series, sets, and discontinuous singularities.)

8. Walter Benjamin, *Gesammelte Briefe* (Collected Letters), vol. 2: *1914–1924* (Frankfurt am Main: Suhrkamp, 1996), 202.

9. This is doubtless the core of the differentiation between a certain Christian messianism, which the Romantics, and in particular Schlegel, secularize in their aesthetics, and a Jewish or Mosaic messianic impulse that informs both the notion of allegory and the poetics and poetry of Hölderlin—an impulse that insists paradoxically on both the radical indissociability of presence and the alterity implicit in finitude.

10. This phrase is translated as "specific linguistic contextual aspects"; in German: *bestimmte sprachliche Gehaltszusammenhänge* (*GS4*, 16; *SW1*, 258).

11. Benjamin, *Briefe*, 2:108.

12. Ibid., 2:252 (January 1921).

13. Martin Heidegger, "Die kategorien- und Bedeutungslehre des Duns Scotus" (The doctrine of the categories and of signification of Duns Scotus), *Frühe Schriften*, vol. 1: *1912–1916* (Stuttgart: Klostermann, 1978), 278–279.

14. On the importance of the notion of *intensity* for Benjamin's thinking about language, see the remarkable text of Werner Hamacher, "Intensive Sprachen," in *Übersetzen: Walter Benjamin,* ed. Christiaan Hart Nibbrig (Frankfurt am Main: Suhrkamp, 2001), 174–235. An English translation of this essay, which places translation at the core of Benjamin's thought, is in preparation.

6. Translatability II

1. Of course the increasing convergence of the two markets since 1999 makes it virtually impossible today to separate them clearly.

2. See Chapter 4, which quotes *The Complete Works of Aristotle,* ed. Jonathan Barnes, vol. 1 (Princeton: Princeton University Press, 1984), 667; 419a, 15–21.

3. Marshall McLuhan's equation of "medium" with "message" marked a first contemporary assault on this tradition. See McLuhan, *Understanding Media: The Extensions of Man* (New York: Mentor, 1964).

4. The Word of God that creates the world, man, and the Garden of Eden is not "placed" within it as are Adam and Eve.

5. The editors of the New Jerusalem Bible (Garden City, N.Y.: Doubleday, 1985) note that the word for "likeness" already introduces a distancing from the more intimate relation implied by "image" (p. 19, note: "'Likeness' appears to weaken the force of image by excluding the idea of equality.").

6. Benjamin's description of the *"dusty* fata morgana" that covers the glass ceilings of the Winter Garden can be read in this context: "dust" appears as the material manifestation of transience. See Walter Benjamin, "Das Passagenwerk," in *GS5*, 217 (F 3,2).

7. See The New Jerusalem Bible, Genesis 1:11.

8. *GS1*, 226; *Origin*, 45. All translations of excerpts from Benjamin's work are my own.

9. Benjamin's word echoes Hölderlin's description of the Rhine in his poem of the same name, *"Reinentsprungenes"*—except that he significantly replaces the past with the present participle.

10. See Chapter 5.

7. Citability—of Gesture

1. It should be noted from the outset that the English edition of *Selected Writings* has translated only the second, 1939 version of "What Is the Epic Theater?" (*SW4*, 302–309), so all references are to the 1939 version. All translations are my own.

2. *GS2*, 1386.

3. Benjamin's figure refers here to the then current, but since largely abandoned, German typographical practice of using *Sperrdruck*—spaced typesetting—instead of italics to emphasize words and phrases.

4. *Oxford American Dictionary* (New York: Avon Books, 1986).

5. For the early, first version of this essay, see Walter Benjamin, *Understanding Brecht* (London: Verso, 1998), 3.

6. Ibid., 3.

7. "Studien zur Theorie des epischen Theaters," in Benjamin, *Versuche über Brecht* (Frankfurt am Main: Suhrkamp, 1967), 31.

8. Benjamin, *Understanding Brecht*, 3.

9. Ibid., 1.

10. Aristotle, *Poetics,* trans. Gerard Else (Ann Arbor: University of Michigan Press, 1967), 34 (51b).

11. Benjamin, *Understanding Brecht*, 3.

12. Ibid., 7.

13. Ibid.

14. See Benjamin, "The Author as Producer," in *GS2*, 698; *SW2*, 779.

15. I explore the "double take" as an eminently theatrical gesture of reflection not coming full circle, in an essay on the dramaturgical writing of Jean Genet; see

Samuel Weber, *Theatricality as Medium* (New York: Fordham University Press, 2004), 295–312.

16. Benjamin, *Understanding Brecht*, 4.

17. See thesis 8 of "On the Concept of History": "The current amazement that the things we are experiencing are 'still' possible in the twentieth century is *not* philosophical. This amazement is not the beginning of knowledge—unless it is the knowledge that the view of history that gives rise to it is untenable" (*GS1*, 697; *SW4*, 392).

18. Aristotle, *Poetics*, p. 34 (52b).

19. "The Author as Producer," *GS2*, 698; *SW2*, 779: The interruptive "stance" *(Zustand)* of epic theater "opposes the dramatic laboratory to the dramatic *Gesamtkunstwerk* (total work of art)."

20. Benjamin, *Understanding Brecht*, 11.

21. Ibid., 12.

22. Ibid., 1.

23. "Being there and then" is my not entirely facetious suggestion for translating Heidegger's notion of *Dasein* into English.

24. Benjamin, *Understanding Brecht*, 13.

25. One articulation of this problem can be found in the film *Sling Blade* (1996), written and directed by Billy Bob Thornton, who also plays the main role, that of Karl Childers, a "retarded" murderer. The attention paid by this film to questions of language is exemplary, beginning with its title.

8. Ability and Style

1. "Gedanke und Stil" ("Thought and Style"), *GS6*, 202. Not translated in *Selected Writings*.

2. See Chapter 4.

9. An Afterlife of -abilities

1. Jacques Derrida, "As If It Were Possible," in *Negotiations: Interventions and Interviews, 1971–2001*, ed. and trans. Elizabeth Rottenberg (Stanford: Stanford University Press, 2002), 352.

2. *PoF*, 38; *Pdl*, 58. Translations have been modified throughout the chapter, but unless otherwise noted, all italics are original.

3. *PoF*, 38; *Pdl*, 58–59; my emphasis in the third and fourth lines.

4. "The theory of the subject is incapable of accounting for the slightest decision" (*PoF*, 68; *Pdl*, 87).

5. See, however, Samuel Weber, "'And When Is Now?' (On Some Limits of Perfect Intelligibility)," *Modern Language Notes* 122, no. 5, Comparative Literature issue (December 2007).

10. Genealogy of Modernity

Epigraph: Benjamin, *GS6*, 98.

1. Alfred Schmidt, *Geschichte und Struktur: Fragen einer marxistichen Historik* (Munich: C. Hanser, 1971).

2. Jürgen Habermas, *Der philosophische Diskurs der Moderne* (Frankfurt am Main: Suhrkamp, 1985), 390.

3. Ibid.

4. Ibid., 297.

5. See Benjamin's *Goethes Wahlverwandtschaften, GS1,* 199–201.

6. The kaleidoscope exemplifies the discontinuous relation of ordered states that characterizes history, according to Benjamin. See *Das Passagen-Werk* in *GS5,* 427–428, and *AP,* 339.

7. Habermas, *Der philosophische Diskurs der Moderne,* 297.

8. Benjamin, *GS1,* 218; *Origin,* 38.

9. From his earliest writings to his latest, Benjamin always conceived "history" and "historical-philosophical" as notions that entail a theological perspective. In his notes to the "Arcades Project" *(Passagen-Werk),* he relates the theological aspect of history to what he calls *Eingedenken,* commemoration, whose transformative (or as we might say today, performative) power he contrasts with the constative stance of science: "History is not simply a science but also and no less a form of commemoration. What science has 'determined' [*festgestellt*], commemoration can modify. Commemoration can make what is unfinished (happiness) into something finished and what is finished (suffering) into something unfinished. That is theology; but what we experience in commemoration prohibits us from conceiving history in a fundamentally atheological manner, just as it excludes that it be written in directly theological concepts" (*GS5,* 589; *AP,* 471). The question thus becomes that of interpreting how "theological concepts," whether direct or indirect, function in the writings of Benjamin.

10. In a note probably written around 1921, shortly before publication of *Kritik der Gewalt,* Benjamin makes explicit his rejection of the Hegelian-Christian notion of "reconciliation" in respect to the question of the moral meaning of time: "The significance of time in the economy of the moral world, in which it not merely effaces the traces of the misdeed [*Untat*], but also through its duration—and beyond all remembering or forgetting—leads in a most mysterious manner to forgiveness, although never to reconciliation" ("The Meaning of Time in the Moral Universe," in *GS6,* 98; *SW1,* 287).

11. "Als Gestaltung des Zusammenhanges, in dem das Einmalig-Extreme mit seinesgleichen steht, ist die Idee umschrieben" (*GS1,* 215; *Origin,* 35).

12. A more idiomatic English rendition of these terms would be "prehistory" and "aftermath," but this translation tends to efface the symmetrical reference to history in the second term.

13. Benjamin's rejection of the implicit teleology of historicism recalls the critique of teleological conceptions of history elaborated by Nietzsche in *On the Genealogy of Morals,* in *On the Use and Abuse of History,* and other texts. In general it should be observed that the relation of Benjamin's book to Nietzsche is far more complex than the occasional, often critical references to *The Birth of Tragedy* would suggest.

14. "The rejection of the eschatology of the mystery plays marks the new drama in all of Europe; nevertheless, the insensate flight into a nature devoid of grace is specifically German" (*GS1,* 260; *Origin,* 81).

15. Carl Schmitt, whose theory of sovereignty as the power of a subject to declare the "state of exception" Benjamin cites in this section, later wrote about the decisive political importance of precisely such "spatial" questions of "access" in a text initially composed in 1947, in response to interrogation by Robert Kempner, prosecuting attorney at the Nuremberg war crime trials. This essay, "The Access to the Ruler, A Central Problem of Constitutional Law," has been reprinted in Carl Schmitt, *Verfassungsrechtliche Aufsätze* (Berlin: Duncker & Humblot, 1985), 430–439.

16. Benjamin designates allegory itself as the scheme of the Baroque era: "Whatever it grasps, its Midas-touch transforms into something significant. Transformations of all kinds were its stock and trade, and its scheme was allegory" (*GS1*, 403; *Origin*, 229). Allegory is a scheme in a dual sense: it transforms the singular phenomenon into a (general) signification; and it imposes this transformation by isolating the phenomenon in its singularity and thus weakening its resistance to allegorical interpretation.

17. "The German mourning play was never capable of animating itself; it was never able to awaken within itself the skewed glance of self-awareness. It remained astonishingly obscure to itself" (*GS1*, 335; *Origin*, 158). Precisely the lack of such self-reflection or meditation *(Selbstbesinnung)* is linked in this passage to the "raw stage" of the baroque: that is, to its distinctive theatricality. The baroque is *theatrical* to the very extent that it does not and cannot be *self-reflective*.

18. *Origin*, 5.

19. In his discussion of tragedy, Benjamin equates "geschichtsphilosophisch" with what he calls "truth-contents," *Wahrheitsgehalt* (*GS1*, 284; *Origin*, 105). Truth, in turn, is defined in the Epistemo-critical Preface as "the resonant relation" *(das tonende Verhältnis)* of those discrete "essences" (*Wesenheiten*) (*GS1*, 218; *Origin*, 37) that are both completely isolated and no less completely independent: the monadological ideas. But however isolated and independent these ideas may be, and however much Benjamin therefore likens their being to that of the Name before the fall into cognition, judgment, and conceptuality (before, in short, the fall into signification, which will reach an extreme in baroque allegory), the resonant relation of these ideas or names is not itself simply another idea or name. It is what goes on among and between them, their "configuration" or "constellation," that constitutes what Benjamin calls "Darstellung," and which in this text will be translated as "staging." It should be noted that Benjamin resorts to an *acoustical* term—resonance—to describe what is generally understood to be a visual structure.

20. The "icy solitude of the self" returns in a later essay of Benjamin's on "The Storyteller," this time, however, to characterize the reader of novels, who "seeks to warm his frosty life on a death about which he reads" (*GS2*, 457; *SW3*, 156). In this essay Benjamin interprets the novel as the modern heir to the classic epic, not tragedy. But given the ostensibly positive interpretation of Greek tragedy as the decisive challenge to "myth," it is interesting to consider the implications of this subsequent equation of "frosty isolation" not with the overcoming of myth, but with a certain form of its return. It is in this direction that this essay seeks to proceed.

21. The Nietzsche of *The Birth of Tragedy* is condemned for an aestheticism that betrays the influence of the "Nihilism" of Bayreuth, which prevented his "genial intuition" from grasping "the hard, historical givens of Greek tragedy" (*GS1*, 282; *Origin*, 103).

22. See Benjamin, "Die Aufgabe des Übersetzers" in *GS4*, 18; *SW1*, 260.

23. Benjamin seems strangely indifferent to the gender of the tragic "hero," as though sexual difference mattered little where heroic self-sacrifice is concerned. The same could be said of "the plotter."

24. Giorgio Agamben has recently called attention to the fact that in one of the manuscripts of his study, Benjamin writes not that the baroque has "no eschatology" (*keine Eschatologie*) but that it has *an* eschatology (*eine Eschatologie*; *GS1.1*, 246). However, if the *end—eschaton—*is no longer a *goal* or *gate* to *salvation*, the difference between the two statements is no longer one of simple opposition or negation. In other words, if the *eschaton* is an end as interruption, *eschatology* is no longer soteriology—a story of salvation (in German: *Heilgeschichte*). Rather it has become an *Unheilgeschichte*.

25. Writing of the "bottomless profundity" of allegorical knowledge, Benjamin observes that "its data are incapable of entering into philosophical constellations" (*GS1*, 404; *Origin*, 231).

26. It is telling that the incident that Benjamin cites in order to introduce this "allegorization of allegory" is drawn from the Catholic instance of Saint Theresa, who in a "hallucination" on her deathbed tells her confessor that the Madonna has placed roses on her bed. When the confessor responds that he sees nothing, she answers: "The Madonna brought them for me." The vision of Saint Theresa announces divine action but as singular "hallucination"—thus leaving its allegorical significance open and uncertain (*GS1.1*, 408; *Origin*, 234).

11. Awakening

1. *GS2*, 158.

2. *Origin*, 45. The translation is mine.

3. "Longtemps, je me suis couché de bonne heure. Parfois, à peine ma bougie éteinte, mes yeux se fermaient si vite que je n'avais pas le temps de me dire: 'Je m'endors.' Et, une demi-heure après, la pensée qu'il était temps de chercher le sommeil m'éveillait." See Marcel Proust, *A la recherché du temps perdu*, vol. 1 (Paris: Bibliothèque de la Pléiade, 1954), 3; English version in *The Way by Swann's*, trans. Lydia Davis (London: Penguin, 2002), 7.

4. "Un homme qui dort tient en cercle autour de lui le fil des heures, l'ordre des années et des mondes. Il les consulte d'instinct en s'éveillant et y lit en une seconde le point de la terre qu'il occupe, le temps qui s'est écoulé jusqu'à son réveil; mais leurs rangs peuvent se mêler, se rompre. Que vers le matin, après quelque insomnie, le sommeil le prenne en train de lire, dans une posture trop différente de celle où il dort habituellement, il suffit de son bras soulevé pour arrêter et faire reculer le soleil, et à la première minute de son réveil, il ne saura plus l'heure, il estimera qu'il vient à peine de se coucher. Que s'il s'assoupit dans une position encore plus déplacée et divergente, par exemple après dîner

assis dans un fauteuil, alors le bouleversement sera complet dans les mondes désorbités, le fauteuil magique le fera voyager a toute vitesse dans le temps et dans l'espace, et au moment d'ouvrir les paupières, il se croira couché quelques mois plus tôt dans une autre contrée." From Proust, *A la recherché du temps perdu*, 5; *Way by Swann's*, 9.

5. Proust, *A la recherché du temps perdu*, 4; *Way by Swann's*, 8.

6. Proust, *A la recherché du temps perdu*, 5; *Way by Swann's*, 8.

7. Proust, *A la recherché du temps perdu*, 5; my translation.

8. Proust, *A la recherché du temps perdu*, 4; *Way by Swann's*, 8.

9. "Space is in itself the contradiction of indifferent being-beside-oneself and of undifferentiated continuity, the pure negativity of itself and the going-over initially into time." G. W. F. Hegel, *Philosophy of Nature*, in *Encyclopedia of Philosophical Sciences, Werke in 20 Bänden und ein Registerband*, vol. 10 (Frankfurt am Main: Suhrkamp, 1970), 55. My translation.

10. "J'avais été intoxiqué moralement par l'odeur inconnue du vétiver, convaincu de l'hostilité des rideaux violets et de l'insolente indifférence de la pendule qui jacassait tout haut comme si je n'eusse pas été là; où une étrange et impitoyable glace à pieds quadrangulaires, barrant obliquement un des angles de la pièce, se creusait à vif dans la douce plénitude de mon champ visuel accoutumé un emplacement qui n'était pas prévu; ou ma pensée, s'efforçant pendant des heures de se disloquer, de s'étirer en hauteur pour prendre exactement la forme de la chambre." Proust, *A la recherché du temps perdu*, 8; *Way by Swann's*, 12.

12. Taking Exception to Decision

Epigraph: Benjamin, *GS1*, 305; *Origin*, 126. I have generally retranslated passages cited from Benjamin in English.

1. "Sie erhalten dieser Tage vom Verlage mein Buch Ursprung des deutschen Trauerspiels. Mit diesen Zeilen möchte ich es Ihnen nicht nur ankündigen, sondern Ihnen auch meine Freude darüber ausprechen, daß ich es, auf Veranlassung von Herrn Albert Salomon, Ihnen zusenden darf. Sie werden sehr schnell bemerken, wieviel das Buch in seiner Darstellung der Lehre von der Souveränität im 17. Jahrhundert Ihnen verdankt. Vielleicht darf ich Ihnen darüber hinausgehend sagen, daß ich auch Ihren späteren Werken, vor allem der 'Diktatur' eine Bestätigung meiner kunstphilosophischen Forschungsweisen durch Ihre staatsphilosophischen entnommen habe. Wenn Ihnen die Lektüre meines Buches dieses Gefühl verständlich erscheinen laßt, so ist die Absicht meiner Übersendung erfüllt" (*GS1*, 887).

2. Walter Benjamin, *Briefe*, ed. Gershom Scholem and Theodor W. Adorno (Frankfurt am Main: Suhrkamp, 1966).

3. "Gerade eine Philosophie des konkreten Lebens darf sich vor der Ausnahme und vor dem extremen Falle nicht zurückziehen, sondern muß sich im höchsten Maße für ihn interessieren. Ihr kann die Ausnahme wichtiger sein als die Regel, nicht aus einer romantischen Ironie für das Paradoxe, sondern mit dem ganzen Ernst einer Einsicht, die tiefer geht als die klaren Generalisationen

des durchschnittlich sich Wiederholenden. Die Ausnahme ist interessanter als der Normalfall. Das Normale beweist nichts, die Ausnahme beweist alles; sie bestätigt nicht nur die Regel, die Regel lebt überhaupt nur von der Ausnahme." See *Politische Theologie, 22.*

4. "Als Gestaltung des Zusammenhanges, in dem das Einmalig-Extreme mit seinesgleichen steht, ist die Idee umschrieben. Daher ist es falsch, die allgemeinsten Verweisungen der Sprache als Begriffe zu verstehen, anstatt sie als Ideen zu erkennen. Das Allgemeine als ein Durchschnittliches darlegen zu wollen, ist verkehrt. Das Allgemeine ist die Idee. Das Empirische dagegen wird um so tiefer durchdrungen, je genauer es als ein Extremes eingesehen werden kann. Vom Extremen geht der Begriff aus" (*GS1*, 215).

5. "Die philosophische Geschichte als die Wissenschaft vom Ursprung ist die Form, die da aus den entlegenen Extremen, den scheinbaren Exzessen der Entwicklung die Konfiguration der Idee als der durch die Möglichkeit eines sinnvollen Nebeneinanders solcher Gegensätze gekennzeichneten Totalität heraustreten läßt. Die Darstellung einer Idee kann unter keinen Umständen als geglückt betrachtet werden, solange virtuell der Kreis der in ihr möglichen Extreme nicht abgeschritten ist. Das Abschreiten bleibt virtuell" (*GS1*, 227).

6. "Immer wieder begegnet in den improvisierten Versuchen, den Sinn dieser Epoche zu vergegenwärtigen, das bezeichnende Schwindelgefühl, in das der Anblick ihrer in Widersprüchen kreisenden Geistigkeit versetzt . . . Nur eine von weither kommende, ja sich dem Anblick der Totalität zunächst versagende Betrachtung kann in einer gewissermaßen asketischen Schule den Geist zu der Festigung führen, die ihm erlaubt, im Anblick jenes Panoramas seiner selbst mächtig zu bleiben" (*GS1*, 237).

7. "Das deutsche Drama der Gegenreformation hat niemals jene geschmeidigte, jedem virtuosen Griff sich bietende Form gefunden, die Calderon dem spanischen gab. Gebildet hat es sich . . . in einer höchst gewalttätigen Anstrengung und dies allein würde besagen, daß kein souveräner Genius dieser Form das Gepräge gegeben hat. Dennoch liegt der Schwerpunkt aller barocken Trauerspiele in ihr . . . Diese Einsicht ist eine Vorbedingung der Erforschung" (*GS1*, 229–230).

8. "Einer Literatur gegenüber, die durch den Aufwand ihrer Technik, die gleichförmige Fülle ihrer Produktionen und die Heftigkeit ihrer Wertbehauptungen Welt und Nachwelt gewissermaßen zum Schweigen zu bringen suchte, ist die Notwendigkeit der souveränen Haltung, wie Darstellung von der Idee von einer Form sie aufdringt, zu betonen. Die Gefahr, aus den Höhen des Erkennens in die ungeheuren Tiefen der Barockstimmung sich hinabstürzen zu lassen, bleibt selbst dann unverächtlich" (*GS1*, 237).

9. Here the question should at least be raised in passing whether the vertigo that Benjamin identifies with the German baroque is not also, in part at least, a result of his own determination of the origin as a *Strudel*, a vortex or maelstrom that "sucks into its rhythm the material of emergence" (*"reißt in seine Rhythmik das Entstehungsmaterial hinein"* (*GS1*, 226; *Origin*, 45). The rhythm of the origin is split between a tendency to restore and to reproduce *(Restauration, Wiederherstellung)* on the one hand, and a certain incompletion *(Unvollendetes, Unabgeschlossenes)* on the other. This split in the origin is

what then articulates itself as the division into pre- and post-history. The origin's lack of a center, fully present to itself, is perhaps the origin of that *Schwindelgefühl* that Benjamin associates with the baroque in general, and with its German version in particular. It remains to be determined, however, whether this connection indicates that the baroque is a particularly originary age, or rather whether the origin itself, as construed by Benjamin, is a peculiarly baroque notion. There is no guarantee that the answer to this question will conform to the schema of an either/or, or permit a simple decision. We will return very briefly at the end of this chapter to the relation between decision and rhythm as articulated in Benjamin's book.

10. "Das ständig wiederholte Schauspiel fürstlicher Erhebung und des Falls . . . stand den Dichtern nicht sowohl als Moralität, denn als die in ihrer Beharrlichkeit wesenhafte, als die naturgemäße Seite des Geschichtsverlaufs vor Augen" (GS1, 267).

11. "Souverän ist, wer über den Ausnahmezustand entscheidet. Diese Definition kann dem Begriff der Souveränität als einem Grenzbegriff allein gerecht werden. Denn Grenzbegriff bedeutet nicht einen konfusen Begriff, wie in der unsaubern Terminologie populärer Literatur, sondern einen Begriff der äußersten Sphäre" (*Politische Theologie*, 11).

12. "Immer noch etwas anderes . . . als eine Anarchie und ein Chaos, [und daher] besteht im juristischen Sinne immer noch eine Ordnung, wenn auch keine Rechtsordnung. Die Existenz des Staates bewährt hier eine zweifellose Überlegenheit über die Geltung der Rechtsnorm. Die Entscheidung macht sich frei von jeder normativen Gebundenheit und wird im eigentlichen Sinne absolut. *Im Ausnahmefall suspendiert der Staat das Recht, kraft eines Selbsterhaltungsrechtes, wie man sagt*" (*Politische Theologie*, 18–19).

13. "Die Autorität beweist, daß sie, um Recht zu schaffen, nicht Recht zu haben braucht" (*Politische Theologie*, 20).

14. "Alle prägnante Begriffe der modernen Staatslehre sind säkularisierte theologische Begriffe. Nicht nur ihrer historischen Entwicklung nach, weil sie aus der Theologie auf die Staatslehre übertragen wurden, indem zum Beispiel der allmächtige Gott zum omnipotenten Gesetzgeber wurde, sondern auch in ihrer systematischen Struktur, deren Erkenntnis notwendig ist für eine soziologische Betrachtung dieser Begriffe. Der Ausnahmezustand hat für die Jurisprudenz eine analoge Bedeutung wie das Wunder für die Theologie. Erst in dem Bewußtsein solcher analogen Stellung läßt sich die Entwicklung erkennen, welche die staatsphilosophischen Ideen in den letzten Jahrhunderten genommen haben" (*Politische Theologie*, 36).

15. "Zu dem Gottesbegriff des 17. und 18. Jahrhunderts gehört die Transzendenz Gottes gegenüber der Welt, wie eine Transzendenz des Souveräns gegenüber dem Staat zu seiner Staatsphilosophie gehört. Im 19. Jahrhundert wird in immer weiterer Ausdehnung alles von Immanenzvorstellungen beherrscht" (*Politische Theologie*, 49).

16. "Der Monarch in der Staatslehre des 17. Jahrhunderts mit Gott identifiziert wird und im Staat die genau analoge Position hat, die dem Gott des kartesianischen Systems in der Welt zukommt" (*Politische Theologie*, 46).

17. "Das metaphysische Bild, das sich ein bestimmtes Zeitalter von der Welt

macht, hat dieselbe Struktur wie das, was ihr als Form ihrer politischen Organisation ohne weiteres einleuchtet. Die Feststellung einer solchen Identität ist die Soziologie des Souveränitätsbegriffes" (*Politische Theologie*, 59–60).

18. "Der Souverän repräsentiert die Geschichte. Er hält das historische Geschehen in der Hand wie ein Szepter. Diese Auffassung ist alles andere als ein Privileg der Theatraliker. Staatsrechtliche Gedanken liegen ihr zugrunde. In einer letzten Auseinandersetzung mit den juristischen Lehren des Mittelalters bildete sich im siebzehnten Jahrhundert ein neuer Souveränitätsbegriff . . . Wenn der moderne Souveränitätsbegriff auf eine höchste, fürstliche Exekutivgewalt hinausläuft, entwickelt der barocke sich aus einer Diskussion des Ausnahmezustandes und macht zur wichtigsten Funktion des Fürsten, den auszuschließen" (*GS1*, 245).

19. On the difficulties of *Beseitigung*—doing away with—as they are explored not by Schmitt but by Freud in his *The Man Moses and the Monotheistic Religion*, see Samuel Weber, *Targets of Opportunity* (New York: Fordham University Press, 2005), 63–65.

20. "Aber ob der extreme Ausnahmefall wirklich aus der Welt geschafft werden kann oder nicht, das ist keine juristische Frage. Ob man das Vertrauen und die Hoffnung hat, er lasse sich tatsächlich beseitigen, hängt von philosophischen, insbesondere geschichtsphilosophischen oder metaphysischen Überzeugungen ab" (*Politische Theologie*, 13).

21. "Der religiöse Mensch des Barock hält an der Welt so fest, weil er mit ihr sich einem Katarakt entgegentreiben fühlt. Es gibt [k]eine barocke Eschatologie; und eben darum einen Mechanismus, der alles Erdgeborne häuft und exaltiert, bevor es sich dem Ende überliefert. Das Jenseits wird entleert von alledem, worin auch nur der leiseste Atem von Welt webt und eine Fülle von Dingen, welche jeder Gestaltung sich zu entziehen pflegten, gewinnt das Barock ihm ab und fördert sie auf seinem Höhepunkt in drastischer Gestalt zu Tag, um einen letzten Himmel zu räumen und als Vakuum ihn in den Stand zu setzen, mit katastrophaler Gewalt dereinst die Erde in sich zu vernichten." Regarding whether Benjamin meant "no Baroque eschatology" or "a Baroque eschatology," see the discussion in Chapter 10, note 24.

22. "Die Ebene des Schöpfungsstands, der Boden, auf dem das Trauerspiel sich abrollt, bestimmt ganz unverkennbar auch den Souverän. So hoch er über Untertan und Staat auch thront, sein Rang ist in der Schöpfungswelt beschlossen, er ist der Herr der Kreaturen, aber er bleibt Kreatur" (ibid., 263–264).

23. "Die Abkehr von der Eschatologie der geistlichen Spiele kennzeichnet das neue Drama in ganz Europa; nichtsdestoweniger ist die besinnungslose Flucht in eine unbegnadete Natur spezifisch deutsch" (ibid., 260).

24. See Alexander Garcia-Düttmann, *Das Gedächtnis des Denkens: Versuch über Adorno und Heidegger* (Frankfurt am Main: Suhrkamp, 1991), 211–213.

25. "Die Antithese zwischen Herrschermacht und Herrschervermögen hat für das Trauerspiel zu einem eigenen, nur scheinbar genrehaften Zug geführt, dessen Beleuchtung einzig auf dem Grunde der Lehre von der Souveränität sich abhebt. Das ist die Entschlußunfähigkeit des Tyrannen. Der Fürst, bei dem die

Entscheidung über den Ausnahmezustand ruht, erweist in der erstbesten Situation, daß ein Entschluß ihm fast unmöglich ist" (*GS1*, 250).

26. "Die Janushäupter des Gekrönten, . . . die notwendig extremen Ausprägungen des fürstlichen Wesens" (*GS1*, 249).

27. "Die Theorie der Souveränität, für die der Sonderfall mit der Entfaltung diktatorischen Instanzen exemplarisch wird, dringt geradezu darauf, das Bild des Souveräns im Sinne des Tyrannen zu vollenden" (*GS1*, 249).

28. "Der Gipfel der Kreatur, ausbrechend in der Raserei wie ein Vulkan und mit allem umliegenden Hofstaat sich selber vernichtend . . . Er fällt als Opfer eines Mißverhältnisses der unbeschränkten hierarchischen Würde, mit welcher Gott ihn investiert, zum Stande seines armen Menschenwesens" (*GS1*, 250).

29. Aristotle, *Poetics*, trans. Gerard Else (Ann Arbor: University of Michigan Press, 1967), 1454a.

30. "So wie die Malerei der Manieristen Komposition in ruhiger Belichtung garnicht kennt, so stehen die theatralischen Figuren der Epoche im grellen Scheine ihrer wechselnden Entschließung. In ihnen drängt sich nicht sowohl die Souveränität auf, welche die stoischen Redensarten zur Schau stellen, als die jähe Willkür eines jederzeit umschlagenden Affektsturms, in dem zumal Lohensteins Gestalten wie zerrißne, flatternde Fahnen sich bäumen. Auch sind sie Grecoschen in der Kleinheit des Kopfes, wenn diesen Ausdruck bildlich zu verstehen gestattet ist, nicht· unähnlich. Denn nicht Gedanken, sondern schwankende physische Impulse bestimmen sie" (*GS1*, 251).

31. Benjamin's figure here recalls Hölderlin's poem, "Halves of Life" (Hälfte des Lebens), as well as certain films of Kurosawa, in particular, *Kagemusha*, which begins with a courier racing down an unending series of stone steps carrying a flag whipping in the wind. The comparison also highlights a characteristic of the baroque: whereas the fluttering of the flags in the films of Kurosawa serves to heighten the tension between enormous and usually self-destructive energy on the one hand, and a certain stability on the other, it is precisely such stability that is utterly lacking in the volatility of the figures Benjamin is describing (and attributing to Lowenstein). It is such stability that the Counter-Reformation Mourning Play seeks to establish—in vain. I hope to explore this unlikely comparison—"unsinnliche Ähnlichkeit" as Benjamin might have called it—elsewhere.

32. "Im Gegensatz zu einem zeitlichen und sprunghaften Verlauf, wie die Tragödie ihn vorstellt, spielt das Trauerspiel sich im Kontinuum des Raumes—choreographisch darf man's nennen—ab. Der Veranstalter seiner Verwicklung, der Vorläufer des Ballettmeisters, ist der Intrigant" (*GS1*, 274).

33. "Seine verworfnen Berechnungen erfüllen den Betrachter der Haupt- und Staatsaktionen mit um so größerem Interesse, als er in Ihnen nicht allein die Beherrschung des politischen Getriebes, sondern ein anthropologisches, selbst physiologisches Wissen erkennt, das ihn passionierte. Der überlegene Intrigant ist ganz Verstand und Wille" (ibid.).

34. "Vom sogenannten Gegenspiel der klassischen Tragödie ist sie durch Isolierung der Motive, Szenen, Typen unterschieden . . . das Drama des Barock [liebt auch] den Gegenspielern in grelles Licht gestellte Sonderszenen einzuräumen,

in denen Motivierung die geringste Rolle zu spielen pflegt. Die barocke Intrige vollzieht sich, man darf es sagen, wie ein Dekorationswechsel auf offener Bühne, so wenig ist die Illusion in ihr gemeint" (*GS1*, 254).

35. "Das Bild des Schauplatzes, genau: des Hofes, wird Schlüssel des historischen Verstehens. Denn der Hof ist der innerste Schauplatz . . . Im Hof erblickt das Trauerspiel den ewigen, natürlichen Dekor des Geschichtsverlaufes" (*GS1*, 271).

36. "Die Christenheit oder Europa [ist] aufgeteilt in eine Reihe von europäischen Christentümern, deren geschichtliche Aktionen nicht mehr in der Flucht des Heilsprozesses zu verlaufen beanspruchen" (*GS1*, 257).

37. "Im ganzen europäischen Trauerspiel ist . . . auch die Bühne nicht streng fixierbar, eigentlicher Ort, sondern dialektisch zerrissen auch sie. Gebunden an den Hofstaat bleibt sie Wanderbühne; uneigentlich vertreten ihre Bretter die Erde als erschaffnen Schauplatz der Geschichte; sie zieht mit ihrem Hof von Stadt zu Stadt" (*GS1*, 298).

38. "Nur die Intrige wäre vermögend gewesen, die Organisation der Szene zu jener allegorischen Totalität zu führen, mit welcher in dem Bilde der Apotheose ein von den Bildern des Verlaufes artverschiedenes sich erhebt und der Trauer Einsatz und Ausgang zugleich weist" (*GS1*, 268).

39. "Man darf wohl den Exkurs in das Juristische noch weitertreiben und im Sinne der mittelalterlichen Klageliteratur von dem Prozeß der Kreatur sprechen, deren Klage gegen den Tod—oder gegen wen sonst sie ergehen mag—am Ende des Trauerspiels halb nur bearbeitet zu den Akten gelegt wird. Die Wiederaufnahme ist im Trauerspiel angelegt" (*GS1*, 315–316).

40. "Die rechtliche Kraft der Dezision ist etwas anderes als das Resultat der Begründung. Es wird nicht mit Hilfe einer Norm zugerechnet, sondern umgekehrt; erst von einem Zurechnungspunkt aus bestimmt sich, was eine Norm und was normative Richtigkeit ist. Von der Norm aus ergibt sich kein Zurechnungspunkt, sondern nur eine Qualität eines Inhaltes" (*Politische Theologie*, 42–43).

13. Violence and Gesture

1. Translations into English are mine.

2. Walter Benjamin, *Gesammelte Briefe, 1910–1940*, vol. 1 (Frankfurt am Main: Suhrkamp, 2000), 206 (my emphasis except for the first two words); *EE*, 104.

3. "Das Mediale, das ist die *Unmittel*barkeit aller geistigen Mitteilung, ist das Grundproblem der Sprachtheorie, und wenn man diese Unmittelbarkeit magisch nennen will, so ist das Urproblem der Sprache ihre Magie." Or: "The medial, which is (to say) the *immedi*acy [more literally, *unmediability*—SW] *of* all spiritual imparting is the fundamental problem of the theory of language, and if this immediacy can be called magic, then the originary problem of language is its magic.)" *GS2*, 142. Unless otherwise indicated, all translations from this work are mine.

4. On the relationship of *Unmittelbarkeit* and *Mitteilbarkeit*, see the remarkable text of Werner Hamacher, "Intensive *Sprachen*," in Christian L. Hart-Nibbrig,

Übersetzen: Walter Benjamin (Suhrkamp: Frankfurt am Main, 2001), 174–235. An English translation of this article is in preparation.

5. See Jacques Derrida, "Le sans de la coupure pure," in *La vérité en peinture* (Paris: Flammarion, 1978), 95–135.

6. This question is already posed by Benjamin's transformation of the common German idiom, which pairs "schalten und walten" in order to suggest unrestricted control or domination. By condemning and rejecting a "mythical" violence that either posits law or sustains and administers *(verwaltet)* it, in the name of a "divine" violence that is neither *schaltend* nor *verwaltend* but rather *waltend,* Benjamin places a heavy burden on this linguistic-semantic distinction, which can also be seen to hang on the presence or absence of the prefix *ver-*: *verwaltend* versus *waltend.* The only other determination provided by Benjamin at the end of his highly enigmatic *Critique of Violence* is not without a certain pertinence for the questions raised by Agamben. For Benjamin does not *end* his distinction of *schaltend* and *waltend* before noting that the latter, by virtue of its being "purely immediate" *(als reine unmittelbare)* is "never the means of sacred execution *(heiliger Vollstreckung)*" but is rather "insignia and seal" *(Insignium und Siegel).* These two words may provide a precious hint as to the distinction Benjamin is introducing between *schalten* and *walten.* Both words involve a certain relation of force. *Schalten,* "switching" or "shifting," presupposes a network of exchanges and circulation and is used today for instance to designate an "integrated circuit board" *(Schaltbrett).* It suggests a change of direction, or of "gears"; both of these meanings preserve what seems to have been its earliest significance, that of "setting or keeping in movement" (as in "shoving" or "pushing" a boat with poles; cf. Duden's *Herkunftswörterbuch,* 2d rev. ed. (Mannheim: Duden Verlag, 1989), 620. *Walten,* on the other hand, which is used far less frequently in contemporary German, derives from words meaning "to be strong, to dominate" and suggests a more direct manifestation of strength, but one that is still, to use Agamben's terms, more "relational" than "substantial." Whereas *schalten* suggests a change in direction, however, *walten* connotes the overcoming of resistances and a certain imposing of *sameness.* What happens when this imposition is construed as "insignia and seal" is a question to which we will return later in the chapter. But even at this point it is impossible to ignore how Benjamin's choice of terms echoes the celebrated formula of Nietzsche: "To *impress* the character of being upon becoming—that is the highest will to power [Dem Werden den Charakter des Seins *aufzuprägen*—das ist die höchste Wille zur Macht]" See F. Nietzsche, *Werke in Drei Bänden* (Works in three volumes), ed. Karl Schlechta, 2d ed., (Munich: Karl Hanser Verlag, 1960), 3:895.

7. Benjamin, *Briefe,* vol. 2, 617.

8. Ibid., 618; cited by Agamben in *EE,* 107.

9. Benjamin, *Briefe,* vol. 2, 618.

10. Hölderlin develops his notion of the "patriotic reversal" *(vaterländische Umkehr)* in his comments on Sophocles' *Antigone,* noting that "patriotic reversal is the reversal of all forms and modes of representation." In his Seminar on Hölderlin's poem, the *Ister* (1942), Heidegger translates *Umkehr* as "catas-

trophe," noting that in the second chorus of *Antigone,* "man is one single catastrophe" but adding that far from being simply a calamity, this may also constitute his most profound possibility.

11. Benjamin, *Briefe,* vol. 2, 618.

12. Although this is probably not the place to go into it, it should at least be noted
that the beggar's wish—and the Jewish joke that it punctuates—operates a convergence between Nietzsche's thought of the Eternal Return and Benjamin's
ambivalent relation to the Messianic. In what way the affirmation of the Eternal Return might "straighten" or "iron out"—*zurechtrücken*—the distortions
and displacements *(Entstellungen)* of time is a question that will have to be addressed elsewhere.

13. This is also a common *topos* of Yiddish (sometimes also Russian: see Gogol)
humor: instead of responding to a question, the question is repeated . . . and
transformed. The "yes"—"Ja"—does not simply affirm but re-affirms what the
question itself seeks to forget.

14. On "keeping," see Peggy Kamuf, "Peace Keeping the Other War," *Traversées
atlantiques, Revue de literature comparée* 312 (October–December 2004):
445–466.

15. Werner Hamacher has convincingly demonstrated that Benjamin's source for
this passage—as well as for many others—is Franz Rosenzweig's *Star of
Redemption.* Rosenzweig there describes the *Tao* as "effecting without acting; only deedlessly . . . It is that which, by being 'nothing,' makes a something 'useful.'" See Hamacher, "The Gesture in the Name," in *Premises,* trans.
Peter Fenves (Cambridge: Harvard University Press, 1996), 333. Hamacher's
reference to this passage from Rosenzweig is also of extreme relevance to
Agamben's most recent publication, *Profanations* (2005), which I will discuss
briefly later. The notion of "profanation" elaborated by Agamben depends entirely on a notion of "use" *(usage)* as a practice cut off from a goal or product,
and thus is very close to what Benjamin, following Rosenzweig, but with a theatrical turn, describes with reference to Kafka.

16. In an earlier discussion of Benjamin, "Benjamin and the Demonic," Agamben
does seem to recognize the decisive importance of repetition for Benjamin's
thinking: "The dialectic of the singular and the repeatable to which Benjamin
entrusts his philosophy of history and his ethics must necessarily reckon
with the categories of origin, Idea, and phenomenon that he develops in the
'Epistemological-Critical Preface' to *The Origin of the German Mourning Play*
. . . The more one analyzes Benjamin's thought, the more it appears—contrary to a common impression—to be animated by a rigorously systematic
intention." See Agamben, *Potentialities,* trans. Daniel Heller-Roazen (Stanford: Stanford University Press, 1999), 155. But Agamben does not seem to
have pursued this insight into the "systematic" significance of the notion
of repetition for Benjamin—perhaps because the soteriology that informs his
thought, even before its turn to Foucault and the critique of a juridically structured "biopolitics," leaves little room for repetition, in sharp contrast to
Benjamin. Thus, his interpretation of Benjamin's notion of salvation opposes
the old to the new as though they were mutually exclusive: "What is saved is

what never was, something new . . . In historical redemption what happens in the end is what never took place. This is what is saved" (*Potentialities*, 158).

17. Already the revised title, *Der Verschollener*, in contrast to its English translation as *The Man Who Disappeared*, suggests a certain repetition: someone who is *"verschollen"* has not been *"heard*" from *again,*" someone whose (acoustical) trace has been lost. The German word connotes the acoustical fading away of a *Schellen* or *Schall*, a *re*-sonance that has become inaudible.

18. Franz Kafka, *Die Romane* (Frankfurt am Main: Fischer Verlag, 1965), 215.

19. Giorgio Agamben, *Infancy and History*, trans. Liz Heron (London: Verso, 1993), 135–140.

20. Ibid., 139.

21. Varro, *De Lingua Latina*, 6:77, quoted in ibid., 139–140. In the English translation, these "Notes" are either truncated or were expanded subsequently by Agamben. The "Notes sur le Geste" that is published in the French edition of *Moyens sans fins* (Paris: Rivages, 1995, 59–71) contain a commentary on the Varro citation that goes very much in the direction I elaborate in this paper. In it Agamben defines the gesture as that which "exhibits a mediality, renders visible a means as such" and relates it to theatrical practices such as "dance" and "mimicry." In an argument that is manifestly indebted to Benjamin—without, however, referring to Benjamin's own theory of gesture, for instance in the essay on Kafka—Agamben defines the gesture with respect to language as that which exposes the mediality of language: "The gesture in this sense is communication of a communicability. Properly speaking it has nothing to say because what it shows is the being-in-language of man as pure mediality" (70). The "purity" of language as medium Agamben then relates to the "gag," as that which "gags" the mouth, preventing it from speaking; and further relates this to "the improvisation of the actor who thereby seeks to compensate for a lapse of memory [*pallier un trou de mémoire*] or the impossibility to speak." Although Agamben thus brings out the *theatricality* of the gesture, as this last example demonstrates, he still thinks of it, in part at least, as the result of a conscious intention of a subject—that of the *actor* seeking to "palliate" a "hole in memory"—rather than as that which, as we will see in a moment, defaces and undoes the very notion of "man," at least in the case of Kafka's "student."

22. The political consummation of the ideal of "self-expression" Benjamin saw in fascism: "Fascism seeks to organize the newly emerging proletarian masses without touching the property-relations that they strive to abolish. It sees its salvation [*Heil*] in helping the masses express themselves." ("Afterword" to "The Work of Art in the Age of its Technical Reproducibility," *GS1*, 506; *SW4*, 269).

23. Franz Kafka, *Der Verschollener (Amerika)* (Frankfurt am Main: Fischer: 2001), 271.

24. Or more literally, "On the 10th recurrence of his death-day" ["Zur 10. Wiederkehr seines Todestages"], *GS2*, 409.

25. *Briefe*, vol. 2, 618; my emphasis.

26. Giorgio Agamben, *Profanations*, trans. Martin Rueff (Paris: Rivages, 2005).

27. In his essay "The Storyteller," Benjamin distinguishes the tale from "informa-

tion" by its reluctance to provide explanations: "It does not exhaust itself." On the example of a chapter from Herodotus, Benjamin notes: "Herodotus does not explain anything. His report is as dry as possible. This is why this story from ancient Egypt is still capable, centuries later, of provoking amazement and reflection." See Benjamin's "Der Erzähler" (*GS2*, 445–446; *SW3*, 148).

28. Agamben, *Profanations*, 120.
29. "In its most extreme form, capitalist religion realizes separation as pure form, without separating anything any more" (ibid., 102).
30. G. Agamben, "The Messiah and the Sovereign," *Potentialities*, 173.
31. G. Agamben, "Benjamin and the Demonic," *Potentialities*, 158.

14. Song and Glance

1. Walter Benjamin, "Agesilaus Santander," in Gershom Scholem, *Walter Benjamin und sein Engel* (Frankfurt am Main: Suhrkamp Verlag, 1983), 40. My translation.
2. "Walter Benjamin und sein Engel," in *Zur Aktualität Walter Benjamins* (Frankfurt am Main: Suhrkamp Verlag, 1972), 87–138. Reprinted with an afterword *(Nachtrag)* in Scholem, *Walter Benjamin und sein Engel*, 35–77.
3. Werner Fuld, *Walter Benjamin: Zwischen den Stühlen* (Frankfurt am Main: Fischer Verlag, 1981).
4. Scholem, *Walter Benjamin und sein Engel*, 73.
5. Ibid., 74.
6. Ibid., 75.
7. In one of the sections of his autobiographical essay "Berlin Childhood around 1900," Benjamin describes an incident that condenses this relationship to Jewish ritual, even in its most moderate forms. During the Jewish New Year, his parents had sent him to pick up a "distant relative" before going to services. Benjamin describes how he lost his way and could not find the relative. Nor did he dare to go to the synagogue alone, "for my protector had the entrance tickets." As the one responsible for his dilemma he cites both his "aversion to the virtually unknown (relative)" as well as "suspicion towards the religious ceremonies, which promised only embarrassment." His situation overcame him in "a hot wave of anxiety," as he realized that "it was too late for the synagogue." But this feeling was quickly overtaken by a sense of being "utterly unconscionable" and "both waves crested irresistibly in a first great feeling of pleasure, in which the desecration of the holiday mixed with the pairing of the street, which allowed me to anticipate the services it would later render to those awakened drives." See Benjamin, *GS4*, 251; *SW3*, 386. Unless otherwise noted, all translations are my own.
8. In "Platonic Love," one of the observations in the collection entitled *Short Shadows*, Benjamin suggests that such love is inseparably bound up with the first name of the beloved, which it leaves "untouched," refusing to replace it by various nick-names and thereby preserving the "tension, the remote inclination that is Platonic love" (*GS4*, 369; *SW2*, 268).
9. Scholem, *Walter Benjamin und sein Engel*, 75.

10. Ibid., 51.

11. Ibid.

12. Ibid.

13. Ibid., 28.

14. Ibid., 29.

15. Elisabeth Weber, *Questions au judaïsme* (Lonrai: Collection Midrash, Desclée de Brouwer, 1996), 45. My translation.

16. Walter Benjamin, "Franz Kafka," *GS2*, 435; *SW2*, 813. The passage is followed immediately by an interpreting of the "nothingness" of "hammering." For a discussion of the passage see Samuel Weber, *Theatricality as Medium* (Stanford: Stanford Stanford University Press, 2004), 74–75.

17. In a very early text, "Dialogue on Religiosity in the Present" (1912), Benjamin has one of the speakers argue that the "modern problem" of religion derives from the fact that discussion considers only "historical religions" rather than attempting to think about what a "religion of the time" might be (*GS2*, 34).

18. For the "the 'original allegorical figure'" see Walter Benjamin, *Ursprung des deutschen Trauerspiels*, in *GS1*, 401; *Origin*, 228. In his early essay on "Language in General and the Language of Man" (*GS2*, 151–152; *SW1*, 70), Benjamin portrays the Fall as one from the language of names, which is still a direct offshoot of the divine creation, into the language of cognitive and moral judgment. The latter sacrifices the singularity of the created to the generality of abstract concepts, above all to "the knowledge of good and evil." This notion is then reinscribed in the book on the *Trauerspiel*, but with an accentuation of the darker side of the language of names: "To be named, even by one who is like the Gods and blessed, still retains an element of mourning . . ." (*GS1*, 398; *Origin*, 224–225). Et in arcadia ego . . .

19. It should be stressed that these two words, "dramatic" and "theatrical," are by no means synonymous, despite their frequent use in this way. "Dramatic" describes a conflict of events, forces, or persons, whereas "theatrical" describes representation-for-another, and consequently, the involvement of every other—"observer," "narrator," "describer"—in what is being recounted. In this text, however, both dimensions converge: the text is *both* dramatic *and* theatrical. For a discussion of recent theater as "post-dramatic," see Hans-Thiess Lehmann, *Post-Dramatic Theater*, trans. Karen Jürs-Munby (New York: Routledge, 2006).

20. Scholem cites Benjamin's remark, in his essay on Karl Kraus, about the "Jewish certitude" that considers language to be "the stage for the consecration of the name" (ibid., 31). Compare Benjamin, *GS2*, 359; *SW2*, 451.

21. Walter Benjamin, "Agesilaus Santander," in Scholem, *Walter Benjamin und sein Engel*, 41.

22. Karl Kraus, *Pro domo et mundo* (München, 1912), 164, cited in Walter Benjamin, "Über einige Motive bei Baudelaire," *GS1*, 647; *SW4*, 354 (fn. 77).

23. Scholem, *Walter Benjamin und sein Engel*, 51.

24. Benjamin, "Agesilaus Santander."

25. Benjamin's "new angel" is a response to the crisis of the old angels, and in particular that of the Christian "Evangiles," which he associates with the Lu-

theran Reformation and its consequences. A "religion of the time"—*Religion der Zeit*—would thus be one that *negotiates* with time rather than seeking to transcend or abolish it.

26. Ibid.

27. It should be noted that the formulation of the text is such as to make no direct assertion about whether or not this is true. The angel "pays me back for being disturbed in his work." This does not assert that the disturbance is the result of anything "I" did, but only that there was an interruption, the angel's "work" was disturbed, and that the angel pays "me" back for that disturbance. The English translation replaces the ambiguity of the German text with certainty.

28. Benjamin, "Agesilaus Santander," 41.

29. *GS1*, 694; *SW4*, 390.

30. Benjamin, "Agesilaus Santander."

31. Scholem, *Walter Benjamin und sein Engel*, 56.

32. Ibid.

15. "Streets, Squares, Theaters"

1. Symptomatic of this reaction, from someone who should have known better, is Foucault's diatribe, in his introduction to the second edition of the book *Madness and Society (L'histoire de la folie)*, in which he inveighs against this tendency as the effort of a "mean spirited pedagogy" ("petite pedagogie") bent on restricting intellectual investigation to the analysis of written texts.

2. In Chapter 5, I discussed the fact that Benjamin initially planned to write his *Habilitation* on the scholastic treatise *de modi significandi* (attributed at the time to Duns Scotus, and in the meanwhile reattributed to Thomas of Erfurt), but that he gave up on the project when he discovered that it had already been made the object of a *Habilitationsschrift* by Martin Heidegger. Far from abandoning his concern with the modes of signifying—a term he uses in his essay "Task of the Translator," Benjamin developed it in his theory of allegory, which he placed at the center of *The Origins of the German Mourning Play*, his unsuccessful attempt to "habilitate" himself.

3. Werner Hamacher has interpreted this as the *Forderungscharakter*—the demand-character, of Benjamin's writings in general. See his essay "Intensive Sprachen," in Christian L. Hart-Nibbrig, *Übersetzen: Walter Benjamin* (Suhrkamp: Frankfurt am Main, 2001), 174–235.

4. Although the published English translation of this text uses "recognizability" to translate *Erkennbarkeit*, I am reluctant to abandon the reference to "knowledge" or "cognition" as such, especially because this connotation is easily lost in the English "recognize." "Recognize" tends in English to take "cognize" for granted, whereas Benjamin is here insisting, I believe, on the fact that cognition itself is involved. It should be noted that although "Erkennen" *can* be used in German to mean "recognize," there is a specific German word for "recognize," *Wiedererkennen*, and Benjamin does not use it. But I readily acknowledge that *both* translations are possible and that each has their advantages and disadvantages.

5. Walter Benjamin, *Das Passagen-Werk*, in *GS1*, 577–578. English translation

by Howard Eiland and Kevin McLaughlin as *The Arcades Project* (Cambridge: Harvard University Press, 1999), 463. Due to the ease of Benjamin's numbering system, only the convolute letter and its number will be used in all subsequent references to this work. The reader who consults the English translation, however, will discover that I have generally retranslated the passages from Benjamin.

6. Benjamin's French is erroneous here in two places: "Cancale" and "provençaux."

7. The association made here by Benjamin has no basis in etymology, even though he suggests that it does: "These meanings must not be overlooked by etymology" [O 2a,1]. According to Duden's Etymological Dictionary *(Herkunftwörterbuch)*, *Schwelle* is etymologically associated with the English, *sill*, whereas *schwellen* is derived from roots cognate with the English, *swell*. My thanks to Michael Jennings, Kevin McLaughlin and countless others for calling this to my attention. On the significance of the *Schwelle* for Benjamin's work in general, see Wilfried Menninghaus, *Schwellenkunde: Walter Benjamins Passage des Mythos* (Frankfurt am Main: Suhrkamp, 1986).

8. William Empson, *Seven Types of Ambiguity* (New York: New Directions, 1966).

9. It should be remembered that in Benjamin's account of the allegorical theater of the German *Trauerspiel*, things and stage-properties are no less important than human characters. See *Ursprung des deutschen Trauerspiels (GS1, 312; Origin, 133)*.

10. What he in fact writes is that "History wanders onto the stage" (*GS1*, 271; *Origin*, 92). The English translation obscures the movement of "wandering": *"Die Geschichte wandert in den Schauplatz hinein"* becomes "History merges into the setting."

16. God and the Devil—in Detail

1. *GS1, 350; Origin, 174–175.* I have generally retranslated passages cited from Benjamin in English.

2. *Monadology,* §1, in G. W. Leibniz, *Philosophical Essays,* trans. Roger Ariew and Daniel Garber (Indianapolis: Hackett Publishing Co., 1989), 213. Future references are found in parentheses in the text by section number. Translations are often modified.

3. "One's own death is of course unimaginable [*unvorstellbar*], and whenever we make the effort to do so, we can ascertain how we actually continue to remain present as spectators. Hence the psychoanalytic school could venture the assertion that at bottom no one believes in his own death or, what amounts to the same, that in the unconscious each of us is convinced of his own immortality." Sigmund Freud, "Thoughts for the Times on War and Death [*Zeitgemäßes über Krieg und Tod*]," in *Gesammelte Werke,* vol. 10 (Frankfurt am Main: Fischer, 1968), 341; English translation in standard edition, vol. 14 (London: Hogarth, 1957), 289. I discuss this essay in Samuel Weber, *Targets of Opportunity: On the Militarization of Thinking* (New York: Fordham University Press, 2005), 52–54.

17. Closing the Net

1. Walter Benjamin, "Capitalism as Religion," in *SW1*, 288.
2. W. Benjamin, "Kapitalismus als Religion," *GS6*, 100.
3. See Martin Heidegger, *Hegel's Concept of Experience* (New York: HarperCollins, 1989), where Heidegger discusses the constitutive gesture of modernity as that of seeking terra firma on which to "take a stand." He also elaborates this argument in "Overcoming Metaphysics," in *The End of Philosophy* (New York: Harper & Row, 1973).
4. "In capitalism, things have a meaning only in their relationship to the cult." *SW1*, 288.
5. This holds for the somewhat earlier "Language" essay, in which language is defined in terms of its "immediate" or "unmediated impartability" *(unmittelbare Mitteilbarkeit)* (*GS1*, 142; *SW1*, 64).
6. See Uwe Steiner, "Kapitalismus als Religion: Anmerkungen zu einem Fragment Walter Benjamins," in *Deutsche Vierteljahresschrift* 72 (1998): 156–157.
7. Charles Baudelaire, *Oeuvres complètes* (Paris: Bibliothèque de la pléiade, 1961), 91. See also Benjamin, *GS4*, 44.
8. See J 64,4 of *Passagenwerk* in *GS5*, 453. See the English version in *AP*, 343.
9. The expression is used in precisely this way by another author whom Benjamin would later, in his notebooks, cite occasionally, Paul Lafargue, who in the introduction to *La droit à la paresse*, written in 1883 while imprisoned, described the situation of the workers in these terms: "La morale capitaliste, piteuse parodie de la morale chrétienne, frappe d'anathème la chair du travailleur; elle prend pour idéal de réduire le producteur au plus petit minimum de besoins, de supprimer ses joies et ses passions et de le condamner au rôle de machine délivrant du travail sans trêve ni merci." Paul Lafargue, *La droit à la paresse* (Paris: Allia, 1999).
10. Walter Benjamin, "Schicksal und Charakter" in *GS2*, 174; see also *SW1*, 203.
11. Benjamin's ambivalence toward Nietzsche recalls in many respects that of Heidegger: both laud and also criticize Nietzsche for his articulation of a certain nihilism. Above all, they seek to put him in his (proper) place, in order thereby better to define their own.
12. Those who would believe that "pagan" *(heidnisch)* is for Benjamin simply a term of reproach or critique would do well to remember his avowed long-term fascination with astrology.
13. Benjamin's citation also changes the gender of death, which in Leopardi's dialogue is feminine: "Madama Morte" rather than "Herr Tod." In Leopardi's text, Fashion reminds Death that they are sisters: "Non ti ricordi che tutte e due siamo nate dalla Caducità?" See Giacomo Leopardi, *Operette morali*, 1.7, viewable online at www.tuttotempolibero.com.
14. See *Das Passagen-Werk*, Convolute B 2,4 (*GS5*, 115; *AP*, 66). See also *Ursprung des deutschen Trauerspiels, GS1*, 244.
15. This is also the formula that comes closest to designating the paradox of Nietzsche's "Eternal Return of the Same." Benjamin was fascinated with the notion of the Eternal Return, which however—once again targeting Nietzsche—he

sought to reattribute to Blanqui's *Eternité par les astres*, written in prison at the end of his life.

16. "Interruption is one of the most fundamental procedures in producing form." See Benjamin, *Was ist das epische Theater? (2)*, in *GS2*, 536; *SW4*, 305. This is, of course, a modern version of the Aristotelian theory of *peripeteia* as an essential constituent of complex tragic plots, but now extended to theater—and art—in general.

17. Benjamin describes Brecht's theater, for instance, as an *"epische Erstreckung,"* which he in turn compares to the action of the Ballet Master on his female pupils, stretching their limbs "to the limits of the possible" (*GS2*, 533; *SW4*, 303). Applied not just to bodies but also to places, *Erstreckung* becomes the *Schwelle* (threshold, swelling) that characterizes the Paris of the Passages. Compare, among many other instances, C 2,4 and C 2a,3 in *AP*.

18. *Gelegen* is the past participle of *liegen*, to lie (down). Benjamin, following Hölderlin, is contrasting two aspects of what in English might be designated as the "lay of the land." To emphasize the temporal aspect of the participle, I have translated *gelegen* not simply as "lay" but as "laid-out."

18. The *Ring* as *Trauerspiel*

1. In an interview Derrida reminds us that "already Luther spoke of *destructio* in order to characterize the necessity of loosening up hardened theological layers which obstructed the originality [*la nudité originelle*] of the evangelical message" (*Le Monde de l'Education*, September 2000, 14). Derrida admits that deconstruction may well refer to something "impossible," but only insofar as this impossibility "is that which is arriving" (or, alternately, which "occurs": *"l'impossible comme ce qui arrive"*). Regarding his own unique contribution to this history, he writes: "Without rejecting or refuting anything, I wanted to emphasize what in the course of deconstruction it has inherited from this memory and how this memory has distinguished it, namely in the same moment at which it re-affirms and respects this inheritance."

2. For a discussion of this admittedly unusual translation, see Samuel Weber, *Theatricality as Medium* (New York: Fordham University Press, 2005), 375, n. 8.

3. Martin Heidegger, *Being and Time*, trans. John Macquarrie and Edward Robinson (New York: Harper & Row, 1962), 44.

4. Wahrig, *Wörterbuch der deutschen Sprache* (Munich: dtv-Verlag, 2006).

5. *GS1*, 317. Throughout I have occasionally altered the English translation, found in *Origin*.

6. Here we should recall Max Weber's distinction between radical Lutheranism and its domestication by Calvin: Calvinism was the earliest pillar of the spirit of capitalism.

7. In his commentary to *Angelus Novus* Benjamin does not go further in remarking on how the angel whose "face is turned toward the past" also looks in the direction of the *observer*, who thereby becomes both a spectator and part of the "past." The "storm" that "is blowing from paradise" and drives the angel "irresistibly into the future" also gusts above the heads of the spectators. By mak-

ing the spectator part of the happenings, Benjamin's reading makes the "picture" a *theatrical scene*. The spectators, who here are also readers, belong to a "past" from which the "storm" rises and against which the angel struggles. In the figure of the angel again the *resistance* to the storm appears, which is now called "progress." See *GS2*, 697, or the English translation, "On the Concept of History," in *SW4*, 392.

8. Of the concept of truth, as it is traditionally understood: that is, as *adaequatio intellectus et rei*.

9. Here one could perhaps find a point of convergence with Klaus Zehelein's idea of having the Stuttgart Opera's Millennial Tetralogy staged by four different directors.

10. "'Opera,' plural of 'opus,' this new variety of 'works' was dubbed; the Italians made a female of it, the French a male, so that the variety seemed to have turned out *generis utriusque*. I believe one could find no more apt criticism of 'Opera' than to allow this name as legitimate an origin as that of 'Tragedy'; in neither case was it a matter of reason *(Vernunft)*, but a deep-set instinct here expressed a thing of nameless nonsense, there a thing of sense indicibly profound." See Richard Wagner, "On the Name 'Musikdrama'" in *Richard Wagner's Prose Works*, vol. 5, trans. William Ashton Ellis (New York: Broude Brothers, 1966), 302.

11. Richard Wagner, "The Festival-Playhouse at Bayreuth, with an Account of the Laying of its Foundation-Stone," in *Wagner's Prose Works*, 5:326. This text includes, among other things, the speech at the laying of the foundation stone of 1872, which is quoted here.

12. Ibid., 334.

13. Ibid., 335.

14. Such an ideality is close to the Evangelical tendency to spiritualization, internalization, and sublimation of corporeality, while in Catholic rites, such as the mass, the spiritual is still linked to a certain localization.

15. The ideality of this theatrical space was marked by the clear and insurmountable separation of the two spaces of which it consisted: the spectator area and the stage area. The proscenia that Wagner placed between them were there not to create a transition or a third space, but rather to reinforce the divide between the two by accentuating the "floating atmosphere of distance" between the spaces. From the spectator "the scene is removed as it were to the unapproachable world of dreams, while the spectral music sounding from the 'mystic gulf' . . . inspires him with that clairvoyance in which the scenic picture melts into the truest effigy of life itself" (335).

16. Adorno analyzed this tendency in *Versuch über Wagner* (Frankfurt am Main: Suhrkamp, 1952). That this aesthetic guiding principle does not necessarily *also* fully determine Wagner's musical-theatrical practice could be demonstrated only through individual analyses.

17. As Adorno has shown, this is also the basis for its usefulness for the commercial media, which were quick to adapt the leitmotifs for their programs, films, and so on.

18. See *Wagner's Ring of the Nibelung: A Companion*, trans. Stawart Spencer (London: Thames and Hudson, 1993), 152. This dilemma would also apply to

music, defined by Wagner as a "female," understood as a "mirror" of man, who therefore can "see in it his very own image" See R. Wagner, *Opera and Drama,* trans. William Ashton Ellis (Lincoln: University of Nebraska Press, 1995), 114; translation modified.

19. In *Opera and Drama* Wagner identifies what he considers to be the essence of music, melody, with self-awareness: "In its significance art is nothing but the fulfillment of the yearning to recognize oneself in a depicted or loved object— of finding oneself again in the mastered appearances of the external world" (ibid., 153; my translation).

20. Ibid., 213.

21. I attempt to investigate this tension in *Theatricality as Medium* (Stanford: Stanford University Press, 2005), esp. 103–110.

22. "This is the resolute, fanatical mien which students have when they study; it is the strangest mien imaginable . . . It may be easier to understand this if one thinks of the actors in the Nature Theater. Actors have to catch their cues in a flash . . . Truly, for them 'hammering is real hammering and at the same time nothing'—provided that this is part of their role." Walter Benjamin, "Franz Kafka" (*GS2,* 435; *SW2,* 813–814).

23. Walter Benjamin, "The Author as Producer" (*GS2,* 698; *SW2,* 779).

19. Reading Benjamin

Epigraph: Benjamin, *GS4,* 433; *SW2,* 727.

1. Walter Benjamin, *Einbahnstrasse* (Frankfurt am Main: Suhrkamp, 1965), 58.

2. Friedrich Hölderlin, "Patmos," in *Hölderlin: Werke und Briefe,* vol. 1, ed. Friedrich Beißner (Frankfurt am Main: Insel Verlag, 1969), 181. English version in *Hymns and Fragments,* trans. Richard Sieburth (Princeton: Princeton University Press, 1984), 96–97; translation modified.

3. Walter Benjamin, *Ursprung des deutschen Trauerspiels, GS1,* 207; *Origin,* 29. References to this book are given in parentheses in the body of the text, first to the German version and then to the published English translation.

4. "Short Shadows," in *GS4,* 425; *SW2,* 699.

5. G. W. F. Hegel, *Phänomenologie des Geistes* (Hamburg: Meiner, 1952), 468–469.

6. Jacques Derrida, *De la grammatologie* (Paris: Editions du Seuil, 1967), 52.

7. Again, on the notion of "intensity" as it operates in the writings of Benjamin, see the remarkable essay of Werner Hamacher, "Intensive Sprachen," in Christian L. Hart Nibbrig, ed., *Übersetzen: Walter Benjamin* (Frankfurt am Main: Suhrkamp, 2001), pp. 174–235. As the title of this volume suggests, and as Hamacher in particular emphasizes, the notion of "translation" is decisive in determining the nature of the signifying relationships that constitute the Benjaminian text. This volume, together with the recently published *Benjamin-Handbuch* edited by Burkhard Lindner (Stuttgart-Weimar: J.B. Metzler, 2006), constitute two of the richest and most thought-provoking collective works of recent Benjamin criticism.

8. Friedrich Nietzsche, *The Birth of Tragedy,* §§ 14–15.

9. Genesis 1.11.

10. This is precisely the point where Hegel, in his *Philosophy of Nature,* sees Nature as the Other of Spirit coming into its own, namely as concept—as the concept of the species, that survives the natural limitations of mortal living beings. In nature, only the genre survives, and hence, the concept as Spirit. It is just this *Aufhebung* of singularity that Benjamin, like Kierkegaard, Marx, and Nietzsche before him, cannot accept. See G. W. F. Hegel, "Philosophy of Nature," *Encyclopedia of the Philosophical Sciences,* pt. 2, paras. (New York: Oxford University Press, 2004), 296–298.

11. G. W. F. Hegel, *Wissenschaft der Logik* (Leipzig: Philip Reclam Verlag Jun, n.d.), 91.

12. G. W. F. Hegel, *Enzyklopädie* (Hamburg: Meiner, 1959), 369.

13. Jacques Derrida, *De la grammatologie* (Paris: Editions du Seuil, 1967), 108.

14. Roman Jakobson, Morris Halle, *Fundamentals of Language* (The Hague: Mouton, 1956), 16.

15. Ibid., 76–78.

16. Gérard Genette, *Figures I* (Paris: Editions du Seuil, 1966), 52.

20. "Seagulls"

1. Walter Benjamin, *GS2,* 158; *SW1,* 101.

2. Unpublished manuscript.

3. Although Benjamin does not mention it, the figure of the "memory palace" has a long history as part of those *hypomnemata,* "external" devices used to assist memory. The Jesuit missionary Matteo Ricci described the technique of "memory palace" in his *Treatise on Mnemonics.* For Benjamin, however, the "palace" is not so much an *aide memoire* as its setting.

4. On the gesture of animals, Agamben quotes Max Kommerell, from the conclusion of the latter's essay on Kleist: "A new beauty begins that assembles the beauty of an animal's gestures, whether tender or threatening." Giorgio Agamben, "Kommerell, ou le geste," in *La puissance de la pentée* (Paris: Rivages, 2006), 206.

Acknowledgments

The chapters in this book span forty years, making it truly impossible to thank everyone who has contributed, in one way or another, to its completion—however incomplete it remains (assuming that completion is even appropriate for such a publication). When I first began writing on Benjamin, what might be described as a "textual" approach to his writings was still relatively rare—and this despite his repeated admonition, that, as with allegory, "writing has nothing servile about it—it does not fall away in the reading process like slag" (*GS1*, 388). In the past decades, however, a remarkable interpretive literature has emerged for which such a statement remains an ineffaceable point of reference and point of departure. If at one point I could still feel that I was engaged in something of a pilot or pioneering project, that has long since ceased to be the case, and I can only hope that this book will add some insights and perspectives to the extremely impressive and still proliferating literature on this extraordinary writer and thinker.

The result of this development is that it would be futile to try and express my indebtedness to those who have contributed decisively to the current understanding and continuing interest in Walter Benjamin. Even in the specific case of Benjamin's "-abilities," it would doubtless be impossible to name all those who helped call attention to this aspect of his work. I will nevertheless mention Peter Fenves, Rodolphe Gasché, and Werner Hamacher as three of those who quite early discerned and interpreted the significance of "-abilities" in Benjamin's writing.

My more immediate debts, however, are first of all to Lindsay Waters, who long ago suggested that I write a book on Walter Benjamin, something that at the time was far from my thoughts but that struck me as an interesting possibility, and that has finally resulted in the present publication, very different from what both Lindsay and I had in mind at the time. Without his extraordinary patience and support, this book would surely never have been written. It also would certainly not be appearing at the time it is, were it not for the generous and capable editorial help supplied by Robert Ryder, who worked his way through the welter of citations and references (many to editions no longer available, and that therefore had to be changed), and helped to prune the repetitions that inevitably spring up in a project lasting as long as this one. A word of thanks is also due Julie Carlson, whose sensitive and precise editing has increased the readability of this book considerably. Eric Jarosinski helped translate the essay on the *Ring* from the German. Finally my wife, Arlette, provided just the right amount of urging and encouragement required to help bring this project to a termination, if not to an end. My gratitude to her exceeds the bounds of this book.

Some of the material here appeared, in different form, as follows: "Benjamin's Style," from *Encyclopedia of Aesthetics* (Oxford: Oxford University Press, 1998), pages 261–264, by permission of Oxford University Press; "The Virtuality of Medium," *Sites* 4, no. 2 (Fall 2000): 297–319, http://www.informaworld.com, by permission of the publisher; "Criticism Underway: Walter Benjamin's Romantic Concept of Criticism," in *Romantic Revolutions* (Bloomington: Indiana University Press, 1990), pages 302–319; "Genealogy of Modernity: History, Myth, and Allegory in Benjamin's *Origin of the German Mourning Play*," *Modern Language Notes* 106 (1991): 465–500; and "Taking Exception to Decision: Walter Benjamin and Carl Schmitt," *Diacritics*, Fall 1992: 5–19, the last two by permission of the publisher, The Johns Hopkins University Press; finally "The Ring as Deconstruction of Modernity: Reading Wagner with Benjamin," in Jost Hermand and Gerhard Richter, eds., *Sound Figures of Modernity: German Music and Philosophy* (Madison: University of Wisconsin Press, 2006), 106–123.

Index

Actuality. *See* Virtuality

Adorno, Theodor, 354nn16,17

Agamben, Giorgio: *State of Exception,* 195–200, 202–207; "Notes on Gesture," 204–205, 347n21; *Potentialities,* 346n16; *Profanations,* 209–210, 246n15

Allegory, 27, 68, 154–155, 158–163, 187, 216–217, 268, 286, 303–307, 320; allegorical script, 307–308; baroque, 68, 151, 155–156, 160–161, 167, 216, 240–243, 248, 286, 304–306, 337n6; and detail, 240–243, 247; and fashion, 269; names as, 233

Aristotle, 34, 46, 81, 98, 104, 105, 128, 142, 151, 233, 234, 294; *On the Soul,* 36, 82; *Poetics,* 100–102, 107–108, 181, 190, 291–292, 353n16; and possibility, 6

Armature, 270–271, 273

Artaud, Antonin, 101

Aura, 119

Babel, story of, 86–88

Baudelaire, Charles, 9, 55, 159; "Le crépuscule du soir," 255–257

Benjamin, Walter, 6; "Agesilaus Santander," 211, 215–226, 286; *The Arcades Project,* 48–49, 65, 167, 169–171, 175, 229–239, 255, 267–273, 314, 336n9; "The Author as Producer," 105, 335n19; "Berlin Childhood around 1900," 348n7; "Capitalism as Religion," 209, 250–267, 274–276; "The Concept of Criticism in German Romanticism," 20–30, 59, 63–64; "Critique of Violence," 163, 195–196; "Destiny and Character," 147, 259; "Franz Kafka: On the Tenth Anniversary of his Death," 200–205, 208, 215, 294–295; "Goethe's *Elective Affinities,*" 77–78, 132; "On Language as Such and on the Language of Man," 38, 40–47, 61, 116–117, 197, 300–302; "On the Concept of History," 107, 120–121, 151, 224, 335n17, 353n7; "On the Image of Proust," 332n17; "On the Program of the Coming Philosophy," 14, 49, 119, 164, 310–313; *Origin of the German Mourning Play,* 7–8, 28, 30, 61, 64, 68, 88–89, 120, 132–163, 169, 176–182, 186–194, 216–217, 239, 240–243, 247, 269, 283–289, 299, 302–309, 313, 329n9, 331n12, 337n16, 352n11; relation to Jewish tradition, 214–215, 217, 218; "Seagulls," 315–322; "The Storyteller," 337n20, 347n27; "The Task of the Translator," 17, 43–44, 53–64, 69–77, 88–94, 329n10, 332n16; "Theological-

Benjamin, Walter *(continued)*
Political Fragment," 225, 332n18; "Two
Poems by Friedrich Hölderlin," 14–19,
276–280; "What is the Epic Theater?"
96–112, 206, 294; "The Work of Art in
the Age of Its Technical Reproducibility,"
17, 59
Body, 171, 292; disarticulation of, 172–174,
289

Communicability. *See* Impartability
Condition *(Zustand)*, 103–108, 111, 114,
183, 250
Criticizability *(Kritisierbarkeit)*, 22, 26, 30,
59, 62, 65
Cult, concept of, 255

Deleuze, Gilles, 31–39, 46, 51, 331nn3,5
Derrida, Jacques, 51–52, 122–128, 231,
301; and deconstruction, 281, 295,
353n1; and the "generalized text," 227–
229; *Limited Inc*, 4–5, 58, 116; and
perhaps, 123–126; and spectrality, 200
Detail. *See* God; Monad; Satan
Determinability *(Bestimmbarkeit)*, 12–13,
16–18
Dialetic, the, 100, 103, 120, 136, 148, 149,
306. *See also* Hegel, Georg Wilhelm
Friedrich: dialectics of; Image *(Bild)*: dialectical
Disjunctive synthesis, 49, 119–120, 165–
168, 230
Doctrine *(Lehre)*, 166, 311–312, 317; in
Kant, 11

Empson, William, 238
Extreme, the, 7–8, 137, 160, 178–180, 182,
188, 190, 230, 254; singularly extreme,
137–138, 179, 313

Fashion, 267–273
Fichte, Johann, 23–24
Form: Romantic concept of, 26, 28–29;
translation as, 56–57, 69–70
Foucault, Michel, 346n16, 350n1; and transcendental historicism, 132
Freud, Sigmund, 78, 170, 244, 245, 259,
265, 266, 342n19; and capitalism, 262–
263; *Interpretation of Dreams*, 45; and
isolation, 329n11; and the unconscious,
244–245
Future, 124; of *Angelus Novus*, 225–226;
and epic theater, 105; future perfect, 37–

38; as imparting the past, 51; and knowledge, 274–275

Genesis, 82–87, 94; Benjamin's reading of,
45–47, 300
Gerund, 66, 171
Gesture, 98–100, 103–104, 163, 203–207,
295, 347n21; of animals, 356n4;
citability of, 97–98, 105–106, 109, 111
Glance, 225–226; and *Augenblick*, 168
Globalization, 81, 113–114, 258
God: and capitalism, 253, 257–261, 275;
commemoration of, 60–61; and detail,
240, 246–247
Goethe, Johann Wolfgang von, 63–65, 70,
214
Guilt *(Schuld)*, 141, 156–157, 280; and
capitalism, 253, 256–268, 274–276; and
Nietzsche, 263–265

Habermas, Jürgen, 131–132
Hamlet, 218, 287
Hegel, Georg Wilhelm Friedrich, 46, 167,
173, 302, 307, 339n9, 356n10; dialectics
of, 35–37, 133, 168, 306
Heidegger, Martin, 33, 72, 123–124, 230,
265, 283, 327n10, 333n13, 345n10,
350n3, 352n11, 353n3; *To Be and Time*,
281–282, 331n3
History, 51, 119, 131–133, 138–142; according to Schmitt, 184–185; as awakening, 169–170; finitude of, 64–65, 67–68;
and the mourning play, 140, 151, 154,
177–178, 181–182, 188–189; natural,
138, 159–161, 163; origin, 88–89, 137–
139; philosophy of, 143–144, 179, 285;
of translation, 81; universal history, 252.
See also Benjamin, Walter: "On the Concept of History"
Hölderlin, Friedrich, 11, 30, 199, 214, 250,
265, 298, 333n9, 334n9, 343n31,
353n18; notion of sobriety, 63–64; translation of Sophocles, 43, 74, 78, 345n10.
See also Benjamin, Walter: "Two Poems
by Friedrich Hölderlin"
Husserl, Edmund, 122

Idea, 7–9, 78, 120, 136–137, 148, 161, 163,
179–180, 302, 313–314; as monad, 138–
140, 303–304, 337n19; Romantic, 70
Image *(Bild)*, 222–223, 313–314; dialectical, 49–50, 121, 134, 229–230; imagistic
dissonance, 279; *Schriftbild*, 309, 313–315

Immediacy *(Unmittelbarkeit)*, 13–14, 19, 38, 41–47, 117–118, 166, 197, 198; of the cult, 254

Impartability *(Mitteilbarkeit)*, 10, 13–14, 38, 40–47, 51, 116–119, 197

Instant *(Augenblick)*, 112, 114, 120; and glance, 168

Intention, 71, 159, 231; death of, 49, 229, 314–315, 332n16

Interruption: and death, 274; of work, 222–223, 272

Iterability, 5–6, 58, 108–109, 116–117, 122, 126

Jakobson, Roman, 307
Jung, Carl, 168

Kafka, Franz, 194, 198–200; Hunter Gracchus, 158; *The Man Who Disappeared*, 201–207, 347n17; "Metamorphosis," 161; "The Next Village," 201; and the Tao, 202, 215, 224, 294–295, 346n15

Kant, Immanuel, 60, 76, 119–120, 124, 164–165, 214, 217, 304, 306–307, 310–312, 314, 333n7; *Critique of Judgment*, 11–14, 39–40, 56–57, 126; notion of transcendental, 58; and style, 11, 16

Kierkegaard, Søren, 101, 122, 127, 168; *Repetition*, 109, 178

Kinship, 54–55, 68, 78

Knowability *(Erkennbarkeit)*, 19, 48–50, 116, 119–120, 169, 229–230, 350n4; now of, 14, 121, 167–168, 229, 314; as possibility, 168

Kraus, Karl, 31, 221, 349n20

Labyrinth, city as, 236–237

Language, pure, 70, 74–75, 77–78, 90–91, 197–198, 302. *See also* Medium: language as; Singularity: of language

Law *(Recht)*, 196, 259, 260; in Kafka, 199–200

Leibniz, Gottfried Wilhelm. *See* Monad
Lévy, Pierre, 31, 33

Life, 33, 62, 65–67, 199, 201, 203; bare life, 259–262, 264, 275; context of, 15–16

Logos, 300–306

Lukács, Georg, 133, 147

Luther, Martin, 93, 218, 219, 247, 269, 284–285, 291, 353n1; faith alone *(sola fides)*, 218, 269, 284–285

Mallarmé, Stéphane, 75–78

Manhood, coming to *(Mannbarwerden)*, 213, 219

Marx, Karl, 262–263

Media, the, 31, 33, 35, 51, 79, 81–82, 94, 95–96, 113–114, 118, 206; theology of, 37–38

Mediality: of language, 42–43, 118, 197–198, 347n21; without end, 196–198

Medium: classical concept of, 34–36, 81–82; Hegelian concept of, 35–37; language as, 38–44, 46–48, 67, 69, 117–118, 165, 197, 311–312, 347n21; theater as, 101–102, 111; of translation, 91, 94

Memory, 6, 10, 205–206, 331n5, 347n21; memory palace, 356n3

Messianism, 333n9, 346n12; of the Romantics, 21

Modernity: definition of, 281–284, 290, 295

Modus significandi, 71–73, 228, 350n2

Monad, 138; idea as, 138–140, 303, 304; relation to the detail, 243–246

Mourning, 119, 143, 156–160, 162, 216, 269, 285, 304

Naming, 45–48, 53, 61, 87–88, 126, 232, 238, 301–303, 349n18; secret names, 211–213, 217, 219–221, 224

Nancy, Jean-Luc, 332n14

Neologisms, 3, 9

Nietzsche, Friedrich, 101, 140, 147, 148, 168, 259, 266, 271, 336n13, 338n21, 345n6; *Beyond Good and Evil*, 123–124; *Birth of Tragedy*, 305, 338n21; and the concept of guilt, 263–265; the Eternal Return, 109, 122, 250, 346n12, 352n15

Non-synthesis. *See* Disjunctive synthesis

Novalis, 20, 21–23, 25, 26

Origin, the, 81–82, 84, 88–90, 132–139, 149, 158, 161, 169–170, 171, 284–285, 300–301, 340n9

Original, the, 17, 43–44, 57–58, 62, 66–70, 73, 81–82, 84–86, 88–90, 92–94, 134, 137, 161, 329n10; afterlife of, 90; and mourning play, 156, 193

Ornamentality, 266, 267, 278

Place: and awakening, 171, 173–174, 319–320; and the Bayreuth *Festspielhaus*, 291; break as, 167; earth as, 82–84; of origin, 135; and room *(Raum)*, 277–279;

Place (continued)
  stage as, 114, 154, 159, 174, 192–193,
  234, 236, 248, 291–292; and threshold,
  233, 236
Plato: anamnesis, 303; cave, 237; dialogue,
  147, 149, 305–306; idea, 302; as judge,
  150. See also Socrates
Plotter (der Intrigant), 141–142, 155–156,
  160, 162, 182, 189, 191–193, 216, 287–
  288
Poetized, the (das Gedichtete), 15–18, 280
Possibility, 5–6, 14, 23, 41, 45, 48, 125,
  126, 331n3; and epic theater, 103, 105,
  109, 113; knowability as, 168; in the
  poetized, 17–18; of self-limitation, 25;
  structural possibility, 6, 39, 58, 116, 123;
  and the virtual, 32; as writing, 298
Presentation (Darstellung), 26, 30, 139,
  148, 303, 337n19
Proust, Marcel, 167, 169–175, 308–309
Purity, 196; and violence, 196–198. See also
  Language, pure

Reading, 175, 180, 205, 207, 208, 210,
  230–232, 298–299, 308–309; readability
  (Lesbarkeit), 19, 48, 50, 229–231, 313–
  315, 321–322
Recognizability (Erkennbarkeit). See
  Knowability
Redemption, 146, 156, 181, 208, 210,
  274
Repetition, 6, 109, 122, 203, 346n16; in
  Leibniz, 245; and mourning play, 153,
  156; and origin, 89–90, 133, 136–137; in
  poetry, 30; and singularity, 170. See also
  Kierkegaard, Søren: Repetition
Reproducibility (Reproduzierbarkeit), 59,
  62, 65, 119
Rosenzweig, Franz, 145, 147, 305, 346n15

Salvation, 9, 290, 346n16; saving, 8; story of,
  285–286, 338n24. See also Redemption
Satan, 215–218, 287; and detail, 240, 248
Saussure, Ferdinand de, 38, 72, 228
Schlegel, Friedrich, 20, 21–25, 62
Schmitt, Carl, 56, 127, 176–179, 182–189,
  193–194, 195, 200, 287, 337n15
Scholem, Gershom, 11, 72, 198, 208, 211–
  215, 217–221, 225–226, 320
Searle, John, 4–5, 58
Self: and the name, 220–221; and other,
  293; parting with, 9, 47, 118, 213; Ro-

mantic reflection of, 24–26, 29; sameness
  without, 270–271, 279; and tragic hero,
  145–149, 152, 156
Shock, 106–107, 110, 131, 285
Silence (Schweigen). See Tragedy: tragic
  hero
Singularity, 170, 203; and awakening, 170,
  172; and the decision, 127; and the extreme, 137–138, 179, 313; and idea, 8,
  139–140; and Kant, 12, 39, 310–312; of
  language, 40, 44, 69, 74; singular tempo-
  rality, 119–120, 164–165, 310; and the-
  ater, 108–109, 113, 144, 259
Socrates: death of, 146–148, 149, 152;
  irony, 146, 155, 158
Sorlin, Pierre, 35–36
Sovereignty, 177–178, 180–191, 194, 205–
  206, 287–290
State (Zustand). See Condition
State of exception, 182–183, 186, 193, 195,
  198, 200
Sterne, Laurence: The Life and Opinions of
  Tristram Shandy, 53–56, 68, 76
Stretching, concept of, 276–278
Study, 199–207
Style, philosophical, 149, 151, 303
Subject, the, 165, 173, 190, 206; in criti-
  cism, 22–23; in writing, 5
Symbol, 9, 65, 91–92

Task (Aufgabe): of the coming philosophy,
  310–311; poetic, 15–16, 18; of translation, 71, 88, 91
Theatricality, 235; and detail, 242–243; of
  mourning play, 190, 337n17
Threshold (Schwelle), 232–233, 235–237,
  318, 322, 351n7; awakening as, 237–238
Tieck, Ludwig, 28
Time: and moral universe, 336n10; narrative versus theatrical, 268–270; as now,
  49–51, 119, 314
Tragedy, 102–103, 143, 150–158, 178, 305;
  tragic hero, 144–149, 151–153, 155, 157,
  305
Translatability (Übersetzbarkeit), 43, 47,
  58–62, 65–66, 68–70, 90–92, 116
Translation, 55–77, 79–94; history of, 81;
  potentiality of, 43, 91. See also Form:
  translation as; Medium: of translation;
  Task: of translation

Undecidability, 126–128

Virtuality, 7, 9, 10, 14–15, 17–18, 31–40, 42, 44, 46, 50–51, 111–112, 114, 168; media as, 113

Wagner, Richard: and the Leitmotif, 292–293; *The Ring,* 288–290, 293

Weber, Elizabeth, 215
Weber, Max, 251, 353n6
Work: concept of, 23, 63, 286, 289–290; *Gesamtkunstwerk,* 288, 290–291; interruption of, 222–223, 272